LEGAL AND
CRIMINAL
PSYCHOLOGY

CONTRIBUTORS

Abraham Blumberg, LL.B.

Jerry S. Cohen, LL.B.

Albert Ellis, Ph.D.

Harry A. Gair, LL.B.

Israel Gerver, B.S.S.

Jacob Goldstein, D.S.Sc.

Charles Hanley, Ph.D.

Albert I. Rabin, Ph.D.

Robert S. Redmount, LL.B., Ph.D.

Earl Rubington, Ph.D.

Alfred C. Schnur, Ph.D.

Robert M. Scott, LL.B.

Thomas S. Szasz, M.D.

Hans Toch, Ph.D.

William W. Wattenberg, Ph.D.

Charles Winick, Ph.D.

LEGAL AND CRIMINAL PSYCHOLOGY

edited by

HANS TOCH

Michigan State University

HOLT, RINEHART AND WINSTON INC.

New York

Printed in the United States of America

To the *Memory* of
A. Ross Pascoe

Preface

Psychology is many things to many people. "Psychology" in the title of this volume is not intended to mean, as one might reasonably suppose, the domain of the professional psychologist. Instead, the word is used literally, in its original sense, as "understanding of the human mind." This broader usage does not exclude academic psychology, but neither does it exclude any academic discipline which can help us to an understanding of people. It also does not rule out practical experience or common sense, insofar as these sources of information can be prevented from misrepresenting freak particulars as general rules.

We can characterize the role of academic psychology in the total enterprise in the words of Sholom Aleichem, taken from the chatty preamble to his short story "The Three Widows":

> "Do you know what psychology is? There is a vegetable called parsley ... To look at it's not bad, it smells nice, tastes good when you flavor food with it. But you try chewing parsley by itself! You don't want to? Then why do you stick psychology down my throat?"

The present volume carries no such intention.

Our effort has the appearance of a "symposium." What may come to mind here is a group of people sitting around a table exchanging views about a subject of mutual interest. Nothing like this holds true of our venture. To be sure, the book is a group effort. But each contribution was written without benefit of interaction with other members of the group. Moreover, the topics range in content, orientation, and level of treatment.

If the product nevertheless has unity, this is only in small part a function of editorial interference, which sometimes imposed a slight semblance of structural uniformity; only minimal unification was provided by occasional cross references in the text, and by introductory chapters intended, in part, for the same end. The reason why this book does show unity lies almost entirely in the composition of our group.

It would be a mistake to classify this volume as an "interdisciplinary" effort; it is not an attempt by representatives of various compartments of the ivory tower to pool their abstractions or to go their separate ways under a common heading. No one here speaks for a discipline or a school of thought or a set of techniques. The members of our group are not congregated as delegates, but as individuals.

As individuals, they fall roughly into three categories. The first category comprises members of that rare group of practitioners in the fields of law and correction who have the willingness and capacity to step outside their profession and to look back at it. They are thereby able to provide intimate portraits of prevailing practices, framed in thoughtful discussions of the purposes and reasons behind these practices. The second set of contributors includes social scientists concerned with these same practices. They attempt to bring to bear information, techniques, and thinking that can increase our understanding beyond the range of practical experience.

The third category of contributors to this volume is that of "practitioner-social scientists" who, equipped with academic training, have tested the applicability and limitation of their training in the courtroom or the penal institution. Thus our group includes lawyers with academic degrees in a social science and a sociologist-turned-prison-warden-turned-professor.

The three orientations I have outlined converge into a sequence of interdependent steps. In thespian terms, our "practitioners" produce the backdrop and cast for our play, our "social scientists" provide the themes and the story, and our "practitioner-social scientists" bring the two together in rehearsal. Thus we can view the result as a collection of efforts geared toward each other. This does not mean that our symposium does not contain divergences of viewpoint. It most assuredly does. These divergences, however, are subordinate to a common concern, that of arriving at understanding and constructive reform.

The book is offered with a dual purpose: It seeks to provide the student, the interested layman, and the specialist with facts about the people involved in the process of criminal justice; more important, it is intended as an attempt to challenge thinking and provoke argument about these facts. To fulfill the first objective, no effort has been spared to provide basic factual information, taking as little for granted as possible. In line with the second aim, several authors were selected who are known to represent refreshing and challenging viewpoints. These contributors were encouraged to make their insights and feelings explicit, no matter how sensitive or controversial the problem.

An effort has been made in the following to spell out and define an area of concern, that of "legal and criminal phychology." This area is intended to comprise problems from a diversity of traditional jurisdictions. It encroaches on the law school, on courses in criminology, on seminars in clinical psychology, and on a variety of other domains.

We have chosen to discuss this miscellany under one cover, because it seemed to provide a common challenge, that of a very broad area of our society which desperately cries for reform. Our effort is intended to fall in step with the current trend toward more rational and humane practices in the administration of criminal justice and the treatment of social offenders. The hope is that a comprehensive discussion of psychological aspects of the process can help in defining problems and suggesting possible solutions.

No author or editor is an island unto himself. In addition to those who lend direct assistance, there are always the unsung ones who have provided a friendly smile at crucial moments, who have shown patience in the face of short temper, or whose casual remarks have triggered elusive ideas. A word of thanks for such support is never superfluous.

The editor is most directly indebted for the help and cooperation he has received from the contributors to this volume. Almost every chapter has entailed work far beyond the call of duty. The editor is grateful for the sensitive understanding of his intentions, and for the kindness with which arbitrary suggestions were received. Very special thanks are due to Robert S. Redmount, Robert H. Scott, and Charles Winick for helpful advice at critical junctures.

Mary Falcsik translated our scribbles into typescript; few others could have performed this miracle. Albert Hastorf is to be thanked for an act of faith in recommending publication of this work. Richard Korn reviewed the entire manuscript and made a number of valuable suggestions.

The editor is personally indebted to the Michigan Department of Correction for their open-door policy over the years. Also valuable has been a Summer Training Institute in the Administration of Criminal Justice presided over by Frank Remington and Victor Rosenblum, under the sponsorship of the Social Science Research Council.

East Lansing, Michigan
June, 1961

H. T.

About the Contributors

Abraham Blumberg is a member of the New York Bar and teaches Social Science at Brooklyn College.

Jerry S. Cohen is on the staff of the Subcommittee on Antitrust and Monopoly of the U.S. Senate. Until recently, he was Assistant Attorney General of Michigan in charge of the Criminal Division of the Attorney General's office.

Albert Ellis is a well-known authority on marriage counseling and criminal psychology. He is the author of numerous books and articles about sexual behavior, and is currently in private practice in New York City.

Harry A. Gair is past President of the Law Science Academy and former Dean of the American College of Trial Lawyers. He has written books about negligence law, a field in which he is a recognized expert.

Israel Gerver lectures in Sociology and Anthropology at Brooklyn College. He has written articles about problems of testimony.

Jacob Goldstein is associated with the New School for Social Research and holds a number of other research positions. He is a social psychologist whose publications deal with a variety of subjects.

Charles Hanley is Associate Professor of Psychology at Michigan State University. He has held a research position in a delinquency prediction study of the San Francisco State College Foundation.

Albert I. Rabin is Professor of Psychology and Director of the Psychological Clinic at Michigan State University. He is consulting psychologist at the State Prison of Southern Michigan. Professor Rabin is the author of approximately seventy journal articles and co-editor of a book.

Robert S. Redmount is Chief Psychologist at the Psychological Services Center of Connecticut, but also practices law in New Haven. Dr. Redmount has published several articles relating psychology to law.

Earl Rubington is affiliated as Sociologist with the Connecticut Commission on Alcoholism and the Yale Center of Alcohol Studies in New Haven.

Alfred C. Schnur is Professor at the School of Police Administration and Public Safety, Michigan State University. Among Dr. Schnur's past positions is a term as Associate Warden at the Minnesota State Prison.

Robert H. Scott is Associate Director of Corrections in charge of the Youth Division, Michigan Department of Corrections. Mr. Scott is a pioneer in the treatment of youthful offenders.

Thomas S. Szasz is Professor in the Department of Psychiatry, State University of New York, Upstate Medical Center, Syracuse. Among Professor Szasz's more than sixty journal articles are many relating to criminal responsibility. Professor Szasz has written a book dealing with pleasure and pain and one on the "myth of mental illness."

Hans Toch is on the faculty of Michigan State University, where he teaches (among other things) a course in Legal and Criminal Psychology. Professor Toch has worked in several areas of social psychology, and has had an interest in problems relating to visual perception.

William W. Wattenberg is Professor of Educational Psychology at Wayne State University. In addition to having written books about adolescence and mental hygiene, Professor Wattenberg is known for his writings on juvenile delinquency.

Charles Winick is a psychologist with many interests. He teaches Applied Psychoanalysis at New York University, and has also taught at MIT, Columbia, and the University of Rochester. Dr. Winick directs the Musicians Clinic in New York and is known for his work in social psychology and drug addiction.

Contents

PART II • CRIMINAL PSYCHOLOGY

PART III • SPECIAL PROBLEMS IN
CRIMINAL PSYCHOLOGY

Part I
Legal Psychology

HANS TOCH

1 Introduction to Legal Psychology

When the man in the street thinks of the workings of the criminal law, he tends to visualize a row of well-oiled machines. First in line is a Law-Passing Machine which acts like a thermostat. It gauges the temperature of society, and passes a law against anything which raises the level of public indignation beyond a tolerable point. Once the law has been passed, an Enforcing Machine enforces it. This contraption surveys the landscape for any signs of disturbance, and clamps iron tentacles on whoever seems to be responsible.

Next in line is the Justice-Dispensing or Courtroom Machine which makes sure that the Enforcing Machine has been functioning properly. This gadget operates like a vending machine. You insert facts about the offense in one slot, and pertinent laws in another. There is a clicking of wheels and a flashing of lights, and "justice" pops out of the dispenser. Justice means (1) a decision as to whether the suspected culprit is guilty of breaking the law and (2) a recommendation as to how he is to be treated if he has been judged guilty. This recommendation is passed on to the Culprit-Processing Machine, which (1) punishes the person in proportion to the damage he has done — and (2) changes him so that he will not offend again.

The civil law, analogously, may appear to take the form of a Damage-Computing Machine, which calculates the monetary value of broken fenders, fractured ribs, loss of income, pain, worry, and the like. Justice would be arrived at when an aggrieved person has been compensated for any harm he may have suffered.

If this picture were accurate, we would not need a field like "legal psychology." In reality, however, the process of passing, administering, and applying laws is in the hands of people — not machines. And "Justice" turns out to be a very human product indeed.

This is where legal psychology enters the picture:

Legal psychology as a *science* studies the process whereby jus-

3

tice is arrived at, examines the people who take part in this process, and looks into their purposes, motives, thoughts, and feelings.

As a *profession*, legal psychology aims at reducing to a minimum those psychological factors which detract from the objectivity of the legal process. The final aim is to make justice as fair and constructive as humanly possible.

The next chapter will examine the problems of legal psychology as a science. In this chapter, we shall illustrate the need for legal psychology as a profession, especially in the process of criminal law. We can start with a look at our mythical Law-Passing Machine.

THE PSYCHOLOGY OF LAWMAKING

People are *motivated* to pass laws. They pass laws which reflect their concerns. Sometimes laws reflect very temporary concerns, as they do when feelings run high because of a crisis which unsettles people or an episode which shocks them.

Antisubversion legislation and witch-hunting laws are examples of crisis-legislation. An example of legislation inspired by a shocking incident is the "sexual psychopathic law" typified by Michigan's Goodrich Act. The Goodrich Act was passed in reaction to a particularly gruesome and repelling sex crime involving a child. It extended, however, to a variety of sexual offenses, and created inequities and enforcement problems (Hartwell, 1950).

Even when laws are not a product of hysteria, they reflect problems which concern people at the time the law is passed. One type of problem which laws may reflect are economic needs, or social and economic relationships. In ancient Rome, land was a very important commodity because it represented wealth and power. The Romans therefore took an extremely dim view of offenses involving land. A person who dug up a boundary stone and transplanted it to a more favorable location could expect to be buried up to his neck and to have his head shaved off with a new plow (Duncan, 1940, p. 77). In England, especially in the days of the Industrial Revolution, property became a dominant concern, and the law showed severity with offenses against property — however slight by modern standards. Many starving children were hanged for stealing a loaf of bread or some exchangeable trifle in an attempt to survive. To this day, the maximum penalty in England for destroying hops or burning a haystack is life imprisonment, and verdicts are at times rendered which reflect such medieval concerns.

A more recent example of a law motivated by socioeconomic relationships is a nineteenth-century San Francisco fire prevention ordinance making it illegal to maintain without a permit a laundry in a wooden building. This ordinance was passed at a time of job competition between Chinese immigrants and native labor. The Supreme Court, in the case of Yick Wo v. Hopkins (1886), found that economic discrimination was clearly the object of the law, since 200 Chinese laundrymen had been unable to obtain permission to operate laundries, whereas 79 out of 80 non-Chinese applications for permits had been granted.

Laws are also passed because of religious or moral standards of the time. Under the reign of Edward III, for instance, there was a strongly worded law against wearing a mustache without a beard (Duncan, 1940). Many communities have passed "blue" laws imposing Sunday curfews on business establishments, which mirror both religious and economic feelings.

Laws also frequently show signs of reflecting feelings of vengefulness or hatred. Psychoanalysts have speculated that such laws may express a hidden desire in the lawmaker to engage in the very practices he proscribes (Weihofen, 1956). In Gilbert and Sullivan's "Trial by Jury" the members of the jury express this type of feeling when they declare:

> "Oh, I was like that when a lad!
> A shocking young scamp of a rover.
> I behaved like a regular cad;
> But that sort of thing is all over.
> I am now a respectable chap
> And shine with a virtue resplendent,
> And therefore I haven't a rap
> Of sympathy for the defendant!"

The extreme manifestation of vengefulness is the death penalty, which one cannot claim to have a rehabilitating effect. As late as March, 1960, a public-opinion poll showed well over half the adult male population of the country favoring the death penalty. Juvenile delinquency also draws its share of vengefulness, with strong public demand for curfews, physical punishment, and "toughness." Such demands become reflected in legislation, and therefore require study.

THE LEGISLATOR AS LAW TRANSCRIBER

The point has been repeatedly stated that legislatures do not make laws. They only record or transcribe the laws which people suggest to them (Chamberlain, 1936). Even in the act of transcribing a law, it is standard practice for legislators to solicit reactions from all manner of people who might be affected. A narcotics law, for instance, might be submitted to physicians and pharmacists who would be hampered by it, and to police officers who would have to enforce it. One result of this process is that organized groups who have an interest in legislation can maintain pressures on legislators in the form of "lobbyists" who promote their biases and interests. (For a discussion and review of lobbying activities in Washington, the reader is referred to Schriftgeiser, 1951.)

Legislators have no way of telling how much public opinion particular lobbying pressure groups represent. It is easy to mistake private desires for public demands. Pressure groups can increase this illusion by stirring up feeling in support of their demands (Zeller, 1938), and by giving the impression that they can vote lawmakers out of office. One former state representative reports that "the legislator can hardly turn around or make a move in the corridors of the State House without being confronted with a veiled threat of the effect on his political fortunes of a vote for or against a particular proposition" (Parkman, 1938, p. 98). The same author describes how the lawmaker "is bound to have a feeling of futility because there is nowhere he can turn for quiet, unbiased reasoning argument, and for impartial information as to the probable effect of the enactment of legislation or the comparative experience of such legislation in other states" (p. 101).

Thus lawmaking is far from an informed, accurate reflection of public opinion. It represents a *distorted* reflection, resulting from the legislators' exposure to lobbyists and interest groups, as well as from their own personal needs and past experiences. These psychological sources of legislation must be exposed and explored.

INTERPRETATION OF LAWS

Demands shift, whereas laws frequently remain. As each wave of public or private pressure washes by, it leaves its deposit of unrealistic or unenforceable laws. Thus, as we shall see in Chapter 17, we have legislation on the books in most states which outlaws sex practices that are extremely common, and therefore cannot be subjected to punishment. Many states also have laws against gambling covering church bingo games, bridge parties, and social poker playing. These types of laws tend to be ignored or are only occasionally invoked for special purposes.

Any prosecutor who did decide to "crack down" on penny-a-point card games would undoubtedly be voted out of office at the earliest opportunity. And, although we would laugh at a judge who followed Herbert's Lord Chancellor's example and proclaimed that

> from this day forth it is my intention to decide such disputes as come before me in accordance with my good sense and judgment, ignoring both precedent and Parliament where they are opposed to me, [Herbert, 1948, p. 158]

we do not expect judges to convict all persons who break all laws. Judges have our full approval when they pretend that some laws do not exist, or when they use them only in emergencies.

Another way of coping with laws which do not meet psychological needs is to pretend to act in accord with them while one is actually "getting around" them. For example, in jurisdictions in which adultery is the only legally accepted ground for divorce,[1] an elaborate pretense of infidelity is generally made in the courts. "Adultery" thus can become a transaction with a young lady like Herbert's "Elizabeth Mugg":

> Elizabeth has been in eighty-nine divorce cases, she tells me, under various names, and has never met one of the parties yet. In this case, of course, she went down to Brighton and stayed a night at the "Cosmopole." Pratt's valet stayed there the same night, and put a pair of Pratt's boots outside Elizabeth's room. During the night her boots met Pratt's, and the next day the valet met one of the chambermaids and identified the boots, and there you are. [Herbert, 1948, p. 39.]

These are the types of arrangements lawyers call "legal fictions." They permit the letter of the law to be followed while its intent is violated. A story which has been cited as a prototype of this process is that of Tom Sawyer digging a hole with a pickax but pretending to use a pocket knife — which "was the right course in such cases" (Pound, cit. Garrison & Hurst, 1956, p. 410).

A third way of adjusting the law to human needs is to determine the most sensible outcome for a given case and then to pick the law or precedent which prescribes this outcome. This does not mean that all laws apply equally to any given body of facts. It does mean that there usually is a choice of laws or previous cases which can be

---

[1] Some jurisdictions in which adultery is the only accepted ground for divorce have a law against adultery. It is obvious that such a law cannot be enforced.

plausibly invoked (see discussion in Chapter 6, pages 133-135). Even the United States Supreme Court "selects" out of several constitutional provisions the one it applies to any given case:

The Supreme Court knows that if it pushes the "deprivation of property without due process of law" button, the answer will come out—unconstitutional. If it pushes the "state police power" button, the answer will come out—constitutional. But the machine of the law does not tell the Court which button to push. [Rodell, 1939, p. 159.]

A verdict may thus be reached on the basis of extralegal consideration, and a legal justification may be selected for it later. Psychologists must be concerned with the motives which in fact inspire legal decisions. In this connection, one basic assumption the psychologist must make is that the purposes for which a law is used should influence the way in which it is perceived. The same law should mean different things to different users. This process is demonstrated by the fact that out-of-date laws can be reinterpreted and applied to situations for which they were not intended. Levi (1949) provides an illustration in the history of the Mann Act. This piece of legislation was passed by Congress on June 25, 1910, and was directed against white-slave traffic, or

. . . any person who shall knowingly transport, or cause to be transported, or aid or assist in obtaining transportation for, or in transporting, in interstate or foreign commerce or in any territory or in the District of Columbia, any woman or girl for the purpose of prostitution or debauchery, or to engage in any immoral practice.

This problem was perceived to be a very serious one. Congressman Mann declared that "all the horrors which have been urged, either truthfully or fancifully, against the black-slave traffic, pale into insignificance as compared with the horrors of the white-slave traffic" (cit. Levi, p. 25). Organized rings of malevolent individuals of alien origin were reputed to have captured young girls in this country and abroad. They were assumed to have coerced their victims by unspeakable means into engaging in unspeakable practices. The Mann Act was intended to curb the importation of the helpless girls as well as their introduction into the red-light districts of American cities.

Whether the problem ever existed, except in the minds of Congress, is a moot point. What matters to us is that the law, once it had been passed, was invoked against a diversity of persons engaged in a variety of unrelated pursuits. As early as 1913, a southern theater manager was convicted under the Mann Act for having made advances to a chorus girl whom he had hired in another state; in 1915, a prostitute was indicted when she changed her residence from Illinois to Wisconsin. The Supreme Court upheld both convictions, although in the first case transportation had occurred for the purpose of employment, and in the second case the woman was admittedly not an innocent victim. In neither case was white-slave traffic involved. In 1944, the Mann Act was invoked against a family that owned a brothel, and was returning there from a vacation trip on which the couple had been accompanied by two of its employees; in 1945, the Supreme Court reaffirmed a conviction arising from a two-block taxi ride in Washington, D. C.; in 1946, the Mann Act was used against Mormons for practicing polygamy.

To be sure, the history of this piece of legislation is not typical. But it does dramatize the general point: Laws are interpreted and reinterpreted in the course of being applied. These interpretations are cumulative, in the sense that a court decision of yesterday can be used by another court today as a basis for a more generous interpretation. This in turn can be used tomorrow, with the result that the law has radically changed its meaning by this time. The judge who finally uses the law may be singularly unconcerned with the problems that motivated its passage. The law is his tool, and acquires (within limits) whatever meanings he may need for his purposes. This creative element in the implementation of law makes the people who apply laws important psychological subjects. This is especially so since judicial interpretations have at times offset progressive social legislation (Goldberg and Levenson, 1935).

SELECTIVE SANCTIONS

The law does not cover different people in the same way, nor is it uniformly enforced against everyone. Psychological factors help to determine who is to suffer the brunt of the law, and who is to remain relatively protected from legal sanctions. A case in point is the selective enforcement against Negroes of the law in parts of the United States. The tendency in several southern states, for example, is to be extremely lenient with a Negro offender who has offended against another Negro, but to throw the book at a Negro who has committed an offense against a white person. It has been speculated that lenience with Negro crime represents an effort to permit Negroes to "let off steam" as long as it does not burn whites. It is the latter whose discriminatory acts are in part responsible for the feelings of aggression expressed in Negro crime (Dollard, 1937).

Another commonly cited illustration of selective law enforcement is the socioeconomic bias of the law. This bias starts with lawmaking, in that acts defined as crimes typically are the antisocial activities of underprivileged persons, such as vagrancy and offenses against property. Large-scale exploitation, misappropriations, and other antisocial activities prevalent in business and industry tend to go unpunished (Sutherland, 1949). Such activities, in fact, are frequently admired as showing initiative and ambition rather than being defined as crimes.

It has also been noted that when two people commit the same crime, the offender from the lower social or economic group is more likely to be arrested, convicted, and committed to prison than his financially favored fellow offender. The police are less likely to suspect the "respectable" citizen, the prosecutor is less prone to charge him, and many judges are less likely to take a serious view of him should his case get into court.

This is not to say that crime is not more prevalent among underprivileged people. As will be noted elsewhere in this volume, slums and poverty do create psychological problems which result in antisocial behavior. However, poorer people don't have the monopoly on crime which they appear to have from an inventory of prison populations or from the guest lists of probation departments.

The inequity in law enforcement dramatizes the importance of studying the perceptions, attitudes, and feelings of people charged with enforcing the law. For our present purposes it will suffice to mention two points in the administration of criminal justice where law enforcers do exercise decisions, and where they thereby affect the rule of law.

Arrest[2]

Police officers do not arrest every offender who is drawn to their attention. Conversely, they sometimes arrest people without having legal grounds. One illustration of overgenerous arrest practices is

---

[2] In formulating the problems of arrest and prosecution I have been aided by the *Pilot Project Report on the Administration of Criminal Justice in the United States* edited by the American Bar Foundation. I am grateful to the Bar Foundation and to Professor Frank Remington for providing access to this material.

the "harassing" of prostitutes, homosexuals, or gamblers. "Harassment" consists of taking likely candidates into custody, and releasing them after a night or two in jail. This involves no effort at enforcing the law, since there is no intention of prosecuting the arrested persons.

Here is an instance in which the police pursue their own objectives rather than trying to act according to legal prescriptions. Feeling that prosecutors or courts do not offer them enough help in their perceived mission, the police may simply take matters into their own hands. The zealousness of the police in their campaign against crime (or sin) is often responsible for serious infractions of freedom or dignity. "Round-ups," overquick shooting, the "third degree," illegal searches and seizures, wire tapping, the use of informers, and even the practice of bribery and graft are illustrations of prevalent abuses of police power (Tappan, 1960). Less dramatic but of similar nature are instances of impolite treatment of suspects and demonstrated lack of sensitivity to human feelings.

As long as such practices occur, the police can never be viewed as a piece of reliable administrative machinery. The people who make up the police must be studied in every respect. Their selection and training is a task to which painstaking effort must be dedicated, and their attitudes and habits must undergo continued scrutiny. This is especially necessary because members of the police are in constant contact with the public. Many people have come to regard the police as arbitrary, sadistic, or merely dishonest. A typical reaction is the suggestion that dogs be substituted for patrolmen because dogs are gentle and understanding. After a recent police scandal in Chicago, patrolmen on their beats were greeted with such remarks as "It takes only one to play cops and robbers." Such unfavorable public reactions create serious consequences even for the police, because they reduce morale and efficiency.

Equally serious consequences result from blindly backing and cheering the police, with no concern for the inevitable side effects of zealous enforcement. Police infringements of law and human rights generally have low visibility (Goldstein, 1960). They come to public attention only as a result of public concern. The newspaper's role is vital in promoting such concern, but the press is more likely to praise toughness than to expose subtle abuses of the rights of unsavory individuals. The problem of educating both the press and the public concerning the human aspects of law enforcement is one of pressing concern.

Charging

Two seasoned felons, Lionel La Fleur and Muggs Pierpont McGee, meet on the grounds of the Shady Brook State Penitentiary. The following conversation ensues:

LL: You just got here?

MM: Yea . . . How long you in for?

LL: One to five years. I'm going out on parole next week. How about you?

MM: Ten to fifteen years. Got a long way to go!

LL: (*respectfully*) I'll say! What did they get you for?

MM: Me and a buddy broke into a gas station in State City one night last November, and the cops caught us.

LL: That's strange! We also got nabbed breaking into a gas station at night. Why do you figure you're in ten times as long as me?

McGee's meditations in response to this question may bring him considerable misery. They may even strengthen his antisocial feelings. And it is, no doubt, of little consolation to McGee that wide discrepancies in sentences are very common.

It would be wrong to assume that sentencing habits of different judges are entirely to blame for this condition. Frequently the prosecutor is equally or more responsible. McGee's prosecutor may have charged him with the offense he actually committed (breaking and entering a business building in the nighttime), which tends to carry a high penalty. La Fleur's prosecutor might have encouraged him to plead guilty to a less serious offense (one not presupposing forced entry, or one specifying daytime as opposed to nighttime). Most prosecutors accept guilty pleas to lesser offenses in a large proportion of their cases.

One important reason for this practice is the sheer volume of pressing business. A guilty plea saves time, since it permits disposal of the case without a lengthy trial. Occasionally, a prosecutor will be delighted to accept a plea to a reduced charge because he may feel that he lacks the evidence to make the original charge stick. Another reason for letting a person plead guilty is to avoid imposing on him an excessive sentence required by law, or to permit him to be placed on probation.

Whatever the reason, prosecutors do not simply apply the law to the facts and rush into court, demanding a conviction. More often than not, they will not take an offender to court at all. And when they do, they may do so for a variety of reasons, many of which have nothing to do with the law. These must be studied.

THE COURTROOM

In the remainder of this section, we shall be concerned with the problem of what happens in the courtroom, and with the human elements that have to be considered in this situation. Chapters 3 and 4 will describe what happens in a typical trial from the point of view of the contending lawyers. It will become evident that advocates involved in the courtroom have to make innumerable assumptions and predictions about the perceptions, attitudes, and motives of other people. It becomes vitally important to them, for example, to guess what goes on in the minds of their judge or jury in the face of every move they or their witnesses make. This, after all, determines the verdict.

Psychological data about *judges* will be discussed in Chapter 6. At this point, we need only indicate that the problem does not confine itself to extreme cases of prejudice. To be sure, judges who are professional sadists, or obviously senile, pose a very special problem, as do the numerous judges who have well-known aversions, preferences, or concerns which lawyers try to manipulate or which they attempt to escape. A problem is obviously also posed by judges with special sentencing habits, such as consistently lenient or perennially "tough" judges. Over and above these dramatic variations, however, one must consider more pervasive and subtle psychological factors, such as the effects of the judge's role. This is the problem suggested by Lady Cicely in Shaw's *Captain Brassbound's Conversion* when she exclaims:

"Bless me! Your Uncle Howard is one of the most harmless of men—much nicer than most professional people. Of course he does dreadful things as a judge; but then if you take a man and pay him £5000 a year to be wicked, and praise him for it, and have policemen and courts and laws and juries to drive him into it so that he can't help doing it, what can you expect?" [Shaw, 1947, p. 646.]

Even more pervasive are the psychological effects of legal training, which will be discussed in the next chapter.

Next to the judge, the trial lawyer is probably most concerned about *juries*, although most criminal cases are tried without them. According to public-opinion polls, a majority of people prefer being heard by a jury rather than by a judge alone, and they tend to rely on juries in their "civil" disputes (the type of trial discussed in Chapter 4). This results in congested court calendars and in high settlements against insurance companies. The reactions of jurors to evidence and to the actions of lawyers become an important social as well as practical problem. The psychology of juries will be taken up in Chapter 5.

Another type of person in whose psychological reactions lawyers have great interest, is the *witness*. The witness is the only access the court has to the facts to which the law must be applied (Frank, 1949). If key witnesses are honestly or dishonestly in error, the wisest court will reach the wrong decisions, and injustice must result. A great deal of courtroom procedure is geared to the problem of evaluating the testimony of witnesses. Legal psychology as a formal discipline started as an attempt to aid in this evaluation.

THE PSYCHOLOGY OF TESTIMONY

In the next chapter (pages 46-47) mention will be made of psychological efforts in the area of testimony. At this point we shall briefly deal with only one book, which more than any other represents the beginning of legal psychology in the United States. This volume is entitled, *On The Witness Stand*, and was first published in 1907. Its author was the German psychologist Hugo Munsterberg, who had been brought to Harvard to head the Psychological Laboratory there. Since Munsterberg was passionately interested in applying psychology to practical problems, his attention soon strayed from the laboratory and centered on the courtroom.

In court Munsterberg noted what to him seemed a very interesting problem: despite the fact that individuals had solemnly sworn to tell "the truth, and nothing but the truth," their version of the truth frequently differed markedly from that of other people who had also sworn to tell the truth. Such differences in the testimony could occur even in simple issues such as the speed of a car, the number of people in a room, the location and distance of a sound, and the general dimensions of a person.

Munsterberg conducted classroom demonstrations and experiments to show that trained observers with generous advance warning could not agree on matters such as the number of squares on a board, the amount of time between two clicks, the pitch of a sound, and the shape of an inkblot. Their testimony, taken immediately after their exposure to an object, would tend to range widely.

Munsterberg concluded that perceptual habits have to be taken into consideration in evaluating testimony. He also showed that a person who flagrantly misperceived one situation was very likely to perform just as badly in another. The demonstration Munsterberg used for this purpose featured two squares — one blue and one gray. He asked his psychology class to judge which square was darker. "The gray was objectively far lighter than the dark blue, and any one with an unbiased mind who looked at those two squares of paper could not have the slightest doubt that the blue was darker. Yet about one fifth of the men wrote that the gray was darker." Having established this, Munsterberg proceeded to the second part of his experiment:

I stood on the platform behind a low desk and begged the men to watch and to describe everything which I was going to do from one given signal to another. As soon as the signal was given, I lifted with my right hand a little revolving wheel with a color-disk and made it run and change its color, and all the while, while I kept the little instrument at the height of my head, I turned my eyes eagerly toward it. While this was going on, up to the closing signal, I took with my left hand, at first, a pencil from my vest-pocket and wrote something at the desk; then I took my watch out and laid it on the table; then I took a silver cigarette-box from my pocket, opened it, took a cigarette out of it, closed it with a loud click, and returned it to my pocket, and then came the ending signal. The results showed that eighteen of the hundred had not noticed anything of all that I was doing with my left hand. Pencil and watch and cigarettes simply had not existed for them. [Munsterberg, 1925, pp. 29–30.]

In comparing the results of the two demonstrations, Munsterberg discovered that *fourteen of the eighteen* men who had given deficient testimony in the color-disk experiment had judged the light gray square to be darker than the dark blue square:

That coincidence was, of course, not chance. In the case of the darkness experiment the mere idea of grayness gave the suggestible minds the belief that colorless gray must be darker than any color. They evidently did not judge at all from the optical impression, but entirely from their conception of gray as darkness. The coincidence, therefore, proved clearly how very quickly a little experiment such as this with a piece of blue and gray paper, which can be performed in a few seconds, can pick out for us those minds which are probably unfit to report whether an action has been performed in their presence or not. Whatever they expect to see they do see; and if the attention is turned in one direction, they are blind and deaf and idiotic in the other. [P. 31.]

Munsterberg advocated that psychologists be permitted to test witnesses and to evaluate testimony. He also pointed out that psychology had acquired much information which could help in sorting reliable from unreliable evidence. According to Munsterberg, "every chapter and subchapter of sense psychology" could clear up testimony problems (p. 33). This contention was amplified by such authors as Burtt (1931). Burtt illustrated his point with facts about sensory defects, distance perception, color vision, adaptation, acuity, auditory space perception, tactual perception, the perception of motion, time perception, and aspects of attention and memory. He attempted to show that in each case, facts known by psychologists could be brought to bear on discrepancies in testimony — discrediting some witnesses, supporting others, or accounting for differences among them.

Psychologists occasionally have been used in the courtroom as experts on testimony. One of the earliest instances occurred in Belgium in 1910. The psychologist involved was Varendonck, who was given the task of evaluating information obtained from two little girls under suggestive questioning in a preliminary examination. To this end, Varendonck devised a series of ingenious experiments incorporating questions similar to those which had been asked of the witnesses. Answers were obtained from children much like the two little girls in age and background. These answers clearly showed that the original testimony could have resulted from the suggestive questions. For instance, eighteen children were asked to name the color of the beard of one of the teachers. Sixteen responded, "Black." The teacher had never worn a beard.

In the crucial experiment,
Written answers were required from 8-year-old pupils. "When you were standing in line in the yard, a man came up to you, didn't he? You surely know who it was. Write his name on your paper." No man had come, but 7 of 22 children gave a man's name. The experimenter continued, "Was it not Mr. M_____?" Seventeen of the 22 answered "yes," and in individual oral examinations gave complete descriptions of the man's appearance and dress. [Rouke, 1957, p. 54.]

The number of psychologists testifying in the courtroom (in a professional capacity) has not increased greatly since 1910. (Chapter 2 takes up some of the reasons for this fact.) Psychiatrists, by contrast, have invested increasing time and effort in the courtroom.

FORENSIC PSYCHIATRY

Chapter 7 of this volume deals with important issues related to psychiatry in the courtroom. A brief word will serve to introduce the subject.

Among the strangest kinds of cases on record are trials in which animals have served as defendants. Swarms of ants, locusts, and mice have been charged and convicted. Cows and pigs have been sentenced to death. One American trial of the thirties resulted in the execution of several dogs. A Spitz was recently placed in four-year probation in New York State. A six-month old puppy named Idaho, also convicted in New York State, was put on probation for two years (Duncan, 1940, p. 41).

Such cases strike us as ludicrous and weird because we make two "common sense" assumptions about human crime which we do not make when dealing with acts committed by animals. The first of these assumptions is that a person acts with *awareness* — that he *knows* what he is doing — whereas an animal does not; the second assumption is that we exercise free will — that we *can help doing* what we do — whereas an animal cannot. These assumptions imply that man may be *held responsible* for his actions, and may be taken to account for them, whereas puppy dogs and cows cannot be blamed for their "crimes": they must be viewed as innocent products of their training and limitations.

Psychiatrists most frequently appear in the courtroom in cases where the argument is raised that a human defendant falls into the same category because of a mental disorder. In the early days this argument exclusively concentrated on the first of the two presumed human qualities. If a puppy was being defended under this formula his counsel might argue:

> Poor Bowser cannot be found guilty of destroying the new mahogany table top because he could not tell that if he stepped on his plate he would cause what we view as a calamity. Since he did not know that the act he was committing would be regarded as wrong, Bowser is clearly not responsible for his crime.

This conforms to the rule of insanity formulated for the British House of Lords in 1843, which is still used all over the United States (except in New Hampshire and the District of Columbia). In fifteen states, this definition (the McNaghten Formula) is supplemented by the "Irresistible Impulse Doctrine," which argues as follows:

Surely you can't hold Bowser responsible for defacing the table, because he could not help doing what he did. After all, Bowser did not *choose* to spill his milk. He acted on a dumb impulse.

Psychiatrists have objected to the use of these definitions of responsibility because psychiatry no longer assumes that people behave with full awareness and free will. A committee of the Group for the Advancement of Psychiatry (1945) poses the issue as follows:

> The rules place a premium on intellectual capacity and presuppose that behavior is actuated exclusively by reason and untrammeled choice. On the one hand, this overemphasizes the importance of the intellect, reason and common sense; on the other hand, it underemphasizes the emotional pressures that energize behavior. [P. 4.]

A psychiatrist testifying under these rules is thus "put to the exercise of relating his medical data to an unrelatable requirement" (p. 5). He must frequently testify that an obviously insane person is "responsible" under the law, because the law ignores the role of the unconscious and of nonrational motives in human behavior.

In response to such arguments by many psychiatrists and some jurists, New Hampshire and the District of Columbia have discarded the so-called McNaghten Rule. In these jurisdictions, a psychiatrist appearing for the defense simply testifies that the defendant is suffering from a known mental disease, and that his crime resulted from his illness. If the jury accepts the psychiatrist's statement, it exempts the defendant from responsibility, and he becomes a medical problem instead of a correctional candidate. If, on the other hand, the psychiatrist does not testify that the defendant is mentally ill, the defendant can be punished.

One troublesome consequence of this new arrangement is that our friend Bowser (unless he suffered from a bad case of rabies) would be declared responsible and punishable for his crime. This fact may prompt one to re-examine the concept of responsibility. If modern pyschiatric views of human nature have shown (as indeed they have) that neither puppies nor people are governed by complete awareness and free will, it should follow that neither puppies nor people may ever be held completely "responsible" for their actions. Certainly, psychiatrists should never attach blame, nor should they exempt anyone from it.

A few psychiatrists have seen this point, and have taken a stand against the use of psychiatric testimony in the courtroom. Szasz (see Chapter 7) has most eloquently argued this position. He has also pointed out that a logical role for psychiatrists would be to bring psychiatric insights to bear on the legal process, rather than to participate in the process:

Psychiatry, as a social science, will do its share of the work in this area if it will make explicit the ethical and psychological premises on which social acts and judgments rest, and if it will contribute to their accurate understanding. [P. 316.]

PSYCHOLOGY AND THE COURTROOM

Szasz (1957) has suggested that psychiatry may have been "over-sold." This possibility presents itself in the case of psychology with equal force. In their zeal to obtain entry into the courtroom as experts, psychologists may make promises which they are in no position to redeem. Dean John Wigmore, one of the greatest legal minds of the century, whose classic on evidence draws heavily on psychological writings, arrived — after thoughtful review — at the conclusion that

there still remains unexploited by psychometry almost the whole field of possibilities in testimonial evidence. In spite of the Munsterberg trumpet-blast of 1909, announcing that "the time for applied psychology is surely near," and that "the judges can test the individual differences of men by the methods of experimental psychology," and "with the same (quantitative) accuracy (as in food materials) can transform their common sense into careful measurements," the record of psychometric achievement with testimony is still meager. [Wigmore, 1937, p. 792.]

If psychologists do enter the courtroom, they also risk falling prey to what Wellman has called "unconscious partisanship," the tendency to "feel complimented by the confidence that is placed in [witnesses] by the party calling them to prove a certain state of facts" and the desire "to prove worthy of this confidence" (cit. Frank, 1949, p. 19).

The same factors which cause psychiatrists to lock horns in the courtroom can create conflicts in psychological testimony. Just as professional witnesses have sprung up in the psychiatric profession, who testify with skillful precision at the drop of a fifty-dollar bill, a comparable fraternity of professional psychological witnesses could easily arise.

The main reason for caution about psychological testimony in the courtroom, however, lies elsewhere. As we have seen, the courtroom and the human foundations which support it are full of points at which scientific inquiry and reform are needed. As a citizen, the psychologist owes the law respect and allegiance. As a psychologist, he must regard law and justice as human products, and he must view them as his subject matter. If he becomes part of the legal process, this view is lost.

The psychologist must cooperate with people active in the legal process by helping them to understand themselves and the human context to which they belong. People active in the field of law are seriously concerned with finding ways of making justice more just. The psychologist and his colleagues can help in this enterprise by locating psychological barriers along the way. They can possibly also join in the task of clearing the road ahead.

References

Burtt, M. E. *Legal psychology*. Englewood Cliffs, N. J.: Prentice-Hall, 1931.

Chamberlain, J. P. *Legislative process*. New York: Appleton-Century-Crofts, 1936.

Dollard, J. *Caste and class in a southern town*. New Haven: Yale Univer. Press, 1937.

Duncan, Y. A. *The strangest cases on record*. Chicago: Reilly & Lee, 1940.

Frank, J. *If men were angels*. New York: Harper, 1942.

Frank, J. *Courts on trial*. Princeton, N. J.: Princeton Univer. Press, 1949.

Garrison, L. K., & Hurst, W. *The legal process*. (Rev. ed.) Madison, Wisc.: Capitol Press, 1956.

Goldberg, L. P., & Levenson, Eleanore. *Lawless judges*. New York: Rand School Press, 1935.

Goldstein, J. Police discretion not to invoke the criminal process: Low-visibility decisions in the administration of criminal justice. *Yale Law J.*, 1960, **69**, 543–594.

Group for the Advancement of Psychiatry, Committee on Psychiatry and Law. *Criminal responsibilty and psychiatric expert testimony*. Report No. 26. Topeka, Kan.: 1954.

Hartwell, S. W. *A citizens' handbook of sexual abnormalities*. Lansing, Mich.: Michigan Department of Mental Health, 1950.

Herbert, A. P. *Uncommon law*. London: Methuen, 1948.

Levi, E. H. *An introduction to legal reasoning*. Chicago: Univer. of Chicago Press, 1949.

Munsterberg, H. *On the witness stand*. New York: Clark, Boardman, 1925.

Parkman, H. Lobbies and pressure groups: A legislator's point of view. *Ann. Amer. Acad. pol. & soc. Sci.*, 1938, **195**, 95–102.

Rodell, F. *Woe unto you, lawyers*. New York: Reynal & Hitchcock, 1939.

Rouke, F. L. Psychological research on problems of testimony. *J. soc. Issues*, 1957, **13**, 50–59.

Schriftgeiser, K. *The lobbyists*. Boston: Little, Brown, 1951.

Shaw, G. B. *Six plays*. New York: Dodd, Mead, 1947.

Sutherland, E. H. *White collar crime*. New York: Holt, Rinehart and Winston, 1949.

Szasz, T. S. Psychiatric expert testimony—Its court meaning and social function. *Psychiat.*, 1957, **20**, 313–316.

Tappan, T. W. *Crime, justice and correction*. New York: McGraw-Hill, 1960.

Weihofen, H. *The urge to punish: New approaches to the problem of mental irresponsibility for crime*. New York: Farrar, Straus, and Cudahy, 1956.

Wigmore, J. H. *The science of judicial proof*. Boston: Little, Brown, 1937.

Yick Wo v. Hopkins, 118 U. S. 366, 1886.

Zeller, Belle. Lobbies and pressure groups: A political scientist's point of view. *Ann. Amer. Acad. pol. & soc. Sci.*, 1938, **195**, 79–87.

2 Psychology and Law

Few men capture the great fascination of law in all of its many leanings. The poet W. H. Auden's[1] effort is noble, and appropriately guides us into the question, What is law?

>Law is the wisdom of the old
>The impotent grandfathers shrilly scold;
>The grandchildren put out a treble tongue,
>Law is the senses of the young.
>
>Law, says the priest with a priestly look,
>Expounding to an unpriestly people,
>Law is the words in my priestly book,
>Law is my pulpit and my steeple.
>
>Law, says the judge as he looks down his nose,
>Speaking clearly and most severely,
>Law is as I've told you before,
>Law is as you know I suppose,
>Law is but let me explain it once more,
>Law is The Law.
>
>Yet law-abiding scholars write;
>Law is neither wrong nor right,
>Law is only crimes
>Punished by places and by time,
>
>Law is the clothes men wear
>Anytime, anywhere,
>Law is Good morning and Good night.
>
>Others say, Law is our Fate;
>Others say, Law is our State;
>Others say, others say
>Law is no more
>Law has gone away.

---

[1] *"Law like love."* Copyright 1940 by W. H. Auden. Reprinted from *The Collected Poetry of W. H. Auden,* by permission of Random House, Inc., and of Faber & Faber Ltd.

And always the loud angry crowd
Very angry and very loud
Law is We,
And always the soft idiot softly Me.

Different perceptions of law lead to different views as to whether law is good or bad, effective or ineffective.

It seems there is little middle ground between judging law's influence on society generally and judging its sharp practical effects in particular, limited situations. For some law is "the true embodiment of everything that's excellent," because it helps to preserve culture, permits continuing and productive relations between men, and provides ethical uplift. It is a part of psychological growth, contributing to the development of individual as well as collective conscience — a thesis particularly developed by the psychiatrist Ranyard West in his book *Conscience and Society* (1945).

Then there is the other view of law which emphasizes its specific and limited practical effect. In this view, law seems unsteady in that it can be manipulated too readily by unscrupulous influence and by devious twisting of its processes. It is primitive and archaic too many times, to the detriment of particular individuals whose fortunes under law seem guided more by the history of society's prior experience than by current needs. And it serves and benefits special and sometimes powerful interests to the detriment of the less favored groups who are unable to muster enough power or wealth to control law's uses.

The point is that there are contradictions in law. For every proposition as to its use and worth there are opposing truths. It is only by reference to a full and systematic catalogue of specific operations and effects of law that one can perceive it most clearly and accurately.

It is the task of the social sciences then — psychology included — to provide studies of the processes and influences of law. But, as Auden notes, law is so vast that one ought to begin with a bit of cartography. There is the need to consider the various operations and effects of law, and we shall do so here from a psychological standpoint. Then, to ascertain clearly some of the problems in the relation of legal and psychological professions, we shall have to consider something of the dispositions of law and psychology which may create problems. And finally, an account of recent experiences in relating law and psychology will help to provide historical perspective. These are the tasks, and this is the outline, of this chapter.

A PSYCHOLOGICAL VIEW OF THE
SPHERES OF LAW

Psychologically, law may be a different experience with a different meaning, depending upon where you grasp it. A person who views the experience and outcome of law in an attorney's office or in a bargaining session, will obtain a different picture of law from that observed in a trial court. The experience of law as a general standard may be something quite different from the experience of law as a set of procedures or as a judicial decree.

Law viewed in terms of the operations and dispositions of a prosecutor may be a different matter from what it is in the hands of a legislator. Judges weave meanings and impacts of law one way, whereas executives, defense attorneys, and office counsel may have quite another influence.

Then, too, the experience and impact of law is likely to be quite different, psychologically and otherwise, depending upon whether one is a litigant or a law student, a criminal aggressor or a victim of sharp economic practices, a subject in court or merely an observer outside.

And finally, the experience of law is different, with different psychological and other consequences, depending upon whether one is trying to fit current law into the history and continuity of legal decision, into the customs and institutions of contemporary society, or into the problems and demands of new frontiers.

Following is some further, more detailed reflection on the psychological challenges in viewing the different operations of law, the persons who operate and engineer law, the parties who are affected by law, and the general contexts in which "living law" operates and has influence.

The Operations of Law

Counseling. One way in which law operates is through the scarcely noted counseling process, in which a client addresses a problem to an attorney. When this occurs, law is personal counseling (Brown, 1950). For instance, a client may enter the counselor's sanctum with a pressing frustration because the house a contractor has built for him under a contract of very general specifications is not satisfactory. He feels he has been defrauded. Should he sue?

In a context of mutual confidence, itself a factor determining the success of counseling, both client and counselor must determine the limits within which the client can be satisfied and the means of satisfying him. The counselor must assess the extent of a client's emotional involvement and the character of efforts he is making to reduce his own tension. Clients may evidence great anxiety because of the uncertainty of their position, or frustration, fear, and aggressive feeling because they have been or may be deprived of some matter of value. The counselor must also consider the strength of a client's position in the specific terms of its legal possibilities. He must elicit information relative to the client's financial ability and willingness to sustain his position. He must find and gauge acts and events, claims, and moods and attitudes that are likely to influence. First, they may be selected to influence a client's antagonist to adjust or abandon his position. Then, they may be reconstituted to influence an individual, perhaps a judge, or a group of individuals, such as a jury (about either of whom selected characteristics and dispositions may be known), to make a particular kind of determination for the client.

Upon the judgments derived from this complicated assessment process, the counselor must determine the kind of information and appeal he will use to encourage or reassure the client in the counseling relationship, or to chasten and console him.

The client's role in counseling is somewhat more than passive and receptive. His initial disposition may be confused and uncertain, or perhaps guilty, or fearful and possibly aggressive. He may use or expect to use the counselor to handle his more intense feelings by having the latter either encourage or discourage them. For this, he requires the counselor's information and judgment, which he then tries to use as a basis for altering or sustaining his life's course, perhaps in a number of particulars. Law as counseling is a highly problematic event, involving uncertainties about the skill, knowledge, and disposition of both client and counselor. Yet this most critical aspect of law is buried in the sanctuary of law offices and is cast in the image of insignificant or innocuous considerations.

Negotiation or Conciliation. Negotiation or conciliation is another important legal process generally obscured from any intensive observation and study. The object of negotiation and conciliation is to bring about decisions and adjustments without resort to the use of legal power. Sometimes only the two parties are involved, through their attorneys; at other times a third party (a mediator) makes of the process a three-party relationship. In one case, two attorneys may get together and try to work out an acceptable marital settlement for their parties in hopes of avoiding unpleasant contested divorce litigation. In another, a judge may hold a pretrial hearing with adversary attorneys to determine the extent to which they can or might agree on the facts and claims relating to an accident, and to find the elements of dispute that really are at issue.

Mostly, negotiation in the hands of lawyers leans heavily on the exploitation of power and the manipulation of feelings of fear. Colloquies between attorneys, advanced in behalf of their clients, scarcely veil the impression of necessary force as the best influence. Formal pleadings which outline the factual and legal nature of a dispute, in anticipation of a trial, are also a kind of power jockeying to expose a weak or weakened position in the opposing party, at least as much as they are a representation of issues in conflict. Pretrial conferences, involving a judge and opposing attorneys, advance similar goals by accentuating positions of strength or weakness.

Influencing, by stressing power and provoking fear, may induce more agreeable solutions if successful, and more violent dispositions if a failure. The full range of psychological skills and values is seldom explored. Appeals to conciliatory types of feelings, for example, bear more careful inquiry. The processes of successful negotiation and conciliation, with or without modified force and recrimination, are scarcely well understood and only fortuitously applied.

The Trial Process. The trial process is the dramatic aspect of law operation that garners the greatest number of references to law. (This is the process with which the remaining chapters in this section deal.) It is particularly the criminal trial process, directly involving relatively small numbers of people but great social interest, that creates and strikes formidable attitudes (Goitein, 1923). Mostly there is interest in the trial as a means of determining truth regarding events and circumstances. Is the accused guilty or innocent of charges against him? The proper measure is said to be the probity of the evidence.

There is also an emotional investment and interest in the trial process as such. It is by dint of this that the spectacle and the emotional persuasiveness in the behavior of attorneys are matters of both selfish concern and universal involvement. Trial tactics (as discussed in Chapters 3 and 4), the modes and skills of attorneys, and their impacts and personalities, become subjects for careful observation and study. The influencing of judges and juries by different rhetorical styles, the strategy of argument in instances of defense, or in prosecution, and the collation of facts and values are matters of particular fascination from this viewpoint.

For some, there is preoccupation with the vestigial characteristics of trial, with its appeal as a form of battle. The attorneys are beknighted in their ancient heritage as champions of causes. Interest focuses on the process of intellectual dueling, including the gouging and emasculation of one by the other. It is a form of discharge for aggressive dispositions both within and outside the trial ring.

The trial process incites feelings of respect and reverence, and suspicion and hostility. With its symbolic trappings, in the dress and figure of the judges, the formality of procedure, and in the stentorian judgments it reaches, it is awesome in both its display and its effects. Rightly, it should be a matter of the most careful psychological study.

The Appellate Courts. The appellate courts are another legal operation submerged in considerable ignorance of its true social and psychological effects. Appellate courts nominally test the use of legal skills, values, and judgments evidenced in "inferior" courts. These are the courts, ordered all the way from district appeals courts to the United States Supreme Court, that receive cases "on appeal." The "appeal" is ostensibly to challenge an application or interpretation of law made in a given case by a "lower court." But these courts, at least by implication if not more directly, have a larger mission of providing intellectual leadership in law, monitoring social change, sensing and disposing of emotional dispositions, and proving ethical merit. In the obscurity of their operations, hedged by all sort of legalism, and in their superior and virtually dictatorial authority, the acts and effects of appellate courts reflect some of the greatest power in society.

Judgments and Decrees. The immediate effects of trial — final orders, rulings, decrees, and judgments — are in themselves worthy of study. Law is judgment or decree, perhaps a death sentence, or an award of X number of dollars for damages, or an injunction preventing a strike. The will of judges is a consecrated magic that invokes the fullest power of "command" and "obey" (Hagerstrom, 1953). Judges' acts are imbued with moral as well as legal significance, and law is hence at its most potent in judicial determination.

The impact and importance of a judicial decision is likely to be more involved and comprehensive than immediate reactions suggest.

It may impede, divert, or encourage a person's behavior, and sometimes may do more than one of these simultaneously. It may inhibit, extend, or incite someone's feelings. And its impact may be felt variously by injured parties, by transgressors, and by third parties whose interests are vested in judicial outcomes by reason of their affinity in some respect to the directly affected parties.

The most discussed field of judicial outcomes is, again, the criminal trial decision (Andeneas, 1952; Redmount, 1959 b, c; Watson, 1958). Trial judgments, notably upon conviction, are intended to have multiple effects upon feelings and actions. They have many peculiarly severe punitive and deprivational qualities. For the convicted, the pronouncement of judgment, backed by the expectation of its execution, is intended to inhibit aggressive and destructive feelings and to impede or eliminate criminal action. The same judgment, perhaps attenuated by other edicts more carefully designed for correction, for example, psychiatric treatment, may also aim at diversion or encouragement into newer channels of behavior. For the victim of the offense, judgment serves to alleviate hostile reaction evoked by the offense. For people not directly involved in the trial, judgment may afford an example to reinforce adaptational and adjustive actions and feelings, particularly so for the person whose dispositions lean toward antilegal behavior.

In civil cases, where severe criminal sanctions are not involved, court decisions may have a less dramatic but more specific effect for many. Insofar as the law acts to support or restrain those who would exploit or develop various facets of social living, trial decisions cause or regulate people's behavior. The highly specific prohibitions in trial decisions which are backed by the power of constituted authority may, for example, inhibit and prevent monopolistic practices that enable one party to own and control the sale and distribution of a large resource or product. But, by the same token, the decision may force the people involved to resort to the practice of some other form of economic concentration, such as through restrictive contractual agreements. What holds for an economic empire is equally true for the proverbial John Doe, for whom a court edict on his divorce petition or plea for compensation because of injury, has the effect of both encouraging and restraining particular behaviors and feelings on his part, with consequences for others as well.

Standards and Rules. Finally, there is the concept of law as the standard and the rule. "Thou shalt not kill" — law relating to homocide — is a fairly primitive instance. Income tax laws, amplified by further rules that guide interpretation, are a more complicated example. Law in this role acts as an ideal and an advice. Or, if one is disposed to exploit or ignore it, it is meant as a warning. It is an instrument of learning premised upon the impact on the person of verbal symbols issued in the form of (authoritative) command (Olivecrona, 1939). The assumption is that declarative law marshals and reinforces attitudes and dispositions that cultivate the habit of doing what one is told. Not only in itself, but also by reason of judicial backing, it is assumed to control feelings, purposes, and actions (Ross, 1946). By reasons of these properties, supported by sanctions, the law is valued as an instrument for defining or securing order. It is also valued in confirming existing ethical aspirations and limitations.

Configurations of Legal Operation

Counseling, bargaining, litigation, judicial decree, and legal standard may be conceived of as successive stages, though they are, in another sense, all contiguous to one another and, in varying degrees, reciprocal in their influence. Legal standards, certainly, are virtually always present, since other legal operations are taken in contemplation of them. And such regulations in turn may bear the mark of the effect and need stemming from certain negotiation practices, litigation procedures, and judicial outcomes. Law, in its operation, is a pattern of influences upon individuals, groups, and larger social forces. And it is in turn a patterned result based upon individual and social needs.

Administrative, Executive and Legislative Operations. The most familiar references to law, and the chapters in this section, contemplate law in terms of the sphere of the courts. But it is also important to study law-making (legislation) and law administration, as distinguished from legal adjudication (trial).

The processes of law-making of interest to the psychologist include (1) the sources and character of motivations to law-making, (2) the process of gathering relevant information, as well as the effect of information on the designing of laws, and (3) the influences and procedures whereby people's plans become reality through law-making. Analysis of the Congress of the United States in such fashion can make fascinating study.

The psychology of law administration would consider how legal missions, determined by legislative standard or judicial decree, are accomplished. Agencies for the administration of particular laws and objectives vary from tax boards to prisons — from welfare commissions to labor relations boards. Some agencies (prisons) are custodial in their function. Some serve mainly to refine and communicate law and policy (for example, Boards of Health, Federal Communications Commission). Still other agencies (such as Workmen's Compensation Boards) exercise a quasi-judicial function. Agencies of law administration can be compared in terms of how they define their goals, how they organize to serve their purpose, and how they influence those who submit to their jurisdiction. Some agencies are distinctly punitive and restrictive. Others may appear as more educational. In still others, the psychological impact of aims and means may be mediational in character. And all are fitted, perhaps competitively, to some hopefully harmonious view of the executive branch of government as a marshaling of force for the purpose of giving direction and expedition to the law.

The Law Operatives

Law is poorly understood without a consideration of the people associated with it. One has to consider various types of people who become vested with certain kinds of functions, and with certain attitudes and dispositions toward their work, toward each other, and toward their constituents.

The Law Enforcers. The law enforcers have in common the responsibility and the psychological disposition to assert control and to limit other people's behavior. This they do under terms of law that are usually rigorously defined. They are the policeman and the prosecutor, the sheriff and the prison guard. Their prime function is to protect the remainder of society against the depredations of violators. To some extent, they may be occupied also in preventive functions.

As greater responsibility for control devolves on the enforcer, the bounds of his discretion are larger. To cite the prosecuting attorney as an instance, he has some range of choice in whether and how to act — in whether or not to prosecute and what charge to bring. But, whether they have freedom of action or their function is defined, law enforcers commonly share the activity, and perhaps the disposition, to be punitive and restrictive. They aggress against others in the name of the law, though they may prefer to be thought of as playing a paternal and protective role. There is the notable tendency among many enforcers to enforce zealously, even rigidly, and there may be considerable intolerance for departure from strict regulations and obedience.

The Law Expediters. The law expediters are the officers and personnel of boards and agencies, such as tax boards, labor relations boards, and the like, whose primary function is to publicize the law, to enlist cooperation with it, and to resolve problems of constituents without the burdensome use of sanctions. The law expediters also implement standards in their decisions and advice, though to a considerably lesser degree and usually with less profound effect and significance than those which occur in the judicial framework.

Characteristic of this group is the need, and perhaps the tendency, to seek conciliatory adjustments between private parties and government agencies. They seek to provide information about legal standards and their operation. They seek compliance with standards without starkly offending those who are involved. As a last resort, they also assume an enforcing role and disposition.

The conciliators require sensitivity in the detection and manipulation of feelings, skills, and insights for the congenial resolution of conflict. They need a larger perspective that affords patience and good judgment. The subtleties that make for success are so great that there is frequent failure. The expediter then tends to move in the direction of overly rigid behavior, akin to the enforcer in his strongest attitude.

The Law Adjudicators. The law adjudicators comprise the highly specific group whose identities and functions are well defined because of their highly dramatized symbolic and practical roles. They are judges, mostly, and also jury. In their juristic function, they mete out the power of the law and visit it upon violators. The judges, particularly, and to a lesser extent the jury, are agents endowed with great measures of strength. Their psychological characteristics are discussed elsewhere in this volume.

The Lawmakers. Legislators, in an ideal sense, are persons who are concerned with distributing values in society, with coordinating and furthering social enterprises, and with balancing and adjusting social experience. In their role as designers of society, lawmakers need large measures of enlightenment and broad perspective. Though involved in choice, they ought to be dispassionate in order to serve the largest number of social interests. They need to be widely sensitive to the experience of others.

In practice, legislators are mostly entwined in the processes of personal influence. They are influenced by others, in response to

the latter's need for their power, for their promise of profit or benefit, or for some other consideration. They also seek to influence
others, as a means of generating support and strength for themselves and their point of view, a point of view that may also be a
reflection of the needs and preferences of others. Legislators barter
in power under the highly principled image of high idealism and
broad creation.

The Law Manipulators. The law manipulators are usually the
attorneys in their common role of advocacy. Whether the advocacy
be in court or in the sanctum of a business office, it is their function
in behalf of their clients to exact the greatest benefits from law and
prevent or lighten the burdens exacted by law. Their job is to
construe law in the light that is most favorable to some particular
interest. They utilize law in selective fashion to satisfy selective
purposes. They must protect clients from the law, if necessary, and
by means of the law, if they can.

The law manipulators have an adversary role to fulfill. They
require the talents of a fighter and a defender. They require an ingenuity for exploitation, perhaps some disposition toward aggression,
a command and convincingness, whether from acting or authority,
and a disposition to feel particular sensitivities and loyalties while
being insensitive to others. They need to be "tough-skinned" but
perceptive, insistent — and yet flexible in the face of frustration.

The Law Promoter-Executives. The town selectman, the mayor,
the governor, and the like, are the advertiser-promoters of law.
Through the publicity they create and are given, they develop a
public awareness of law, and of possibilities and prospects regarding
law. Their further function is to suggest and direct courses of law.

The law promoter-executive needs to be a sensitive tuning board,
responsive to values and preferences, but at the same time a determined person instilled with a sense of authority and responsibility.
In his highly exposed and complicated role, he must be capable of
developing various postures. Nevertheless, there must be sufficient
substance in each so that he does not appear as purely synthetic. The
need is for a highly marketable but not a shallow personality,
variously attractive but with an individual intensity and integrity.

In summary, law operatives are, and are required to be, diverse
personalities in their particular roles. Nominally, there are important
similarities in that many may share investigative and fact-finding,
decision-making, and evaluative functions. There are overlapping
activities and dispositions even among the seemingly discrete roles

we have described. But, there is sufficiently separate identity in terms of role and personality needs to suggest highly particular and significant associations between law operatives and law operations and effects.

Parties Affected by Law

The effects of law are various, and the kind and degree of impact is scarcely known. Law may deprive people of freedom of movement and even of life itself. Or deprivation may consist of decrements in power, or wealth, or prestige, or the like.

Law may benefit people by providing learning, and by re-reflecting values concerning what is proper and necessary. It may enlarge and reassure the range of a person's actual personal freedom — as in civil rights matters — or his economic freedom by permitting or encouraging particular means of exploitation.

Law, on the other hand, may do no more than seek to preserve values concerning what is proper and necessary. It may protect a person's rights and integrity. There may be compensation for injury, monetary compensation, or emotional satisfaction in the harm visited upon malefactors. There may be limitations on marauding and exploitative behavior, so that injunctions will result if a party's conduct is unduly offensive or threatening. For example, labor unions may be prevented from carrying on secondary boycotts, and a separated husband may be enjoined from annoying his spouse.

Any particular operation of law may have both immediate and remote effects. These may be direct and visible, at one extreme, or they may occur on anonymous, hypothetical parties, at the other.

Aggressors. The greatest familiarity as to the impact of law exists in relation to apprehended aggressors. Whether they are engaged in burglary or monopoly, the punishment for and containment of their behavior is rather obvious. But even as to this publicized group, more remote effects of law — changes in actions and attitudes as a result of the operation of law — are not as well identified and catalogued.

Victims. The impact of law on victims of offenses is the subject of some knowledge and some educated guesses (Hentig, 1948). In some instances, as in accidental injury, there is compensation, but this is only one type of effect of the actions or inactions of law. In some instances, as in the criminally violated, the law may provide an opportunity for emotional discharge, particularly for feelings of frustration and then hostility, when the aggressor is punished. Satisfaction may take the form of an injunction, as a safeguard against being violated in the future, or there may be no relief at all. There may be no visible or considered impact of the law on individual victims, and effects on their behavior may not be discerned carefully.

Litigants. The impact of law on litigants, particularly where neither party can be defined as an aggressor or a victim, also invites consideration (Redmount, 1959). The effects of the process witnessed in the courtroom, and of its results, actual or probable, may have a considerable impact on litigants. Their view of law, their behavior, and their decisions — both immediate and subsequent — may be determined in large measure by their experiences and observations. Behavior may be designed specifically to avoid future litigation, as in setting up procedures or representation in business enterprise because of knowledge of the difficulties and risks of litigation. On the other hand, behavior may be tailored so as to draw the benefits of litigation, and persons may learn the importance of representing themselves in a favorable light, as in court proceedings, however the truth of the matter.

Law Operatives. Another identifiable group for whom the impacts of law may be critically important consists of law operatives. Their skills and attitudes require that the law should operate with fairly specific, predictable outcomes. For a policeman, law must have the impact of expediting and reinforcing his use of power. For an attorney, customary structure in handling and presenting cases, a systematic pattern in considering evidence, and a predictable result predicated on the procedures used are necessary to skill and competence. Problems are introduced when the impacts of law are not systematic, predictable, and identifiable for this group.

Particularly Susceptible Third Parties. The effects of law on those nearly involved is perhaps of greatest moment (Andenaes, 1952). Those on the threshold of behavior and consequence that invite the spotlight of law, and those who have not yet been apprehended, may be particularly sensitive to the impacts of law. Prospective rapists and their victims, tax dodgers, litigious paranoiacs, and law students all contemplate the law's operations and effects in highly specific ways that are meaningful and frequently may critically affect their behavior. The frustrations or reassurances, the limitations and permissions, afforded by law may have very dramatic significance in its impact on the attitudes and behavior of such people.

The Anonymous General Public. The more remote impact of law, particularly on parties not specifically identified or spotlighted, is a more contentious and uncertain matter. Many people may be parties for whom law has only a very general import. The prospect of their seeing law in a highly specific and involved manner, based upon strong personal exposure, is remote. They may be the victims of unfair trade practices, of corporate mismanagement, or of malfeasance in public office. If they are aggressors, they may be speeders or tax manipulators, so much like a large class of persons that they are perhaps unlikely to be specifically and individually identified or apprehended. Yet, even here, "law" has some general meaning and impact on behavior. Such speeders and manipulators, for instance, are close to abiding by regulations, and are aware of and respond to regulation.

Some Social Contexts of Legal Influence

A fuller understanding of law must recognize that current legal operation has a direct and continuous relationship with its historical antecedents. It would also consider that law has a large place (among its other roles in society) in the ordering of human behavior and in the solution of conflicts. It must take into account the fact that law reflects social customs, values, practices and purposes. It must take note of the fact that law helps form aspirations, insights, and trends that are prime movers in the behavior of people and that tend to broaden human experience.

Legal Precedents and Traditions of Legal Behavior. Understanding development and change in the precedents and practices of law is a source of responsible feeling for and interpretation of the law (Oliphant, 1928). One can recognize in law patterns of thinking and feeling. They are reflected in the insistence that any current case or problem apparently can be decided by means of clear reference to and connection with principles of decision in similar problems in the past. And they are seen in the rigorous rules of procedure and rules relating to ascertaining facts and presenting evidence — guided by strict authority — through which a case or problem must pass to gain the benefit of a legal decision. These are habits, attitudes and operations that are intended to safeguard the consistency and continuity of law. The abandonment of experience to special logic constitutes a mode or habit of law for permitting development and change. Law is therefore taxed with highly intellectual and limited interpretations of experience. The novel and the immediate have obstacles to overcome or to infiltrate in the shape of stubborn dispositions designed to preserve order and regularity, precedence and familiarity. Codifications of rulings and statutes, together with stringent definitions and procedures, create strong, built-in psychological dispositions. These need to be identified for their unique character and their influence on human experience.

Then, too, there is the distinction between the nominal and formal procedures to which law is dedicated for its continuing development, and the "underground" behavior that stitches the law and reflects other aspects of disposition under it. In the latter instance, one perceives that dedicated habits are also attended by less obvious but equally strong exploitative and manipulative behavior. Thus, lawyers routinely exploit emotional propensities while using the words of law in order that partisan interests may be served. In these instances, rational consistencies in law may be undermined and historical continuities in legal decision may be severely attenuated.

Law and Custom. The relation of law to social custom also helps to define characteristics of law (Ehrlich, 1936). In some instances, law is the enactment of custom, and safeguards the latter with its power. In other instances, law may define, or seek to define, practices independent of custom. Custom may dictate a high degree of individual prerogative in ownership rights, but zoning laws may insist on the pre-eminent importance of community benefit. The result may be interesting and complicated shifts in feeling and perhaps in behavior where law is concerned and where individual "rights" are involved. Law may serve to negate particular custom; perhaps the most dramatic instance is the enactment of desegregation policies in southern United States.

Law and Social Institutions. Law is in itself an institution and, by its constituted power, dominates other institutions. It may augment conscience in the commercial world, for instance, by drawing rein on overly grasping or deceptive practices. It may encourage self-discipline and self-critical feelings in the field of medicine, if only by reason of the threat of malpractice suits and close court questioning of medical findings.

On the other hand, law may prove a deterrent or a stimulant to institutions in ways that would not be considered beneficial. Rehabilitation programs of the medical institution for criminal behavior deviants may be frustrated when law insists on a punitive disposition toward offenders. (See Chapter 13.) To some elements of religious institutions, at least, law may appear to undermine spiritual support given to marriage by its secular approach and lax, insensitive treatment of divorce matters. From another point of view, it may encourage deceit and misrepresentation because of its inflexibility relating to divorce and the need to allocate blame to one party or another before a divorce is granted.

Law as an institution bears the mark of influence from other institutions with which it deals. Penal units are increasingly dedicated to rehabilitation objectives nurtured by forces outside the law. Adjudication procedures are liberalized so as to accommodate the needs of the commercial institution to settle disputes with greater dispatch and provide for more conciliatory dispositions. Formal mediation and arbitration procedures are the result. In fact, laws, law operations and law operatives are frequently guided or persuaded by the pressures and needs of other institutionalized elements of society.

Law and Modern Problems. The creative and leadership role of law in sponsoring and promoting human aspirations and social development is not well perceived by its critics. Transnational law, including the unique problems of the space age, creates a challenge to evolve concepts and operations that bridge vast differences in social values and loyalties, differences in cultural behavior, in information, in emotional disposition, and so on (McDougal 1952; McDougal and Lipson, 1958). Leadership in determining or establishing values, as in the development of regional and community concepts to cope with mutual problems (zoning, municipal redevelopment, transportation authorities), or in the moral enterprise of desegregation, or in the instrumentation of social welfare purpose (income or health protection), or in the preservation of individual freedom with the pressure of social change, casts law in complex psychological functions. The diversities, uncertainties, and rigidities of attitude and behavior on the part of those involved provide an interesting set of relations which law must manipulate.

FUNDAMENTAL CHARACTERISTICS OF LAW AND PSYCHOLOGY

The psychologist, or group of psychologists, who confronts law in all its estate is bold indeed. In fact, he does not yet exist. That there is plenty of psychology in law, and plenty to be studied, is plain to behold. Lawyers themselves are students of psychology — most conspicuously in their manipulations of actions and reactions to bring about trial decisions. But psychologists as such have been rather more timorous in their infiltration into law than into medicine or education. The reasons are historical, political, and philosophical.

Historical Influences

Law. The emergence of law is through the collection and codification of authoritative decision. This is characteristic, whether one has reference to ancient law in the Hammurabic code of Babylon or to more recent Anglo-Saxon law emanating from the codes of Justinian and King Edward the First, and the Yearbooks of the fourteenth and fifteenth centuries. Law is also closely tied to logic, in the tradition of Aristotle and Saint Thomas Aquinas, who saw reason as the protector of ethical values. Lord Coke (1832), a most famous English jurist, referred with reverence to the premise that "law is logic. It has its own special logic." Even Coke's great antagonist, Francis Bacon, construed all law, as he did all knowledge, as a matter of classification based largely on Aristotelian precepts of logic. It is in this tradition that law attained its firmness of dedication, its limits of understanding, and the basic consistency and intractability of its substantive decisions and its procedures. Continuity became a matter of carrying on traditions in prescribed ways.

The spirit of the law became fixed. It began to go about its business with the appearance of autonomic regularity. In the gravity of its responsibility to society it is aloof, austere, and superior. It orders and transcends experience, and is not mistress to mere temporal fixations. It is THE LAW.

This is the basic fiber of law, its fundamental disposition and the character of its tradition. There are divergencies, of course, but these provide only some attenuation to the basic values in law. Mostly in the past century, and then notably in the less tradition-bound United States among "Westernized" countries, law has increasingly become conscious of, and has subserved, experience and social reality. The radical influence of the utilitarian legal and political philosophies of Bentham (1823) and Jhering (1879) are the important forebears in what today may be called grossly a "sociological law." The implications of Roscoe Pound's pathfinding paper, "A Theory of Social Interests" (1921); Holmes's famous epigram "The life of the law is experience not logic," (1881, p. 1) and his dedication of a career of juristic service and monumental legal decisions to this proposition; Cardozo's subtle exposition (1921) and application of legal (judicial) decision as a complex of behavior in a social world; and Brandeis's original use of legal briefs stuffed with social and economic data (Muller v. Oregon, 1908), and his emphasis on the association between economic policy and legal responsibility (1956) — all these are important landmarks in law's evolutionary trend.

Consciousness of economic, political, and broadly social result is more than ever a characteristic of American law. There is greater diversification in law's methods than ever before and a larger sensitivity to experience. There are laws to protect people from their own ignorance and to prevent shady exploitation. Unconscionable sales and contracts, though technically correct, may be struck down. There are food inspection laws, arbitration procedures, and compensation boards to expedite the use and enhance the social value of law. But the pervasive qualities of law's traditions have first call and still make the most profound impression in the character of law.

Psychology. The emergence of psychology — modern psychology, at least — stems predominantly from the shattering social and intellectual impact of Darwin particularly, and more generally from the traditions in philosophy of Descartes, Locke, Condillac, and others. The soul of psychology is inquiry, not authority; its end is understanding, not security. Inquiry into experience characterizes the sweat of great modern forebears of psychology, such as James and Freud. If, as it is claimed, inquiry aspires ultimately to control human behavior, then a natural association will evolve between law and psychology, but this appears still a long way off. At the moment, only a reasonable predictability in behavior is the objective which guides psychological endeavor.

Armchair inquiry into the nature of personal experience has given way to efforts to develop more accurate interpretation by means of controlled observation and analysis. The process of knowing in psychology means observing from a specific point in a specific way and making a specific finding. Definition and certainty is the result, at least the present aim, whether the reference is to physiological behavior, a sense of well-being, or social behavior, such as law-abiding or law-violating attitudes and actions. Increasingly, both clinical and experimental investigators are becoming more concerned with and more involved with more of the individual and more of his milieu. Necessarily, in this connection, the concern with milieu is becoming more systematic and more important in the complete investigation of individual experience. This concern becomes apparent, for example, in discussions of criminal behavior in this volume.

Political and Social Influences

Law. The role and influence of law in social experience, and consequently in individual behavior, is a matter of immense political significance. Law has the last word in an exceptionally wide area of human decision, both directly and indirectly. Of all the agencies of human control, it is vested with the greatest and unsurpassable authority. The authority is formally constituted and may control any human decision.

The power of law is installed in its institutions, in its decisions, and in its agents, each according to the definition of its particular function and limits. These identifications of law reflect a quality, perhaps the most important quality, of its strength: formally constituted power is its very existence and expression. The human instrumentalities of law, in their manipulation of legal processes, are disposed to view themselves with a consciousness of authority, of supreme social importance, and of an intelligence based upon centuries of accumulated human judgment. It is a traditional point of view zealously safeguarded against the encroachment of all other claim to dominance.

Psychology. The role of professional and scientific psychology in personal and social experience is less formidable. Its power of influence is great and inevitable only among the severely debilitated who must rely on the psychiatrist or psychologist for help. Increasingly, however, its widening scope of application and self-promotion results in an advisory influence in social affairs that is frequently binding in its impact. Its opinions relating to the general range of human behavior, particularly its emphasis on individual and growth values, and its applications in industry, education, and medicine, serve notice that it will be distinctly heard. Thus while law holds the bulk of authoritative power in a wide range of social operations, psychological infiltration frequently makes of itself a superior force. Its political strength is without office, but its popular hold can compete with the more static views of vested authority.

Characteristically lacking assigned social responsibility, psychology can afford to be more imaginative in social and personal matters. This is partly a matter of refreshing ingenuity and inquiry, and partly a matter of being somewhat poorly informed and unburdened by pressing demands. Psychologists are likely to be forthright and encouraging in their view of social problems and political responsibility, but also quite naive in any sphere beyond that immediately pertaining to the individual. Thus, psychologists are likely to be extravagant in their claims and expectations. They are impatient where lawyers seem fixed and recalcitrant, and ambitious and inventive where lawyers seem cautious.

The difference in the measure of political responsibility reflects limits or limitation in both legal enterprise and psychological applications. Where psychology aspires, sometimes rashly, law withholds, sometimes grudgingly and with undue parsimony. Where psychology is adventurous, law must frequently be unmoved and even stern. Where law is responsible, psychology may be unperceptive, even foolish.

Factors of Intelligence and Knowledge

Knowledge and intelligence are also matters on which law and psychology tend to differ. Intelligence perhaps is best thought of here as the way in which one knows and the extent to which one endeavors to find out. Knowledge would be the assured product of our intelligence — evidence upon which we can rely.

Law. In law only the method of logic is formally recognized as a way of guiding our knowing and experiencing. To know is a matter of identifying fixed historical antecedents and then establishing connections between some specifics of past and present by means of logic. To construct an example, airplanes are "known" because of their similarity as a means of transportation to horse-drawn vehicles and railroads of the past. This is perhaps more fundamental than that they are aspects of a technological or atomic age. Where logic does not span gaps in experience so as to identify the new experience in a plausible manner, "common sense" or simple fiat (command) may be used (Fuller, 1946). The essential characteristics of "common sense" and fiat are uncertain, except that they make for efficiency and some explanation.

A few words need to be said, too, of what constitutes the experience to which logic can be applied. As a matter of deliberate policy, experience, in law, is required to be grounded in certainty. Mere feelings, personal opinions, and surmise — however intense or correct — generally count for very little. Observables and the possibility of concrete observation are important. Experience that has specific dimensions — dimensions that identify it in a social context — is better than and more than experience that is vaguely "known" and personal. Experience that has demonstrable effects is also more certain and therefore more real than in the instance where the effects are more difficult to demonstrate.

The result in law is knowledge with a high degree of familiarity and order. As intelligence is substantially a matter of logic, the connection between law's knowledge and intelligence is fairly clear. It is further secured by the tendency to give permanence to both its efforts and results in decisions that are absolutely binding and persistent in social experience. By such power, it seems almost to construct a knowledge of its own, essentially impervious to efforts at intelligence and knowledge that come from other sources.

By constricting experience as a matter of convenience, and particularly by singling out ordinary logic as the means of identification and analysis, law is able to establish an intelligence and knowledge, both for its own institutional operation and for a larger society.

Psychology. The view of psychology about knowledge and intelligence is, in a sense, opposite. Behavioristic psychology (academic learning theory, as an instance) and psychologies of consciousness, such as psychoanalysis, combine in the effort to know experience more intimately, more completely, and in more ways. The striving, as in law, is for certainty, but certainty comes here more from exploration and less from restrictive convention. There is less concern for the social consequence of findings, and, as a result, there are fewer "sacred cows" and there is less need to "doctor" inquiry in order to produce quickly an appearance of completeness and invincibility. For instance, the social contributions of behavioristic psychology are not impressive. More is known about learning nonsense syllables than about adjusting in complex social organization. Yet, because of the specificity of both inquiry and result, behavioristic psychology breaks down experience so as to allow for insights and possibilities that would not otherwise be observed.

Psychologies of consciousness also espouse the aims of clarity and certainty, but their more certain emphasis is upon experience. "Experiencing" is a matter of combining the contributions that come to us not only from our senses, but particularly from our feeling and thinking. The consequence is a more sensitive awareness of experience and a broader intelligence than characterizes law's approach. Yet, at the same time, interpretations are less certain and may appear to be radical and unusual. This is because emotion, when accounted for in terms of logical meaning, produces its own versions of experience. These are often more significant and meaningful to the experiencing person than to the observer who is without special training in the vicissitudes of emotional living.

Psychologies of consciousness, by the very reason of their unique exploratory and discovering mechanisms, introduce facets of experience that are otherwise unobserved and ignored. The operation of the "unconscious" in behavior is a case in point. The contribution is a broader but less certain knowledge of behavior, ranging beyond commonplace comprehension, familiar to those who share the requisite intelligence for understanding, comforting to the experiencing individual, but the despair of those who rely almost wholly upon logic and familiar historical interpretation as the means of "knowing."

Differences in intelligence and knowledge become very apparent in prevalent thinking about personal deviancy, such as crime and mental illness. Historical and commonplace views draw crude and gross impressions of the deviant related mostly to the social effects of his experience. The outcome is an emphasis on order and responsibility. Note is taken of the extent to which order has been subverted, and judgment emphasizes the importance of discipline and punishment. Thus, the criminal is reprehensible because of his crime. Its effect justifies his being severely hurt and deprived. He has not followed the logical and consistent mode of social behavior.

As will be noted farther along in this volume, psychological intelligence and knowledge give a different accent to deviancy. Crime and mental illness are observed in more refined dimensions of personal experience, so that specific antecedents as well as their effects on experience are important, and so that personal meanings as well as general effects may be observed. Deviancy becomes a matter of modifiability. It is seen as a cause or an effect from complex circumstances, manipulable to the degree that one can alter some of the circumstances to produce change in experience. The emphasis is on the objective of rehabilitation rather than punishment. The basis and understanding is, or can be, somewhat more complete.

However, notably in other spheres of social experience, law's views may prove the more sophisticated and intelligent. There may be neither enough reliable investigation and knowledge in behavioristic psychology nor enough pertinence in the multiphasic interpretation of psychologies of consciousness, to contribute to a substantial understanding of complex economic and political problems, for example. Here, history and commonly interpreted experience may provide a better basis for achieving understanding than anything psychology now offers. Problems of political authority, economic enterprise, and individual welfare, juxtaposed to one another as they are in courts, legislatures, and political administrative offices, need to rely on the familiar intelligence and knowledge of law. The intelligence of psychology applied to this arena commands some attention but there is no present basis of decision regarding any unique value it may hold.

EXPERIENCES IN THE RELATIONS OF LAW AND PSYCHOLOGY

Efforts from Law

The fruits of psychological inquiry into law are sparse, and they are less of a tribute to the psychologist than they are to the lawyer. Speculative inquiry into the nature of law, postulating that it is fundamentally psychological, is the mark of a group of Scandinavian philosophers and jurisprudents. The intellectual patron of the group, Hagerstrom (1953) found, in the psychological conditions of "command," "duty," and "rights" the basis and the essence of law-abiding behavior. Olivecrona (1939) perceived the sense and significance of law as the taking-within-oneself by the individual of the values and conditions declared in legal standards. It is some element of consciousness about law and not the immediate direct effect of measurable external pressure that creates personal response to law. Thus, the person's response and disposition toward law is a product of his internalized attitude rather than of external pressure upon him, though this may not have been the case early in his experience. (One detects in Olivecrona's formulation some simulation of the identification process known to Freudian psychology.) Lundstedt (1955) stressed what he regarded as the instinctual and emotional character of law-responsive and law-violative behavior.

A Polish jurisprudent of the turn of the twentieth century, Petrazycki (1955), reflected a unique genius in constructing a highly personal and difficult theory of both psychology and law. He conceived of law in the broadest sense, as consisting of regulations and guides ranging in experience all the way from the rules in games for fun to the rules in complex political government. The basic and psychological support of law is the "impulsion," a widely shared inclination of uncertain origin that makes people respond similarly in situations calling for regulative behavior. The impulsion is imbedded in the person and, if properly sampled in relation to a variety of problems, serves as a basis for the effectiveness of formal standards.

The trial and judicial process has come in for its share of speculative psychological inquiry by notable legal scholars. Frank, whose ideas reflect the impress of Freud and Piaget particularly, scored the "quest for certainty" in law and on the part of lawyers as an effort to seek psychological security (1930). Virtually alone among students of law, he was specifically concerned with the vagaries of individual behavior — judge's, counsel's, litigant's, and witness's — that contribute to uncertainty in the trial process (1949). Thurman Arnold (1935, 1937), seldom identified for his psychological viewpoint, nevertheless reflected and acknowledged this influence in distinguishing and relating symbolic and practical operations in legal process. He pointed out that symbols, formalities, feelings, words, and appearances persist as a psychological necessity even after much substance and meaning in a viewpoint or an operation have changed.

Psychology as a means of *reflection* upon the trial process has not been attempted nearly as much as psychology as a means of *exploitation*. Almost legion are the handbooks and accounts by lawyers of psychological exploitation of the trial process in order to produce successful partisan results. (See Chapters 3 and 4 for a detailed discussion.)

The psychological denominators of facts and fact finding in the trial process have been subjected to some systematic intellectual inquiry as well as to partisan inquiry. A generation ago, the fertile mind of Robert Hutchins, then Dean of the Yale Law School, saw the possibility of bridging academic and scholarly interest in the probity of legal "rules of evidence," with inquiry into the contributions of burgeoning "scientific" psychology in "perception," "memory," "emotion," and so on. Hutchins and a psychologist, Slesinger, combined to produce a series of law journal articles "testing" rules of evidence in terms of specific psychological studies and observations (Hutchins and Slesinger, 1928, 1929). Rules and judgments in the assessment of memory, emotion, intelligence, and so on, in testimony were tested and checked in terms of psychological findings.

Hutchins's effort was to enlist the knowledge of psychology in aid of law, particularly in connection with the trial process. His was an instance in a movement among some American "legal realists" to place law on a firmer scientific footing. Some of these legal scholars appropriated, not the *facts* of psychology, but the psychological *approach* in contemplating problems of law. Most notable, in this first generation of empirical social science in law, was Underhill Moore's abstruse effort to study the legal problem of parking behavior and sanctions by means of specific experimental design and through the use of principles of learning theory (Moore and Callahan, 1943). Recently, legal scholars aided by social scientists — particularly sociologists skilled in survey methods — have embarked upon a diversity of projects using empirical social science in the study of behavior relating to law and legal problems. Beutel (1957), as an exercise in what he refers to as "experimental jurisprudence," applied this means to study behavior and particularly deviant behavior connected with bank drafts. Cohen, Robson, and Bates (1958) applied the survey method to ascertain the attitudes of parents in relation to the control, including legal control, of children. Largest of all in the scope and intensity of inquiry is the continuing study of the jury system being conducted by a research team at the University of Chicago Law School (see pages 102-105).

Efforts from Psychology

By comparison, efforts at inquiry into law directed by psychologists have been narrower in scope and, at the same time, more concentrated. Very early in the modern history of academic psychology, students of individual psychological behavior made specific experimental inquiry into the methods of obtaining testimony in order to discern the impact of these methods on perception, emotion, memory, and the like. Implicitly, they were investigating truthtelling propensities vital to factual inquiry in courtroom operation. Landmark efforts of this type are the studies of Wilhelm Stern (1930), Whipple (1909), and of the legally trained investigator into the truth process, William Marston (1924), as well as the work of Munsterberg described in the preceding chapter. Inquiry into the truth propensities of individuals, or more generally into the impacts upon people of "natural" and induced stress, has continued and enlarged in psychology. However, such inquiry has largely shifted away from the law for a variety of reasons, one of which is probably the inaccessibility of the courtroom for experimental purposes.

Coextensive with the development of systematic and theoretical psychology, there also developed an interest in "applying" the growing reservoir of psychological facts and ideas to a variety of settings. Medicine, education, and industry were beneficiaries of this "applied" emphasis. To a lesser extent, there were also contributions to law, notably in such treatises on legal psychology as those of Burtt (1931), and McCarty (1929) a generation ago. Primarily, they concerned behavior processes as they were understood in the psychological currency of the time and as they presumably could be applied to the trial process. (See reference to Hutchins and Slesinger, above.)

Currently, systematic efforts in the application of psychology to law reflect the immense growth trends of clinical psychology and psychiatry, with their emphasis upon personality study, analysis of deviancy, and psychological remedy. The consequence for law has been a trend of most consistent application to the study of criminal offenders and to the development of correctional processes. Efforts are concentrated on learning more about causes, characteristics, effects, and modifications in individuals who show antisocial propensity and usually have been apprehended for notable aggressive or sexual behavior.

Psychology's swelling concern for and with the deviant, and law's dramatic involvemnt with the deviant (because such striking values as individual freedom, social security, and the like are at issue) combine to make personal deviancy the meeting ground of law and psychology. Because of the opposing approaches and emphases cited earlier in this chapter, the interaction is predominantly hostile in character. The highly dramatized arena that sparks and symbolizes the elements of conflict is the trial court. The most specific operation at issue is the testimony of the psychiatric and psychological expert. Examination and argument is conducted in the context of law about matters of deviancy that arise where criminality and mental illness are in question. The role of the psychiatric expert and his view of deviancy, and the historical position and slight evolution of law in the matter, have been the subject of a flood of contentious writing. Chapter 7 deals with the substance of this controversy between psychiatry and law.

The role of the psychologist as an expert witness in court, as distinguished from the psychiatrist, has recently been explored comprehensively by Louisell (1955). Since the testimony of the psychologist is most frequently solicited on matters of behavior deviancy and personality, the issues and struggles are similar to those in the psychiatrist-and-law involvement. However, Louisell also cites occasional instances where psychologists have been called upon to assess and report on general reactions of a public to trademarks, in infringement cases, and to certain business practices, in monopoly suits. And, with increasing frequency, professionally conducted surveys of various kinds are being solicited in connection with a variety of legal decisions. Perhaps the most celebrated role of the psychological expert in law, currently, is in connection with United States Supreme Court and lower court decisions affecting racial segregation policies (Brown v. Bd. of Education, 1954; Cahn, 1955).

References

Andenaes, Johannes. General prevention—Illusion or reality. *J. crim. Law, Criminol. & pol. Sci.*, 1952, **43**, 176.

Arnold, Thurman W. *The symbols of government*. New Haven: Yale Univer. Press, 1935.

Arnold, Thurman W. *The folklore of capitalism*. New Haven: Yale Univer. Press, 1937.

Auden, W. H. *The Collected Poetry of W. H. Auden*. New York: Random House, 1945.

Bentham, Jeremy. *Principles of morals and legislation*. (Rev. ed.) London: Oxford Univer. Press, 1823.

Beutel, Frederick K. *Some potentialities of experimental jurisprudence as a new branch of social science*. Lincoln: Univer. of Nebraska Press, 1957.

Brandeis, Louis D. *The Brandeis reader*. (Pollock ed.) New York: Oceana Publications, 1956.

Brown, Louis M. *Manual of preventive law*. Englewood Cliffs, N. J.: Prentice-Hall, 1950.

Brown v. Board of Education, 347 *U. S.* 483, 1954; (Appendix to Appellant's Briefs).

Burtt, Harold E. *Legal psychology*. Englewood Cliffs, N. J.: Prentice-Hall, 1931.

Cahn, Edmond. Jurisprudence. *New York Univer. Law Rev.*, 1955, **30**, 150.

Cardozo, Benjamin N. *The nature of the judicial process*. New Haven: Yale Univer. Press, 1921.

Cohen, Julius, Robson, Reginald A. H., & Bates, Alan. *Parental authority: The community and the law*. New Brunswick, N. J.: Rutgers Univer. Press, 1958.

Coke, Sir Edward. *Institutes of the laws of England*. (19th ed.) London: J. & W. T. Clarke, 1832, Pt. I, 97b.

Cook, Walter Wheeler, in *My philosophy of law: Credos of sixteen American scholars*. Boston: Boston Law Book Co., 1941, p. 49.

Ehrlich, Eugen. *Fundamental principles of the sociology of law*. (Moll trans.) Cambridge, Mass.: Harvard Univer. Press, 1936.

Frank, Jerome. *Law and the modern mind*. New York: Brentano, 1930.

Frank, Jerome. *Courts on trial*. Princeton, N. J.: Princeton Univer. Press, 1949.

Fuller, Lon L. Reason and fiat in case law. *Harvard Law Rev.*, 1946, **59**, 376.

Goitein, Hugh. *Primitive ordeal and modern law.* London: Allen & Unwin, 1923.

Hagerstrom, Axel A. T. H. *Inquiries into the nature of law and morals.* (Olivecrona ed.) Uppsala: Almquist & Wiksells, 1953.

Hentig, Hans von. *The criminal and his victim.* New Haven: Yale Univer. Press, 1948.

Holmes, Oliver Wendell, Jr. *The common law.* Boston: Little, Brown, 1881, p. 1.

Hutchins, Robert M., & Slesinger, Donald. Some observations on the law of evidence—Spontaneous exclamations. *Columbia Law Rev.,* 1929, **28**, 432.

Hutchins, Robert M., & Slesinger, Donald. Consciousness of guilt. *Univer. of Penn. Law Rev.,* 1929, **77**, 725.

Hutchins, Robert M., & Slesinger, Donald. Family relations. *Minnesota Law Rev.,* 1929, **13, 625.**

Hutchins, Robert M., & Slesinger, Donald. State of mind in issue. *Columbia Law Rev.,* 1929, **29, 145.**

Hutchins, Robert M., & Slesinger, Donald. Competency of witnesses. *Yale Law J.,* 1938, **37,** 1017.

Hutchins, Robert M., & Slesinger, Donald. Memory. *Harvard Law Rev.,* 1938, **41,** 860.

Jhering, Rudolf von. *The struggle for law.* (Lalor trans.) Chicago: Callaghan, 1879.

Konefsky, Samuel J. *The legacy of Holmes and Brandeis: A study in the influence of Ideas.* New York: Macmillan, 1956.

Levi, Edward H. *An introduction to legal reasoning.* Chicago: Univer. of Chicago Press, 1949.

Louisell, David W. The psychologist in today's legal world. *Minnesota Law Rev.,* 1955, **39,** 235.

Lundstedt, Anders V. *Legal thinking revised.* Stockholm: Almquist & Wiksell, 1955.

McCarty, Dwight G. *Psychology for the lawyer.* Englewood Cliffs, N. J.: Prentice-Hall, 1929.

McDougal, Myres S. Comparative study of law for policy purposes. *Yale Law J.,* 1952, **61,** 915.

McDougal, Myres S. & Lipson, Leon. Perspectives for a law of outer space. *Amer. J. int. Law,* 1958, **52,** 407.

Marston, William M. Studies in testimony. *J. Amer. Inst. crim. Law Criminol.,* 1924, **14,** 5.

Moore, W. Underhill, & Callahan, Charles C. *Law and learning theory: A study in legal control.* New Haven: Yale Law Journal Co., 1943.

Muller v. Oregon, 208 *United States Reports* 412, 1908; (Appellant's Brief).

Oliphant, Herman. A return to stare decisis. *Amer. Bar Ass. J.,* 1928, **14,** 71, 159.

Olivecrona, Knut H. K. *Law as fact.* London: Oxford Univer. Press, 1939.

Petrazycki, Lev I. *Law and morality.* (Babb trans.) Cambridge, Mass.: Harvard Univer. Press, 1955.

Pound, Roscoe. A theory of social interests. *Papers & Proc. Amer. sociol. Soc.*, 1921, **15**, 16.

Redmount, Robert S. Psychological discontinuities in the litigation process. *Duke Law J.*, 1959, **4**, 571.

Redmount, Robert S. Psychological views in jurisprudential theories. *Univer. of Penna. Law Rev.*, 1959, **107**, 472.

Redmount, Robert S. Some basic considerations regarding penal policy. *J. crim. Law Criminol.*, 1959, **49**, 426.

Redmount, Robert S. Perception and strategy in divorce counseling. *Conn. Bar J.*, 1960, **34**, 249–269.

Ross, Alf. *Toward a realistic jurisprudence.* Copenhagen: Einar Munksgaard, 1946.

Stern, Wilhelm. *Beitrage zur psychologie der aussage.* Leipzig: J. A. Barth, 1930.

Watson, Andrew S. A critique of the legal approach to crime and correction. *Law and contemp. Probs*, 1958, **23**, 611.

West, Ranyard. *Conscience and society.* New York: Emerson Books, 1945.

Whipple, Guy M. The observer as reporter: A survey of the "Psychology of testimony." *Psychol. Bull.*, 1909, **6**, 153.

JERRY S. COHEN

3 Trial Tactics in Criminal Cases

Tired from a long day of work, a housewife sits on the front steps of an apartment house in a midwestern city waiting for the evening breeze to cool the hot, humid air. As the darkness closes around her, a car pulls up to the curb. A man steps out of the car, walks toward the sitting woman, and without warning grabs her and attempts to drag her into his waiting automobile. Fortunately, a policeman in the neighborhood hears the commotion and is able to apprehend the attacker before he has a chance to drive away, but not before the housewife suffers bruises, cuts, a broken nose, and a ripped dress. Later the assailant is identified as a well-to-do businessman who can give no reason for his actions.

From this situation both a criminal and a civil case arise. The woman may sue her assailant in a court of law for sufficient money to compensate herself for doctor and hospital bills, a new dress, pain and suffering, possible humiliation, and other damages flowing from the attack. If she successfully convinces the court or jury by a "preponderance of evidence" that this man caused the damages she claims, a judgment in the form of a sum of money will be awarded her. This is the primary purpose of a civil law action: to compensate one by means of money for damages suffered because of the wrongful act of another. (See Chapter 4 for a discussion of civil actions and the precise meaning of "preponderance of evidence.") However, a criminal case also arises from the same situation because the general public has a primary interest in protecting itself from this type of antisocial conduct.

This chapter will discuss tactics used in such a criminal trial. It will do so from the point of view of the prosecutor and the defending attorney, contrasting where possible the difference in approach to trial problems inherent in these opposing roles.

No attempt will be made to discuss the procedure involved from the time of arrest to the trial itself. The chapter will deal only with those psychological factors involved in the trial which are utilized by the prosecutor on behalf of the state and the defense counsel representing the accused.

For the purposes of this chapter, it will be assumed that the trial is heard by a jury, although the defendant may waive the jury and have his case heard by a judge if he so desires.

NATURE OF THE PROCEEDINGS

The purpose of the criminal law is to protect society. This is done by providing for sanctions against those who break rules passed to protect public safety. Society thus hopes to deter its citizens from engaging in behavior which the state believes is harmful to the general well-being of its citizens. However, the public has still another vital interest at stake.

The liberty and freedom of American citizens have always been a matter of prime concern in our democratic process. Because of this concern for the individual and his freedom, the prosecutor in our criminal case must convince the court or jury "beyond a reasonable doubt" that the defendant was the man who attempted to drag the woman into the car with the intention of harming her. This is in sharp contrast to the "preponderance of evidence" burden the plaintiff must sustain in a civil action for damages based on the same facts. The prosecutor in a criminal case, in other words, must convince the jurors of the defendant's guilt to a much greater degree of certainty than would be necessary in a similar civil action. As a further protection for the liberty of the defendant, the law gives him a "presumption of innocence" which he carries with him throughout the trial. When the defendant appears in the courtroom the jurors must consider him innocent, and it is the task of the prosecutor to remove from around the shoulders of the defendant "beyond a reasonable doubt" this mantle of innocence with which the law has clothed him. "Presumption of innocence" and "proof beyond a reasonable doubt" create psychological factors which favor the defendant. However, other factors inherent in the nature of the trial favor the prosecution.

A criminal case is prosecuted by the state on the complaint of an individual. When the title of the case is read in the courtroom it is always "The People of the State of Michigan v. John Doe." Or "The United States of America v. John Doe." This factor is one which the prosecutor or the district attorney will always stress. He is on the side of the people of the state for the purpose of protecting the public from a menace in the form of the defendant.

A juror is also likely to believe that the state would not go to the trouble and expense of prosecution unless it was convinced of the defendant's guilt. This is particularly true in federal courts when an FBI agent or a secret service agent is likely to testify for the government. The general public represented by the jurors tends to have explicit faith in such testimony because of the favorable reputation of the agencies for which these officers work.

Thus, even before the trial is under way, there are already factors at work (inherent in the trial process) which may have an effect on the final outcome, depending to a degree on how they are utilized by the prosecutor and the defense counsel.

THE PROSECUTOR AND THE DEFENSE COUNSEL

To understand the trial process itself, it is necessary to recognize the differences of approach to the same problem by the prosecutor on the one hand and the defense counsel on the other. Among lawyers this phrase is often heard: "Once a prosecutor, always a prosecutor." On the other hand, it is also widely assumed that lawyers whose primary practice has been as defense counsel have a great deal of difficulty in becoming prosecutors. The basic reason is that each approaches his duty from a different point of view, and once the point of view has become solidified by experience it becomes difficult for the attorney to change his approach.

The job of the prosecutor is generally to construct or build a case. A man is dead, a store is robbed, a forged check is cashed. The prosecutor must evaluate all the facts and circumstances which can possibly illuminate the incident. From these he must construct a plot which precludes doubts about the innocence of the person ultimately accused. To do this requires the ability to weave together methodically all the threads of evidence into a finished tapestry of guilt.

Defense counsel, on the other hand, approaches the same case differently. He must tear down, pick apart, rip holes in the finished product of the prosecutor. He must have a mind that can find flaws and hammer away at them until the foundation of the case crumbles.

The prosecutor in the case of the housewife, for instance, methodically builds his case by discovering other witnesses who may have observed the car or its license number, or who may be able to give a description of the driver. He evaluates testimony by the police officer as to what he saw when he approached the scene, and any statement made by the defendant at the police station. He utilizes the physical evidence: the torn cloth in the woman's hand matching that in the assailant's shirt; the human hairs underneath her fingernails matching those in the attacker's head. He may produce witnesses who can testify to similar acts committed by the defendants. He pieces together the testimony of witness after witness, weaving a web of guilt from which it would seem that the defendant can never escape.

Then the defense attorney goes to work. Did any of the witnesses actually see this man, the defendant, lay a hand on the woman? If the answer is no, then it is merely her word against his. He checks the general reputation and background of the woman. Did she know the man previously? Did she in fact provoke him? Did she make overtures to him rather than he to her? Did she grab him in a fit of anger instead of he grabbing her? The mind of the defense counsel thus searches for the points that he can hammer at the jury to raise a reasonable doubt about his client's guilt in their minds.

Even if a client admits that he has performed the act upon which the prosecutor predicates guilt, the defense counsel still has avenues open to him. He may build his defense on the grounds that the act was innocent in its inception and no criminal intent was present. Or he may attempt to convince the jurors that his client has committed a lesser offense (in terms of ultimate penalty possible) than the one charged.

For instance, suppose that, as in a recent Michigan case, a wife shoots her husband through the head twice with his .45 Colt revolver. She freely admits that she has shot him. But does this mean that she is guilty of a crime? Not necessarily. She may have shot him in self-defense or may have shot him accidentally. Her mind may have been so deranged at the time of the shooting that she cannot be held responsible for her act. And if none of these possibilities fits her case, she may still be guilty of different grades of homicide, depending upon the state of her mind. Was she in such a state of anger at the time as to reduce the offense to manslaughter? Did her mind function sufficiently to form the malicious intent necessary for second-degree murder but not for the premeditation necessary for first-degree murder? Such are the questions her defense counsel will raise.

As a result of prosecuting many cases it is true that a prosecutor may become somewhat calloused to the rights of the individual. After observing the results of many heinous crimes, he may be tempted to give his primary concern to the protection of the public.

On the other hand, the defense counsel is more likely to think in terms of the individual human being he defends, and whom he learns to know well. His orientation leans more strongly toward the protection of the rights of the individual. This is why it is sometimes said that the defense attorney must be a humanitarian or the prosecutor must be calloused. These conditions, however, generally arise as a result of experience, rather than from some inherent characteristics of personalities.

Be this as it may, these are the advocates who face each other when the clerk bangs his gavel on the first day of trial, saying, "Hear ye, hear ye, the circuit court for the County of Chippewa is now in session."

SELECTING THE JURY

The defendant in a criminal case may elect to be tried either by a jury or by the judge. If the defendant decides that he wants a jury trial, the process of selecting the jury is the first step in the trial of his case. Today in many jurisdictions, the judge himself questions the prospective jurors as to their qualifications to sit on the jury. In such areas the function of the prosecutor and the defense counsel in the process has been greatly curtailed. However, in the many jurisdictions where the attorneys themselves conduct the questioning of the prospective jurors, this procedure is still an important factor in the ultimate outcome of a case.

When conducted by the prosecutor and defense counsel, the process of selecting a jury known as "*voir dire* examination" has three general functions: first, to select jurors most favorable to the position of the attorney asking the questions; second, to create a favorable atmosphere for the presentation of evidence by the same party; third, to prepare the jurors for some of the problems that opposing counsel feel may arise during the trial which could be detrimental to their case.

In regard to selecting favorable jurors, many writers of textbooks in this field emphasize the differences between nationalities and types of employment of individual jurors. Sweeping generalities have been made concerning the type of person most likely to convict or to acquit. It is often said that a defendant is better off with jurors of a southern European background because they are likely to be more sympathetic toward the individual. On the other hand, northern Europeans have been said to be less likely to shed tears over the plight of the defendant who has broken the law. On closer examination, such recommendations have little value in the selection of a jury. Psychologists and sociologists have aptly demonstrated that generalizations of this nature are far too broad to be accurate. Factors which motivate individuals are far more complex and important than nationality or type of employment.

Other authors have spoken about the intuitive sense which an attorney must have about potential members of the jury. It has been said, "If you don't like the looks of a juror, chances are that he doesn't like the looks of you." In my opinion this generalization also is a poor guide. Most trial lawyers have had the experience of discovering that an intuitive friend on the jury has turned out to be his worst foe, or that a supposedly unfriendly juror has supported his client to the end.

There is only one sound method by which a choice of jurors can be made: a thorough knowledge of their individual backgrounds and histories. If he is able through investigation to obtain full information on the backgrounds, likes and dislikes, habits, prejudices, and past experiences of the candidates for his jury, the attorney is able to choose intelligently a juror who is likely to be sympathetic to his point of view. If he cannot obtain this information, the attorney is greatly handicapped by the limitations inherent in receiving information from the prospective juror's own lips in open court. In such cases, a large dose of luck is a necessary supplement to the lawyer's educated guess as to whether he is faced with a favorable juror. This does not mean, however, that there is nothing to be gained from the *voir dire* examinations.

The *voir dire* examination is the first opportunity which the juror has to appraise the opposing attorneys. The impressions which the attorney creates at this point therefore become very important to the atmosphere of either good or bad will in which he will present his witnesses. Should the attorney decide he does not want a particular member of the jury panel to sit on the case, he must be careful to excuse him in such a way as not to alienate other jurors on the panel who might tend to identify themselves with their unwanted colleague. There may develop an initial atmosphere of unfriendliness toward the attorney who excuses a juror. To forestall this many techniques have been developed by attorneys whereby a juror is made to believe that the attorney is doing him a favor by excusing him from the jury, when in fact the attorney simply does not want him sitting on the case.

An example of how the unskilled dismissal of a member of a jury panel in a criminal case can affect an entire trial occurred recently in Detroit. It developed during the examination of the proposed juror that she was of the same religious faith as the defense counsel. The prosecutor promptly excused her, leaving the impression that her religion was the only reason why he did not want her on the jury. Unfortunately, the girl wore steel braces on both legs as the result of polio. Moreover, because of her warm personality, she had become well liked by the other jury members. From the inside of the jury box she had to stumble over the legs of five jurors in order to get out. The remaining members of the panel were indignant at the prosecutor for humiliating the girl in the courtroom. This incident created a fertile field in which the defense attorney could plant his testimony and other evidence.

In anticipation of some of the problems which may arise during the trial that could be detrimental to the lawyer's position, the prosecutor or defense attorney, by his questioning of the jury panel, will attempt to prepare the jury for the role he hopes the jury will play in the trial ahead. For instance, if the prosecutor knows that the defendant is of such a personality as may arouse the sympathy of the jury, he may ask the panel, "Mr. X, regardless of any feeling of sympathy you might develop for the defendant, would you, if the facts so warrant, do your duty as a juror for the protection of society and not hesitate to convict the defendant if it appears beyond reasonable doubt that he has committed the crime charged against him by the people of this state?"

On the other hand, if the defense counsel knows that his client has a criminal record, he may question the jurors as to whether or not they would have any prejudices against a man who may have been convicted previously for a mistake he made a long time ago. He might then follow up with the question, "Will you do your duty as jurors to decide this case on the basis only of the facts which are presented at this trial and to consider this man innocent until proven guilty beyond reasonable doubt regardless of any mistake he may have made years ago?"

The jury having been chosen from the members of the jury panel, the twelve jurors "tried and true" then take their places in the jury box, both the prosecutor and defense counsel loudly proclaim (so that the jurors can hear) that they are satisfied with the jury selected, and the case proceeds to the opening statement.

THE OPENING STATEMENTS

Prosecutor

The opening statement performs three functions: it acquaints the jury with the testimony to be presented; it may help to create or sustain the type of atmosphere that will put the jurors in the frame of mind to convict or acquit; and it prepares the jurors for testimony which the prosecutor or the defense attorney knows will occur during the trial and which might appear detrimental to their side of the case. The prosecutor is the first to address the jury. He generally makes a simple, direct statement of the evidence to be presented, emphasizing at all times the seriousness of the crime charged. He will not engage in an emotional appeal at this point in the trial. This would generally make the jurors less alert in following the testimony.

The statement must be kept simple, logical, and free of irrelevancies: if the jurors cannot follow what is said in the opening statement, they will not be able to follow the testimony. The testimony to be given by the witnesses who will soon take the witness stand must be outlined so that the jurors are prepared to understand it and put it in its proper perspective. The best prosecutors generally attempt a matter-of-fact attitude and make no wild claims that will not be substantiated later. At the conclusion of his opening statement the prosecutor wants the jurors to be prepared to understand the testimony and eager to hear it. At the same time he wants them to be impressed by the seriousness of the crime and the great danger to the public caused by the acts with which the defendant is charged.

If the prosecutor has witnesses who he suspects will be repulsive to the jurors, he will tell the jury so during the opening statement to prevent the jurors from being shocked or surprised when the witnesses take the stand. In such a case the prosecutor will explain that it is his duty to present all witnesses who have any knowledge pertaining to the alleged crime; that in presenting these witnesses he must take the good with the bad; that often in vicious crimes the associates of the defendant who have knowledge may be no better than the defendant himself. After all, it is this type of witness who knows most about the type of crime with which the defendant is charged. If the prosecutor does this task well, the jurors will regard him with respect and friendliness and will fully understand why it is necessary to believe the testimony of some of the witnesses who would otherwise have appeared to be disreputable.

Defense Counsel

At the conclusion of the prosecutor's opening statement the defense counsel may either make his opening statement or reserve it until such time as he is ready to present his witnesses. Generally, the defense attorney does not choose to make an opening statement at this time. There are many reasons for this. The most important is that by the time the prosecutor has concluded the presentation of his case, the defense attorney's opening statement would have been forgotten. There may, however, be occasions when the defense attorney may wish to make an opening statement at the commencement of the trial. If he does not intend to put any witnesses on the stand himself, this is the only chance he has to address the jury prior to closing argument. Or, if the defense counsel feels that the prosecutor's opening statement has been unusually effective, he may wish to provide an antidote to its effect at this early stage in the proceedings. When alibi or temporary insanity is to be the defense, some defense attorneys feel it advisable to make the jury aware of this fact at the beginning of the trial. However, these occasions, where defense counsel makes his opening statement immediately following the prosecutor's, are exceptions to the general rule.

In his opening statement, the defense attorney — like the prosecutor — will first make a simple, logical, direct statement of the defense he will present. However, unlike the prosecutor, he may introduce collateral matters into his statement for the purpose of obscuring the primary issues involved. He will also minimize the seriousness of the offense. He may, for instance, point out that the act with which the defendant is charged could happen to anyone, including, by inference, any member of the jury. He may point out that, if indeed, the defendant did commit the act, he had no intention of harming anyone. Or he may merely deny that the defendant participated in the acts constituting the offense. Underlying the opening statement is an attempt to develop sympathy for his client. If successful, he has further prepared the field for the planting of his defense in the minds of the jurors.

EXAMINATION AND EVIDENCE

To understand the proceedings about to take place — the questioning of witnesses and the introduction of evidence — a few comments are necessary about the ground rules governing these proceedings. The questioning by the prosecutor and defense counsel of their own witnesses is "direct examination" — probably one of the most overlooked of an attorney's skills, often taking a back seat to the more dramatic cross-examination to follow. "Cross-examination" in this case is the questioning of the prosecutor's witnesses by the defense attorney.[1] A full explanation of the methods and tactics used by attorneys in direct and cross-examination are covered thoroughly in the following chapter, "Trial Tactics in Civil Cases." For the purpose of this chapter it is only necessary to note the essential difference between the two. During direct examination no question may be asked which leads the witness by suggesting an answer. The usual questions in direct examination are "Please tell us what happened"; and "Then what followed?" Yet the attorney must so arrange and phrase these seemingly innocent questions as to bring forth a clear, logical, lucid story from the witness while not appearing to suggest any particular answer. He must know when to ask questions requiring only a short answer, when to interrupt a witness who begins to ramble or to make statements dangerous to his position, and how to prod the memory of a witness when he seems to have forgotten vital testimony.

In cross-examination, the questioner may ask leading questions (questions which suggest an answer). He may ask, for instance, "Isn't it true that you visited Mary's Bar and Grill on the day of the crime?" Such a question is logical in cross-examination since the purpose of this type of examination generally is to test the truth or accuracy of the testimony given by the witness, or to show prejudice or bias. It is, of course, illogical on direct examination, when the jury is entitled to hear the story of the witness in his own words unaided by the suggestions of his attorney.

---

[1] Generally speaking, when an attorney questions his own witnesses he is involved in direct examination, and when he questions the witnesses called by the opposing counsel he practices cross-examination.

During the trial itself, objections at times will be made by attorneys on the grounds that testimony is immaterial, irrelevant, incompetent, hearsay, or, possibly, not responsive. Some laymen have been unkind enough to suggest that this is merely a magical mumbo jumbo conjured up by attorneys to obstruct the free flow of testimony to the jury. Nothing could be further from the truth. The rules of evidence have developed, and continue to develop, because they have proved themselves in the crucible of experience to be well suited to the search for truth, which is the function of the criminal trial.

Materiality, for instance, means that testimony can be given only if it has some bearing on the issues to be decided. Relevancy assures that these material facts have sufficient significance in determining vital issues of the case to make it worth while to allow them in evidence. Competency fulfills two purposes. First, it protects areas of public policy in which some overriding public interest outweighs the importance of getting all the facts pertaining to the issues important to the trial. Thus communications between a doctor and his patient, or a lawyer and his client, are privileged, so that neither the doctor nor the lawyer is "competent" to testify as to these conversations told them in confidence; second, the rule of competency keeps out testimony which may not be reliable because of the defective or puerile condition of a person's mind. Thus, a witness with intelligence on the level of a moron or an idiot, or a child who is not sufficiently mature to differentiate truth from falsehood, may not be competent to testify.

The hearsay rule simply means that if you don't hear it, see it, smell it, or touch it yourself, you can't testify about it. This rule again is designed to keep unreliable testimony from being admitted into the trial. If cross-examination is the law's most effective weapon for asserting truth, this weapon is useless when examining a witness who does not have firsthand knowledge of the facts to which he is testifying. There are many exceptions to the hearsay rule which have developed in areas where by its nature the evidence is so reliable that it is not materially affected by the fact that the person who knows about it at firsthand cannot be present to testify. Thus, certain government records, bookkeeping entries, and the like, do not require the person who made the entries to be present

An objection on the grounds that an answer is not responsive means that the witness has not actually answered the question asked him. If a witness is asked what time an incident occurred and he answers by telling me what he had for dinner, the answer would thus be objectionable as being "not responsive."

These, then, generally speaking, are the ground rules which guide the conduct of the trial insofar as testimony and evidence are concerned. Having mentioned them, we are now ready for the prosecutor to call his first witness, as our jury looks expectantly toward the witness chair.

TRIAL

Role of the Prosecutor

In most states, the prosecutor has the duty of calling to the stand all witnesses having knowledge of the circumstances surrounding a crime, whether or not they are friendly to the prosecution side of the case. This increases the chance that some of his witnesses will be good and some will be bad, insofar as the presentation of testimony is concerned. Some will be truthful and some will exaggerate. Some will make good impressions on the jurors and some will irritate the jury by their very presence. This is the raw material with which the prosecutor must mold this case. From these witnesses he must present to the jury a clear story of a crime, including all its elements. It is a cardinal rule for the prosecution that the jury must not become confused, which implies the need to present one's case as simply and directly as possible.

With this basic rule in mind the prosecutor will select the order of his witnesses much as a director stages a play. He must get the maximum psychological impact out of the material with which he has to work. Usually he will put one of his best witnesses on the stand first, if he can, because he wants to make an immediate impact on the jury. He must have a witness who will initially make a good impression and who will stand up under cross-examination. His very best witness, however, will probably be saved for last, because the jurors are most likely to remember this last witness when the case is closed. In between, strung out in the order necessary to evolve a logical sequence, will be the rest of the witnesses.

In addition to presenting a case through witnesses in an unconfused, simple, and direct manner, the prosecutor must maintain an attitude of seriousness, keeping humor out of the proceedings as much as possible. Humor in a criminal case can cost the prosecution a conviction. For example, in a murder case tried some years ago a police officer had followed his wife and her paramour from a local bar to his home, where he observed them getting into his bed together. He then proceeded to empty his service revolver into the two bodies. He was tried for the murder of his wife — on the face of it a vicious, cold, and calculated crime. At the trial the prosecutor introduced into evidence large blown-up pictures of the dead wife, which he lined up facing the jury box so that the jurors could not look forward without observing the gruesome scenes. Naturally the initial impact on the jury was great. But during the prosecutor's examination of the witness, defense counsel without a word arose quietly to his feet, walked to the pictures and turned them about with their backs facing the jurors. A few minutes later the surprised prosecutor turned them back to their original position. In another few moments the defense attorney again quietly turned the pictures with their backs to the jury. After this procedure had been repeated three or four times, the jurors began to smile. One could almost see them mentally making bets as to how long it would take before the pictures would be turned around again. Finally one of them broke into loud laughter and the rest joined in. This was hardly an atmosphere in which to convict a man of first-degree murder and probably contributed toward the final verdict of not guilty by reason of temporary insanity.

In another hearing in Michigan, the prosecutor was pounding home his point and at the crucial moment banged his fist on the table shouting, "Why, defense counsel's contention is nothing but minutiae!" The defense attorney leaped to his feet and roared an objection to the prosecutor for using such vile and vulgar language in the presence of the court. By the time the dictionary had been taken from the shelf and the jurors had been told that "minutiae" was just another word for "small unimportant details," the spell was broken and the jurors, defense counsel, and the judge were chuckling loudly. It is difficult for laughing jurors to take seriously the prosecution's claim that the defendant is a dangerous man who must be found guilty for the public's protection.

Another general rule for the prosecutor is not to show signs of friendliness toward the defendant. In cross-examining the defendant the prosecutor will not refer to him by his first name, nor associate with him during recess. Such conduct would be noticed by the jurors. If the prosecutor feels kindly disposed toward the defendant, why should the jurors feel otherwise? This point is well illustrated by a recent case in which a local jury brought in a verdict of not guilty for an unusually vicious crime, a decision which surprised both the attorneys and the court. One of the jurors said afterward, "Well, when I saw the prosecutor with his arm around Jim's shoulder [Jim being the defendant] out in the corridor, I figured he must not have done anything or the prosecutor wouldn't be chatting with him so friendly like."

Another important task facing the prosecutor is to keep the defendant and his unlawful act in the center of the trial at all times, never allowing himself to be distracted to collateral matters. This is essential. It is the defendant who is on trial. He must be the star of the show. He and his crimes must be kept in the center of the stage. The jurors must be continually aware that this defendant is being prosecuted for doing unlawful acts. An example of how a prosecutor accomplished this is provided by a recent California case in which two defendants were on trial for killing the wife of one of them. After an unusually eloquent plea by the defense counsel, both defendants were sobbing and many of the jurors were crying sympathetically. The prosecutor quickly rose to his feet and said, "Perhaps someone should shed a tear for the dead wife of the defendant, who is unable to be here today to cry for herself." The side excursion of sympathy for the defendants by the jurors was abruptly stopped by this one statement and the fact that a woman had been killed was once again the center of the proceedings.

Another example occurred in a hearing in which defense counsel, in making an objection, argued quite eloquently that the prosecutor was trying the wrong man; that his client was "but a small potato in the whole proceedings." The prosecutor replied without hesitating, "I agree that the defendant is a small potato, but he is the only potato we are interested in." Again defense counsel's attempt to direct the proceedings into a siding was halted and the trial was back on the main track.

In presenting his case the prosecutor must maintain a demeanor of complete fairness. Such an appearance is very important. If the prosecutor becomes obstreperous, the alert defense counsel has a new opening. "Persecutor Jones is at it again, trying to persecute my poor client." The fact that the average juror expects fairness from the prosecutor is a detriment for the prosecuting attorney who forgets his manners when he walks into court. Today's jurors will not tolerate the vitriolic, sharp-tongued table-pounding prosecuting attorney made famous by the movies.

A few years ago I watched a prosecutor browbeat a thoroughly frightened witness, a young woman who had perhaps loved too often and not wisely. The prosecutor first pounded away at her by bringing out vividly her unsavory background. On further cross-examination he showed "beyond all doubt" that she "could not possibly" have seen the incident to which she had testified. He hammered away at his point: where the girl had been standing, the time of night, the amount of light, and other physical factors to which she had testified would have made it "impossible" for her to have seen the defendant at the location as she had claimed she had done. The prosecutor became more and more vitriolic, his face flushed, his words dripped sarcasm, and the frightened witness cowered in her chair, her eyes darting hopelessly around the room. At this point, when in his own mind he had completely demolished this witness, the prosecutor stopped momentarily and looked slowly around for dramatic effect. Into that momentary stillness was heard the quavering, pitiful voice of the witness saying, "But Mr. Prosecutor, if you had been standing where I was standing you would have seen the defendant as clearly as I did." The tables were turned. The jury smiled in relief. The bully had been beaten by the neighborhood weakling. The prosecutor lost control of the trial, which eventually resulted in acquittal. This case emphasizes that courteous and impersonal treatment of witnesses by the prosecutor is not only good manners but good trial tactics.

Finally, the prosecutor must give the jurors the impression that he wants them to know the entire story. In other world, he must make no needless objections. Constant interruption of a witness's narrative tends to arouse a feeling of hostility in the jurors. Inexperienced prosecutors will often make objection after objection to testimony which has practically no effect insofar as the issues of the case are concerned. When, after many needless objections, the inexperienced prosecutor begins to feel the anger of the jury at his constant interruptions, he may feel it unwise to object to a matter that really goes to the very heart of his case.

Although keeping out testimony or evidence is the general purpose of an objection, both prosecutors and defense counsel may use objections to achieve other purposes. For instance, when the cross-examination of a friendly witness causes the witness to become hesitant or flustered, the opposing attorney may make an objection for the purpose of giving his witness a chance to compose himself. In stating their objections some attorneys may also hint to the witness what answer is proper. On other occasions the attorney may state an objection of the purpose of letting the jury hear matters favorable to his client which might be legally inadmissible in the trial. As an illustration, in arguing to the jury, a prosecutor in a small Michigan county actually cited as evidence a short speech he had made while objecting to a question asked his witness. He was behaving as if the witness had said what he had wanted him to say in the first place.

With the objection serving so many purposes during the course of the trial, it is doubly important that the prosecutor save his objections for those instances when they will do the most good.

Role of the Defense Counsel

The primary task of defense counsel is to develop sympathy for his client, if possible. After all the legal dust is settled, it is claimed by experienced court personnel that they can predict what a jury will do by whether or not they themselves feel sorry for the defendant at the conclusion of the trial.

A trial was held recently in which a college student at a small Michigan college was tried for having brutally beaten his roommate to death with a stock end of a shotgun. As the prosecution unfolded its case and the jury studied the picture of the dead boy, one could almost feel the hatred directed at the defendant who had done this dastardly act. The defense was temporary insanity and the defense counsel cleverly and ably brought out the background of the defendant to show what an exemplary student he had been and what a fine upstanding young man he had always appeared to be to his friends and family. He was dissipating the hatred and ill feeling of the jurors in preparing to put his client on the stand. Finally, when the boy himself testified, and haltingly told the story of how the voice of Satan had overpowered him and had compelled him to do this terrible thing to his dearly beloved friend, tears came to the eyes of many of the jurors. At this point, acquittal could be predicted.

Defense counsel may also develop sympathy for his client by alleging that he was a victim of circumstances. In such cases the defense attorney will bring out through his witnesses how the web of circumstances closed tighter and tighter around the defendant through no fault of his own. If he can do this to the extent that the jury begins to feel, "There, but for the grace of God, go I," his client is on the road to acquittal.

If his client has a criminal record, the defense attorney may try to develop the thesis that his client was the victim of unjustified persecution by the police; that every time a crime occurred, his client was arrested simply because he had once made a mistake; that the case under consideration could be viewed as just another example of how police authorities had hounded this poor, unfortunate man. If the defendant has any physical deformities, or is of low mentality or of small or grotesque statute, the defense attorney may attempt to develop the jurors' natural sympathy for the underdog, the man who has never had a chance.

In addition to attempting to develop sympathy for his client, the defense attorney will generally also try to keep the major issues of the case as vague as possible. To try to raise a reasonable doubt in the jurors' minds as to the guilt of the defendant, he may also bring matters into the trial which have no real bearing on the ultimate issues. The defense counsel may do this in many ways. He may focus his attack on the motives or character of the complaining witness, in an attempt to leave the impression that it is not the defendant that should be on trial, but the complaining witness, who out of spite and bias is responsible for the predicament of his unfortunate client.

If policemen or other prosecuting witnesses appear interested in convicting the defendant, defense counsel may direct his attention to their attempts to force a conviction of his client. An example of this occurred in a negligent homicide case in Detroit when a police officer — in the hope of strengthening the case against the defendant — stated that he had found glass from one of the headlights of the defendant's car at the scene of the accident. Defense counsel knew that this could not be true. Through cross-examination, he was able to put the police officer in the position of admitting that he had lied when he made the statement. In his final argument, defense counsel had his collateral issue ready-made. If his client was in fact guilty, why did the police officer have to lie in an attempt to convict him? He completely discredited an officer of the law who was so anxious for a conviction that he would perjure himself in a courtroom. By the time he was finished, it was no longer a question of his client's guilt or innocence. Rather, it was the police officer who was on trial, and the defendant's own reckless driving was largely forgotten by the jurors in their indignation against this officer of the law.

In homicide cases, a favorite target of defense counsel is the party whom the defendant is accused of killing. In a proper situation the defense attorney will put the dead man on trial. If the deceased can be shown to be a wife-beater, a braggart, a generally undesirable character, he becomes the center of the trial instead of the defendant. And if the jurors can be brought to the state of mind where their feelings of hostility are turned against the dead person (instead of against the defendant who is alleged to have killed him) an acquittal is possible. Once a jury can be made to believe that "he had it coming to him," the dead man's ill fortune may become the defendant's good fortune. If the prosecutor himself is overzealous in his prosecution, the defense counsel may make him the collateral issue by pointing to obviously improper and vicious tactics. He will accuse the prosecutor of being more interested in lengthening his string of convictions than in seeing that justice is done in a particular case.

The defense counsel is like a boxer sparring for an opening, and when he sees a weak spot, a collateral issue, a vital flaw, he will seize the advantage and tenaciously develop it to the utmost.

Humor, as stated previously, is a great ally of the defense counsel. If he can introduce humor into the trial without playing the part of the clown, he increases his client's chance of acquittal. A good example of this technique occurred in a negligent homicide case where the defendant's car drove into a safety zone, striking an elderly woman and breaking her left leg. Three days later she died of a blood clot in her heart. The question was whether the breaking of her leg was the direct cause of her death. The experienced medical examiner testified that the clot had formed in the area of the break and had traveled inexorably to the heart and caused her death. His testimony had obviously impressed the jurors and defense counsel's only chance was to discredit it. Inasmuch as the medical examiner was testifying to what actually had happened, this appeared to be an impossible task. However, the medical examiner himself gave the defense attorney the opening he needed.

Defense counsel had noticed in the autopsy report that the medical examiner had not internally examined the right leg, although the report indicated there were bruises on it. In desperation he asked the type of question which attorneys are never supposed to ask in cross-examination. "*Why* didn't you examine the right leg internally?" The witness could easily have told the truth — that based on his long experience and the clear evidence uncovered in his autopsy, further examination was not necessary. Instead, much to defense counsel's surprise, the medical examiner launched into a flag-waving speech about the responsibilities of his office and the patriotic duty of the medical examiner not to mutilate the human body.

Defense counsel then questioned the witness as follows. "Wasn't the top of the head first sawed off?" "Yes." "Weren't the ribs sawed through on both sides?" "Yes." "Wasn't the stomach slit down the middle with a knife?" "Yes." "Weren't the vital organs pulled from the body?" "Yes." "Then wasn't the left leg sliced open and the arteries jerked out?" "Yes." "But the reason you didn't look into the right leg was that you didn't want to mutilate the human body?" "That's right." The medical examiner's testimony was laughed out of court and the prosecutor's case went with it. The jurors could no longer take the proceedings seriously. The tragic death of an elderly woman was forgotten because of the ludicrous testimony of the medical examiner.

It is also sometimes possible for defense counsel to develop the possibility that an unknown person, instead of his client, committed the alleged crime. If handled properly, the man who wasn't there can often become the big factor in a criminal case. He can become the real defendant. If the jurors reach the point where they begin to question whether or not there might have been another party involved instead of the defendant, the nagging voice of reasonable doubt is once more present.

The defense of insanity raises problems of its own for defense counsel. As pointed out above (pp. 17-18), the law historically has held that a man is not responsible for his own acts when because of a mental disease he is unable to differentiate whether his acts were right or wrong (McNaghten Rule). In two jurisdictions, the rule has been modified so that if the guilty act is the result of a mentally diseased mind, a defendant is not responsible for his acts, even if he could tell the difference between right and wrong (Durham Rule). In other jurisdictions irresistible impulse is considered a defense for an otherwise guilty act, provided the impulse was in fact irresistible and was caused by mental disease. (See Chapter 7 "Criminal Responsibility and Psychiatry.")

These various definitions of temporary insanity mean little when translated into the actual drama of a trial. Usually the prosecutor will have present a psychiatrist to testify that the defendant was not legally insane when the crime was committed, and the defendant will have a psychiatrist to testify that he was. Whom do the jurors believe? If the jurors during the trial develop sympathy for the defendant and particularly if they develop a dislike for the party killed in a murder case, they will seek means of acquitting the defendant. And if the psychiatrist testifying for the defendant can reasonably rationalize his position regarding the defendant's insanity, the defendant's chance of acquittal by reason of temporary insanity is good. Insanity is thus a favorite defense in murder cases where the deceased "had it coming" or where the defendant has a history which elicits sympathy. There are practically no limits to the admissibility of evidence where insanity is the defense, since any fact is admissible which bears on the mental condition of the defendant at the time the crime was committed. If, for instance, the dead wife was a philanderer, all the sordid incidents of her past can be brought out to show their deteriorating effect on the defendant's mind, if he knew about them.

In a Michigan case tried in a small county, a mother was on trial for first-degree murder for killing her four-week-old baby by smashing it against the wall. Defense counsel was able to pick a jury composed almost entirely of mothers, many with several children. The prosecutor was happy to cooperate. The defense was temporary insanity. Defense counsel was able to bring out the facts that the defendant's husband was a habitual drunkard; that he beat his wife regularly; that they had five children, one of whom had had polio and three of whom had been continually sick for a period of months; that just prior to the alleged crime the husband had disappeared, leaving the defendant destitute; that on the night in question three of her other children had been crying continually and the infant had been screaming without let-up for almost an hour. It was thus easy to show that this defendant had come to the breaking point, that her mind could stand no more. Since she had to stop the screaming she lashed out, and all of her frustration and pent-up emotions emerged in one wild moment of fury. As the trial concluded, the impact of a heinous act had been dissipated and the defendant had become an object of sympathy and pity. She was acquitted, not because of the technical definitions of the legal defense of insanity; not because of the brilliant testimony of the psychiatrist for the prosecutor or of the psychiatrist for the defense (who had come to irrevocably different positions from the same set of facts), but only because the jurors could understand and sympathize with the poor woman upon whom they were sitting in judgment.

FINAL ARGUMENT

Role of Prosecutor

The defense having rested its case, the prosecution having no rebuttal testimony and therefore also resting, the attorneys proceed to final argument. The prosecutor opens the final argument and, following the defendant's presentation, gets the last word in rebuttal argument.

During the course of the trial, the prosecutor has on many occasions elicited the testimony which he desired from a witness and then has gone on to some other subject, so that the witness would not have an opportunity to change or modify his testimony. Usually these little nuggets of fact are overlooked by the jurors in relation to the total significance of all the testimony. In the prosecutor's initial closing argument, therefore, each item is plucked from its place in the testimony and set into a crown of guilt. Suddenly facts which seemed insignificant assume their true place and weave an unbroken rope of evidence to convict the defendant. If the prosecutor does his job well, the jurors often see for the first time the full picture of unfolding guilt as the meaning of the testimony and evidence accumulated during the trial is pointed out.

While presenting these pertinent pieces of testimony and evidence in a logical and sensible sequence, the prosecutor is also careful to develop an atmosphere in the courtroom conducive to a finding of guilt. Therefore, as an undertone to his argument, he weaves into it the seriousness of the offense, the need to protect the public safety, the duty of the jury not to allow sympathy to enter into its deliberations, and the fact that once the jurors have performed their sworn duty of rendering a verdict, the sentencing is the sole responsibility of the judge.

As he does this the prosecutor is careful to avoid intemperate, inflammatory, and prejudicial statements. His is the voice of conscience, clearly and coolly pointing out for all to see the guilt of the defendant. Possibly in his rebuttal argument, the prosecutor may be excused if for the first time in the trial he allows passion and emotion to enter his voice. Up to this point he has appeared to act without malice, without ill feeling toward the defendant, and with only the cool detachment of a man doing the duty he has been sworn to perform. But in rebuttal some of the revulsion he feels for the defendant comes into his voice and in his final few minutes of argument he may make an impassioned plea for the conviction of the defendant.

Role of Defense Counsel

Defense counsel starts with the same testimony and evidence as the prosecutor, but he must come to an opposite conclusion. From the same facts which the prosecutor claims point irrevocably to guilt, the defense counsel must find that the defendant should be acquitted.

He will begin as the prosecutor did by examining and explaining the testimony and evidence.

However, he is not as interested in a clear, logical presentation of testimony. He is more interested in raising a reasonable doubt concerning his client's guilt. Therefore, he will generally not answer the argument of the prosecutor on a point-by-point basis. He may do any of the following, singly or in combination: emphasize as most important those fragments of testimony or evidence that favor his case; interpret apparently unfavorable facts in a way favorable to the defendant; hammer at the weak link in the prosecution's case, and attack the credibility of a principal prosecution witness. In a murder case, if possible, he will try to discredit the deceased.

Underlying defense counsel's argument are the recurring themes "reasonable doubt" and "presumption of innocence." These are treated against the background of appeals for sympathy for the defendant.

Moreover, defense counsel is not as dispassionate an advocate as the prosecutor may appear to be. Many defense attorneys tend to identify themselves with their clients. Therefore, defense counsel is pleading a cause which is his own — the freedom of an individual against the faceless, emotionless state attempting to crush one of its citizens. He must convey to the jurors the justice of this cause, which generally necessitates an appeal based on both emotion and logic. Emotion is utilized to drive home the logic of reasonable doubt.

EPILOGUE

Prosecution and defense counsel having finished their closing arguments, the judge charges the jurors as to the law. The jurors retire for their deliberations, then return to the courtroom. "What is your verdict?" the judge intones.

Then an eternity of silence follows for both attorneys and the defendant before the foreman of the jury gives the answer that will determine whether a human being will go free or be branded for life.

CONCLUSION

In criminal trials man's most precious gift — his liberty — is at stake. And what does this liberty depend on? Too often on the skill of opposing counsel. Yet, to date, no better system has been devised to test guilt or innocence than this adversary system. With all its imperfections, the trial has progressed a long way since the rack and the trial by ordeal.

However, as long as imperfections remain, our judicial system must continue to improve in its quest for truth. Fortunately, our courts have not been blind to new scientific techniques and ever-increasing areas of knowledge. When the techniques receive general acceptance by the experts in the discipline most closely related to them, and when new fields of knowledge are substantially verified, the law has generally proved willing to utilize such techniques and knowledge. This is done by incorporating improvements into the existing framework of legal procedure and the adversary system.

One factor slowing improvement has been the sketchiness of the contributions of the social scientists to the legal profession. While the biochemists and bacteriologists have been giving the medical practitioner new tools with which to work, the social scientists have given the lawyer little. Some pilot projects have been initiated, particularly in the area of reliability of perception of witnesses. But experiments have not progressed to the stage where they can be put to work in the courtroom. It is heartening that some interest is now being shown by the social scientists in this area; however, their progress to date is disappointing.

The criminal trial is a fascinating drama which should challenge the most creative minds among the social scientists to develop improved methods and techniques to help determine the guilt or innocence of those before the bar.

References

Appleman, John Alan. *Successful jury trials: A symposium*. Indianapolis: Bobbs-Merrill, 1952.

Baer, Jules H., & Balicer, Simon. *Cross-examination and summation— Containing the principles and practice of trial procedure*. New York: Modern Law Publ., 1933.

Cornelius, Asher L. *The cross-examination of witnesses: Rules, principles and illustrations*. Indianapolis: Bobbs-Merrill, 1929.

Cutler, A. S. *Successful trial tactics*. Englewood Cliffs, N. J.: Prentice-Hall, 1949.

Elliott, Byron K., & Elliott, William F. *The work of the advocate*. (2d ed.) Indianapolis: Bobbs-Merrill, 1911.

Goldstein, Irving. *Trial technique*. Chicago: Callaghan, 1935.

Stryker, Lloyd Paul. *The art of advocacy: A plea for the renaissance of the trial lawyer*. New York: Simon and Schuster, 1954.

HARRY A. GAIR

4 Trial Tactics in Civil Cases

As has already been indicated, the vital difference between the trial of a criminal case and the trial of a civil case lies in the nature of the burden of proof that is required of the proponents; the people in the criminal case, the plaintiff in the civil case. In a criminal case the people or the prosecution is required to prove its material claims "beyond a reasonable doubt." The moment a jury feels that there is a reasonable doubt about a fundamental issue, the defendant is entitled to the benefit of it with a subsequent acquittal.

In a civil case the burden of proof is different. The plaintiff, literally "one who complains," i.e., one who begins a lawsuit before a tribunal to obtain a remedy for an injury to his rights, needs to prove his contentions not beyond a reasonable doubt but only by a "preponderance" of the evidence. The classic explanation of preponderance of the evidence is the analogy to scales — if the evidence advanced by the plaintiff is put on one side of the scales and the evidence advanced by the defendant is put on the other, and if the plaintiff's evidence in quality, not in quantity, weighs more than the defendant's evidence, then it matters not how much the outweighing is, it can be by a feather's weight, he has sustained his burden of proof and must prevail. The necessary corollary of the rule is that if the plaintiff's evidence is of equal quality to that of defendant — if the scales are balanced — he has not met his burden of proof and must lose. Obviously, the same result must follow if the defendant's evidence weighs more than the plaintiff's.

In other words, in a criminal case the proponent's burden is to convince beyond a reasonable doubt. That need poses its own peculiar brand of psychological problems and tactics to deal with them; in a civil case the plaintiff's burden is to persuade that his position is the more likely one — this gives rise to a different set of psychological problems and a different set of tactics to cope with them.

75

The trial tactics of a plaintiff's advocate in a civil case are directed to the task of persuading a jury that his client's position is more tenable, more credible, and more likely than the defendant's. The trial tactics of the defendant's advocate are directed to persuade the jury that his client's contentions are at least as likely as, if not more so than, those if the plaintiff.

What tactics a civil trial lawyer utilizes, and why he utilizes them in his efforts to persuade a jury that his client's position is the more likely one, is the subject matter of what follows.

Although applicable to both sides of the counsel table, the matter is being presented mainly from the point of view of the plaintiff's attorney since his is the burden of proving the issues and he has the greater task of persuasion.

EVALUATION OF THE CASE

Basic to the proper presentation of a case as well as to its persuasiveness, and basic to the dissection of the defense offered against it and its substance or lack of it, is the acquisition of as thorough a body of facts concerning the matter in controversy as can possibly be obtained. That is a pedestrian pursuit, laborious and often boring. It is boring because clients are often not able to hold to what is relevant in their narration. They generally engage in rambling tales replete with unnecessary tidbits. However, it is far wiser for a lawyer to amass too much data than too little, trusting to his own ability to discriminate and discern what is needful and persuasive.

The tactics that the lawyer pursues to gain this information from his client depend on his evaluation of the client's temperament, intelligence and motivations. He must understand the psychological factors that color a client's narrative — the desire to put one's best foot forward, the instinct to place the blame on someone else, the reluctance to reveal something seemingly discreditable, the self-interest, the frequent assumptions by a client that *he* knows what is important, with the attendant suppression of material which might depress his lawyer's interest in his case. The client must be told that no matter how harmful some past incident may appear to him, it may not be so at all; that in any event, since the adversary may discover all about it, only awareness can enable his lawyer to arm against such matters. Often it is necessary to prod him into such disclosures by relating the disastrous experiences which have occurred because of client reticence.

It is good catharsis for the client — besides being comforting — to know that there is nothing so bad in one's past which, if it cannot be excused or explained, can have its effect greatly attenuated by simple admission if need be. It is the dragging out of the information by the adversary that is catastrophic.

So it must be learned whether the client has been in other accidents, and how they affected him. All records reflecting his prior health and his activities must be obtained.

In good part this applies to witnesses as well. Here additional and other motivations must be considered — the tendency of a witness to feel important and to become positive about matters of which he cannot be really certain, the predilection of witnesses to become partisan for the side that calls them, with the consequence that "helpful" assumptions are substituted for observations.

Accordingly, witnesses' recollections must be checked against their comprehension of time, distance, and direction as well as their awareness of the relation between claimed observations and indisputable physical facts.

Trial tactics, therefore, begin in the lawyer's office long before he gets to the courtroom. In fact, he has to make a decision very early as to whether he is to take his case to court at all.

SETTLEMENT TACTICS

It was long ago said by a learned judge that pain has no market value and suffering no scale of prices. In a modern frame of reference this means that one cannot take a list of injuries, press the appropriate buttons of a Univac machine, and come out with an answer as to what a case should be settled for.

Settlement negotiations must take into account how the jury may be expected to react to the particular facts of a case: the nature of the injury, the nature of the liability, who it is that is being sued and who it is that is suing.

For instance, there is a well-nigh universal feeling that it is not sporting of a guest to sue his host. True, the law is no respecter of persons, and it says that if A has negligently hurt B, B is entitled to be compensated in full for the damages he has sustained, no matter what the relationship between A and B. But nine chances out of ten the jury will apply its own law — if A is nice enough to invite B for a ride, and B sues him, well .... For a lawyer not to take into account this possible prejudice of a jury in his negotiations is to ignore a simple psychological fact — that jurors, who are no different from other people, do not think it right for the beneficiary to sue the good Samaritan. In another situation A lends his car to B and B negligently injures C. B, for some reason or other, cannot be sued, so C sues A as the owner of the car. How angry can a jury be with A when he did nothing more heinous than lend his car to B? Certainly the law says he is liable, but the jury will not think much of the law and will discount the real value of the damages accordingly. The antidote to this prejudice will be discussed later, but any lawyer who thinks that this antidote will necessarily work, and who will not take into consideration in his settlement negotiations the possibility that it might not work, is engaging in poor trial, or pretrial, tactics indeed.

How the jury will react to the plaintiff is also an important consideration in settlement negotiations. It is a commonplace that careful drivers dread motorcyclists, bicyclists, and children on skates. It can be assumed as a certainty that the jury will have a number of people on it who at some time or other have cursed out a bicyclist or a child on skates or a passing motorcyclist. To insist on full damages when such a one is injured is to ignore the well-known mental attitudes of the everyday citizen — it is bad settlement tactics.

Another factor to be weighed in settlement negotiations is the manner in which the accident happened — again the lawyer must bear in mind how a jury would feel about the particular kind of accident. If A breaks a leg while riding in a train that collides head-on with another, the jury will undoubtedly give him full compensation — the fault of the defendant cannot be in doubt. No railroad could ever justify head-on collision of its trains. However, if B sustains the same fracture while driving a car that is involved in a right-angle collision with another car, each driver claiming the lights to have been in his favor, of necessity the jury will feel that the chances probably are that each was in some degree to blame. Settlement negotiations which do not take that fact into consideration are not good tactics.

A jury's reaction to a particular type of injury must also be considered. Disability consequent upon hysteria, shock, or neurosis may be just as disabling as that produced by an organic damage. But will a jury think so? It may, and it may not. The contempt with which the average citizen regards "psychos" — the very word bespeaks it — suggests in many cases an award far less than the full measure of damages sustained.

In other words, although settlement negotiations are conducted out of court, the specter of the jury's psychological attitudes, mental sets, and feelings hovers over the negotiations. The arrival at a fair value for settlement requires awareness of how the jury and the judge, in the area of judgment, regard the particular type of liability involved in the case, or how they appraise the nature of the injury suffered, or how they might regard the antagonists.

Since the outcome of the trial may be called a gamble, it is good tactics to weigh the offer made in settlement against the ultimate chances of a better recovery. The possible mental attitudes of the jury require evaluation, and allowances must be made for those possible attitudes. The question to be answered by the lawyer is not whether it is worth while for him to gamble on a trial, but whether it is worth while for the client.

JURY SELECTION

Jurors, as do all human beings, have many set, preconceived notions and major and minor biases and prejudices. They do not shed them when the wheel turns, their names are called, and they gingerly step behind the rail into the jury box. Accordingly, selection of a jury requires that the lawyer be certain that the jury does not have unshakable attitudes against the very heart of his case. If a lawyer is trying the case of a victim of an aviation disaster, where will he be if he has a juror who, never having been in a plane himself, feels that whoever does fly, and crashes, has assumed the risk?

This points up the fact that the jury must be made aware of the precise charges which are made against the defendant. Every lawyer knows that if there is a feature in his case which will provoke a juror's wrath or antipathy, he does not keep it to himself as a source of worry if he is adept in trial tactics. He finds out whether the jurors can surmount their feeling and judge the issue objectively. He can rely on the fact that in an American court all jurors will understand that no one wants to come to bat with one strike or two already called on him. Examples of such cases are legion. Boys on skates, bicyclists, motorcyclists, a guest in an automobile suing his host for negligence, as I have said earlier, are not usually benevolently viewed by jurors. Each juror must be asked to agree that he will follow the law given him by the judge, despite his own view of what the law should be. The challenge to a juror's ability to be fair usually gets a responsive reception.

Has the juror ever been involved in a similar case with a result adverse to the lawyer's present position? Would the nature of his work prejudice his judgment?

What a man does every day, how he makes his living, with whom he associates necessarily condition his outlook. Policemen become inured to complaints, bank employees become hardened to requests for money, employees of utility, transportation, and realty companies become calloused to claims of fault, to grievances of the consumers. Jurors with these attitudes carry them into the jury box. Therefore, when a plaintiff's attorney selects a jury he must bear this carry-over in mind and bring it out by questioning, and if the carry-over is denied he may use a peremptory challenge to rid himself of the ex-policeman, the utility company employee, and any others whose daily work has inured them to pain, complaint, and grievance.

On the other hand, salesmen, people in the entertainment world, artists, people who frequently do more than just lend an ear to hard-luck stories or to a request for help, who are not impervious to the challenge of righting a wrong, also carry their attitudes into the jury book. Their presence on a jury is the defendant's worry.

In other words, at all times the lawyer must keep in mind the particular facts of his case in all its aspects — injury, liability, who the parties are — when he is selecting a jury. He must keep in mind the nationality of his client, of his witnesses, of the defendant, lest any facet in the background of the juror, or of the witness, or of the party, may affect a juror's appraisal of the case, the client, and the issues.

Then there are certain intangibles that a lawyer has to consider when selecting a jury. Without analyzing the whys and wherefores, or making psychological excavations into the subconscious, everyone is familiar with the fact that he can dislike a person, a total stranger, on sight. We may remember the lines, "I do not love thee, Doctor Fell, the reason why I cannot tell, but . . . I do not love thee, Doctor Fell."

One thing a lawyer tends to assume, in selecting a jury, is that if he does not like the juror's looks, the chances are that the juror may not like his — he will frequently let such a juror go.

As pointed out in Chapter 3, there are also psychological factors to be considered in *how* to let a juror go. The feeling of kinship among the members of a group, with a concomitant resentment toward a real or fancied slur against some fellow member, is a well-known phenomenon. Westerners do not like Easterners to criticize a Westerner. New Yorkers take a dim view of Chicagoans deriding other New Yorkers. This feeling of kinship, of loyalty to a particular group that a man may be associated with, no matter how temporary that association may be, is often present in a jury panel. When, therefore, a lawyer excuses a juror, he does so with tact, with graciousness, almost as if he were saying, "You would do the same if you were in my position"; otherwise the next juror called, who might have had lunch with the excused juror, or agreed with his politics in a casual discussion in the hall, may feel a vicarious slight.

Peremptory challenges are limited in number. These are the challenges which can be made arbitrarily, as distinguished from a challenge for cause, where the juror has acknowledged something in his background that would make him unfair. The lawyer must keep in mind how many challenges he has used, for when there is one challenge left the lawyer's views of who is a bad juror must be restricted. The use of the last challenge may result in the calling of a juror much worse than the one just excused. A lawyer uses his last challenge only if he feels that whoever is called cannot possibly be as bad as the one he has just bidden to depart.

In other words, the psychological problems of selecting a jury revolve about attitudes, prejudices, biases, and mental sets that color the processes of decision, not so much as to how a thing is proved (testimony, exhibits, summations), but more as to what the proof will be and who the people involved are. The selection of a jury, therefore, involves a consideration not so much of the reasoning powers of the jury but of its attitudes toward the kind of case it will have to decide, and what will be necessary to produce conviction.

OPENING STATEMENT TO THE JURY

The capacity of jurors to be interested in a case before them is a noteworthy thing. During the war, when terrible events were taking place, it was amazing to see how jurors could narrow their field of interest, shut out the world outside, and focus on the case on trial.

The lawyer starts off with the great advantage of a listening audience. It is his task to retain that attention. This he does not by purple oratory, for exaggeration will bring the attorney nothing but grief if his proof fails to measure up to what he has promised. For a lawyer to make a claim in his opening statement that he will not be able to prove, or which the judge might eliminate by a ruling, may prove catastrophic to his case.

The objective of the opening statement of the plaintiff's counsel is to challenge the jury's sense of injustice. He wants to evoke not only a sympathetic reaction of outrage, resentment, or anger because something has occurred which should not have occurred, but a feeling that something should be done about it. This is accomplished by an attorney's telling a jury that what befell his client was due to the wrongful actions of the defendant and telling it to the jury with such organization of detail as to make the point stark and clear.

Where the case for either side rests on scientific evidence the opening statement must be used to make the scientific aspects of the case comprehensible to the jury. The jury will then not be plunged into the expert's exposition without preparation and understanding.

If reliance is going to be placed on an inarticulate witness the jury must be prepared for him. The jury will doubtless agree to the suggestion that to find out what a witness knows is more important than how beautifully he can talk about it. The lawyer in his opening statement tells the jury what his inarticulate witness is going to say so that the jury, when they hear the witness, can discount his incoherence. In this way the jury can be conditioned to the proposition that if a witness is telling the truth his faults of expression are relatively unimportant.

ORDER OF PROOF

To rouse a jury's sense of injustice effectively and to evoke its desire to remedy what has happened means more than an indiscriminate presentation of the facts. The sooner the jury appreciates that a wrong has been done, the stronger will be its desire to repair its consequences. Few plays survive a first act that does not quickly point up the conflict to be met in the play. The reception of evidence is most sympathetic if it is heard after the plaintiff's right to recover has been shown. A proper order of proof requires that, apart from preliminary testimony as to maps, models, and so on, necessary for the development of the proof, the first witness be the one who fastens the liability on the defendant. If the plaintiff himself cannot do so, he should not be the first witness. Under such circumstances, the plaintiff would be practically confined to narrating his injuries at a time not most beneficial to him. To illustrate with a case: The plaintiff was a grocer's helper. While he was delivering an order via the dumb-waiter, it fell and fractured his skull. He had never been on the premises before. The case turned on a defect in the dumb-waiter machinery, about which the plaintiff could offer no evidence at all.

Such a case only marks time if the plaintiff is put on first. But if the first witness tells of frayed ropes or of broken bolts in the machinery, the jury will be eager to get at the wrongdoer, and the plaintiff's testimony is most sympathetically awaited. Otherwise, the intelligent members of the jury will be listening to the testimony with divided minds, since they are still in doubt as to whether the defendant is liable to the plaintiff. The picture is one of "Too bad, but whose fault was it?"

In another example, an action recently tried involved an airplane wreck, with no survivors. The theory of the action was that the designer of the plane had installed a faulty fire-extinguisher system, based on CO_2 as the extinguishing agent; that in the course of flight, because of a threatened fire, the extinguishers were discharged and their fumes entered the cockpit and disabled the crew. Illustrating what has been said about the order of proof, long before any evidence was offered as to what had happened on the wrecked plane the jury had already been shown the dangers of CO_2 in this kind of extinguisher system.

It had been proved that on test flights of this type of plane, fumes of CO_2 had seeped into the cockpit when the fire extinguishers had been discharged, and had so affected the members of the crew that they lost control of the plane. When the proof introduced at the trial reached the plane on which the deceased was a passenger, the hand of doom hovered over the plane as it was taxiing down the runway for what was to be its final take-off.

Airplane cases frequently pose a dilemma to the lawyer because they know that juries need simple, stark, clearly defined issues.

In airplane cases it is very frequently difficult to make a direct proof of negligence. The plane is destroyed, its occupants are killed, there is no one to relate what it was that had happened aboard. The law, recognizing the difficulty of proof in such a case and in some similar situations, has evolved what is called the doctrine of *res ipsa loquitur*, a Latin phrase meaning "the thing speaks for itself." This rule says that where an accident occurs which would not occur in the ordinary course of events had due care been exercised, the jury may infer negligence from the very fact of the accident itself. The defendant then comes forward with evidence which offers some explanation for the accident that exonerates him. The trouble with relying on the *res ipsa loquitur* doctrine is that many jurors do not understand its implications. They still want to know what act is claimed to have been negligent, and no one has told them. It is an especially weak reed to rely on when the defendant comes forward with a plausible explanation of the accident. A defendant offering a vivid explanation of an accident, as against a passive description of it, may cause the contest to fail by inanition. There is no spark, no clash of issues to rouse the jury. It is not for nothing that statistics disclose that when airplane cases have been tried on the *res ipsa loquitur* theory, 80 percent have resulted in a verdict for the defendant.

Most lawyers rarely have more than two fact witnesses, and do not have to worry about having any burden of riches in that respect. The lawyer knows, however, that every witness put on the stand is a potential hazard because he is subject to collapse on cross-examination. The danger always threatens that one witness may cancel out some important testimony of another, and the admonition given in every field of endeavor to "quit when ahead" applies equally in the calling of witnesses. By the same token, making proof of matters other than the issue that the lawyer is interested in is only to invite trouble, of which there is no lack in any event.

It is a psychological fact that it is the first witness who establishes liability that will draw the heaviest fire of cross-examination.

Good tactics recognizes that, and the first witness on liability should be the one best capable of withstanding cross-examination.

DIRECT EXAMINATION

Most lawyers, while eager to absorb the principles of cross-examination from masters of the art, feel that they have nothing to learn about direct examination. When they are battered in court by objections sustained as to the relevancy or materiality or competency or form of their questions, all it proves to them is that they are plagued by an overtechnical lawyer, possibly abetted by a judicial accomplice. In many cases such ineptness results in failure to get all the facts before the jury; moreover, it distracts the jury's attention and concentration so necessary to the success of the plaintiff's case.

A proper direct examination of a witness in court requires direct questioning of the witness before trial, out of court. Otherwise, the witness may not understand the meaning of the questions. Where the witness has been accustomed to answer leading questions in preparation for trial, he may not get the point of the properly framed direct question.

A classical example occurs where a witness in court is asked whether he saw defendant's car prior to the accident. The witness simply doesn't know what "prior" means. When the lawyer tries again, by asking him if he didn't see it before the accident, he will find that his witness thinks "before" means the day before yesterday. He does not consider the matter of seconds during which he saw the car as being "before," so back comes the answer, "No." All further efforts to straighten out the witness are then met by strident objections against repetition. Only too often a well-meaning judge puts a quietus on the whole business by turning to the witness and saying:

Q: You did not see the car UNTIL the accident happened?
A: Witness (*gratefully*): That's right.

Counsel should be certain to warn his medical witness that effective presentation of his testimony requires that the doctor remember that he is trying to persuade a jury.

He cannot hide behind a scientific barricade on the assumption that all he is required to do is to give what he calls the facts. Facts they should be, but couched so that those who must judge them can understand them. Some doctors do not seem to recognize the difference between a clinic and a court, and will use terms which are entirely incomprehensible and meaningless to the jury. They must be taught that if technical phrases are to be used they should come after the nature of the injury has been conveyed to the jury and not before.

The jury is disturbed by such lack of consideration, which is a costly psychological error. It does not advance the plaintiff's case at all for his medical witness ponderously to inform the jurors that plaintiff is suffering from a traumatic exacerbation of a spondylosis into a third-degree spondylolisthesis at the level of $L5$ and $S1$ and then trying to get an English translation, when the intelligence of the jury would have instantly grasped and responded to testimony that the plaintiff is suffering from a forward dislocation of the last lumbar vertebra onto the bone below, which has so disturbed and distorted the normal relationship of the vital functioning parts as to inflict pain and disability. The doctor can then let the jury in on the meaning of the medical diagnosis by explaining that the term "spondylo" means vertebra and "listhesis" means slipping forward; hence this type of dislocation gets the name "spondylolisthesis." The jury will be informed on the two levels of lay and medical understanding.

How a witness talks in the courtroom has no relation to how a witness talks in the outside world. In the outside world he says what is on his mind, he is not inhibited from giving opinions, advancing conclusions, using adjectives, or digressing when the spirit moves him.

In the courtroom narration is broken up by questions and circumscribed by objections to conclusions, operations of the mind, assumptions, hearsay, to name a few of the restrictions on what a witness may talk about. To take a witness unfamiliar with courtroom procedures, with his own special style of communication and without previous preparation to learn to talk a new language — for that is what the question-and-answer form is — is not only bad tactics; it is bad psychology. No one likes to be thrust into an unfamiliar milieu, particularly in public where a failure induces not only a feeling of rejection, but, what is worse, a feeling of being made to sound ridiculous.

It is, therefore, the function of the lawyer to know as much about his witness in advance as possible, lest the witness be subjected to this psychological trauma of having every statement he makes objected to as a conclusion, or as an operation of his mind, or as something else which plainly suggests that he doesn't know how to express himself properly.

As noted above, a proper examination out of court is necessary so that the witness may understand what the lawyer is getting at. It is also needed so that the lawyer may learn what the witness is trying to say. This requires a knowledge by the lawyer of the idiosyncrasies of his witnesses. Some witnesses must be asked for the information that they can give in some definite and precise way; otherwise they do not yield it. Merely because a lawyer has interviewed even trained intelligences, such as actuaries, does not ensure that their testimony will sound as persuasive in court as it did in the informal give-and-take of an office conference. Asking such a witness the precise questions which will have to be put to him in court is no remedy; a formula that enables the witness to give the lawyer the essential facts must be found.

Some witnesses start to answer before the question is finished. A series of such answers to questions, hanging in the air — besides the effects they have on the lawyer's poise — will seem to a jury a lesson too well learned. Frequently, a story has in fact been memorized. The classical exposure of this type of recollection is to be found in the cross-examination by Max D. Steuer, one of the great trial lawyers of all time, in the Triangle Waist Company fire case. In that case a fire had occurred in a factory building with the result that many working girls were killed in attempting to escape. The tenants were charged by the District Attorney's office with responsibility for the catastrophe.

It was necessary for the prosecution to prove that one of the doors was locked, that this precluded the escape of the occupants and thereby caused the tragedy. The last witness called by the prosecution was asked to tell her story, and she gave a long, graphic description of how, when the fire was seen, she tried to get out, how other people were trying to get out, how the door was closed and could not be opened, how one of the girls had caught fire, how the flames spread, and many other details.

When Mr. Steuer cross-examined he asked her a number of questions which avoided the basic issue, so that she had the opportunity to forget about the main story. He then asked her to tell the jury what happened. She repeated her story practically word for word, comma for comma. The imagery was the same, the expressions were the same, the chronology was the same. Again Mr. Steuer drew her away from the crucial element of the case until the passage of time should have dulled the recollection and the words she had just said. When sufficient time had passed in other questioning, he again asked her what happened, and once more came the same story, word for word, image for image, point by point. After she had repeated the story a third time Mr. Steuer did not question her any more. Nothing she said was contradicted, nor was the witness's character impugned in any way, but the value of her testimony was destroyed: obviously what she was saying was not a true recollection of the facts but a memorized and touched-up version of what she recalled.

Some witnesses ramble and wander away from the question. The lawyer has a clear duty to warn the witness about embarrasing himself and others by these mannerisms.

Since the witness must do the narrating, counsel must determine how fitted the witness is by intelligence and articulateness to do it. To the extent that the witness must narrate a sequence of events, if what he says sounds stilted and studied, or rambling and incoherent, it is far wiser to get his testimony by a series of questions addressed to the various phases of his observations. If the questions are not obnoxious as leading, nor asking for conclusions, they and the answers will constitute the narrative.

BAD PRACTICES IN EXAMINING WITNESSES

Good, practical courtroom psychology differs sharply from courtroom practices associated in the minds of many people with the questioning of witnesses, and actually practiced by some lawyers.

For instance, the persuasiveness of a narrative can be spoiled by the habit of some counsel of repeating the answers of the witness. Associated with this is the tendency to polish and embellish a good answer, by restating it, as one twirls a good diamond to get different gleams of light from it. A witness is not so dependable. The witness may not answer as well or as convincingly the second time, and objections by counsel as to answer being repetitious, and possibly some caustic comment by the Court as to what it thinks of repetition — all this will mar the effect on the jury of a witness's answer.

Nor is it a good idea to try to make an answer more convincing by asking the witness in a raised, challenging voice, "Are you sure about that?" Nothing is gained. The jury may think that the lawyer himself doesn't believe it; the witness may feel that he has perhaps made an error.

It sometimes happens for one reason or another that the witness does not get the point of the question and simply does not know what to answer. A good lawyer does not press him. The witness will become disturbed, lose confidence, feel that he is failing in what is expected of him, and may decide what is wanted in the strangest way.

A good lawyer also knows that he should not ask leading questions. The other side does not like it. The judge frowns on it and, in fact, the jury would not like it even if no one objected. Any intelligent juror can see that it is the lawyer who is chanting the prayer and the witness giving out with the Amen. Hence, a proper presentation of a case avoids leading questions on any material matter save in certain exceptional cases.

SETTING THE STAGE FOR
CROSS-EXAMINATION

Carelessness often results because of failure of counsel to warn his witness of some catch questions which may be asked of him. The typical one is whether the witness has discussed the facts of the case prior to coming to court. Many witnesses hearing this question for the first time in court, asked in a tone suggesting the commission of a high misdemeanor, feel that they are being charged with perjury and deny having had any communication with counsel. They should have been advised of the procedures customary in a forum in which they are strangers. Similarly, the tendency of a witness to say that an event took a minute or two to occur, when it actually occurred in a matter of seconds, should be corrected so that the witness will be more accurate in his testimony. It is unfair to have a witness, who meant a second and said a minute, harried by a remorseless cross-examination.

All lawyers tend to overanxiety about the weaknesses in their cases which they hope their adversary knows nothing about; yet they are afraid of being too optimistic about such a possible ignorance. It is good psychological practice for the plaintiff's counsel to make the disclosure rather than to have a cross-examination uncover it. Such a disclosure takes the sting out of any cross-examination on the issue. When something is dragged out in cross-examination the jury may feel that it must have been something wrong or reprehensible and so was concealed.

The client may have had a previous accident which, however, did not involve the injuries in suit. The lawyer weighs the type of accident it was, the apparent if not real similarity of injury, or its real relevance, and brings it out on direct examination in the manner best calculated to reduce its import or significance on the particular issue being litigated. If the lawyer has any lurking doubts about the effect of a forced revelation he does not wait for the development of suspicion and doubt raised by defendant's questions — he brings it out himself. He casually and briefly, by his direct questioning, brings out the dissimilarity between the injuries without making it appear that there is a vexing problem. A poker face can be just as important in a trial of a lawsuit as it is in poker. The rule of revelation is followed in any matter which counsel feels would give the adversary the opportunity to cloud the atmosphere of the trial. A first impression can be so very powerful, that great effort is necessary to eradicate it. Sometimes redirect examination, when such an attempt can first be made, may be too late.

DEMONSTRATIVE EVIDENCE

In recent years there has been a widespread practice to dramatize jury trials in personal injury actions. All types of devices have been employed — from dropping artificial legs in the laps of jurors to using lurid moving pictures of brain surgery. The simplest device used is the blackboard, where the economic loss is computed.

The theory behind demonstrative evidence is that one picture or one model is worth a thousand words. When limited by the dictates of good taste and objectivity, demonstrative evidence can help to make a medical claim clear to the jury. If too lifelike, however, or too dramatic, there may be a revulsion — jurors do not like to be shocked any more than does anyone else.

Other types of demonstrative evidence are demonstrations and tests made in court. Here the lawyer must have great regard for what is known in the engineering profession as "Murphy's Law," which states that if anything can go wrong it will.

From a jury's standpoint the ridicule engendered by a failing experiment or demonstration is disastrous to the side presenting it. The psychological bases of a universal subject of laughter, a man slipping on a banana peel, are strongest when it is an expert that slips. Ridicule is anathema to a position urged in court, and any lawyer who refuses to be restrained by Murphy's Law is flirting with grave trouble.

In a case recently tried, the plaintiff's claim was that a ladder had been manufactured by the defendant with inadequate materials and improper design, that as a result it collapsed on anticipated use. The defendant had a whole host of experts to testify to the excellence of the design, the superior quality of the material, and the thoroughness with which the tests and inspections were made before the ladder was distributed for sale to the public. All the experts were estimable gentlemen, highly qualified, and very articulate. To demonstrate how right they were, the defense obtained the Court's permission to test out a similar ladder outside the courthouse. The ladder was placed up against the wall of the building, and mechanics were sent up the ladder to show that it could carry weight far in excess of that exerted by the plaintiff when the accident happened. The intent was to demonstrate that the ladder broke not because of any deficiency in it but because the plaintiff had misused it. Unfortunately, the defense had not had the foresight to judge the effect of the rather soft soil on which the ladder rested during the experiment. Long before the loads on it had reached the amount that plaintiff had testified to, the ladder began to buckle ominously and the experiment ended ignominiously.

CROSS-EXAMINATION

What is it that the cross-examination seeks? Generally speaking, there are two things: to prove "recollection" of events from "reconstruction"; and to test motivation and interest. The cross-examiner seeks a lever with which to pry apart the opposed testimony. He centers upon the tendency of witnesses to be favorable to the side which calls them and to suppress what is helpful to the other side. Since the jury will decide on what it considers the probabilities of the case, as well as the fitness of things, the aim of cross-examination is to downgrade the story or the storyteller. The art of "cross-examination" is prostituted by "examining crossly." If it is offensive to the jury, it makes no difference how successful it is.

There usually is a demolition plan in the mind of the cross-examiner: Does the witness know too much? How did he have the time to observe all of it? When and how was it all pieced together and with whose help? A lawyer must feel his way. The aphorism that a lawyer must know what answer he is going to get before he puts his question does not always hold. There are situations where counsel must cross-examine because the witness's testimony has seriously damaged his case. The questioning is aimed at mitigating the force of the testimony, not by asking for its repetition, except in very rare instances where it seems to be a carefully rehearsed story committed to memory. Where the lawyer knows who the witness will be, the cross-examination must be carefully prepared with an appreciation of the psychological moment to stop. In a famous trial in which a woman was charged with her stepmother's murder, the prosecution called the housekeeper, whose testimony showed that the defendant was the only one who had been in the house and therefore had the sole opportunity to commit it. It was vital for the defense to show a family atmosphere making murder an incredible supposition. The housekeeper was of fine character, bright and intelligent. She had to be questioned and her answers could not be forecast. How the defense lawyer formulated each question to demonstrate a peaceful household, but poised to drop the subject if any answer betrayed his hopes, was a masterpiece of psychological preparation. He had one hard fact on which to commence his cross-examination: the maid had been employed in the family for three years. Listen to his questioning:

Q: "Did you have any trouble there?" If she said "Yes," the cross-examiner could retort without fear of contradiction, "But you did stay there for three years," and then, accepting the answer as a warning, go to some other topic, as if he had scored a point. But she said, "No, sir." He went on to exploit this gain with the next suggestive question.

Q: "A pleasant *place* to live?" If he got a "Yes," it would certainly suggest that things were not only all right for the maid, but with the household too. If she said "No," he still had his retreat open and he could say, "But you stayed there three years *and* you never had any trouble." But the first "Yes" she had given suggested another "Yes" to the question which seemed so similar, and that was her reply. Now came the most delicate point in the defense. It was the danger spot. Note the artless way in which the question was phrased.

Q: "You never saw anything out of the way?" What could she say? A respectable, religious girl like the housekeeper does not describe places as "pleasant" where "out of the way" things occur, as the lawyer would be quick to remind her if her answer were disappointing. She said, "No, sir," and a gem in the cross-examiner's art was on the table. Certainly he could never, without careful preparation, have risked asking the witness if she had ever observed quarreling between the daughter and the stepmother. (Lustgarten, 1950)

The lawyer must know enough to stop while he is ahead, to let well enough alone. The cross-examiner must constantly sniff the atmosphere for signs of danger. It may be a paradox, but he is at once inwardly apprehensive and outwardly confident. He never cross-examines just to hear once more some evidence which delighted him, either on the witness's direct or on his cross-examination. He may not hear it again. Only too often the witness may rephrase his answer so as to rob it of its original effect. He may guilelessly and with the jury's sympathy explain away his answer.

THE FINAL ARGUMENT

One often hears the statement that the case was won on summation. Although not strictly true, this is a concise way of pointing out that it is not enough to hear the testimony and listen to the evidence. The material in many cases is in the record to justify the verdict, but the facts must be selected and woven into a convincing pattern.

We have advanced a long way in jury persuasion in the past fifty years. The old hell fire and brimstone won't do. True enough, the average juror does not go through laborious mental processes to form his usual judgments. This, however, is by no means to say that he does not conform even in a simple way to what he conceives to be some logical process in his thinking.

No adult admits even to himself that his opinions and judgments are childish, immature, prejudiced, and baseless. However poorly supported his premises are, however blind his interpretation of the facts he deals with, he in some way vests them with what he conceives to be a logical validity. For these reasons, to use the logical method frankly and avowedly with a jury is in most cases to disarm the jurors from their suspicions, always alive, that the speaker or advocate is trying to get the ball past them.

To be logical is not the same thing as to be dry as dust or boring. Logical thought can be conveyed in the language of moving eloquence, and the tones of sincerest advocacy are not inconsistent with fiery zeal. It is far more often than not true that a jury will be brought to conviction by a logical approach to its intelligence rather than by any other method. No one likes to be thought unintelligent or so gullible that the wool can be pulled over his eyes by glib and meaningless talk.

The summation must be guided by what one knows the Court is going to charge the jury. The Court must charge the preponderance of evidence rule. Long before that, the plaintiff's counsel should have carefully explained to the jurors what it means and have proved to them that he has established his case far beyond even preponderance of evidence. If the jurors have not been told about the preponderance of evidence rule during the summation and hear it for the first time from the Court in its charge, they frequently misunderstand it. Many judges do not deal with the subject any further than to say that the plaintiff is entitled to recover if the preponderance of evidence is in his favor. Only too often the jurors interpret such a charge as meaning that if they have any doubts about the facts they must find against the plaintiff.

Some jurors, while sitting in a criminal case, may have heard the Court's charge on the reasonable doubt rule. The lawyer in a civil case must emphasize to his jury that the law in its wisdom puts no such burden on any plaintiff in a civil case. It should be pointed out to the jurors that the law recognizes the impossibility and injustice of requiring one to prove his case beyond a doubt; that all of us daily decide on actions and conduct, by weighing the pros and cons — the doubts — one way or the other. Shall I take this job — or buy this house — or take this partner? No course of action is so illuminated, so clear, that there is never any doubt. We make up our minds on the whole issue and on the weight of the arguments.

Counsel must always remember that after all the speeches are over, the "dread" charge on contributory negligence must be given. Depending on the jurisdiction, the law holds that an injured person may not prevail in whole or in part if his injury is contributed to by his own fault or omission to take care. This is known as the doctrine of contributory negligence. When the judge charges that doctrine, particularly in a jurisdiction where the slightest degree of contributory negligence bars recovery, no matter how negligent the defendant may have been, it never sounds good to the plaintiff. Many jurors — especially women — search meticulously and minutely for evidence of contributory negligence. Counsel should demonstrate on summation that there was none.

He makes clear to the jury that everyone could do something better the second time if he had the God-given power of hindsight, that hindsight has 20/20 vision. People injured in the course of their daily activities should be judged from the point of view of one going about his normal business — and not from the scientific and detached observation of the jury box — removed from all the other activities heightening and distorting the atmosphere and surroundings in which the accident happened. One does not go up and down the stairs of his home or walk on the streets with his attention as alert as it would be if he were rowing a boat in shark-infested waters.

Nor is he called on to be an animated guide in the tenement house he lives in — and to ever and always remember that on the second step of the first section of the stairway leading to the first floor the step is loose on the wall side, and that on the banister side near the second step from the top on the final section leading to the top floor there is a scooped-out spot on the step where he could easily turn an ankle.

Counsel does not try to answer every point raised by the other side. In the first place, it makes for a wholly defensive attitude and disrupts the proper presentation of his own case. The jury is certainly not keeping score of every point to see whether it is properly answered or not. In many cases a summation can forcefully be made for either side on the proof advanced by that side without taking up the adversary's proof at all. This fact is mentioned, not because it is recommended as the summation of choice, but because it illustrates that it is not essential that a summation segregate each point made by the adversary in order to answer it fully.

In actual practice a very strong argument may be raised by one side to which there is really no adequate reply. Rather than spend a lot of time assailing a strong position with insufficient ammunition, it would be wiser to ignore it and rely entirely on the strength of one's own case. It is the over-all picture of the case that must be shown to be important and controlling and not any one particular part of it.

A lawsuit is not a disinterested investigation but a bitter duel between adversaries. However, zeal is no cloak for offensiveness. No argument was ever made more persuasive by vituperation or other coarse *ad hominem* approach. No one should forget that the trial is being conducted in a forum of law before a jury intent on justice. On this note the case may well be left to the jury.

Reference

Lustgarten, E. M. *Verdict in dispute.* New York: Charles Scribner Sons, 1950.

5 The Psychology of Juries

Approximately one million Americans are called for jury duty each year. They are participating in a procedure which has been described by Blackstone as "the glory of the English law," and which distinguishes both English and American trials. Beginning in ninth-century France, the jury was originally a group of men compelled by the king to take an oath. The Normans brought it to England, where the jury was a body of men used in an inquisition or inquest and not part of the administration of justice. The oath was a guarantor of veracity, and only the king could compel the taking of the oath. The beginning of the modern use of juries was an order by Henry II, by the Grand Assize, that a litigant in a dispute about title to land could summon a royal jury. The men on the jury were called because they knew the facts in the disputed case, and were rejected if they did not. A litigant won when he got twelve oaths. This was the origin of the trial, of the requirement of unanimity, and of the use of twelve jurors. Twelve jurors are needed because of the traditional English abhorrence of the decimal system and because of the English preference for twelve, as in the twelve pennies in a shilling.

In 1215, Pope Innocent II effectively prohibited trial by ordeal — the previous procedure — by forbidding ecclesiastics to participate in ordeals. In his 1166 Assize of Clarendon, Henry II started what we know today as the grand jury and the bill of indictment, by requiring a jury to report any of its members suspected of committing certain crimes. For some time after the jury supplanted the ordeal as a method of trial, the jurors who brought the indictment were also the persons who tried the case. In 1352, Edward II ruled that no indictor should also try a case. The jury gradually changed from a group deciding a case on the basis of its pretrial knowledge to a group which got information from outside. This information was initially given haphazardly, privately to one or two jurors, or publicly in response to a general invitation. Gradually, procedures for

96

admission of evidence developed, until today a person with prior knowledge of the facts of a case probably would not be permitted to serve as a juror.

The judge and the jury were never formally created as separate institutions. The jury derived its powers from the judge's willingness to accept its verdict. In theory, the jury is still an instrument used by judges to reach a decision. The jury's verdict has no legal effect until the judge's judgment is entered.

Ever since the jury system began to flourish in America, after complaints by colonists that the king was depriving them of trial by jury, there has been a considerable debate over its relative merit. There is no clear statement in the law of the kind of cases for which juries are and are not suited. Opponents of the jury system have pointed out that the two countries which gave rise to the jury, France and England, have been using it less and less. Hardly a year goes by without a national magazine publishing a strong attack on our jury system, or a distinguished jurist praising it. Every attack on juries seems to elicit an equally vigorous defense.

Although there have been considerable changes in civil and criminal codes, there have been practically no changes in the jury system. Its many alleged imperfections have been discussed, but such discussion seems to have had little effect on jury procedure, possibly because of the power of custom or possibly because of the lack of any effective alternate procedure. Attempts to change the jury system have been attacked in some quarters as attempts to upset the system of checks and balances which judge and jury present to each other.

The subject has occasioned novels (Postgate, 1940), first-person accounts (Sutliffe, 1925), best sellers by judges (Bok, 1941), and motion pictures like the 1959 success "Twelve Angry Men," in addition to extensive scholarly discussion (Busch, 1949; Williams, 1955), especially since the growth of the "legal realist" movement of the last half century (Green, 1930; Arnold, 1935; Frank, 1949). The "legal realists" have called attention to what actually happens in the courts, in contrast to the theory of what happens (see Chapter 2).

HOW THE JURY SYSTEM WORKS

What is the jury system and why has it attracted such extravagant praise and blame? Trial by jury is an integral part of the federal court system (Judicial Conference, 1942). The state legislatures have established their own procedures for juries on the local level. On federal and local levels, jury selection is covered by the equal protection clause of the Fourteenth Amendment, which entitles all litigants to have prospective jurors selected from a cross section of the community. This does not mean that a Negro litigant, for example, must have a Negro on a jury which is trying his case, but it does mean that the panel of prospective jurors should include Negroes.

Uniform qualifications for federal jury duty are prescribed by law (United States Code, 1952). Jurors in state and local jurisdictions are usually selected by commissioners specifically charged by law with this responsibility. Among the criteria used for selection of jurors are age; citizenship; lack of a criminal record; ability to read, speak, and understand English; taxpayer status; good health; mental capacity; and a fair education (Note, 1956). Some states, such as Nebraska, Tennessee, and Virginia, have relatively many specific requirements. Other states, such as Massachusetts, Ohio, and Delaware, permit jurors to be selected on the basis of their possession of relatively few of the many possible requirements for jury service.

The core of most of the lists of citizens from which jurors are often chosen is the roster of registered voters in the community. It thus usually excludes persons under twenty-one. Most jurisdictions require prospective jurors to execute a questionnaire which may include their attitudes toward various kinds of punishment. Many occupational groups, such as teachers and lawyers and other professionals, are often exempt from jury duty. Other prospective jurors may be sick, or have business out of town, or be otherwise unable to be present at the specific time that they are called. Groups that are underrepresented in juries include those with very low income and the poorly educated. Exemptions and excuses usually eliminate from 60 to 80 percent of the persons on the original list of prospective jurors.

The juror may be called either in a civil case, in which only private rights are involved, or in a criminal matter. Trial by jury is required by federal and state constitutions in most criminal and many civil cases. The defendant in a criminal case may waive a jury and be tried by judge alone, and both parties in a civil suit may give such waivers. It is thus the consent of litigants which keeps the jury system in use. The lawyer for either side is permitted to determine whether a juror has any attitudes which might prejudice a fair trial for his client, in a pretrial or *voir dire* examination of jurors. The lawyer has a much greater opportunity to screen jurors in a state or local court than in a federal Court, where the Court is likely to be more active in selecting the jury than it is in a state or local court. The judge conducts the pretrial examination of prospective jurors in ten states, the lawyer does in eleven states, and both do in the other states. If the preliminary interview indicates a specific reason for believing that a prospective juror will be prejudiced, his presence on the jury may be challenged by a lawyer for either side. Each lawyer is permitted an unlimited number of such challenges "for cause." Each lawyer is also permitted a fixed number of peremptory challenges, which permit him to disqualify a prospective juror without giving a specific reason for doing so. Lawyers typically engage in many more peremptory challenges than challenges "for cause."

The jury of twelve men and/or women thus consists of jurors who have been "qualified" by the lawyers so that they can come to a fair and impartial verdict. The life of a jury is usually two or three weeks, or until the completion of the case for which it has been assembled and at the conclusion of which it is dissolved.

The jurors elect their own foreman, who presides over their deliberations. Once the trial has begun, the individual jurors are forbidden to interrogate witnesses, because their questions may be improper or antagonistic. Most jurisdictions forbid jurors' taking of notes, because jurors differ in their note-taking ability and the juror of superior note-taking ability may have an unfair advantage over his colleagues. When all the testimony is completed, the judge's instructions to the jury include a detailed explanation of the law which is relevant (Plucknett, 1929). First formulated in 1585 in Coke's famous phrase, the Court's function is to determine which laws are necessary for the jury to know about, and it is the Court's role to advise the jury what the law is. The jury's function is to apply the law to the specific evidence and facts in the case and to determine what the facts are.

The theory of the jury holds that it does its job best in an atmosphere of secrecy, and only jury members may be present at its deliberations. Almost all jurisdictions require the jury to return a unanimous verdict. A mistrial is declared and the case retried if there is a hung jury which cannot reach unanimity. In those few civil cases in which unanimity is not required, a majority of nine or ten is required.

No juror can be forced or threatened to sign any verdict, and no one has the right to influence his judgment or decision. There are some jurisdictions in which the jury fixes the penalty in a criminal case; in others, the judge fixes the penalty after the jury has given its verdict. In a civil action involving a suit for a fixed sum, the jury decides how much money will be awarded.

RESEARCH ON JURIES

Probably the first serious research on the jury system was conducted in 1924 by lawyer-psychologist William M. Marston (1924). He executed several well-designed studies which used simulated juries, and most subsequent jury research has also been based on simulated juries. He concluded that one trained individual is a better fact finder than either a female or a male jury, in terms of the judge versus jury problem, and that female were better than male jurors. The individual juror's previous professional training and experience were related, Marston found, to his skill at fact finding. Marston reported that written evidence was superior to oral evidence, and that the self-confidence of a witness might be more effective on a jury than the logic or psychological soundness of other testimony. In Marston's simulated juries, female jurors used more care in considering testimony than did male jurors. Direct examination proved to be a more complete and accurate method of presenting testimony than cross-examination. Marston recommended that the results of his study be used to improve the current jury system rather than to emphasize its futility.

In 1935, two law professors made the first empirical study of what happens in a jury room (Hunter, 1935). After a trial they questioned jurors on various phases of the litigation on which they had rendered a verdict. They concluded that the typical juror does not understand the rules of law involved in a lawsuit and does not apply them to the relevant issues. Two federal judges, some twelve years later, published the results of a questionnaire they had sent to 375 jurors on federal and state courts in three midwest states (Hervey, 1947). Of the 185 jurors who answered, 73 said that they had not understood the judge's instructions.

The value of a discussion among the members of a jury has been documented by two experiments (Dashiell, 1935). An incident occurred in front of a college class, two members of which reported it to 7 jurors. Each juror wrote out his individual version of the story and then each jury reported on a version on which all the jurors agreed. The two original witnesses reported 62 and 55 percepts, respectively, with 5 and 8 errors. The individual jurors reported 44 percepts and averaged 10 errors. After discussion, each jury agreed on an average of 32 items, but averaged only 4 errors.

In a related experiment, a number of individuals saw a short film and reported its contents to 24 juries, each of which had from 12 to 15 members. Each jury member wrote his own narrative and answered the standard questionnaire; each of the juries then reached a group decision on the same material. In each of the juries, the individual jurors did worse than did the individual witnesses. In all 24 juries, however, jurors did better as a group than they did individually. A typical witness scored 65, an individual juror 32, but the juries reported a group consensus of 50.

Psychologists have studied not only the effects of discussion but also the effect of having the last word in a trial. They have explored the hypothesis that the opinions of a jury vary in the course of a trial (Weld and Roff, 1938). The evidence in a famous bigamy case was read to a group of listeners, who rated the defendant's guilt or innocence after each installment, using a scale of 1 for certainty of innocence to 9 for certainty of guilt. At the beginning of the presentation, the subjects felt strongly that the defendant was guilty and felt so even more strongly after the prosecution presented its case. They were less certain as the defense progressed. When the prosecution spoke again, they again began thinking in terms of guilt. After the next and last defense presentation, the subjects again began thinking in terms of innocence and the average final evaluation was 2, or innocent. In the next version of the experiment, all the defense material was presented first, followed by all the prosecution material — and the subjects voted 4.4. When all the prosecution material was presented first and followed by all the defense material, the voting was again 2. The experimenters conclude that the usual order of presentation, with the defense coming last, is favorable to the defense. They noted that some were heavily influenced by new evidence.

One study of how a jury's verdict was reached was conducted by two psychologists with a mock trial (Weld and Danzig, 1940). They found that the first witness for a side was usually the most effective, and that the prestige of the opposing counsel was quite influential in influencing juror judgment. Only 1 of 41 jurors changed his mind about a case in the jury room.

More recent attempts to conduct similar experiments have cast some doubts on the extent to which the side of a two-sided issue that is presented first necessarily has the advantage (Hovland, 1953, 1957). However, these recent studies are based on classroom experiments, in contrast to the earlier studies which simulate courtroom situations, in which the two sides are clearly labeled as opposing each other.

Another empirical study was conducted with juries sitting in mock trials at the Yale Law School (Hoffman and Bradley, 1952). The Yale researchers concluded, on the basis of their experiments, that juries seem to try the lawyer rather than the litigant whom he represents. Juries seem to ignore a judge's instructions to disregard a statement previously made. Once the statement has been made it has been perceived, and instructions not to consider it have little effect. The researchers also found that the mere fact of someone's being indicted and brought to trial tend to make him suspect, in spite of the presumption of innocence in our court system. They also found jurors very reluctant to emerge from their deliberations saying that it had not been possible to reach a verdict. Confirming earlier research, it was found that juries tend to disregard the rules of law and that the recollection of great masses of testimony was extremely difficult. They concluded that juries need more orientation than they now receive.

The most elaborate empirical research undertaken on juries has been under way since 1953 at the University of Chicago Law School, where a team of social scientists and lawyers has been engaged in studies of the behavior of experimental juries as well as of activities of actual juries. A series of studies has examined various phases of status and role in their expression in the jury room. One study of 127 jurors in a mock trial of an automobile negligence case compared the relative activity of men and women in the jury room (Strodtbeck and Mann, 1956). Its examination of twelve different groups of jurors suggested that men jurors initiate relatively long periods of activity directed toward the solution of the jury's task. Women tended more to react to the contributions of others. This difference is probably a reflection of the role differences between the sexes in our culture.

Another study with mock juries examined the manner in which the status of the jurors in a number of mock trials affected their work as jurors (Strodtbeck, James, and Hawkins, 1957). In over half the cases studied, the foreman was nominated by one member and quickly accepted by the others. In all the cases, the foreman was selected quickly. When the mock jurors had completed their deliberations they were asked what kind of person they would like to have on a jury trying a member of their family. All the different occupational groups except laborers would prefer to have a member of their family tried by a jury which consisted largely of proprietors. Laborers preferred skilled workers on the jury trying a member of their family, with proprietors in second place. All groups except laborers placed laborers in last place as potential jurors for members of their family. The face-to-face experience on the mock jury caused the lower-status groups to be evaluated more highly. In general, jurors of higher status participate more than jurors of lower status, have more influence on other jurors, derive more satisfaction from their service, and are perceived as being more competent by other jurors. Jurors can size up the status of other members of their panel by obvious cues such as dress, speech, and references to previous experience.

Another Chicago study continued the examination of the effect of status of jurors (James, 1959b). A recorded criminal trial was presented to panels which totaled 204 jurors. In electing a foreman, the jurors usually selected someone of relatively high status. Male jurors and those with a college education participated most actively in group discussion. The jurors in this study spent about 50 percent of their time exchanging experiences and opinions, 25 percent of the time on procedure, 15 percent reviewing facts, and 8 percent on court instructions. The more educated jurors interpreted the court's instructions more accurately and more effectively, and facilitated group discussion more than did the more poorly educated jurors. The jurors' education did not seem to be a factor in whether they concurred in the majority decision, were pressured into going along with the majority, or had any tendency to be dissidents. All the jurors showed real concern for doing their job, and there was no evidence that one or two "strong men" had undue influence on other members of their panel. Jurors evaluated the participation of others without regard for their educational background, although jurors with only a grade school education spoke significantly less accurately and more disruptively than others.

An attempt was made, in another Chicago study, to evaluate jurors' assessment of criminal responsibility in a trial (James, 1959b). The same recorded criminal trial was played to twenty juries. Half the juries were instructed in terms of the McNaghten Rule, which involves the defendant's ability to distinguish right from wrong. The other half were instructed in terms of the Durham Rule, which involves the question of whether the crime was the product of mental illness. A thorough discussion of these concepts can be found in the Chapter 7, "Criminal Responsibility and Psychiatry." Both sets of instructions were given serious consideration by the two groups of juries.

One study involved interviewing a larger number of jurors after they had served in an actual case (Kalven, 1957). In 71 percent of the cases, there was no unanimity on the first ballot. In 36 percent of the cases the split was at least 8 to 4. In 90 percent of the cases where the majority voted guilty on the first ballot, the verdict was guilty. In 97 percent of the cases where the majority voted not guilty on the first ballot, the verdict was not guilty. Hung juries which could not reach a verdict occurred only when the initial balloting showed a substantial minority. Since hung juries did not occur frequently, the perennial fear that one "strong man" could lead to a hung jury was not confirmed. A hung jury seems to reflect the closeness of the case and of a juror's feeling that his minority view can get several other supporters.

One survey addressed itself to the question of whether jury service provides an important point of contact with the court system. It found that 6 percent of the general population had jury service during their lifetime and that 3 percent had their only direct contact with the court as a result of jury service (Kalven, 1957). Some 55 percent of the public, however, had been in court in some capacity, including 23 percent who had been a party to litigation, and 21 percent who were witnesses. Fifty-five percent of the public had known someone who had been a juror.

The same study provided some data on the impact of jury service. Of those who did not serve, 36 percent would like to serve, 48 percent would not like to serve, and 16 percent were undecided. Of those who had served in the previous year, 94 percent said they would like to serve again, and only 3 percent said they would dislike it, with 3 percent willing to serve again as a duty. In the Chicago survey the great majority of the jurors who actually did serve in a case, and did not suffer economic hardships from serving, said that they would like to serve again.

Economic hardship and being called but not serving on an actual jury decreased enthusiasm for jury duty. Some citizens may dislike jury duty because they are uneasy about judging others and uneasy in a new experience. Actually serving on a jury tends to make jurors more enthusiastic about its use in criminal cases and less so in civil cases.

The focus of one study was the extent to which ten different experimental juries would make awards for damages (Kalven, 1958). This problem is important because of the widely held belief that the amount of damages which is "right" for personal injuries is "Law written by the jury," rather than by statute. The specific case which was presented to the experimental juries had actually been settled, in a real situation, for $42,000. The average award made by the ten experimental juries was $41,000. The range was from $17,500 to $60,000. This experiment suggests that a particular jury may make an award which may appear to be relatively high or relatively low, but that in the long run such awards tend to approximate an average.

Another phase of the Chicago study has examined regional variations in civil suit awards by juries (Kalven, 1957). San Francisco juries, for example, give higher awards than do Los Angeles juries, and Brooklyn more than Queens juries in New York City — in both cases the margin is 20 percent. One phase of the Chicago research involved polling federal and state judges on how they would have decided a number of jury cases. Judge and jury agreed in 41 percent of the cases; the judge favored the defendant more than did the jury in 33 percent of the cases; and he favored the plaintiff more than the jury did in 25 percent of the cases — contradicting the usual view that the jury favors the defendant.

THE PSYCHOLOGY OF THE JURY

For a case to get into a court at all, it is a reasonable presumption that both sides have something to say which, from their points of view, should lead the jury to a verdict in their favor. What will lead the jury to a verdict one way or the other will be a reflection of the motivation of the jurors, and their perception of the evidence in terms of how the jurors relate to the lawyers, litigants, judge, and the other members of the jury. It would be difficult to find a subject which lends itself more directly to psychological analysis than the motivation, memory, perception, and interrelationships of jurors.

Lawyers have long been aware of the importance of the psychological dimension in jurors' behavior, on a kind of anecdotal or impressionistic basis. They have sought areas within the prospective juror's personality which could be exploited by building bias into the make-up of the jury, arousing its feelings, and influencing the terms of its decision (Goldstein, 1935; Nizer, 1946–47; Cutler, 1949; Belli, 1956). Chapters 3 and 4 of this volume deal with some of the assumptions lawyers make about juries. There is no way of knowing whether the observations of lawyers are generalizable without conducting more special psychological research than has been available to date. In some instances, the assumptions of lawyers are valid if viewed in the light of discoveries made by psychoanalysis. Juries, for instance, can clearly be induced to "identify" with the lawyer's client (Belli, 1956).

Another psychoanalytic mechanism which may be helpful in understanding what jurors do is "projection." In evaluating the extent to which psychological factors enter into the work of the jury, the traditional lawyers' adage that aged and infirm jurors make the defendant pay for their ills as well as for those of the plaintiff is relevant. It may be difficult for jurors to avoid putting *themselves* into their observations of what the merits and demerits of each litigant's case might be, projecting some of their own needs onto litigants. Some jurors may not project their needs directly onto a litigant but may engage in the related mechanism of "displacement." Their behavior as jurors is an expression of feelings which they did not express in other situations, such as at work or in the home. They might not be able to express their feelings about an employer directly to the employer, but they might transfer such feelings into a courtroom situation in which an employer is a litigant.

Another dimension of behavior to which psychoanalysts have addressed themselves, and which is relevant to the work of the jury, is the enormous range of thoughts and feelings which people experience (Freud, 1915), even when they are concentrating on something. The attention of a juror may wander, either when he is listening to testimony or when he is deliberating with his colleagues in the jury room. Psychoanalytic findings would suggest that the fantasies of a juror might be stimulated by persons connected with the trial who remind him of someone who had been emotionally significant to him in the past.

Our understanding of the psychology of the jury can also be improved by considering the findings of psychological research on how people form impressions of other people, because the juror's evaluation of the case is essentially his evaluation of the people who are involved in it. For instance, a number of studies have documented the extent to which people tend to value traits which resemble their own traits (Fensterheim and Tresselt, 1953).

One summary of many psychological researches on what enables people to judge others accurately, which is surely relevant to the work of the juror, concluded that fellow feeling, the ability to use information, detachment, social adjustment, intelligence, and a global approach to people are likely to be found in persons who can judge others accurately (Bruner and Taguiri, 1954). How the individual judges other people is likely to affect his impression of how others should behave, and what is "reasonable" for them. In a negligence case, the whole issue may hinge upon whether a litigant behaved in a "reasonable" or "prudent" manner (James, 1951). The juror's evaluation of this is likely to involve his self-concept, how he perceives other people, and his expectations of the behavior of people at different age levels who possess different physical and emotional characteristics. Many studies in perception have documented how complex the processes are by which the perceiver selects from the evidence of his senses that which is uniquely meaningful to him. What he selects is a reflection of his needs, aspirations, life situation, prejudices, previous experience, and many other factors. It is logical to expect that Juror X will perceive the world very much as he did when he was Mr. X, and he will not overnight become a judicious evaluator of evidence merely because he is sworn in.

Many of the studies in the psychology of memory are relevant to an understanding of the work of the jury (Bartlett, 1932). The jury's examination of evidence is based on its ability to recall what is presented to it. It is reasonable to assume, for example, that jurors will tend to recall emotional and dramatic incidents more clearly than they will recall less startling evidence.

Studies in "set" (expectations based on past experience or needs) also are relevant to jurors' performance of their jobs (Piaget, 1937). Cartoons have made us familiar with how the set of jurors can change when a pretty girl trips to the witness stand. The set of jurors may change less dramatically when other witnesses go to the witness stand, but it is certainly subject to change. A special kind of set is that of a juror prejudiced for or against a particular kind of witness or litigant. How important this may be can be seen in the derivation of the word "prejudice" from the Latin for prejudgment. Prejudiced jurors may not wish to admit that they are prejudiced when being qualified in routine pretrial examination. Their prejudice may assert itself during the trial, even though jurors are required to consider the evidence without regard for race, creed, or color. The psychology of prejudice is thus a central source of clues to how a jury functions (Allport, 1954).

A major source of data to enhance our understanding of the psychology of the jury is the considerable experimentation on small groups during the last two decades (Cartwright and Zander, 1953). The findings of these researchers into group dynamics may be almost directly applicable to the jury's task, because the typical small group studied by group-dynamics researchers consists of persons who have not previously met and who are assembled for the purpose of solving a specific problem, much as a jury is.

Many findings of such research may be relevant to the jury. For example, a study of groups in problem-solving situations has reported that such groups tend to move through time from a relative emphasis on problems of getting used to the situation to problems of evaluation, and subsequently to problems of what to do about these evaluations (Bales and Strodtbeck, 1951). It is possible that juries go through the same steps in addressing themselves to their task. Other research suggests that group members who talk a lot are regarded by their fellow group members as functioning more effectively than those who are quiet, even when the group accepts the solution of the latter (Riecken, 1958).

Another kind of psychological research that may sharpen our understanding of jury functioning is the examination of the kinds of people who can most easily be persuaded. Recent research has demonstrated that there are certain kinds of people who have a general susceptibility to persuasion and social influence (Janis, 1954). These persons are likely to have high social inadequacy, high "inhibition" of aggression, and feelings of depression. By contrast, persons who are resistant to persuasion are likely to manifest persistent aggressiveness, social withdrawal, and acute neurotic symptoms.

Apart from these predisposing personality characteristics, there is considerable evidence to support the proposition that people are likely to be more receptive to the suggestions and views of certain persons than to those of others. Jurors would presumably tend to carry into the jury room preferential views toward high-status persons. A reflection of this presumed greater wisdom which high-status persons possess could be seen when the armed forces, after World War II, revised their court-martial procedures so as to give enlisted men the right to have other enlisted men on their trial boards. Most enlisted men still preferred to be tried by officers.

One experiment in the realistic setting of a conference confirmed the hypothesis that group members of low status behave toward group members of high status in a way which will reduce their uneasiness with the highs (Hurwitz, 1953). The low-status persons tended to participate relatively little in group discussion. This finding suggests the possibility that low-status jurors would tend to be less active than those of higher status, which is being confirmed in the Chicago jury studies.

The possibly enormous power of group pressure in modifying a minority view is illustrated in one experiment in which members of an experimental group were instructed to lie about their impression of the length of a line (Asch, 1952). One subject in each group was not aware that the other persons were lying, and thus was faced with a situation in which the group unanimously contradicted the evidence of his senses. About one third of the subjects made errors in the same direction as did the majority. In a jury situation, this experiment suggests the possibility that a minority view might be swayed by the pressure of the majority. The possible importance of minority views in a group situation has been demonstrated in other studies in which the opinions of persons with minority views upgraded the group's solution of a problem (Maier and Solem, 1952; Kadis and Winick, 1960).

It would thus seem that many kinds of psychological research on individuals and groups can be applied to the study of the jury. Since so many central areas of psychology are relevant to what jurors do, much psychological data from many different sources may be constructively used in helping us to understand how the jury works. Such data can assist us in translating our knowledge of the jury into practice. Collecting data on practice can in turn add to our knowledge of individual and group psychology. Since there is good reason to believe that our knowledge of the psychology of the jury will tend to improve its functioning, both psychology and the jury system would benefit from their collaboration.

CONTROVERSY OVER THE JURY SYSTEM

Ranging from the suggestion that juries be abolished and that cases be tried by a judge, to modifications in jury procedure, the debate over the merits of the jury system has assumed much momentum. The jury has been said to be the epitome of the democratic process, with citizens gathering to evaluate the merits of the contention of another citizen. Others have claimed that the jury is the antithesis of democracy because it is responsible to no one, is completely anonymous, and is not required to give any grounds for whatever verdict it reaches, in contrast to the judge, who gives the reasons for his decision.

The traditional defense of the jury system emphasizes that juries are especially qualified to perform their critical function of fact finding (Bell, 1940). It is emphasized that the mode of selection of jurors and their representativeness, disinterested approach, and open-minded discussion contribute to jurors being able to weigh the possibilities and to reach a sound decision in a case. Critics have pointed out that lawyers usually use peremptory challenges in order to disqualify potential jurors who have any special knowledge of the subject matter of the litigation. They also note that the best-qualified potential jurors in the community either are exempt from serving or are likely to avoid jury duty because of the considerable economic loss it may represent to them. Professor George Braden has observed that the practice of judges in "directing a verdict" in cases in which there is so much evidence on one side that no reasonable man could fail to decide for it, suggests that courts themselves do not regard juries as especially competent arbiters of debatable factual matters. Whether controverted factual issues are best resolved by discussion among citizens who have no specific experience in handling disputes has also been questioned by various critics.

One of the most frequently heard arguments for the jury system is that the jury is a kind of legislature which wisely corrects the law by applying extralegal considerations and popular attitudes to the issue under consideration (Wyzanski, 1952). This has been further expressed as the jury's refusal to apply a particular law if it believes the law to be unjust. Opponents of the jury system believe that it is curious that we should support a jury's nullification of the work of elected legislators, and they believe that such a viewpoint assumes a degree of sophistication which the average jury does not possess. Since the deliberations of the jury are secret, there is no way of knowing whether the jury nullifies the law on the basis of serious consideration or on the basis of caprice. Juries' prudence may not necessarily be superior to jurisprudence, and it is difficult for some critics of juries to understand how, in the same 1946 report, the American Bar Association could say that the jury must "let the law prevail," as well as that "the jury often stands as a bulwark" between an individual and an unreasonable law.

Another point at issue between friends and critics of the jury system is whether jury service is an educational experience which provides participation in a democratic activity and helps to create confidence in government and law (Curtis, 1952). Critics aver that this experience usually lasts for only two weeks, and that the education of the jury occurs at the expense of the litigants. They feel that jury duty may lead to cynicism about the workings of the courts, and that the confidence of the public in the democratic processes by which juries work has been undermined by juries' acquitting notorious criminals who were obviously guilty, or convicting the innocent (Borchard, 1932). The reluctance of many citizens to serve on juries is cited by critics as the best evidence that many citizens are actually not interested in the educational experience of jury duty and will avoid it whenever it is possible to do so.

Another point at issue is whether the jury represents one way of counteracting bias and corruption of judges (Haynes, 1944). Critics point out that we have avoided giving sentencing powers to juries because of fear that they would abuse such powers. They also feel that the judge in criminal cases, even if there is a jury, can still express his bias or corruption in his sentence.

Juries have traditionally been said to be more reliable in criminal than in civil proceedings because they are sensitive to the special circumstances of the alleged crime. Opponents of the jury system believe that alleged criminals who are members of certain minority groups may not experience this benevolence of the jury. They also note that the public needs protection against "groundless acquittals."

Proponents of the jury have praised the procedure whereby the judge gives instructions on the relevant law to the jury, and the jury interprets those instructions and applies them to the facts at hand (De Sloovere, 1933). Critics of juries feel that it is almost impossible for the judge to present the law in a way which is understandable to the untrained mind (Farley, 1932). They also complain that the judge sometimes mixes questions of law and fact in his instructions to the jury and that the instructions may not be useful, even if they are intelligible. Other critics have observed that many issues of fact have legal status, and any attempt to distinguish law from fact is unreal. Some students of juries have complained that it is naïve to have the jury listen to all the evidence before the judge explains the relevant law, because it then must try to recall the evidence retrospectively in terms of the judge's explanation. Other critics feel that some lawyers may request a great many kinds of instructions from the judge, not to help the jury in its deliberations but so that when the case is appealed they can claim that some of the instructions were ignored. Even if a jury has not followed the judge's instructions, in many criminal cases the judge is required to follow the jury's verdict.

Critics of the jury system have maintained that there are cases in which the jury does not apply the judge's instructions and instead does what it would like to do, without heeding the law. Other proponents of juries have denied that juries can avoid following the judge's instructions. One famous handwriting expert, who testified in cases all over America for over three decades, had so little confidence in juries that he recommended that a difficult case not be given to a jury relatively late in the day (Osborn, 1937). He felt that the jurors would be likely to be so interested in getting home that they might render a hasty decision.

One noted trial lawyer has summarized the reactions of many lawyers to the jury system as practiced today by saying that the jury is right in 99 percent of the cases, even though it may be right for the wrong reasons. The typical jury in this view forms a judgment and then rationalizes that judgment. Some critics have objected that to find reasons for confirming a decision which has already been arrived at is a kind of exaltation of irrationality, and that to say that a jury is right for the wrong reasons is essentially illogical. There is no way of knowing just how and why juries reach a verdict.

It has been alleged that some juries reach their verdicts in a capricious way, like flipping coins or rendering a quotient verdict, in which the award favored by each juror is averaged arithmetically (Skidmore, 1948). If the judge learns that a verdict was reached in such a way, he is likely to reject the jury's verdict. In most jurisdictions nothing is done about such a verdict if the irregular manner in which it was reached is disclosed after the jury has been discharged.

Lawyers often demonstrate their true feelings about juries, according to critics, when they have occasion to represent a client in a relatively complex matter, such as an antitrust action. They seldom ask for a jury in such a case because they generally do not have confidence in a jury's ability to grasp complex ideas in a rational manner. Standard textbooks on trial procedure by experienced lawyers seldom encourage beginning lawyers to select impartial jurors. Instead, they generally encourage them to select jurors who will be responsive to emotional appeals (Turney, 1924; Keeton, 1954).

The debate about juries has thus been vigorous and continual, with equally eminent lawyers and judges on both sides of the argument.

Some of these debates have given rise to specific suggestions for reform.

SUGGESTED REFORMS IN JURY PROCEDURE

Many reforms have been suggested to keep jury practice abreast of knowledge and experience. One reform which has been urged would begin with the selection of the jury itself (Note, 1956). The proponents of reform in selection have stated that the traits desired in effective jurors are relatively easy to measure objectively. These traits would include physical integrity, a fund of general information and of information on legal institutions, personal stability, reasonable critical judgment, and reasonable attitudes. At the present times, Los Angeles County is perhaps the only jurisdiction to use standardized tests of intelligence, memory, and perception in jury selection. Some students of juries have recommended that such valid psychological tests to screen jurors might be used to serve a number of purposes.

The use of standardized tests might mean that less time would be spent in *voir dire* examinations, and thus decrease court calendar congestion. Another benefit which has been foreseen is that attorneys would tend to stress rational rather than emotional appeals. If litigants knew that jurors were relatively tough-minded, flimsy cases should be less likely to get to court. The exclusionary rules of evidence which limit the evidence that can be presented in court could be liberalized if relatively alert jurors could be assumed. It is urged that the prestige of the jury system and of jury duty would increase if jurors were selected more carefully.

The kind of objective psychological tests recommended for jury selection have proved their usefulness in screening personnel in the armed forces and in industry. No new legislation is required to use such tests, it is said, and a ruling by a commissioner of jurors or courts is all that would be required. Although one decision held that a procedure which screened out many prospective jurors would violate the constitutional requirement of trial by a "cross section of the community" (Glasser, 1942), later decisions have approved the setting of high qualifications for jurors (Fay, 1947). The courts have held that the constitution guarantees the jury mode of trial but not its specific features or procedures (Robinson, 1950).

Some reformers of the jury system have felt that even more widespread use of the screening procedures may fall short of the mark. These reformers recommend that there should be regular use of jurors who are specialists in the matter under consideration, who would be able to consider relatively technical or complex matters in a presumably more efficient way than would ordinary juries. These reformers believe that it is foolish to exclude from a jury the very people who know most about a particular problem or area. A related recommendation is the greater use of the special or "blue ribbon" jury, in order to get more jurors from the upper socio-economic brackets than normally serve (Baker, 1950).

In addition to more precise procedures for selecting jurors, there has been considerable discussion about the desirability of training citizens in the procedures and mechanics of courts and juries, so that they would have a background of knowledge before being called as jurors. A number of judges have urged that adult education groups as well as students in public schools receive formal, scheduled instruction in the nature of jury activity as well as fact finding in the context of jury activity. It has been recommended that successful completion of such a course be a prerequisite to any jury duty. One procedure for improving the performance of juries, which has been used in a number of jurisdictions, is the orientation booklet that describes the workings of the court and jury (Miner, 1946). Some judges give orientation talks to groups of prospective jurors. Because of the lack of any controlled experiments there is no way of knowing how effective these orientation procedures have been. It is certainly possible that the citizenry's increasing awareness of and interest in jury functioning may lead to the dissemination of more accurate information about juries and to more effective juror performance.

Another focus of discussion for improving juries has been the possible effects of newspaper dissemination of information which may interfere with a fair trial. Such information may affect the prospective juror's ability to be objective, especially in criminal trials. It has been urged that there be stricter enforcement of the contempt of court laws against newspapers that publish incorrect statements of fact or express biased opinions that can hinder a fair trial in a case to be tried by a jury (Goodhart, 1935). Contrary to popular belief, the American law is similar to the British law on this subject. English practice goes back to 1742, when Lord Hardwicke sent a publisher to jail for printing a libel against a witness in a pending case. In 1924, the editor of the *London Evening Standard* was fined a thousand pounds and costs for publishing the reports of special investigators sent by the newspaper to interview some witnesses in connection with a famous crime. These procedures ensure that there will be no "newspaper conviction or acquittal." However, even though they have the power to do so, few American judges have had the hardihood to punish the press.

The admissibility of psychiatric concepts of personality for witnesses for both plaintiffs and defendants has been urged as a necessary reform. It has been suggested that jurors may be helped by having expert testimony about a witness, because jurors may not perceive a mentally abnormal witness to be abnormal (Comment, 1950). Thus, in the second trial of Alger Hiss, Dr. Carl Binger testified for the defense that prosecution witness Whittaker Chambers was a psychopath who might make "false accusations." If the psychiatrist has an opportunity to conduct a clinical examination of a witness, this would clearly be preferable to his reporting on observations. Under present laws, however, a witness's privacy is jeopardized by his submitting to such an examination.

Another suggestion for improving the performance of juries would encourage the judge to call in a variety of experts to render expert testimony (Beuscher, 1941). This would give the judge more latitude than he currently has. It is now possible for the judge, in certain circumstances, to refer complex testimony to an expert, who may report on the testimony to the jury, which may or may not accept his report. If the judge is encouraged to call on expert testimony, it is urged, the quality of testimony would improve.

A procedure suggested for improving the ability of juries to evaluate evidence is to give judges the right to comment on the evidence, although this would obviously contradict the traditional role of the judge. One suggestion made is the wider use by judges of cautionary instructions to the jury, in which the judge makes suggestive comments on testimony that may have occasioned an emotional ferment in the jurors. The purpose of the judge's doing this would be to bring into the open some of the emotional factors that may be influencing the jurors.

The wisdom of excluding some of the kinds of evidence which are not permitted under current procedures has been questioned (Morgan, 1936) by some legal scholars, who have suggested that such evidence may help juries. Others have questioned the desirability of forbidding jurors to take notes during a trial (Comment, 1948).

A number of suggestions for improving the performance of juries focus on the procedure by which verdicts are reached. It has been urged by one judge that there be a stenographic record of jury deliberations so that the judge can scrutinize the record in order to determine how the verdict was reached (Galston, 1943). If it were reached by improper means, he could set the verdict aside. Polling the jury on the method by which it reached its verdict is another procedure which has been urged in order to make the jury system work better. It has been suggested that such polling would make jurors more likely to behave in a responsible way. A related procedure which has been recommended is the interrogatory, a written statement by the jury about specific questions on specific facts, which is provided by the jury along with a verdict. The interrogatory permits the judge to obtain an insight into the jurors' reasons for the verdict they render.

Some proponents of jury reform have recommended the greater use of the special rather than the general verdict (Sunderland, 1919). The general verdict is an either/or decision, and is thus either all right or all wrong. The special verdict requires the jury to determine specific issues of fact raised at the trial. It thus maximizes the separation of the three dimensions of the law, the facts, and the application of the law to the facts. It enables errors to be localized and may improve the jury's morale by its abandonment of secrecy. The trial judge applies the appropriate law to the facts which are established by the special verdict, and thus the jury is less able to tell which side will benefit from its finding and is thus less likely to be swayed by nonrational considerations. The special verdict would require greater singleness of allegation and greater precision of presentation. The special verdict and the interrogatory have been authorized for the federal courts and in some states, but judges have made little use of either procedure, in spite of what their advocates believe to be direct relevance to many civil actions.

The size of the jury itself has been questioned. It has been said that twelve jurors are too many, and that six to nine jurors would do just as effective a job and save money and time (Clark, 1934). There has been relatively little experience reported with juries of less than twelve. The widespread requirement for unanimity of decision has also been called into question by some students, who believe that unanimity imposes an unreal requirement that may influence some jurors to abandon their convictions because of the great pressure on them to reach a verdict.

Another suggested reform has attempted to combine the positive qualities of the group decision with the experience and wisdom of the judge by having several judges deciding each case instead of a jury. This would temper the possibility of a judge's being capricious or arbitrary and at the same time ensure that the litigant's case would be discussed by several people.

The variety of suggestions on how to improve juries suggests that these recommendations have been based less on data than on speculation. Further research of the kind we have reviewed in this chapter may help decide the relative merit of various suggestions to improve juries.

References

Allport, Gordon W. *The nature of prejudice.* Cambridge, Mass.: Addison-Wesley, 1954.

Arnold, Thurman W. *The symbols of government.* New Haven: Yale Univ. Press, 1935, pp. 128–138.

Asch, Solomon. *Social psychology.* Englewood Cliffs, N. J.: Prentice-Hall, 1952, pp. 450–501.

Baker, Richard C. In defense of the blue ribbon jury. *Iowa Law Rev.,* 1950, **35,** 409–421.

Bales, Robert F., & Strodtbeck, Fred L. Phases in group problem solving. *J. abnorm. soc. Psychol.,* 1951, **46,** 485–495.

Bartlett, Frederic C. *Remembering.* Cambridge, England: Cambridge Univer. Press, 1932.

Bell, Laird. Let me find the facts. *J. Amer. Bar Ass.,* 1940, **26,** 552–555.

Belli, Melvin. *Ready for the plaintiff.* New York: Holt, Rinehart and Winston, 1956.

Beuscher, J. H. Use of experts by the courts. *Harvard Law Rev.,* 1941, **54,** 1105–1127.

Bok, Curtis. *Backbone of the herring.* New York: Knopf, 1941.

Borchard, Edwin M. *Convicting the innocent.* New Haven: Yale Univer. Press, 1932.

Broeder, Dale W. Functions of the jury: Fact or fiction? *Univer. of Chicago Law Rev.,* 1954, **21,** 386–424.

Bruner, Jerome S., & Taguiri, Renato. The perception of people. In Gardner Lindzey (Ed.), *Handbook of social psychology.* Cambridge, Mass.: Addison-Wesley, 1954.

Busch, Francis X. *Law and tactics in jury trials.* Indianapolis: Bobbs-Merrill, 1949.

Cartwright, Dorwin, & Zander, Alvin (Eds.) *Group dynamics.* Evanston, Ill.: Row, Peterson, 1953.

Clark, Charles E., & Shulman, Harry. Jury trial for civil cases. *Yale Law J.,* 1934, **43,** 867–885.

Comment: Should juries be allowed to take notes? *J. Amer. Judicature Soc.*, 1948, **32**, 57–59.

Comment: Psychiatric evaluation of the mentally abnormal witness. *Yale Law J.*, 1950, **59**, 1324, 1341.

Curtis, Charles P. The trial judge and the jury. *Vanderbilt Law Rev.*, 1952, **5**, 150–166.

Cutler, A. S. *Successful trial tactics*. Englewood Cliffs, N. J.: Prentice-Hall, 1949, pp. 76–81.

Dashiell, John F. Experimental studies of the influence of social situations. In Carl Murchison (Ed.), *Handbook of social psychology*. Worcester, Mass.: Clark Univer. Press, 1935, pp. 1097–1158.

De Sloovere, Frederick. The functions of judge and jury. *Harvard Law Rev.*, 1933, **46**, 1086–1110.

Devlin, Patrick. *Trial by jury*. London: Stevens & Sons, 1956, pp. 5–11.

Dewey, John. *Essays in experimental logic*. New York: Holt, Rinehart and Winston, 1916, pp. 402–406, 419–435.

Farley, R. J. Instructions to juries—Their role in the judicial process. *Yale Law J.*, 1932, **42**, 194–225.

Fay v. New York, 332 U. S. 261, 291, 1947.

Fensterheim, Herbert, & Tresselt, Margaret E. The influence of value systems on the perceptions of people. *J. abnorm. soc. Psychol.*, 1953, **48**, 93–98.

Frank, Jerome. *Courts on trial*. Princeton, N. J.: Princeton Univer. Press, 1949, pp. 126–146.

Freud, Sigmund. *Psychopathology of everyday life*. New York: Macmillan, 1915.

Galston, Clarence G. Civil jury trials and tribulations. *J. Amer. Bar Ass.*, 1943, **29**, 195–198.

Glasser v. New York, 315 U. S. 60, 86, 1942.

Goldstein, Irving. *Trial technique*. Chicago: Callaghan, 1935.

Goodhart, Arthur L. Newspapers and contempt of court in English law. *Harvard Law Rev.*, 1935, **48**, 888–895.

Green, Leon. *Judge and jury*. Kansas City, Mo.: Vernon Law Book Co., 1930, pp. 153–185, 395–417.

Haynes, Evan. *Selection and tenure of judges*. Newark, N. J.: National Conference of Judicial Councils, 1944.

Herbert, Alan P. *Misleading cases in the common law*. London: Methuen, 1927, pp. 9–21.

Hervey, John G. Jurors look at our judges. *Oklahoma Bar Ass. J.*, 1947, **18**, 1508–1513.

Hoffman, Harold M., & Bradley, Joseph. Jurors on trial. *Missouri Law Rev.*, 1952, **17**, 235–251.

Hovland, Carl I., *et al. Communication and persuasion*. New Haven: Yale Univer. Press, 1953, pp. 269–281.

Hovland, Carl I., *et al. The order of presentation in persuasion.* New Haven: Yale Univer. Press, 1957, pp. 269–281.

Hunter, Robert M. Law in the jury room. *Ohio State Law J.,* 1935, **2,** 1–19.

Hurwitz, Jacob I., Zander, Alvin F., & Hymovitch, Bernard. Some effects of power on the relations among group members. In Dorwin Cartwright and Alvin Zander (Eds.), *Group dynamics.* Evanston, Ill.: Row, Peterson, 1953, pp. 483–492.

James, Fleming. The qualities of the reasonable man in negligence cases. *Missouri Law Rev.,* 1951, **16,** 1–26.

James, Rita M. Jurors' assessment of criminal responsibility. *Soc. Probs.,* 1959, **7,** 58–69.

James, Rita M. Status and competence of jurors. *Amer. J. Sociol.,* 1959, **64,** 563–570.

Janis, Irving L. Personality correlates of susceptibility to persuasion. *J. Pers.,* 1954, **22,** 504–518.

Judicial Conference of Senior Circuit Judges. *Report of the Committee on Selection of Jurors,* 1942, pp. 13–45, 66–88.

Kadis, Asya L., & Winick, Charles. The role of the deviant in the therapy group, *Int. J. soc. Psychiat.,* 1960, **6,** 277–278.

Kalven, Harry, Jr. A report on the jury project of the University of Chicago Law School. *Insurance Counsel J.,* 1957, **24,** 368–381.

Kalven, Harry, Jr. The jury, the law and the personal injury damage award. *Ohio State Law J.,* 1958, **19,** 158–178.

Keeton, Robert E. *Trial tactics and methods.* Englewood Cliffs, N. J.: Prentice-Hall, 1954.

Maier, Norman R. F., & Solem, Allen R. The contributions of a discussion leader to the quality of group thinking. *Human Relat.,* 1952, **5,** 561–572.

Marston, William M. Studies in testimony. *J. Amer. Inst. crim. Law and Criminol.,* 1924, **15,** 1–31.

Miner, Julius H. The jury problem. *J. crim. Law & Criminol.,* 1946, **37,** 1–15.

Morgan, Edmund M. The jury and the exclusionary rules of evidence. *Univer. of Chicago Law Rev.,* 1936, **4,** 247–258.

Nizer, Louis. The art of the jury trial. *Cornell Law Quart.,* 1946–1947, **32,** 59–72.

Note: Psychological tests and standards of competence for selecting jurors. *Yale Law J.,* 1956, **65,** 531–542.

Osborn, Albert S. *The mind of the juror.* Albany, N. Y.: Boyd, 1937.

Piaget, Jean. Principal factors determining intellectual evolution from childhood to adult life. In *Factors determining human behavior.* Cambridge, Mass.: Harvard University Press, 1937, pp. 32–48.

Plucknett, Theodore F. *A concise history of the common law.* Rochester: Lawyers' Cooperative Publishing Co., 1929, pp. 104–131.

Postgate, Raymond W. *The verdict of twelve*. London: Collins, 1940.

Riecken, Henry W. The effect of talkativeness on ability to influence group solutions to problems. *Sociometry*, 1958, **21**, 309–321.

Robinson, W. S. Bias, probability and trial by jury. *Amer. sociol. Rev.*, 1950, **15**, 73–78.

Skidmore v. Baltimore & Ohio, 167 F. 2d, 1948. Opinion of Judge Frank.

Strodtbeck, Fred L., & Mann, Richard D. Sex role differentiation in jury deliberations. *Sociometry*, 1956, **19**, 3–11.

Strodtbeck, Fred L., James, Rita M., & Hawkins, Charles. Social status in jury deliberations. *Amer. sociol. Rev.*, 1957, **22**, 713–718.

Sunderland, Edison R. Verdicts, general and special. *Yale Law J.*, 1919, **29**, 253–267.

Sutliffe, Robert S. *Impressions of an average juryman*. New York: Appleton-Century-Crofts, 1925.

Turney, Raymond T. *Court room psychology: A work on jury trials*. Los Angeles: Times Mirror, 1924.

Ulman, Joseph N. *A judge takes the stand*. New York: Knopf, 1933.

United States Code, 28 U. S. C. 1P1861, 1952.

Weld, H. P., & Danzig, E. R. A study of the way in which a verdict is reached by a jury. *Amer. J. Psychol.*, 1940, **53**, 518–536.

Weld, H. P., & Roff, M. A study in the formation of opinion based upon legal evidence. *Amer. J. Psychol.*, 1938, **51**, 609–628.

Williams, Glanville. *The proof of guilt*. London: Stevens & Sons, 1955, pp. 190–272.

Wyzanski, Charles E. A trial judge's freedom and responsibility. *Harvard Law Rev.*, 1952, **65**, 1281–1304.

Zeisel, Hans, Kalven, Harry, Jr., & Buckholz, Bernard. *Delay in the court*. Boston: Little, Brown, 1959, p. 103.

CHARLES WINICK, ISRAEL GERVER,
and ABRAHAM BLUMBERG

6 The Psychology of Judges

De Tocqueville wrote over a century ago that in America most major, as well as minor, problems ultimately find their way into the courts (De Tocqueville, 1945). For example, in one year 1,330,000 people used the courts in the states of New York and California alone (Blaustein and Porter, 1954). Of the 7,903 judges officially reported in the courts of America, 621 are on the federal bench, 5,041 are state or county judges, and 2,241 sit in city courts (Bureau, 1958). Many other thousands of judges serve in police courts or as justices of the peace, although many of them may have other occupations. Perhaps as many as 5 percent of the country's approximately 250,000 lawyers are thus serving as judges at any one time.

The judge represents one of the few occupations which enjoys extremely high status in practically all modern cultures. The exceptionally high status of judges and their removal from ordinary interpersonal contact is underscored by their robes of office, the judges' sitting above the general room level, and the rather absolute power of judges in their courtrooms. Great respect is generally shown for the office, which is usually designated by very honorific titles. Judges indicate awareness of the reification and depersonalization of their offices by referring to themselves as "the Court" or "the Bench." Many if not most lawyers see judgeship as a proper climax to a career in the law.

The image of the judiciary is thus, at least since Old Testament days, of a group of aloof holders of great power. In some ways they are analogous to revered theologians who interpret Scripture, and they have been instrumental in developing the law into a kind of secular theology. Just as the meaning of Scripture is continually being modified by commentators, the meaning of the law is continually being modified by other judges (see Chapter 2).

The enormous prestige of the judge in America is exemplified in two situations involving judges which have resulted in much popular and other reaction. The discussion over the mysterious disappearance in 1930 of New York's Justice Crater continues to this day because it is inconceivable that a judge would disappear voluntarily. When Federal Judge Manton — an exponent of Natural Law — was found guilty in 1939 of accepting bribes, the expectations of his high office were stridently violated, and the case occasioned much comment. A federal judge, in contrast to more ordinary mortals, was assumed to be immune from such temptation.

The great importance of the work of judges makes it curious that there is relatively little agreement on the qualities of a good judge or on how judges reach their decisions. This lack of agreement, however, helps to explain why the judiciary is the only profession in our society for which there is no specific training or preparation. Inasmuch as the great majority of our judges are elected and not appointed, it is the voters of America who are regularly called upon to evaluate the background of candidates for the bench.

THE JUDGE'S JOB

Although there is not complete agreement on the exact qualities of a good judge, Hobbes's discussion has been the basis for most later commentators: "The things that make a good judge . . . are, first, a right understanding of that principal law of nature called equity, which depends . . . on the goodness of a man's own natural reason, and meditation. . . . Secondly, contempt of unnecessary riches and preferments. Thirdly, to be able in judgment to divest himself of all fear, anger, hatred, love and compassion. Fourthly and lastly, patience to hear, diligent attention in hearing, and memory to retain, digest and apply what he has heard" (Hobbes, 1950).

These qualities are relevant to the work of the judge. The judge is the umpire in the courtroom warfare known as the trial. The trial judge has a role in jury selection and in the admission of evidence; by his rulings on specific applications of law, he is contributing toward the record of the trial that will be necessary in any appeal which may be taken. The judge's subpoena powers enable him to compel the production of records and the appearance and testimony of witnesses. The judge maintains order and discipline and exerts extraordinary control over the conduct of attorneys and other participants in a trial. The judge's power to set aside verdicts, to direct verdicts, to rule on the various motions of counsel, and to effect settlements enables him to dominate the course of litigation.

The judge has a major role in connection with the historic doctrine of judicial review, by which the judge can declare legislative acts unconstitutional (Marbury, 1803). The judge's sentencing power in criminal cases enables him to reinforce the values of society and the distinction between the transgressor and the society which exercises the sentencing power. Ross has stressed that "punishment must not appear as natural brute violence, but as the act of God or of Justice. It must firmly ally itself with the religious and moral ideas of the time, and avoid the appearance of being a blow dealt by a victor to his prostrate foe" (Ross, 1926).

In spite of the enormous importance of the judge's sentencing power in criminal cases, the bulk of the work of the courts is devoted to civil cases and to the resolution of disputes affecting property. In the prestige hierarchy of judges and lawyers, those engaged in the criminal courts are generally on lower levels of prestige, however important their work is. The civil courts oversee the orderly transfer of wealth in our society by their appointment of receivers, executors, administrators, trustees, guardians, and other caretakers of property.

THE MAKING OF JUDICIAL DECISIONS

One of the central activities of the judge is making decisions. The decision has both a public or manifest and a private or latent aspect. The public aspect consists of what the judge communicates publicly, either orally in the courtroom or in a written opinion. An opinion is a statement by a judge in which he explains why he decided as he did. He states the facts as he sees them and the legal rules he applied. Any such public communication of a decision is likely to be made by the judge in accordance with the well-established principle of social psychology that a communicator's message is modified by his perception of his audience (Pool and Shulman, 1959).[1]

---

[1] The judge's opinion generally has two parts — the "holding" and the "dictum." The "holding" consists of judicial observations necessary to the decision of the case. The "dictum" consists of comments not necessary to the actual decision. The opinion is an intellectual rationale which is buttressed by a hierarchy of legal precedents, usage, and case law synthesis, which lead up to the "holding" or *ratio decidendi*.

Different judges may be talking to different audiences in their decisions and opinions. Some judges seem to be talking to the general public in comments associated with decisions in the sentencing of criminal offenders. These comments may be reflections of the judge's belief in the power of his observations to deter future criminals, a desire to maintain a particular reputation, a wish to cater to public pressures, or a desire to keep his name before the voters for purposes of re-election or election to other office. Those judges who seem to be communicating with their colleagues may be demonstrating, for several reasons, their awareness of the human condition, or their flair for fine reasoning, apt citations, or legal scholarship. These reasons may include the edification of other lawyers in the courtroom or they may include unseen audiences or "hidden perceivers" — posterity, other judges, other colleagues who may be instrumental in helping the judge in his career, and so on. Or the judge may be giving his opinion in order to avert posible higher judicial reversals or to obtain agreement and support for his opinion at peer levels and from superiors. The specific audience to which the judge is addressing himself is seldom explicitly stated in his decision and can only be inferred on the basis of the context and circumstances of the decision.

SOME CONTEXTUAL PRESSURES ON JUDICIAL DECISIONS

The specific context and level of jurisdiction of a court may be related to the kind of decision which its judges typically make. The higher the level of a court, the more scrupulous is the care likely to be shown to procedural matters and the greater the concern for all legal rights and protocol. The area of responsibility of a court may be relevant to how its judges perceive their cases. A lower court, such as a magistrate's court in a large city, can, and almost invariably does, pass a case along to another court if there is any indication that the case is problematical, thus postponing its role in the entire decision-making process. A traffic court or a justice of the peace in a smaller community may dispense rough and ready justice which often violates the rights of defendants, but this may seldom be discovered because such cases are only rarely appealed to a higher court. Such a judge is likely to be relatively freewheeling in his decisions.

In addition to this dimension of the level of the court at which the judge presides, there is the important dimension of whether a court has original or appellate jurisdiction. The judge who sits in the court of original jurisdiction, in his role as trial judge, arbiter, sentencer, or awarder, is likely to become involved in the legal, interpersonal, and emotional dynamics of the small group in the courtroom of which the judge is the hub. Even though they are together for a short time, the members of the courtroom group interrelate with each other. The judge in the court of original jurisdiction not only is reacting to witnesses and lawyers, but may also be aware of the shadow of an appellate court passing on any actions or decisions of his which are dubious. He must thus maintain professional impassivity in the courtroom and make his decision with the possibility that the "hidden perceivers" may engage in an appellate review and possibly rebuke him, either because of his application of a specific rule of law to specific facts or because of the facts he has selected as important in a given case or because he has behaved arbitrarily and unreasonably.

The appellate judge is more removed from the original dispute or offense and is therefore relatively unconcerned with the actual interpersonal dynamics in the case. He studies not only the case record on appeal but also what the judge did with the case and whether the original judge behaved with propriety and in accordance with the law. The great majority of cases, however, are not appealed beyond the trial judge's decision; hence the trial judge is a very important figure. In spite of this, the great judges of American tradition are almost always found in appellate courts rather than in courts of original jurisdiction.

Another component of the context within which judical decisions are made is the pressure upon the judge to reduce a sentence, in response to a request by the prosecuting attorney that he do so in return for a defendant's pleading guilty to a lesser charge. The prosecuting attorney can enter upon discussions with a defendant to plead guilty to a lesser charge only if he has support from the judge. The judge is usually satisfied to do so so long as he regards the sentence for the lesser offense to be adequate punishment (Ohlin and Remington, 1958). The prosecutor initiates such a request in order to avoid overcrowding of trial calendars and long delays. The defendant is usually told that no promises about a lesser sentence can be made to him in response to his plea of guilty, but he is informally advised that it is likely that he will get special consideration.

Another variable related to the social structure of the court is the role of the judge's law clerk or legal secretary. He is usually a lawyer, and either may have political connections or may have graduated from a law school with distinction. Some members of the Supreme Court have been attacked for giving too much responsibility to their law clerks, who are usually recent honor graduates from the national law schools. Whether or not these attacks are justified, they have served to focus attention on the exact role of the law clerk, which may range from legal errand boy and citation searcher through being a sounding board for the judge and actually participating in making decisions in important cases. There is reason to believe that these anonymous law clerks may be important contributors to some decisions. One former law secretary to Justice Holmes has discussed the clerks' influence on the Supreme Court (Konefsky, 1956).

Political pressures may also be among the larger social factors contributing to the context of the judge's decision. There may be some pressures, visible or invisible, on the judge for reasons of partisan politics or business. Even though there may be no pressures on specific cases, the judge may not wish to offend those who have contributed to his past, or may control his future when he comes up for reappointment or renomination. Only federal judges and some trial and higher appellate state justices are appointed for life and are thus presumably above political pressures; yet even they may be interested in promotion. Inasmuch as most judgeships are often likely to be political rewards, there is likely to be an assumption of repayment by the judge for the reward, although such assumptions are apt to be tacit on both sides. Appropriate repayment may be in the form of judical sympathy for the interests of the sponsors or former associates of the judge when litigation involving such interests comes before him. Probate court judges in ten states are permitted to practice law, and it is easy to see how the pressures of the private practice of such judges might affect their judical functioning.

In order to help judges cope with this kind of difficult contextual situation, the legal profession, through the American Bar Association, has promulgated its own Canons of Judicial Ethics (Cheatham, 1955). These moral guidelines to judical conduct are based on sources like the Magna Charta (XLV), the Bible (Deuteronomy 16), and Francis Bacon's essay on judicature. The canons range from precepts on the virtues of promptness to the evils of ex parte communication (communication from one litigant without an equal opportunity being afforded the other). The twenty-eighth canon almost spells out the necessity for a judge to avoid political party responsibilities. It flatly prohibits partisan political activity by the judge and urges him to be content with his judicial position rather than use it as a lever to run for another office. Conforming to this canon or avoiding it can both cause problems for the judge and be reflected in his decisions. The thirtieth canon, on how to handle candidacy for office, is also likely to lead to conflict between individual pressures and the normative imperative.

There is some question about the extent to which judges are guided by the Canons of Judicial Ethics, but the relationship between the formal ethic and actual practice is a fascinating one for the psychologist to observe. First-person and other accounts by judges generally make it clear that the relationship is also one which is of concern to judges (Botein, 1952; Ulman, 1933; Lummus, 1937). It is difficult to tell whether judges' conduct is ever evaluated dispassionately by others in terms of how judges face these conflict situations. The fact that in the last thirty years *not one* judge has been removed from office by impeachment, which is the appropriate procedure for removal from judical office, suggests that either judges' handling of these conflicts is impeccable, or there is a feeling that judges' behavior is above reproach and their handling of conflicts of interest is best left unscrutinized.

SOME PERSONAL VARIABLES IN THE JUDGE'S CAREER

A number of personal characteristics of judges may be presumed to enter into the process whereby they make decisions. The age of the judge as well as the age of the litigant before him may be relevant. Observers in criminal courts have noted, for example, that younger offenders are likely to get more lenient treatment from some judges than are older offenders.

A career on the bench has its own life cycle, and a judge who has just assumed his robe of office may perceive his duties and responsibilities quite differently from the way an older judge perceives his. In contrast to an older judge, the younger man may be very eager to make his mark. It has been noted that many judges tend to become more cautious with age. Other judges tend to become more confident and less susceptible to pressures as they grow older. The older judges, as do ordinary citizens, may become more conservative and tradition-oriented and less experimental. With the experience of years on the bench, some judges tend to be more reserved than they originally were in giving the specific rationale behind a decision. Aging is doubtless a factor in aberrant behavior of judges, and is particularly important because judges are generally named to the bench fairly late in life. There is sometimes a conflict between the relative youth of judges' law clerks and the relative age of the judges themselves.

Ethnic, nationality, religious, and race factors may help or hinder a judge in being appointed or elected or promoted. In American political life, judgeships are often regarded as offices which should be allocated on the basis of these factors. Certain judgeships often seem to be especially available for persons of specific backgrounds that seem to be underrepresented on the bench, especially at election time. Political leaders often make a tacit assumption that the bench's ethnic composition, writ large, should be the same as the electorate's. These background factors may also be very relevant to the judge's judicial behavior. It is likely, for example, that a judge from a minority group might be very harsh on litigants of the dominant ethnic group, perhaps as one means of demonstrating some of his feelings about the dominant group. Another judge from such a group might be "soft" on litigants of the dominant ethnic group as one way of expressing his identification with the regnant group. But to avoid any imputation of favoritism a judge from the minority group might be especially harsh with a litigant from the same group.

Still another judge from the same minority group might be an exceptionally hard worker in order to demonstrate that he made his way to the bench on the basis of merit alone. In all these cases, the specific background of the judge would be directly related to his judicial behavior.

The number of women judges is increasing, especially in courts concerned with family matters and children. There is some reason to believe that a woman who becomes a judge is likely to be a relatively superior person, because of the general prejudice against women lawyers and judges. Some women judges may overreact to this stereotype and be exceptionally rigorous in their decisions, as if to demonstrate that clichés about women's emotionalism are false.

The marital status of the judge may enter into his decisions, especially in matters involving paternity actions, family difficulties, separation or divorce, neglected children, or juvenile delinquency. The divorced judge's attitude toward a divorce action may be quite different from that of a bachelor judge. In one jurisdiction, lawyers representing the husband in marital action are delighted when a particular judge is assigned to the case because the judge's difficulties with his own wife — which are known to the lawyers — often make him especially sympathetic to the husband's side of the story. Whether the judge has any children himself may enter into his decisions involving children, ranging from oversentimentality to avoidance (the judge might say that his "hands are tied by the law"), to extreme vigor in punishing either parents or children for violations of the law.

The socioeconomic status from which the judge came may be relevant to his decisions, depending on the extent to which he has internalized the biases of his particular group. Thus a judge whose father was a sucessful attorney or a member of any other elite occupation is often likely to have adopted the conservative point of view of his father's occupational group. A judge whose father was a small retail storekeeper, or had some other equally marginal status, may have resented his background and have sought the elite status of a judge and so be ultraconservative. One judge who is the son of a conservative father may be relatively radical, whereas a judge who is the son of radical may be relatively conservative on the bench, although both men are reacting to their fathers' backgrounds. This kind of inconsistency between social class background and judicial attainment may have resulted in some unusual decisions and opinions.

The law school which the judge attended may have a considerable effect on his decisions. It is curious that the typical judge is more likely not to have attended law school than is the typical lawyer, and of those judges who did go to law school, there are proportionately more among graduates of unapproved law schools than among graduates of approved law schools (Blaustein and Porter, 1954). The bench clearly is not getting the lawyers with the best training, although this situation may be changing for the better.

The kind of legal practice in which the judge engaged before his appointment undoubtedly has some relationship to the type of decisions he gives. A judge who has been a corporation lawyer is likely to see things difierently from the way a judge who has been a criminal lawyer sees them. Individual differences are important because a judge who was a criminal lawyer, as in one case, may become an extremely harsh and tough-minded judge when dealing with the kind of criminals he used to defend, whether because he is reacting against his past or because he believes in severe punishment or because of other reasons. Another judge who was a criminal lawyer may be relatively lenient toward his former clients because he does not believe in severe sentences, as one means of identification with his past, or because of other reasons.

A judge who as a lawyer represented insurance companies in negligence actions, and a judge who used to represent people suing insurance compainies are likely to approach a negligence case with different kinds of prebench points of view, which may or may not enter their work as judges. If the financial status of a litigant or lawyer is unusual, whether the judge is relatively wealthy or just struggling along on his salary may enter into his attitudes toward such litigants or their lawyers.

Previous political activity is also often a factor in the context within which the judge will make his decision. A number of similar dimensions of the judge's career lines can be distinguished. They seem to suggest a typology of at least three different kinds of judge. The existence of such types has possible importance because it is likely that each of the different kinds of judge perceives the bench differently and has different motivations for it, and thus may behave differently as a judge.

What can be called the Lower Level of judicial career development is the course followed by perhaps the great majority of lawyers who become judges. Such a person has usually attended a low-level law school and has joined a political club as well as a variety of fraternal, benevolent, and religious organizations. This kind of lawyer will generally take all kinds of cases, perhaps even including some at the suggestion of political leaders. After years of faithful service to his party, such a lawyer will be given a vacancy on the bench. This kind of "ideal type" pattern is likely to be found in many courts of first instance and appearance, such as justices of the peace, traffic courts, and magistrates.

A Middle Level career pattern would typically include graduation from a law school which is accredited but above the level of the "factory" and below the level of the national law schools. Such a lawyer is likely to have a moderately successful and discriminating practice, more dignified than "ambulance chasing," but he is not with a first-rate law firm. He is likely to exhibit political leadership substantially above the routine service of the Lower Level judge, and to get a Higher Level judgeship.

The Upper Level judge is likely to have come from an elite family, to have been graduated from a national law school, and to have been a member of a well-regarded law firm (Miller, 1951; Mills, 1951). He is also likely to have held relatively important political office and to have demonstrated exceptional ability before getting a relatively High-Level judgeship.

There are, of course, many judges who do not fit into these "ideal types." No typology can adequately capture the range of judicial career patterns. Some lawyers may get to the bench because they are special friends of an unusually well-placed politician. Some lawyers may be wealthy enough to be able to give a large sum to their political party and, all other factors being equal, such a lawyer is more likely to get to the bench than an equally qualified lawyer who has not given any money to the party in power. Two scholars recently reported that it was "rumored" that the "going rate" for judgeships in New York City was the equivalent of two years' salary for the office (Sayre and Kaufman, 1960). Some lawyers may be singled out for the judiciary merely because of their brilliance and knowledge. Some law school professors who have not practiced may be tapped for the bench, but this is relatively infrequent.

There is some reason to speculate on the way in which the judge's career pattern is related to the kind of decision he makes. Of special interest are atypical cases, where a lawyer with one kind of background gets a judgeship that is not one it would be logical to expect him to get. Deviant behavior on the part of judges, like intemperate language or actual crime, as in the case of a recently convicted former Westchester County Surrogate, seems to occur mainly in judges whose position on the bench does not flow naturally from their previous careers. As we would expect from studies into the causes of other forms of deviant behavior, the dissonance between the individual's life style and the demand of his role, may lead to problems (Zajonc, 1952).

DIFFERING VIEWS ON THE BASIS
FOR JUDICIAL DECISIONS

Some four thousand years ago, when the Code of Hammurabi was promulgated, it was believed that judges' decisions and the law came directly from the gods. By the time of Holmes's pioneering studies in the late nineteenth century, it was becoming clear that law was the result of human experience. Up to the early twentieth century, writers on jurisprudence had generally held that judges were able to keep their personalities out of their decisions. Soon after the turn of the century, some students of the courts who were less "tough-minded" than the legal realist school (which held that the law was the decision of judges in particular cases — in contrast to the traditionalist view that the law consists of general rules) were developing the thesis that law is a form of social control. Some of the great exponents of what has been called sociological jurisprudence noted that even distinguished Supreme Court judges like Marshall and Taney differed in their interpretation of the Constitution, and that such differences are partially attributable to the different social, economic, and political backgrounds of the judges (Pound, 1923). These scholars were not suggesting that judges were making decisions on the basis of their economic backgrounds. They were suggesting that the judge's professional education and experience were influential in his decision.

The anthropological approach to judges' decisions has been followed by some writers. Llewellyn has pointed out that there is a procedure for getting rid of precedents which are troublesome and another procedure for using precedents that seem helpful. The same doctrine may be used for a specific purpose as well as for its exact opposite (Llewellyn, 1951). He has suggested that the main function of the courts is not to resolve disputes but to establish "working rules" for society (Llewellyn, 1925). He has urged the study of what judges and courts actually do, and Dean Roscoe Pound has added his great prestige to encouraging the application of the social sciences to the study of what the courts are doing (1938).

Other writers have said that it was less important to study the courts than to study the judges, in terms of what can be called the latent or private aspects of their decisions. As long ago as the sixteenth century, Montaigne commented that the judge's mood and humor varied from day to day and were often reflected in his decisions. Legal scholars have occasionally mocked the importance of such nonrational aspects in a decision and referred to them as "gastronomical jurisprudence," or an explanation of a judge's decision in terms of factors like gastronomical ailments. Such factors doubtless do enter into many judges' decisions, but they are hardly likely to be explicitly stated in the formal decision.

Candid statements about the way in which the judge's personality enters into his decisions have been made by some of America's leading judges. One of the great American judges, who was an outstanding figure in the development of law in New York State, Chancellor James Kent, said well over a century ago, in explaining how he reached a decision: "I might once in a while be embarrassed by a technical rule, but I almost always found principles suited to my view of the case . . ." (Frank, 1930). Even the famous legal philosopher, Justice Oliver Wendell Holmes, who is perhaps the classical exponent of the modern approach to law, has said that "a decision is the unconscious result of instinctive prejudices and inarticulate connections," and "even the prejudices which judges share with their fellow men have a good deal more to do than the syllogism in determining the rules by which men should be governed" (Holmes, 1881). Justice Cardozo stated that forces which judges "do not recognize and cannot name have been tugging at them . . . and the result is an outlook on life . . ." (Cardozo, 1921).

One federal judge, after years of service, concluded that he reached his decisions by hunch or feeling: "I . . . give my imagination play, and brooding . . . wait for the feeling, the hunch — that intuitive flash of understanding . . ." (Hutcheson, 1929). Writing a few years later, a distinguished judge said that a judge reaches his decision "by a 'hunch' as to what is fair and just or wise or expedient . . . the personality of the judge and the judicial hunch are not and cannot be described in terms of legal rules and principles" (Frank, 1932). Frank has pointed out that the "sentence" which the judge pronounces comes from the Latin verb *sentire*, which means "to feel," and that the judge experiences his decision on an emotional level. In a decision, he wrote that "much harm is done by the myth that merely by putting on a black robe, and taking the oath of office as a judge, a man ceases to be human . . . If the judge did not form judgments of the actors in those courthouse dramas called trials, he could never render decisions" (Frank, 1946).

The English jurist Lord Macmillan also underscored that "the judge's mind remains a human instrument working as do other minds" (Macmillan, 1937).

A Supreme Court justice frankly stated: "I know that in this great mass of opinions by men of different temperaments and qualifications and viewpoints, writing at different times and under varying local influences, some printed judicial word may be found to support almost any plausible proposition" (Jackson, 1944). This suggests that the judge first reaches his decision and then may look for a precedent to document his "decision," in contrast to the usual view that the precedent search precedes the decision. Just how much of an opportunity a judge has to find the "judicial word" with which he is comfortable can be seen in Justice Stone's estimate that a good law library, as of 1923, would have about 18,500 volumes of reports and 5,500 volumes of statutes, with 350 new volumes of reports and 250 new volumes of statutes each year (Stone, 1924). He estimated that a good law library around A.D. 2023 would have 1,850,000 volumes of reports and 550,000 volumes of statutes. Judges have pointed out that the judge is a human being and does not "clink out" decisions as a computer does (Tate, 1958), but is practicing an art (Yankwich, 1957).

A number of judges have thus stated quite frankly that instead of following a formal logical scheme, they reach their decisions by a kind of intuitive Gestalt impression of the case and its issues. If there are many judges who do reach their decisions in this way, it is important to know this as well as to know how many judges do so. Its implications for juridical science are central: it is like the difference between explaining a particular learning phenomenon in Gestalt principles in contrast to the traditional theory that judges reach their decisions by a logical process akin to learning theory. Among the possible implications for the student of the bench is that the precedents and legal reasoning cited by the judge may not actually be the private rationale for some decisions.

One authority who conducted psychological studies of judicial decisions said flatly that every judicial opinion "amounts to a confession" by the judge (Schroeder, 1918). He presented a hypothetical case in which the judge's decision was a direct reflection of "fearful phantasies from his own past," instead of a wise adjudication. A pioneering student of personal factors in judges' decisions examined the way in which different New York magistrates, in 1916, were handling the same offense (Haines, 1923). He found that the proportion of cases dismissed ranged from 6.7 percent for one magistrate to 73.7 percent for another. One magistrate discharged 18 percent of his disorderly conduct cases and another discharged 54 percent. Haines reasoned that personality factors in each judge were probably responsible for the huge spread between the sentencing behavior of one judge and another. The fate of a litigant who appeared in this court was thus clearly a function of the judge before whom he was fortunate or unfortunate enough to appear. Another empirical investigation of court behavior found "criminal courts in Chicago today . . . twisting the law and inventing fictions to attain results they regard as just" (Hall, 1935). Other studies have suggested the possibility that some judges have favorite numbers which they use in establishing sentences (Burtt, 1931; Gaudet *et al.*, 1934).

Legal scholars have discussed the personal and even idiosyncratic components in the work of the bench. Dean Roscoe Pound has praised Bergsonian intuition in a judge as a desirable quality (Pound, 1925). One noted student of the logic of law admitted that "unmistakable directions, irresistible implications, are few" for the judge (Radin, 1925). One member of what can be called the realistic school of judicial interpretation said that the behavior of judges exhibits a "predictable uniformity" because human values of judges suggested the kinds of decisions they would render (Cohen, 1935).

A related viewpoint is that many judicial decisions are essentially fictions because "many of the most beautifully intricate and subtle of legal theories are merely a form of legal rationalization or fiction. . . . Theories are now recognized as often a means of jusifying decisions rather than as reasons for making them" (Bohlen, 1935). Another scholar presented the view that judges engage in a kind of mental gymnastics or "jurisprudential fictions," which they use in order to justify and rationalize their decisions (Fuller, 1931), and he established a typology of legal fictions. One scholar has frankly stated that judges seldom give the "real motives and reasons" behind their decisions (Rohrlich, 1931), although he believes it is best that the public not know of these "real" motivating factors.

Even though experienced jurists and scholars have repeatedly emphasized the personal factors which are related to the judge's decision, the more formal point of view toward judicial decisions has also been a continuing tradition (Radin, 1925; Dewey, 1924). Some legal scholars have suggested the possibility that law can some day be made almost as precise as geometry (Cairns, 1941). Justice Frankfurter has repeatedly urged that the message of the statutes is clear and that judges should do as the statutes suggest (Frankfurter, 1947). He has urged that a judge "move within the framework of relevant legal rules and the covenanted modes of thought for ascertaining them. . . . This is achieved through training, professional habits, self-discipline and that fortunate alchemy by which men are loyal to the obligation with which they are entrusted. . . ." (Frankfurter, 1952).

Justice Frankfurter has urged that, in the absence of obvious constitutional defects, courts be loath to overturn legislative judgments as embodied in statutes. He has also indicated in the strongest terms that judges desist from substituting their proclivities, tastes, and notions of justice or goodness for that of the people as they have expressed themselves through their legislatures.

Another point of view on the judge's function sees the decision as an instrument of social control in the hands of a completely rational judge (Michael and Adler, 1933). Justice Douglas is representative of what can be called a social control or libertarian view on the current Supreme Court, and has clearly stated his belief that the judge is not an impersonal arbiter (Douglas, 1959; Schwartz, 1957). The widely discussed differences between the "liberal" and "conservative" (Larson, 1955) members of the Supreme Court have made it clear that even on this highest level, judges may perceive their function differently, and that a study of the personal and social backgrounds of the men on the Court would be as realistic an approach to their decisions as the more usual legal approach (Carr, 1942; Lerner, 1957).

THE PSYCHOLOGY OF THE JUDGE

The frequent references by legal scholars to the "personality" of the judge are almost never carried into an extended discussion of the subject. If we define "personality" as everything about a person which has relevance to his relations with other people, then it is obvious that many different dimensions of the personal and social background of the judge are relevant. His possible interest in dominance, his needs, his self concept, his ways of achieving security, and his use of unconscious defense mechanisms like projection, rationalization, sublimation, repression, and suppression may all be important.

The behavior of the judge represents a kind of natural convergence between the area of "decision theory" and the area of "role theory" in social psychology. The judge is a person who must make a decision, but under circumstances in which his role as a judge is a reflection of his other and previous roles and of his several group memberships. Any kind of multiple group identification creates problems for the individual (Hartley, 1951). Different judges may have different reference groups (groups with which they identify and which provide standards for decisions). These groups may include the great leaders of the judiciary like Holmes, their colleagues on higher courts, the common man seeking justice, the impersonal majesty of justice, the established power structure of society, an ideal of social amelioration, the lawyers who appear before them, and many others. Conflict between the judge's reference groups may be reflected in his decisions.

The power over other persons which judges wield has been a source of concern to many students of the bench. Some may glory in the power, some may dislike it, and others may be ambivalent about it. It is possible that the power and dominance of the judge's role attracts persons who have an authoritarian inclination. Psychological research has extensively documented that the authoritarian persons are likely to see things in an either-or fashion, rather than in the balanced and democratic manner which is traditionally associated with the judicial temperament (Adorno, 1950). The process of socialization in office may temper the power strivings of judges.

There are courtroom observers who have suggested the perhaps overenthusiastic generalization that some judges are basically insecure people who seek security in the ritualized power embodied in the judicial robe. Other observers have called attention to the latent psychological functions which may be served for some judges by sentencing.

Since our courts are based on the adversary system, in which points of difference and conflict are explicitly the foci of courtroom discussion, it is possible that there is some self-selection of lawyers who seek the bench because of their interest in this kind of expression of disagreement. Many years ago, in his famous novel *Bleak House*, Charles Dickens expressed the view that there is a specific kind of judge who enjoys the battle of the courts. If Dickens's vision were found to apply to any considerable proportion of the American judiciary, this would certainly be relevant to the study of the psychology of the judge.

The courtroom may provide an outlet for the kind of exhibitionism which has traditionally characterized actors and other near exhibitionists. The judge has a captive audience, in contrast to the actor whose audience may walk out on him at any time, or not even buy a ticket to the theatre. No matter how egocentric the judge's behavior becomes, the lawyers for either side are hardly likely to complain about it. As is true of most professionals, but perhaps especially because his name is affixed to his opinions, the ego of the judge is likely to be deeply involved in his work.

Judges' perception may be very important because their alertness in a trial is of critical importance to both sides. The psychology of perception is as applicable to a judge as to any other person

(Bruner and Tagiuri, 1954). One outstanding example of idiosyncratic perception of judges occurred not long ago when a federal trial judge revealed, after years on the bench, that he always assumed that any witness who rubbed his hands while testifying was a liar (Frank, 1949). It is only possible to speculate on the number of unfair decisions which such a judge gave.

The well-established difficulties of memory and cognition which plague witnesses are likely to be multiplied in the case of a judge, who is a witness of the witnesses, and thus perceives at two removes from the reality of the circumstances which gave rise to a trial. One noted student of the law has reported that his task as a young lawyer was to drop books on the floor when a judge began getting drowsy (Gross, 1947).

PREDICTING DECISIONS

Professor Oliphant of Columbia Law School was not the first who believed that judicial decisions could be predicted by studying the stimuli, or facts, which were presented to the judge. Oliphant first presented his views in 1928. A well-known mathematician, at about the same time, was exploring the possibility of establishing a science of prediction of judges' decisions (Keyser, 1929). More recently a lawyer and a political scientist have suggested the feasibility of a science of judicial prediction, even though they recognize the role of personality factors of judges and others connected with the trial (Lasswell and McDougal, 1943). One scholar has called for appropriate statistical and probability techniques to summarize how individual judges behave in different kinds of cases (Loevinger, 1949).

One study identified several areas of judicial action to which quantitative methods have been applied with meaningful results (Schubert, 1958). Another study has attempted to quantify any rule of law that makes a decision dependent on combinations of specified controlling circumstances (Kort, 1960). These promising starts have made the possibility of a science of prediction of judicial decision much more realizable.

SUGGESTED CHANGES

Many recommendations have been made for improving the quality of the work of judges. Such recommendations are usually made very cautiously because of the established tradition of being very reluctant to criticize the judiciary, even inferentially. One such recommendation is that trial judges make written findings of fact (Note, 1948). This might help in the review of a case, define the scope of the decision, increase public confidence in the courts, and reassure the litigants that their case had been carefully considered by the judge. Findings of fact will, it has been suggested, act as a partial check on the judge's subjectivity.

A number of students of the courts, including the Survey of the Legal Profession of the Amercian Bar Association, have recommended that courts use more of the method of relatively informal conferences of all the parties in chambers with the judge (Blaustein and Porter, 1954). It is interesting that judges have often met the recommendation that they seek consonances rather than arbitrate among dissonances with less than marked enthusiasm, a fact which suggests that there are judges who enjoy the combat of the courtroom.

Another suggestion made by an imaginative lawyer and judge urged that prospective judges undergo some kind of psychoanalytic treatment (Frank, 1949), as one way of recognizing the great power of the judge's "personal equation." Such self-exploration, he felt, should be of great help in reducing judicial bias and prejudice. Ideally, such treatment would be repeated throughout the judge's career on the bench. The same student has questioned the whole system of precedent-following by judges, saying that it has roots in emotional immaturity and a need for certainty. Good judges "will not talk of 'rules' and 'principles' as finalities while unconsciously using them as soporifics to allay the pains of uncertainty" (Frank, 1930).

Federal Judge Julian Mack refused to wear a robe when presiding at a trial, and often conducted trials in his chambers, sitting on the same level with the witnesses and lawyers. Others have recommended that judges not wear robes, pointing out that Thomas Jefferson was opposed to any distinctive costume for federal judges. Robes have priestly connotations which many observers believe to be irrelevant to modern life, and which may help lead to stilted and awkward testimony. Other students of the courts have suggested that, as part of becoming more informal, courts abandon the complicated language which they currently use in decisions and speak more plainly, so that they can be both understood and criticized more directly. As long ago as 1898, Justice Brewer suggested the possible value of being critical of the Supreme Court, noting that "the life and character of its Justices should be the objects of constant watchfulness by all." The robe is a symbol of the judge's sealing himself off from criticism.

One suggestion for improving judicial decisions which has been made by a number of legal students is to incorporate more behavioral science into court findings, and possibly train judges in the nature of behavioral science. Critics have observed that classical sources, like Wigmore on Evidence (Wigmore, 1940), do not appear to take any cognizance of what modern behavior science says on subjects like perception and consciousness. Judges daily deal with subjects on which the behavioral sciences have collected much data, and they almost never refer to such data. The 1954 Supreme Court desegregation decision was a major decision that did draw on such materials (Brown, 1954). In another series of decisions the Court has stated that a jury must be representative of the community from which it is drawn if it is to be impartial, thus recognizing dimensions similar to those used in selecting a sample by survey technicians (Robinson, 1950). Such use of behavioral science is rare.

Despite some of the statements made about the wisdom of integrating social science findings with legal materials in the desegregation decision, such materials were used in the courts over a half century ago. In an epoch-making brief (Muller, 1908), Brandeis successfully urged that economic and social data were as relevant in a case involving the constitutionality of a law limiting the working hours of women as the legal principles. Ever since, the Brandeis Brief has been the designation for a brief which includes nonlegal material of probative value to the propositions being urged upon a court. Since such procedures are established, their relative nonuse by judges leads to speculations on the reasons for their nonuse.

One such reason is that judges may be afraid of being considered "unlawyerlike" and possible overruled. Another reason is the nature of law school training and the history and development of legal institutions including the common law. The writings of legal philosophers and judges, beginning with Henry De Bracton in the thirteenth century, express an overt or covert yearning for predictability and certainty. As Redmount points out in Chapter 2 of this volume, the law often appears to be a closed system of great orderliness that manifests a grand design which rules the legal relations of men. Judges trained in such a system and accustomed to the doctrine of *stare decisis*, or the following of precedent, may understandably be reluctant to use social science materials which are seldom as precise and definitive as statements in the law. The long struggle between lawyers and psychiatrists is a good example of the "legal ethnocentrism" which has characterized judges' attitudes toward the materials of behavioral science. Judge Bazelon's recent decision in the Durham case, which is discussed in detail in Chapter 7, "Criminal Responsibility and Psychiatry," represents a sign of some rapprochement between the bench and modern knowledge of mental hygiene. The increase of such rapprochement will be the best counter to the fears of some judges that their status and power will diminish if they take advantage of cognate materials from other fields.

Suggestions for improving the functioning of the courts have included modification of the procedures whereby judges are selected. All federal judges are appointed for life, but judges are elected in about three fourths of the states, for terms ranging from 2 years in Vermont to 21 in Pennsylvania (Institute, 1956). It has been alleged that the electorate is not competent to appraise the qualifications of a given candidate for judicial office, and the appointive system has been attacked because of the element of political patronage. The American Bar Association has favored a plan (the Missouri Plan) whereby a state governor would select a candidate from a panel of names submitted by a nonpartisian judicial nominating commission, and the candidate would then be confirmed by the electorate at the next general election. The California Plan calls for appointment by the governor and confirmation by the majority of an ex officio commission as well as subsequent confirmation by the electorate. Another plan would have local bar associations nominate candidates who would be recommended to the political parties

The more actively the work of the courts is discussed, the more likely is it that we shall begin to bring theory and practice together in the optimum selection and functioning of judges. It is to be hoped the introduction of the concepts of psychology and other social sciences into the discussion of the work of the bench will lead to ever-improving methods for the administration of justice in the courts — a goal which all believers in the democratic process can only endorse.

It is necessary to realize that progress in improving court procedures is likely to be relatively slow. Almost twenty years after the American Bar Association, in the late 1930's, had adopted minimum practical standard of judicial administration, complete conformity to these standards had not been achieved in even a single state, with the possible exception of Alaska. The enormous importance of the judiciary in the lives of men makes it urgent that continuing effort, from all relevant disciplines be continued with the patient cooperation of all who are interested in improving the work of the courts. The judge, after all, is a key link between the individual and the agencies of social control.

References

Adorno, Theodore W., *et al. The authoritarian personality*. New York: Harper, 1950.

Blaustein, Albert P., & Porter, Charles O. *The American lawyer*. Chicago: Univer. of Chicago Press, 1954, pp. 131, 198, 136–138.

Bohlen, Francis H. The reality of what the courts are doing. In Max Radin (Ed.), *Legal essays in tribute to Orrin K. McMurray*. Berkeley: Univer. of California Press, 1935, p. 44.

Botein, Bernard. *Trial judge*. New York: Simon and Schuster, 1952. Brown v. Board of Education, 347 U. S. 483, 1954; 349 U. S. 294, 1955.

Bruner, Jerome S., & Tagiuri, Renato. The perception of people. In Gardner Lindzey (Ed.), *Handbook of social psychology*. Cambridge, Mass.: Addison-Wesley, 1954, pp. 637–654.

Bureau of the Census. *Statistical abstract of the United States*. Washington, D. C.: U. S. Government Printing Office, 1958, p. 149.

Burtt, Harold E. *Legal psychology*. Englewood Cliffs, N. J.: Prentice-Hall, 1931, p. 263.

Cairns, Huntington. *The theory of legal science*. Chapel Hill: Univer. of North Carolina Press, 1941.

Cardozo, Benjamin N. *The nature of the judicial process*. New Haven: Yale Univer. Press, 1921.

Carr, Robert K. *The Supreme Court and judicial review*. New York: Holt, Rinehart and Winston, 1942, pp. 235–237.

Cheatham, Elliott E. *Cases and materials on the legal profession*. Brooklyn: Foundation Press, 1955.

Cohen, Felix S. Transcendental nonsense and the functional approach. *Columbia Law Rev.*, 1935, **35**, 809–849.

de Tocqueville, Alexis. *Democracy in America*. New York: Knopf, 1945, Chaps. 6, 15.

Dewey, John. Logical method and law. *Cornell Law Quart.*, 1924, **10**, 17–27.

Douglas, William O. On misconception of the judicial function and the responsibility of the bar. *Columbia Law Rev.*, 1959, **59**, 227–233.

Frank, Jerome. *Law and the modern mind.* New York: Brentano, 1930, pp. 104, 166.

Frank, Jerome. What courts do in fact. *Illinois Law Rev.,* 1932, **26,** 762–776.

Frank, Jerome. In re J. P. Linehan and Company, 138 F (2d), 651–654, 1946.

Frank, Jerome. *Courts on trial.* Princeton, N. J.: Princeton Univer. Press, 1949, pp. 250, 270, 335.

Frankfurter, Felix. Some reflections on the reading of statutes. *Columbia Law Rev.,* 1947, **47,** 528–546.

Frankfurter, Felix. In Public Utilities Commission v. Pollack, 343 U. S. 451; 72 S. Ct. 813, 1952.

Fuller, L. L. Legal fictions. *Illinois Law Rev.,* 1931, **25,** 513–546.

Gaudet, G. F., Herrick, G. F., & St. John, G. W. Individual differences in penitentiary sentences given by different judges. *J. appl. Psychol.,* 1934, **18,** 675–686.

Gross, Hans. A psychological theory of law. In Paul Sayre (Ed.), *Interpretations of modern legal philosophies.* New York: Oxford University Press, 1947, pp. 766–775.

Hains, Charles G. General observations on the effect of personal, political and economic influences in the decision of cases. *Illinois Law Rev.,* 1923, **17,** 96–116.

Hall, Jerome. *Theft, law and society.* Boston: Little, Brown, 1935, p. 264.

Hartley, Eugene L. Multiple group membership. In John H. Rohrer and Muzafer Sherif (Eds.), *Social psychology at the crossroads.* New York: Harper, 1951, pp. 371–387.

Hobbes, Thomas. *Leviathan.* New York: Dutton, 1950, p. 242.

Holmes, Oliver Wendell, Jr. *The common law.* Boston: Little, Brown, 1881, p. 35.

Hutcheson, Joseph C. The judgment intuitive: The function of the "hunch" in judicial decisions. *Cornell Law Quart.,* 1929, **14,** 274–278.

Inkeles, Alex, & Rossi, Peter H. National comparisons of occupational prestige. *Amer. J. Sociol.,* 1956, **61,** 329–339.

Institute of Judicial Administration. *Selection, tenure and removal of judges in the 48 states, Alaska, Hawaii and Puerto Rico.* New York: Institution of Judicial Administration, 1956.

Jackson, Robert. Decline of stare decisis is due to volume of opinion. *J. Amer. Judicature Soc.,* 1944, **28,** 6–8.

Keyser, Cassius J. On the study of legal science. *Yale Law J.,* 1929, **38,** 413–422.

Konefsky, Samuel J. *The legacy of Holmes and Brandeis.* New York: Macmillan, 1956, p. 94.

Kort, Fred. The quantitative content analysis of judicial opinions. PROD, 1960, **3,** 11–14.

Larson, Arthur. The lawyer as conservative. *Cornell Law Quart.* 1955, **40**, 183–194.

Lasswell, Harold D., & McDougal, Myres S. Legal education and public policy: Professional training in the public interest. *Yale Law J.*, 1943, **52**, 203–295.

Lerner, Max. *America as a civilization.* New York: Simon and Schuster, 1957, p. 446.

Llewellyn, Karl. The effect of legal institutions upon economics. *Amer. econ. Rev.*, 1925, **15**, 665–671.

Llewellyn, Karl. *The bramble bush.* New York: Oceana Publications, 1951.

Loevinger, Lee. Jurimetrics. *Minnesota Law Rev.*, 1949, **33**, 455–494.

Lummus, Henry T. *The trial judge.* Chicago: Foundation Press, 1937.

Macmillan, Hugh P. *Law and other things.* Cambridge, England: Cambridge Univer. Press, 1937.

Marbury v. Madison, 1 Cranch 137, 1803; 2 Lawyers' Ed. 60.

Michael, Jerome, & Adler, Mortimer J. *Crime, law and social science.* New York: Harcourt, Brace, 1933.

Miller, William. American lawyers in business and in politics. *Yale Law J.*, 1951, **60**, 66–76.

Mills, C. Wright. *White collar.* New York: Oxford Univer. Press, 1951, pp. 121–128.

Muller v. Oregon, 208 U. S. 412, 1908.

Note: The law of fact: Findings of fact under the federal rules. *Harvard Law Rev.*, 1948, **61**, 1434–1444.

Ohlin, Lloyd E., & Remington, Frank J. Sentencing structure. *Law & contemp. Probs.*, 1958, **23**, 495–507.

Pool, Ithiel de Sola, & Shulman, Irwin. Newsmen's fantasies, audiences and newswriting. *Pub. Opin. Quart.*, 1959, **23**, 145–158.

Pound, Roscoe. A theory of judicial decision for today. *Harvard Law Rev.*, 1923, **36**, 940–959.

Pound, Roscoe. *An introduction to the philosophy of law.* New Haven: Yale Univer. Press, 1925, pp. 101–130.

Pound, Roscoe. Fifty years of jurisprudence. *Harvard Law Rev.*, 1938, **51**, 777–812.

Radin, Max. The theory of judicial decisions. *J. Amer. Bar Ass.*, 1925, **11**, 357–362.

Robinson, W. S. Bias, probability, and trial by jury. *Amer. sociol. Rev.*, 1950, **15**, 73–78.

Rohrlich, Chester. Judicial technique. *J. Amer. Bar Ass.*, 1931, **17**, 480–481.

Ross, Edward A. *Social control.* New York: Macmillan, 1926, p. 112.

Sayre, Wallace S., & Kaufman, Herbert. *Governing New York City.* New York: Russell Sage Foundation, 1960.

Schroeder, Theodore. The psychologic study of judicial opinions. *California Law Rev.*, 1918, **6**, 89–113.

Schubert, Glendon A. The study of judicial decision making as an aspect of political behavior. *Amer. pol. Sci. Rev.*, 1958, **52**, 1007–1025.

Schwartz, Bernard. *The Supreme Court.* New York: Ronald, 1957, p. 363.

Stone, Harlan F. Some aspects of the problem of law simplification. In *Lectures on Legal Topics.* New York: Macmillan, 1924, p. 209.

Tate, Albert. The judge as a person. *Louisiana Law Rev.*, 1958, **19**, 438–447.

Ulman, Joseph N. *A judge takes the stand.* New York: Knopf, 1933.

Wigmore, John H. *Wigmore on evidence.* Boston: Little, Brown, 1940, II, 41–190, 244–293.

Yankwich, Leon R. The art of being a judge. *Univer. of Penn. Law Rev.*, 1957, **105**, 374–389.

Zajonc, Robert B. Aggressive attitudes of the "stranger" as a function of conformity pressures. *Human Relat.*, 1952, **5**, 205–216.

THOMAS S. SZASZ

7 Criminal Responsibility and Psychiatry

In many trials, including famous murder cases with which the reader will undoubtedly be familiar, the defense has revolved around the proposition that, although the defendant may have committed the acts with which he was charged, he was nevertheless innocent. This defense tactic rests on the premise that a harmful act is considered a criminal offense only if it is perpetrated knowingly and willfully — that is, with "criminal intent." It is held that if a man is "insane" or "mentally ill" he may not be responsible for his actions. Hence an accused who successfully pleads insanity may be acquitted with the verdict "not guilty by reason of insanity." Such a defense involves psychiatrists testifying for one or both sides. In the present chapter, our task will be to examine critically the problem of so-called criminal responsibility, and especially its relationship to psychiatry.

WHAT IS CRIMINAL RESPONSIBILITY?

A vast criminological, legal, and psychiatric literature is devoted to expositions of what is understood by the term "criminal responsibility." Thus the impression is created that this concept has a clear-cut and generally accepted meaning. After its constant use over a period of half a century or more, many contemporary students of crime, as well as the laity, have come to *assume* that criminal responsibility is indeed a workable concept. All that is needed is the psychiatrist who will ascertain whether an offender does or does not possess the trait of criminal responsibility.

But criminal responsibility is neither an object nor a phenomenon found in nature, such as, say, the Grand Canyon or a rainbow. This may seem rather like stating the obvious, and, in a way, it is. Since

146

there is a persistent effort, however, to find "objective criteria" for criminal responsibility as though it were an object, it is necessary to emphasize that it is nothing of the sort. Also, criminal responsibility is neither a disease nor a disability. The concept is not synonymous with, nor can it be derived from, the concepts of physical or mental illness. Pneumonia, hypertension, paresis, schizophrenia, neurosis are terms designating such diseases, yet none provides a definite clue to the "criminal responsibility" of its bearer.

Despite this, it is possible to give an approximate answer to the question, What is criminal responsibility? We could say that it is "punishability," meaning by this society's right to enforce certain negative sanctions against the offender. It is clear, then, that the concept of criminal responsibility refers to a complex notion concerning the *relationship between offender and society*. Accordingly, it is a mistake to think that criminal responsibility is a quality *residing in just one of the parties involved* (the offender), and that it is merely a task for accurate observation to detect the presence or absence of this "factor."

Types of Responsibility

It is also necessary to note, by way of preliminary clarification, that the simple term "responsibility" (or "responsible") is used in everyday language in three different ways. First, *in the descriptive mode*, as when we assert that "the avalanche at X was *responsible* for the death of three skiers." This is a statement of what happened. It contains no evaluation of the ethical quality of the event, nor any suggestion of what should be done. In contrast to this, we may use the word "responsible" in the *prescriptive mode*, referring not so much to what happened but rather to what should be done. When used in this way, "responsible" means "bad" (or less often "good") and carries with it the command to change the situation, or to prevent (or encourage) its recurrence. For example, if we say that cigarette smoking is *responsible* for a higher than average incidence of lung cancer, implied is the suggestion that cigarette smokers should give up this habit. It is important to emphasize that this command is only *implied*, for it hinges on another tacit premise, namely that smokers value or should value longevity more than the pleasure derived from smoking.

The concept of responsibility (whether as adjective or noun) commonly is used in still another sense. This usage has been called *ascriptive*, to designate the ethical quality ascribed to the act (of a particular person) by the observer (Stoljar, 1959). Ascriptive responsibility is often mistaken for descriptive responsibility. This confusion runs through and vitiates a great deal of what has been written on the problem of criminal responsibility. The specialized languages of jurisprudence and psychiatry use all three types of responsibility, usually without making explicit the necessary distinctions among them. A brief illustration may clarify the subject.

Let us take the statement, "John killed James." In the descriptive mode, this simply means that either we are truthful or we are lying (excluding the possibility of making a mistake, to simplify the matter). Evaluation of the correctness of this statement requires the listener to verify or falsify it. Accordingly, if it is asserted that "John killed James," we can respond in one of three ways: Yes, no, and I don't know.

Criminology and law do not, however, deal with physical facts *as such*. That is a subject for physics, chemistry, biology, and so forth. Criminology and law deal with social relations, with ethics, or, most generally, with rule-following behavior. District attorneys are not interested in death as a biochemical phenomenon; they are interested in death *only* insofar as it presents a specific psychosocial and ethical problem.

The question thus becomes, *"How* did John kill James?" and "Is John *guilty* or *innocent?"* In regard to the first question, further fact finding and often motive finding becomes necessary. Did John kill James in cold blood to rob him? Or did James throw himself in front of John's truck? Or did John "kill" James by failing to save him from drowning, after James jumped in the river to commit suicide? And so forth. The point is that special psychological, social, and legal inquiry is often required to establish precisely under what circumstances John killed James. Under some circumstances this is *not* a matter for the law at all — for example, if John was a soldier and James was the enemy. Under others, it is unquestionably necessary that John be prosecuted. And under still other circumstances — for example, when the distinction between suicide and homicide is unclear — it may be a matter of *choice* for the legal authorities whether they take action or not. The issue of *responsibility as guilt* arises only in a legal context. (It may also arise in a religious setting. This, however, is basically similar to the legal situation and is, in fact, its prototype.) Hence, if we are asked whether John did in fact kill James, our answer will depend, in part, on whether we are asked in the capacity of naturalistic observer or jury.

Responsibility for a bit of action may be ascribed, or attributed, to someone "truly" or "falsely," meaning that in the first instance the person is descriptively responsible, whereas in the second he is not. Furthermore, each of these ascriptions may be publicly (that is, by a jury) verified or falsified. Hence, for each charge of "responsibility," there are four alternative possibilities. The following illustrative example will show more clearly what each of these alternatives is.

The charge is that John Doe killed James Smith, in Columbus, Ohio, on January 30, 1957. Is John Doe responsible (or "criminally responsible") for James Smith's death? The four basic outcomes of such a criminal prosecution and the defense against it are as follows. First, John Doe's responsiblity for the act may be both descriptively and ascriptively true. This is the case of the apprehended and successfully prosecuted criminal. Second, Doe may have committed the act, but to ascribe responsibility to him might have been false (that is, judged false by those empowered to verify the matter). This is the case in accidental homicide. Third, the description of John Doe's responsibility might have been false (that is, he may, in fact, have been nowhere near Columbus, Ohio, on that date), but the ascription of responsibility to him could, nevertheless, be made to "stick." This is the successful "frame-up" or the conviction of an innocent man as scapegoat. The Dreyfus case is a classic example (Paleologue, 1957). Fourth, and last, Doe's responsibility for killing Smith may turn out to be false both descriptively and ascriptively. This is the unsuccessful frame-up, or the case of the innocent man's finding justice in the courtroom. A summary of these four contingencies is presented in Table 1.

TABLE 1

Classification of Acts According to Types of Responsibility

	I	II	III	IV
Descriptive Responsibility	True	True	False	False
Ascriptive Responsibility	True	False	True	False

I = The apprehended and successfully prosecuted criminal
II = The accident
III = The successful frame-up, or conviction of the innocent person (the scapegoat)
IV = The unsuccessful frame-up, or acquittal of the innocent person

So far nothing has been said about the psychiatric aspects of the problem of criminal responsibility. This was intentional, because a logical clarification of the subject is necessary before psychiatric complications, so to speak, can meaningfully be introduced into the picture. We are now ready to consider still another type of so-called irresponsibility for crime. First we shall be concerned only with the logical status of this concept. Later we shall examine its history and present status.

Irresponsibility Due to Insanity

Typically, the defense of insanity is raised only in those criminal cases in which the descriptive responsibility of the offender for the alleged antisocial act is accepted as true. That is to say, in such a case there is no doubt in anyone's mind that John Doe *did* commit the illegal act with which he is charged (killing James Smith). Logically, then, the argument falls in Group II, Table 1. These are the cases characterized by true descriptive responsibility, and supposedly false ascriptive responsibility. The American verdict "Not guilty by reason of insanity" states precisely this. It could be rendered in the form: "John Doe is not guilty (ascriptively) of killing James Smith (although he did cause his death) because of X." X may here stand for any number of things, but most typically for one of these three: accident, self-defense, insanity (Hart, 1958). Irresponsibility for a harmful act by reason of insanity is thus entirely similar logically to irresponsibility for such an act because it happened accidentally or in self-defense. The notion of insanity has simply been added to other excusing conditions, exculpating, as it were, the commission of otherwise criminal acts. We shall return to this later.

The handling of the insanity plea in English law is somewhat different. There, in a comparable situation, the verdict is, "Guilty, *but* insane." As a practical matter, both maneuvers leave much to be desired. American lawyers have advocated adopting the English tactic, while some British jurists have expressed preference for the American version (Weihofen, 1933). The logical analysis presented is helpful in this connection, for it shows that the British way of looking at the "insane criminal" tends to place his behavior in Group I, whereas the American viewpoint places it in Group II. In both cases, the focus is on ascriptive responsibility. The main difference between the two positions is that the American verdict obscures the factual (descriptive) issue more than does the English version. The former simultaneously denies and reasserts the antisocial character of some aspects of "insane" behavior. This is accomplished, first, by asserting that the offender is "not guilty (by reason of insanity)." This renders the act akin to accidents and noncriminal behavior. The offender's subsequent commitment, however, belies this assertion, and recodifies the behavior as grounds for his involuntary detention (now called "hospitalization" rather than "imprisonment") (Hall and Glueck, 1958, pp. 313–14).

HISTORICAL AND SOCIAL ASPECTS OF CRIMINAL RESPONSIBILITY

The idea that some people are "insane" (or "psychotic") and hence irresponsible for their actions has been held only in some cultures and only during certain periods. According to this notion, which is very popular in contemporary America, there are basically two types of human conduct. One is so-called ordinary, rational human behavior. The other is so-called irrational behavior. In the latter mode of conduct, men allegedly do not (fully) understand their own actions and are governed by powerful impulses rather than by reason. The shortcomings of this dualistic concept of behavior are well known and will not be discussed here. Let us note only that if behavior is classified as either rational or irrational, the observer is involved in ethically judging rather than in merely describing his observations.

The Concept of Madness in Ancient Greece

While the general concept of "insanity" or "madness" can be traced to antiquity, there is no clear evidence that it was an excuse for criminal behavior either in ancient Greek or in Roman law. The Greeks, as a matter of fact, were fascinated with the notion that man is not the active creator of his own destiny, but rather that he is, as it were, lived by fate. (This view was rekindled by Freud's early concepts of Id psychology.) In the view of the great Greek tragedies, man is essentially helpless vis-à-vis fate (Dodds, 1957). Such a concept of human behavior makes all men slightly mad. The Sophoclean plays, and particularly their central themes (which became psychoanalytic "complexes"), thus served as admirable models for the elucidation of mental illness, conceived as not consciously willed action. This view of human conduct lends itself poorly or not at all to classifying certain antisocial actions as nonpunishable because of madness: first, because all behavior is regarded as basically of this type, and second, because man is held responsible (in some sense) even for the involuntary, fate-willed actions that he commits. This, at least, is the message of Oedipus's tragedy. Freud explicitly reasserted this principle when he said that man is "responsible" for his dreams and for his unconscious wishes. (In this context, however, "responsible" is used only descriptively; that is, the sources, or causes, of our dreams lie within us and we cannot attribute them to the machinations of others. This kind of responsibility should not be confused with moral or legal responsibility.)

Accordingly, it is not surprising that in ancient Greece, madness was not regarded as a defense against criminal charges. This cannot be attributed to the absence of the notion of "mental incompetence" in classical Greek thought, for this was an accepted charge in cases of civil litigation. It is alleged, for example, that this charge was brought against Sophocles himself by his son Iophon (Encyclopaedia Britannica, 1947). Yet, apparently no one suggested that Socrates's "treasonous" teachings were due to madness, and that, therefore, he should be treated as a harmless lunatic. We cannot assume that it would have even occurred to anyone at that time to "explain" Socrates's behavior in this way. Roman law, too, does not deal with the issue of insanity.

From McNaghten to Durham

According to Glueck (1925), the real beginning of the legal treatment of mental unsoundness can be traced to early English law. Insanity was officially admitted to law as an "excuse" for criminal action during the reign of Edward I (1272–1307). The details of the subsequent history of this subject, until the trial of McNaghten, need not concern us here.

The most famous and important forensic-psychiatric case in the annals of Anglo-American law is undoubtedly that of McNaghten (1843). The facts were that in 1843, Daniel McNaghten shot and killed Drummond, private secretary to Sir Robert Peel, believing him to be Peel. The defense was insanity. *Medical* evidence was introduced showing that McNaghten was "laboring under an insane delusion" of being hounded by enemies, among them Peel. The jury found him "Not guilty, on the ground of insanity" (Weihofen, 1933, p. 25).

Following this verdict, the question of unsoundness of mind as an excuse for crime was made a subject of debate in the House of

Lords. The judges of England were asked to present their views on the criteria for such an acquittal. The most important part of the judges' answers was the following:

> The jury ought to be told in all cases that ... to establish a defense on the ground of insanity, it must be clearly proved that, at the time of committing the act, the party accused was labouring under such a defect of reason, from disease of the mind, as not to know the nature and quality of the act he was doing, or if he did know it, *that he did not know he was doing what was wrong.* [Weihofen, 1933, p. 28.]

It is clear that in saying this the judges had an entirely reasonable idea in mind — namely, that the purpose of the criminal law is, or should be, to "punish" so-called willfully committed wrongdoings. An act that results in harm to someone cannot be judged simply by looking at *what* happened. We must also evaluate *how* it happened. Consider two hypothetical cases. In the first, a man has an epileptic seizure while driving his car; as a result, he loses control of the vehicle, and runs down and kills another man. In the second, a man loses a considerable sum of money in a card game that, he believes, was crooked; he waits for the winner, and, when the latter crosses the street, runs over him and kills him. In the first case, the man "did not know the nature or quality of the act he was doing"; in the second, he did. The idea underlying the McNaghten Rule was that there may be many conditions of the type illustrated by the case of the "epileptic accident," and that these should be distinguished from deliberate acts of mischief. It is difficult to see how anyone could quarrel with this intention. The actual implementation of this rule, however — and especially the *means* used to assess whether an offender knew what he was doing, and whether he knew that it was wrong — resulted in vast difficulties. Most of the difficulties derive from the fact that so-called mental illnesses were conceived as basically similar to neurological defects. Hence the belief that "mental illness" causes a lack of appreciation of what one does.

This unrealistic emphasis on reason in mental disease, as well as other principles of the McNaghten Rule, has often been vigorously and heatedly debated. We shall not enter into this discussion — which, particularly when it is concerned with the finer points of distinction between degrees of "mental disease," is reminiscent of scholastic debates about theological doctrines. We shall instead indicate the principal issues to be kept in mind in studying this subject.

1. McNaghten's Case codified (as law) the notion that certain acts are the results of "mental illness." Moreover, such illness was

conceived as being essentially similar to bodily disease. No distinction was made between organic brain defects (for example, congenital idiocy), acute intoxications, deliria (that is, drunkenness), and ideationally motivated actions (political crimes). This global and undifferentiated conception of mental illness has been accepted even by most of the critics of the McNaghten Rule.

2. The postacquittal fate of the defendant was left unclarified. Tacitly, however, it was accepted practice in McNaghten's day, as it still is in many parts of the world, that at least some patients who are said to be mentally ill may be treated *as though* they were criminals; that is, they may be forcibly restrained and involuntarily segregated from society ("hospitalized"), sometimes for life (Szasz, 1957).

3. The socioeconomic, political, and ethical implications of deviant behavior were obscured in favor of its so-called medical causes. This, too, has remained a significant issue to our day, even in the modifications of the McNaghten Rule.

Much has been made of the psychiatric dissatisfactions with so-called tests of insanity, such as are implicit in McNaghten's Rule. In this connection, Isaac Ray's argument against these tests is usually approvingly quoted, to show that "enlightened" psychiatric knowledge militates against the use of such tests (Overholser, 1959). Isaac Ray's views had a profound impact on American psychiatry, especially on forensic psychiatry, and hence deserve careful study. For our present purposes, it should suffice to recall that he was strongly *opposed* to reforms advocating nonrestraint in treating mental patients! In general, he was more interested in the so-called legal applications of psychiatry than in psychiatry as a science. He was frequently sought as an expert in criminal cases. Ray's forensic-psychiatric views found expression in the New Hampshire Rule. In two celebrated decisions, handed down by the Supreme Court of New Hampshire in 1869 and 1871, the relation between "mental disease" and "criminal responsibility" was defined as a problem of weighing evidence to be decided by the jury. In the Jones Case (State v. Jones, 1871), the court expressed itself as follows:

> Enough has already been said as to the use of symptoms, phases, or manifestations of mental disease as legal tests of capacity to entertain a criminal intent. They are all clearly matters of evidence to be weighed by the jury upon the question whether the act was the offspring of insanity. If it was, a criminal intent did not produce it. If it was not, a criminal intent did produce it and it was crime.

Under this rule it suffices for a psychiatrist to testify that the defendant is classifiable under a particular category of mental illness, by virtue of having certain standard symptoms. Further, the psychiatrist must testify that the crime was caused by this condition of the defendant. Now, it must be admitted that this does *sound* better than McNaghten's Rule. But the improvement is deceptive. The change, in fact, may be an ethical retrogression. This rule retains many of the difficulties of its predecessors; it, too, treats some kinds of deviant behavior as "illness" and is silent on the disposition of the acquitted "criminal patient." Perhaps the most deceptive but most significant feature of the New Hampshire Rule is the positive valuation it places on the absence of a *predetermined test of insanity*. It is only logical that those who have claimed that mental illness is basically no different from physical illness should be required to "put up or shut up." Ordinary diseases, such as syphilis, lobar pneumonia, epilepsy, and so forth, may all be defined in such a way that *publicly demonstrable tests* can be used to establish their presence or absence. For legal and ethical purposes, moreover, it is more important that there be such tests than that they be very accurate. For without the tests, expert opinion ceases to be scientific (in the instrumental sense of this word), and instead becomes oracular. I would argue, therefore, that it is decidedly not enough for a psychiatrist to testify concerning his "diagnosis" of a case, and perhaps also how, in his opinion, the defendant was "not responsible" for his acts because of "mental illness." Unless he also explains how he arrived at this conclusion — which in essence means making the tests used explicit — his testimony runs counter to the ethic of a rational, democratic jurisprudence. For in the absence of such *publicly verifiable* criteria of rendering judgment, psychiatric expert testimony will be accepted or rejected not on the merit of the scientific argument presented but rather on whether the psychiatrist, as an authoritative person, is accepted or rejected. (See Chapter 3.) But it is the expert *testimony* not the expert (person) that should concern the jury! This is the situation when other technical experts, for example, a toxicologist or a pathologist, testify. I submit that the very fact that the high public reputation of such men as Isaac Ray (and others who followed him) was necessary to bring about the progressive "psychiatrization" of the law should make us wary of their claims. If their claims had been scientifically sound and verifiable, men of lesser repute could have established them equally well. Beginning with the New Hampshire Rule and culminating in the Durham Decision (see page 157), the oracular pronouncements of eminent psychiatrists have taken the place of publicly verifiable facts (and of scientifically acceptable theories). The change from McNaghten to New Hampshire and Durham is thus a move away from a Rule of Law toward a Rule of Men.

At this point, before proceeding to a discussion of the Durham Rule, it is necessary to mention the so-called "irresistible impulse" test, which exempts from responsibility acts committed as a result of irresistible impulse. The moral basis of this test rests on the fundamental proposition that "freedom of the will" is essential to criminal responsibility. Those who have advocated this test have assumed, further, that there exist human conditions or situations in which men are irresistibly driven to act in certain ways. Such "irresistibly" committed actions are then placed in the same category as accidents. Neither is purposefully planned and executed. The foregoing statements must not be regarded as descriptions of facts concerning observable human behavior. On the contrary, in the case of the notion of irresistible impulse — as in so much of forensic psychiatry — theories of human behavior and prescriptions of conduct are presented as if they were empirical observations. We need not be concerned here with a criticism of this principle. It should suffice to note that the idea of an act committed as a result of an irresistible impulse presupposes that action is impulse-motivated, and that some impulses can be resisted whereas others cannot. "Sanity" is then conceived as the ability to resist (antisocial) impulses. These statements have, of course, only the remotest sort of connection with psychosocial facts.

Rather than consider this concept further, it will be more pertinent for us to note the historical context in which this test arose and the reasons given in support of it. The irresistible impulse doctrine is of American origin and dates from 1834 (Weihofen, 1933, p. 46). It was adopted in several states and received its strongest support in a decision handed down in Alabama in 1886. There is a vast literature concerning these decisions and the irresistible impulse doctrine generally, most of it dealing with the test's advantages over the McNaghten formula (which it usually "supplements"). The main point, as I see it, is that to many persons the McNaghten Rule implied a principally *cognitive or intellectual definition* of "insanity." Accordingly, there has been a constant agitation, mostly on the part of psychiatrists, for the recognition of the so-called *emotional aspects* of "mental illness." The irresistible impulse test is probably best viewed as an early expression of opposition to the McNaghten formula, on the basis of the latter's alleged overemphasis on the role of reason in personality functioning. The Durham Rule is a logical sequel to the irresistible impulse test. It reveals a persistent preoccupation with the question of which part of the personality is "sick," and with a refutation of the significance of the rational in human behavior.

The Durham Rule (1954) was handed down in a decision of the United States Court of Appeals for the District of Columbia in 1954. Its most significant assertion is that "an accused is not criminally responsible if his unlawful act was the product of mental disease or mental defect." Evidently, this is simply a semantic modernization of the New Hampshire Rule.

This decision has been widely hailed by both jurists and psychiatrists. It is said to represent a great scientific advance in criminal jurisprudence. A few legal scholars (notably, Hall, 1956), and an even smaller number of psychiatrists (Szasz, 1958b) have expressed criticism of the decision and its implications.

Clearly, the Durham Decision represents the final culmination of what could aptly be called the "psychiatrization" of some aspect of the criminal law. It is an attempt to transform the preconceived notion that there are two modes of existence — one sane, the other insane — into legal "reality." Since this rule has had a powerful impact on contemporary American jurisprudence, its psychiatric, legal, and ethical aspects will be examined in detail.

THE DURHAM RULE AND ITS IMPLICATIONS: A CRITICAL ANALYSIS

According to the jurists who formulated the Durham Decision, it was based on the general ethical principle that "our collective conscience does not allow punishment where it cannot impose blame." This seems like an idea that is at once self-evident and wholly commendable. In fact, it is neither.

In its naked form, the above-quoted assertion lays claim to a general principle as a *regulatory force* in social behavior. Obviously, such a statement cannot be regarded as a description of a natural law. It is, rather, a prescription about the principles that *ought to* govern social living (in the society intended by the speaker). As I pointed out some time ago (Szasz, 1956), a logical corollary of the rule "No punishment without blameworthiness" is that there should likewise be "No reward without praiseworthiness." The fact is, of course, that our society is not constructed along these lines at all.

Indeed, to reform it in accordance with these principles would turn it into a type of human organization quite unknown to us and one that is hardly imaginable.

Another source of difficulty is encountered when we consider that ignorance of the law is no excuse in the eye of the Anglo-American (as well as the Roman) philosophy of law. How can a person ignorant of the law be held responsible for breaking it? How can he be blamed for committing an act that he did not know was prohibited? The answer is, of course, that the well-being of a democratic social order depends upon every adult person's knowing what he can do and what he cannot. *Legal responsibility* is thus an expectation. It is an *expectation*, first, that people will learn the laws of the land in which they live, and, second, that they will try to adhere to them. Thus, should they break the law, we will be entitled to consider them blameworthy.

If we apply this reasoning to offenders who are alleged to be mentally ill, we shall come to similar conclusions. That is, if such persons are "ill" in some sense resembling a state of bodily illness, this shall not excuse them from adherence to the law. If, on the other hand, "mental illness" is a phenomenon in some ways similar to ignorance (which, indeed, it is), then this state — and its correction — shall also ascriptively be regarded as falling within the primary responsibility of the adult citizen. Thus, from a purely *logical point of view*, there are no good grounds for the rule that there should be two types of laws, one for the mentally healthy and another for the mentally sick.[1]

MENTAL ILLNESS AS AN EXCUSING CONDITION

The discussion so far has presupposed two conditions which must now be further analyzed: the notion of mental illness, and the judicial status of such illness as a so-called excusing condition. We shall examine each of these separately.

The Nature of "Mental Illness"

I began this discussion by stating that "criminal responsibility" and "psychiatry" are ambiguous terms. We are now ready to identify

---

[1] The psychiatric aspects of this problem were analyzed in detail in several previous publications (Szasz, 1956, 1958b, 1958c), to which the interested reader is referred.

and briefly illustrate some of the problems attending the concept of psychiatry.

The scope and subject matter of psychiatry are ill defined. To some, psychiatry means the study of diseases of the brain; to others, the study of diseases of the mind; and to still others, the study of behavior, diseased or otherwise. Nor is there agreement on the scientific and technical methods that characterize this branch of knowledge. Some rely on physicochemical methods; others on psychosocial methods. Accordingly, the terms "psychiatry" and "psychiatrist," as employed in contemporary America, may be used to identify a variety of scientific disciplines and their practitioners.

It is generally assumed that so-called mental illnesses exist. It is further assumed that the phenomena so designated belong in the same logical class as bodily illnesses. In the legal thought of the past century, moreover, these assumptions have been treated as though they were simple, well-established, empirical observations or so-called facts. Probably the first, and undoubtedly one of the most effective proponent of this "common-sense" view of psychiatric illness was Isaac Ray. Under his guidance and influence, the New Hampshire court, in State v. Pike (1869), asserted that "all symptoms and all tests of mental disease were purely matters of fact to be determined by the jury." The concept "mental disease" was here defined, by legislative fiat, as fact, rather than as interpretation (based on facts) or as theory (designed to explain facts).

Critical inspection of the phenomena called mental illnesses and the actual operations of psychiatrists reveal that the term "mental illness" designates a concept quite unlike that suggested by the above-mentioned definition. To put the matter succinctly, I believe we would be justified in asserting that there is no such thing as a mental illness. In other words, the alleged existence of such illnesses, as naturally occurring phenomena, similar to, say, fractures and cancers, is a myth. Mental illness is a metaphorical expression, referring to disturbances or deviations in *social behavior*. The basis for this view of so-called psychiatric illnesses was presented elsewhere (Szasz, 1959a, 1960b) and cannot be detailed here. Suffice it so say that a clarification of this conception has far-reaching practical implications. I shall mention only two of these, which are pertinent to our present concern.

1. There is a distinction between illness as *happening* and as *action* (Peters, 1958). Bodily illness — for example, developing a brain tumor — falls in the logical happening class. Having such a disease is not the result of a (willed) action, but is rather in the nature

of a passively incurred occurrence. The disease-conception of mental illness places certain behavioral acts in the category of such passively incurred occurrences. In this view, for example, a so-called paranoid schizophrenic person's shooting his "persecutor" would be regarded as a happening. The view here proposed, on the other hand, treats the crime as an action. (This is not to say that it is an action in every way similar to, or identical with, all other types of action. But it is an action, nonetheless.) It is clear that this consideration has a profound bearing on mental illness as an excusing condition. This will be discussed presently.

2. According to traditional definition, psychiatry is the study and treatment of mental illnesses. A more accurate and serviceable definition would be to regard psychiatry as one of the sciences (both pure and applied) dealing with *human (social) behavior*. As such, psychiatry would be principally a social science, rather than a medical science. Its sister sciences would be anthropology, ethics, psychology, and sociology. Medicine in general and neurology in particular are the sciences concerned with man's physical or bodily behavior, rather than with his social behavior. The problem of "sanity" thus ceases to be a purely medical concern.

If we seriously believe that the *human experiences* of certain offenders are significant data for juries and judges to consider in sentencing them, then we should have to conclude that it is *not* the offender's alleged mental illness that is really relevant, but rather his *human circumstances* — his upbringing, family situation, values, and the like. This would mean that psychiatric testimony would be only one among several types of expert testimony to be considered. The courts would thus be thrown open to behavioral scientists of all sorts, all of whom could contribute, each in his own special way, to the jury's understanding of what happened, and why, in a given criminal case. If this were implemented, psychiatrists would have to relinquish the prestige and authority vested in their medical degrees, which now enable them to be experts in so-called mental illnesses or psychopathologies. As toxicologists need not be physicians, so experts in human behavior need not be psychiatrists. The psychiatric expert's status has traditionally been based on his affiliation rather than on his usefulness. This, I submit, has been one of the factors that has undermined, and rightly so, the value of psychiatric expert testimony in the eye of the law and the public. A respectable and self-respecting expert must be one whose expert status derives from special skills and knowledge, not from membership in a special group. This is especially true in the case of psychiatry, since membership in various professional groups may be gained on the basis of criteria quite unrelated to the skills required for, say, assessing variations in social or ethical behavior. Hence it is logically and empirically possible for a person to be an expert in psychiatry without being an expert in the science of human behavior.

Excusing Conditions

The concept of an excusing condition was most clearly formulated by Hart (1958):

It is characteristic of our own and all advanced legal systems that the individual's liability to punishment, at any rate for serious crimes carrying severe penalties, is made by law to depend on, among other things, certain mental conditions. These conditions can best be expressed in negative form as excusing conditions; the individual is not liable to punishment if at the time of his doing what would otherwise be a punishable act he is, say, unconscious, mistaken about the physical consequences of his bodily movements or the nature or qualities of the thing or persons affected by them, or, in some cases, if he is subjected to threats or other gross forms of coercion or is the victim of certain types of mental disease. This is a list, not meant to be complete, giving broad descriptions of the principal excusing conditions; the exact definition of these and their precise character and scope must be sought in the detailed exposition of our criminal law. If an individual breaks the law when none of the excusing conditions are present, he is ordinarily said to have acted of "his own free will," of "his own accord," "voluntarily"; or it might be said, "He could have helped doing what he did." [Pp. 81–82.]

It is clear, from Hart's subsequent discussion as well as from inspection of the administration of Anglo-American law, that the *logical prototype* of an excusing condition is an accident. In this case, no responsibility can be ascribed to the offender. It is important to note, however, that this principle is no longer adhered to, as in cases of compensation for industrial accidents. The employer need not be at fault for the worker to be awarded compensation for injuries so incurred. In practice, no legal system admits without qualifications that all criminal responsibility is excluded — automatically, as it were — by any particular excusing condition. Hence, mental illness — like accident, provocation, or duress — may or may not constitute an excuse for a given criminal act. Here we need not be concerned with the problem of *what factors, in addition to the psychiatric ones, affect the court's judgment* concerning whether mental illness is or is not an excusing condition. What will interest us is only the logic and psychology of *why* mental illness should ever be considered an excusing condition.

Should "Mental Illness" Be Considered an Excusing Condition?

Those who consider mental illness an excusing condition do so because they regard so-called mentally ill persons as falling in a class distinct from and different from those who are mentally well. This distinction is supposed to rest on psychological or psychiatric criteria. As outstanding a legal authority as Professor Glanville Williams (1953) has stated, apropos of considering the restraining effects of punishment, that "Mentally deranged persons, however, can be separated from the mass of mankind by scientific tests, and can be given treatment instead of being subjected to punitive sanctions. Being a defined class, their segregation from punishment does not impair the efficacy of the sanction for people generally" (p. 347).

I submit that this view embodies a grave error. That no scientific distinction between mentally sick and mentally healthy persons exists — at least at present — is evident from the psychiatric literature. Another, perhaps simpler, source of evidence to support this contention is the well-known battle of the psychiatric experts. It is possible, in virtually any case in which psychiatric testimony is introduced, to secure psychiatric testimony in opposition to it. How are we to reconcile this fact? If we compare psychiatric to, say, toxicological testimony, a comparable situation would be one in which the toxicologist for the prosecution testified that a body contained a lethal amount of arsenic, whereas the toxicologist for the defense testified that it did not. This, of course, never happens, because one of the experts could be, and would be, proved guilty of perjury.

How, then, can a similar sort of situation happen in psychiatric testimony? Psychiatric experts can render conflicting opinions, I believe, because the standards or criteria for their opinions always remain unexplicit. Thus, they can testify to virtually anything — as expert *opinion* (not as fact) — and they cannot possibly be proved wrong. Neither can they be proved right. It is as if both toxicologists in the example cited could be right, one because he considered the lethal dose of arsenic to be x milligrams, the other because he considered it to be y milligrams. As long as we do not seek to ascertain the criteria that the experts use — and demand that these be framed in objective, descriptive terms — we encourage them to influence and lead us, rather than to *inform* us! It is my thesis, briefly, that mental illness is not the sort of phenomenon whose presence or absence can, at least according to current practices, be easily identified by scientifically impartial methods. Since there are no scientifically accepted ethical and social criteria of mental health — a concept corresponding to the permissible level of arsenic in the human body in our analogy — there can be no scientifically acceptable criteria of mental illness.

In addition to this chiefly logical argument against regarding mental illness as an excusing condition, we should also consider the argument, presented earlier, that "mentally ill" behavior is more akin to action than to happenings. Now, it may correctly be argued that, in some part, such behavior is also similar to happenings. To the extent to which a person "acts" *in an involuntary fashion,* to precisely that extent, however, he cannot be regarded as a "human being" (in the social sense of the term). This, then, leads to the apparently insoluble dilemma in which much of contemporary forensic psychiatry finds itself. Either we regard offenders as "sane" and punish them, or we regard them as "insane," and, though officially excusing them of "crimes," punish them in the most serious way possible, namely, by treating them as beings who are "inhuman" or "less than human" (Guttmacher and Weihofen, 1952; Weihofen, 1956). In this dilemma, it seems to me that the most dignified, and psychologically and socially most promising, alternative is not to consider mental illness an excusing condition. Treating offenders as responsible human beings, even though sometimes they may not be individually "blameworthy," offers them the only chance, as I now see it, of remaining "human" and possibly becoming more so.

Many contemporary forensic-psychiatric authors tacitly adhere to the premise that illness is bad and that virtually any method that is likely to prove therapeutic may justifiably be employed, with or without the consent of the patient. Wertham (1955) called this "psychoauthoritarianism" because it substitutes the psychiatrist's authority for the patient's responsibility for and self-determination of his own fate. Another appropriate descriptive label for this sort of orientation would be to call it the "medical" or "therapeutic" attitude. In contrast to it, we may speak of the ethic of responsibility and democracy — or, more precisely, of the ethic of the "open society" (Popper, 1950) —which places higher value on personal integrity and self-determination than it does on health. For instance, it is illegal for a physician to treat a patient, if he is of age and conscious, without his consent. Legally, unauthorized treatment is assault and battery. Now, those adhering to the ethics of therapeutism could object and say: "But if the physician could show that the patient was sick, and that he did properly treat him, should this not exonerate the physician from the charges?" In fact, such a physician might even argue that he should be regarded as the patient's (and society's) benefactor, rather than as a lawbreaker. It seems to me that both positions rest on reasonable arguments. How we decide will depend on which values, among several conflicting ones, we prefer. Decreeing the supremacy of health as a value, will, in many such situations, result in serious losses in individual self-determination and personal freedom. Conversely, if it is decreed that dignity, self-responsibility, and freedom are supreme values, even more important than health, then, in some situations at least, the health of persons may suffer as a consequence. This is the case, for example, in the widely publicized instances in which members of the sect known as Jehovah's Witnesses may die following an operation, because the use of blood transfusions is prohibited by the religious teachings of this group. It has often been asserted, and it remains true, I believe, that such diversity is not only the price of democracy but its very essence.

The converse of this situation (that is, the converse of the ethical primacy of individual choice, responsibility, and its consequences) characterizes the practices of contemporary forensic psychiatry. This includes the uses to which psychiatric testimony is put in criminal trials, and also the tactic of committing persons charged with criminal acts who had been acquitted by reason of insanity. What I have earlier called the psychiatrization of the law means precisely this: *the subordination of the ethics of the "open society" to the ethics of medical-therapeutic considerations and arguments.* Thus, in the legal adjudication of a case, claims concerning the mental state of an offender may be given more weight than his actual participation in the act, his self-confessed reasons for it, his gains from it, and so on. Likewise, in committing an acquitted "criminal" to a mental hospital, supremacy is given to the notions of mental illness and therapy, while injury is done to the value that no one should be detained without being proven guilty of criminal activity. By the same token, the ethically odious conception of an indefinite sentence (particularly for a person unconvicted of any crime) is made tolerable, at least for some people, by disguising it as serving the interests of a *higher* ethical goal, namely, the goal of *good individual and public health!* Clearly, we must make a choice between the ethics of the "open society" and the ethics of therapeutism.

EPILOGUE

I should like to add a brief note to what I have said concerning the potential practical implementation of the point of view I have expressed.

I submit that a great deal of the complicated machination that now goes on in the name of pleading insanity in criminal cases could be obviated if all persons were treated *as though* they were responsible for their actions. (Needless to say, the death penalty would have to be abolished before such a viewpoint could seriously be entertained. So long as it exists, it exerts a powerful temptation on psychiatrists, lawyers, and everyone else to use the insanity plea for no other purpose than to avoid this penalty.) I would further propose that there should be only two types of institutions: jails and hospitals. No hybrids would be permitted. This would mean the elimination of *all* involuntary hospitalization *as* hospitalization. (Some persons now dealt with in this way probably would have to be sentenced to jails, which could then function therapeutically.) Accordingly, persons charged with criminal offenses would be either acquitted or sentenced to jail. Acquittal would be complete and unconditional, as the term implies. Psychiatric, sociologic, ethical, and other considerations could be weighed in determining the sentence and in carrying out the penal disposition. The latter could, conceivably, range from neutral segregation — just putting in time — to a full-fledged psychiatric rehabilitation program. Since the persons to whom such therapy would be administered would be restrained by law, and since the treatment itself might be administered against their wishes, it would seem to me more honest, and hence more desirable, to codify this type of incarceration as jailing rather than as hospitalization. What is being advocated, in brief, is a more consistent, candid, and forthright separation of self-defined illness with self-responsibly undertaken treatment on the one hand, and of other-defined "illness" or criminality and legally imposed "treatment" or confinement on the other hand.

References

Dodds, E. R. *The Greeks and the irrational*. Boston: Beacon Press, 1957.

Durham v. United States (1954) 214 F. 2d 862 (D.C. Cir.).

Encyclopaedia Britannica. Unsigned article on "Sophocles." 1949, **XX**, 1003.

Glueck, S. S. *Mental disorder and the criminal law: A study in medico-sociological jurisprudence.* Boston: Little, Brown, 1925.

Guttmacher, M. The quest for a test of criminal responsibility. *Amer. J. Psychiat.,* 1954, **3**, 428–432.

Guttmacher, M. S., & Weihofen, H. *Psychiatry and the law.* New York: Norton, 1952.

Hall, J. Psychiatry and criminal responsibility. *Yale Law J.,* 1956, **65**, 761–785.

Hall, L., & Glueck, S. *Cases on criminal law and its enforcement.* (2d ed.; American Casebook Series, E. N. Griswold, General Editor.) St. Paul: West Publishing Co., 1958.

Hart, H. L. A. Legal responsibility and excuses. In S. Hook (Ed.), *Determinism and freedom in the age of modern science.* New York: New York Univer. Press, 1958, pp. 81–104.

McNaghten's Case (1843) 10 Cl. & F. 200, 8 Eng. Rep. 718 (H.L. 1843).

Overholser, W. Major principles of forensic psychiatry. In S. Arieti et al. (Eds.), *American handbook of psychiatry.* New York: Basic Books, 1959, II, 1887–1901.

Paleologue, M. *An intimate journal of the Dreyfus case.* New York: Criterion Books, 1957.

Peters, R. S. *The concept of motivation.* London: Routledge & Kegan Paul, 1958.

Popper, K. R. *The open society and its enemies.* Princeton, N. J.: Princeton Univer. Press, 1950.

State v. Jones, 50 N. H. 369, 1871. (Quoted in Overholser, 1959.)

State v. Pike, 49 N. H. 399, 1869. (Quoted in Weihofen, 1933.)

Stoljar, S. Ascriptive and prescriptive responsibility. *Mind,* 1959, **68**, 350–360.

Szasz, T. S. Some observations on the relationship between psychiatry and the law. *A.M.A. Arch. Neurol. & Psychiat.,* 1956, **75**, 297–315.

Szasz, T. S. Commitment of the mentally ill: "Treatment" or social restraint? *J. nerv. & ment. Dis.,* 1957, **125**, 293–307.

Szasz, T. S. Scientific method and social role in medicine and psychiatry. *A.M.A. Arch. int. Med.,* 1958, **101**, 228–238. (a)

Szasz, T. S. Psychiatry, ethics, and the criminal law. *Columbia Law Rev.,* 1958, **58**, 183–198. (b)

Szasz, T. S. Politics and mental health: Some remarks apropos of the case of Mr. Ezra Pound. *Amer. J. Psychiat.,* 1958, **115**, 508–511. (c)

Szasz, T. S. The classification of "mental illness": A situational analysis of psychiatric operations. *Psychiat. Quart.,* 1959, **33**, 77–101. (a)

Szasz, T. S. Psychiatry, psychotherapy, and psychology. *A.M.A. Arch. gen. Psychiat.,* 1959, **1**, 455–463. (b)

Szasz, T. S. Moral conflict and psychiatry. *Yale Rev.,* 1960, **49**, 555–566. (a)

Szasz, T. S. The myth of mental illness. *Amer. Psychologist*, 1960, **15**, 113–118. (b)

Weihofen, H. *Insanity as a defense in criminal law*. New York: The Commonwealth Fund, 1933.

Weihofen, H. *The urge to punish: New approaches to the problem of mental irresponsibility for crime*. New York: Farrar, Straus and Cudahy, 1956.

Wertham, F. Psychoauthoritarianism and the law. *Univer. of Chicago Law Rev.*, 1955, **22**, 336–338.

Williams, G. *The criminal law*. London: Stevens & Sons, 1953.

Supplementary References

Discussions of the Durham Rule

Douglas, W. O. *Law and psychiatry*. New York: The William Alanson White Institute of Psychiatry, Psychoanalysis and Psychology, 1956.

Fortas, A. Implications of Durham's Case. *Amer. J. Psychiat.*, 1957, **113**, 577–582.

Hall, J. Mental disease and criminal responsibility: McNaghten versus Durham and the American Law Institute's tentative draft. *Indiana Law J.*, 1958, **33**, 212–225.

Sobeloff, S. E. Insanity and the criminal law: From McNaghten to Durham, and beyond. *Amer. Bar Ass. J.*, 1955, **41**, 793–796, 877–879.

Watson, A. S. Durham plus five years: Development of the law of criminal responsibility in the District of Columbia. *Amer. J. Psychiat.*, 1959, **116**, 289–297.

Ethics, Law, and Sociology

Cahn, E. *The moral decision: Right and wrong in the light of American law*. Bloomington: Indiana Univer. Press, 1956.

Friedrich, C. J. *The philosophy of law in historical perspective*. Chicago: Univer. of Chicago Press, 1958.

Hall, J. *Studies in jurisprudence and criminal theory*. New York: Oceana Publications, 1958.

Morris, C. *The open self*. Englewood Cliffs, N. J.: Prentice-Hall, 1948.

Parsons, T. *The social system*. Glencoe, Ill.: The Free Press, 1952.

Popper, K. R. *The poverty of historicism*. Boston: Beacon Press, 1957.

Pound, R. *An introduction to the philosophy of law*. New Haven: Yale Univer. Press, 1922, 1954.

Pound, R. *Social control through law*. New Haven: Yale Univer. Press, 1942.

Williams, G. *The sanctity of life and the criminal law*. New York: Knopf, 1957.

Psychiatry and Criminology

Alexander, F., & Staub, H. *The criminal, the judge, and the public: A psychological analysis.* (Rev. Ed. with new chapters by F. Alexander. Original ed. trans. G. Zilboorg.) Glencoe, Ill.: The Free Press and the Falcon's Wing Press, 1931, 1956.

Board, R. G. An operational conception of criminal responsibility. *Amer. J. Psychiat.,* 1956, **113,** 332–336.

Cahn, E. N. (Ed.) *Social meaning of legal concepts. No. 2: Criminal guilt.* New York: New York Univer. Law School, 1950.

Davidson, H. A. *Forensic psychiatry.* New York: Ronald, 1952.

Group for the Advancement of Psychiatry, Committee on Psychiatry and Law. *Criminal responsibility and psychiatric expert testimony.* Report No. 26. Topeka, Kan.: 1954.

Hakeem, M. A critique of the psychiatric approach to crime and correction. *Law and contemp. Probs.,* 1958, **23,** 650–682.

Menninger, K. The psychiatrist in relation to crime. In *A psychiatrist's world: The selected papers of Karl Menninger, M.D.* New York: Viking, 1926, 1959, pp. 729–736.

Menninger, K. A. *Man against himself.* New York: Harcourt, Brace, 1938.

Ross, H. A. Commitment of the mentally ill: Problems of law and policy. *Michigan Law Rev.,* 1959, **57,** 945–1018.

Szasz, T. S. Psychiatric expert testimony: Its covert meaning and social function. *Psychiat.,* 1957, **20,** 313–316.

Szasz, T. S. Recent books on the relation of psychiatry to criminology. (A review article.) *Psychiat.,* 1958, **21,** 307–319.

Wertham F. *The show of violence.* New York: Doubleday, 1949.

Zilboorg, G. *The psychology of the criminal act and punishment.* New York: Harcourt, Brace, 1954.

Part II
Criminal Psychology

HANS TOCH

8 Introduction to Criminal Psychology

It is widely assumed that a convicted felon must be punished by the law in proportion to the seriousness of his offense. It is also assumed that an effort must be made to "rehabilitate" or "correct" the errant culprit so that he becomes a congenial and law-abiding member of the community.

Chapter 13 will discuss the fact that we cannot really accomplish both aims at the same time. One reason for this is that if we share the Mikado's sublime object of making "the punishment fit the crime" we have to punish in the same way every person who has committed the same crime. If we send one forger to prison for five years, we must send the next forger to prison for five years. If we maintain that first-degree murder deserves a life sentence, anyone found guilty of murder in the first degree must spend the remainder of his life in prison.

But as we shall see later in this section, the same offense can be committed by a variety of people for a variety of reasons. One of our two forgers, for instance, may have stumbled into the profession accidentally — through an unfortunate choice of acquaintances, as a misguided outlet for artistic leanings, under the temporary influence of alcohol, or in a period of despondency over a financial crisis; once detected or after a few weeks of sobering prison life, he may never etch anything more objectionable than bathing beauties or wild flowers. The second forger may be a chronic offender with a string of convictions stretching back to his eighth birthday. His personality may be so warped that only prolonged psychiatric attention may hold out hope of preventing the continuation of his annoying criminal career. If our aim is to "correct" these two culprits, we must clearly take their differences into account. If we do, we may rehabilitate both; if we don't — and if we "punish" both of them in proportion to their offense—we may rehabilitate neither.

171

We may convert the first forger into a bitter, antisocial person, and we may release the second before we have made the necessary impact on him.[1]

The same point holds for our murderers. In general, persons guilty of first-degree murder are the safest people to release from prison — they seldom commit further offenses beyond traffic violations. Occasionally, however, such a person is a very serious menace to society by virtue of his strong, uncontrolled impulses. From a correctional or rehabilitative point of view, this type of offender may well have to be confined for life, whereas his fellow murderers might at best be wasting many years in which they could make constructive contributions to society.

Criminal psychology is a discipline which shares with others the problem of rehabilitation or correction of offenders:

As a *science*, criminal psychology studies the causes of criminal behavior. It attempts to isolate, describe, and understand the particular combinations of factors which lead particular people to commit particular crimes. It seeks to arrive at general statements or laws about patterns of causation of antisocial behavior.

As a *profession*, criminal psychology aims at reducing crime by treating offenders. The concern here is with finding ways of changing people so that they refrain from antisocial behavior.

THE CONCEPTION OF MAN AS FREE MORAL AGENT

Rehabilitation as an objective in dealing with criminals has gained acceptance only very recently. Less than two hundred years ago, the prevalent form of treatment of convicted offenders was corporal punishment. Favorite forms of punishment included flogging, mutilation, branding, and the stocks and pillory (Barnes, 1930). Capital punishment was applied with horrifying frequency. According to one estimate, 200,000 witches were executed in Europe in the sixteenth and seventeenth centuries. Henry VIII slaughtered 72,000 of his subjects, and legalized boiling to death as one means of doing so (Lawrence, 1928). Before the revision of the English penal code in the first half of the nineteenth century, 222 types of offenses could result in hanging.

---

[1] Most forgers actually fall into the second category. The chances of their rehabilitation in prison are negligible. Upon release they generally relapse easily into forgery.

This is not to say that there was anything uniform about the application of punishments. In most instances the offender could expect little mercy, but the nature of his offense gave him no information about the severity of the punishment he could anticipate.

Judges were concerned not only about punishing the offender for his misdeeds, but also about deterring others from turning to crime. Hangings were considered to be highly educational, and were widely advertised. Branding and mutilation in part served the same purpose, in that each victim, if he survived, could provide a roadside warning to others. Thus William the Conqueror decreed "that no one shall be killed or hung for any misdeeds, but rather that his eyes be plucked out and his feet, hands and testicles cut off, so that whatever part of his body remains will be a living sign to all of his crime and iniquity" (Barnes, 1930, p. 61).

Both the aim of punishment and that of deterrence were firmly rooted in a religious conception of human nature. Man was viewed as a free moral agent. He was seen as being able to choose between righteous behavior sanctioned by God, and evil conduct of which God took a dim view. Severe *punishment* could thus be regarded as a pious act.

A philosophy of *deterrence* followed from the premise that the potential criminal could choose *not* to commit his evil act. Deterrence also was a sacred obligation from the religious viewpoint, since a crime deterred represented a soul saved.

DIVINE INTERVENTION IN THE COURTROOM

The religious conception of crime was implicit in the very nature of medieval trials. Until 1215, for instance, the favorite method of adjudication in Europe was Trial by Ordeal, in which God was presumed to deliver the verdict by intervening on behalf of the defendant or by not doing so. If God intervened for the defendant (making it possible, for instance, for him to be boiled without blistering, or to float when weighed down with stones, or to walk between fires, or to touch a corpse without flinching) he was declared innocent. If God failed to intervene, he was declared guilty. A series of prayers and invocations was prescribed for every form of ordeal. Boiling water, for instance, was sometimes "adjured" as follows:

"O holy water, O blessed water, water which washest the dust and sins of the world, I adjure thee by the living God that thou shalt show thyself pure, nor retain any false image, but shalt be exorcised water, to make manifest and reveal and bring to naught all falsehood, and to make manifest and bring to light all truth; so that he who shall place his hand in thee, if his cause be just and true, shall receive no hurt; but if he be perjured, let his hand be burned with fire, that all men may know the power of our Lord Jesus Christ, who will come, with the Holy Ghost, to judge with fire the quick and the dead, and the world! Amen!" (Cit. Wigmore, 1941, p. 11.)

Civil cases were also divinely decided. One type of trial took the form of a sporting event in which champions of plaintiff and defendant (sometimes monks) would compete, and God presumably selected the winning team.

An obviously insane offender was not considered — even in the Middle Ages — as exercising free will. This far from mitigated the severity of his treatment, however, because the devils which were assumed to inhabit and control him were usually harassed by torturing and burning their unfortunate host.

HEDONISM AND CLASSICAL ANTHROPOLOGY

Early versions of criminal psychology developed against this background. One such development is the application to crime of Bentham's theory of hedonism. Jeremy Bentham anticipated modern behaviorism by asserting that "Nature has placed mankind under the government of two sovereign masters, pain and pleasure" (Bentham, 1907, p. 1).

Crime, like other human conduct, was seen as representing an effort to gain pleasure. The criminal was a special case because he derived pleasure at the expense of the community: his search for happiness provided pain to others. Punishment must be designed to deter this type of effort by making it unprofitable. This could be accomplished by making the punishment "not less in any case than what is sufficient to outweigh [the value] of the profit of the offense" (p. 179). The pain inflicted by the punishment must equal the pleasure to be derived from the offense. By the same token, arbitrariness or cruelty would serve no purpose: "The punishment ought in no case to be *more* than what is necessary to bring it into conformity with the rules here given" (p. 182). Bentham thus provided "rules" for making the punishment fit the crime in equitable fashion.

Bentham's attempt is very closely paralleled by Cesare Beccaria's *Essay on Crimes and Punishments*, which represents the cornerstone of the so-called Classic School of Criminology. Beccaria, like Bentham, believed that "pleasure and pain are the only springs of actions in beings endowed with sensibility" (Beccaria, 1819, p. 21). He also argued that crime constituted an injury against society and was "to be measured by the injury done to society" (p. 32). And he, too, concluded that punishment should be determined by the extent of the injury, and should not exceed it. Thus crimes against property should be punished by fines, if at all possible. Beccaria took a strong stand against capital punishment, against torture, and against unfair trial procedures resulting in inequitable sentences. These views occasioned strong attacks from contemporary jurists, who "accused Beccaria of being the protector of robbers and murderers, because he wanted to abolish the only means of compelling them to a confession, the torture" (Ferri, 1910, p. 19).

Both hedonism and classical criminology were firmly based on a psychology of volition. They assumed that every criminal act resulted from a decision of free will in the face of a temptation. They assumed that this temptation varied with the offense. Punishment, therefore, also had to vary with the offense.[2] This would increase both its equitability and its effectiveness as a deterrent.

THE POSITIVE SCHOOL OF CRIMINOLOGY

The Positive School of Criminology, which was inaugurated in 1872 by Cesare Lombroso, denied the role of free will in causing crime, and maintained that crime was *determined*, by factors which could be isolated and measured:

The positive school of criminology maintains... that it is not the criminal who wills; in order to be a criminal it is rather necessary that the individual should find himself permanently or transitorily in such personal, physical and moral conditions, and live in such an environment, which become for him a chain of cause and effect, externally and internally, that disposes him toward crime. [Ferri, 1910, p. 22.]

The positive school of criminology took a strong stand against any system in which the law or the judge fixes the prison term of the offender in accord with his offense:

---

[2] Bentham made one allowance for individual differences among offenders: since all were not equally sensible to pain, he felt that in fixing the punishment "circumstances influencing sensibility ought always to be taken into account" (Bentham, 1907, p. 182).

Add your sums and subtract your deductions, and the prisoner is sentenced to one year, seven months, and thirteen days. Not one day more or less! But the human spectator asks: "If the criminal should happen to be reformed before the expiration of his term should he be retained in prison?" The judge replies: "I don't care, he stays in one year, seven months, and thirteen days!"

Then the human spectator says: "But suppose the criminal should not yet be fit for human society at the expiration of his term?" The judge replies: "At the expiration of his term he leaves prison, for when he has absolved his last day, he has paid his debt!" [Ferri, 1910, pp. 84–85.]

THE "CRIMINAL" MAN

As an alternative to this system, the members of the positive school of criminology advocated the study of all factors which might influence a given person's criminal career. This included his social and economic conditions, his ethnic group membership, and the state of the weather at the time of the crime. Lombroso and his followers, however, concentrated on the "anthropological factor," which "represents the organic and psychological condition of the criminal" (Ferri, 1910, p. 61). Within the "anthropological factor" the positive criminologists were primarily concerned with anatomical differences.

Thus Lombroso (1911a) ascribes the birth of his system to the following event:

I... began to study criminals in the Italian prisons, and, amongst others, I made the acquaintance of the famous brigand Vilella. This man possessed such extraordinary agility, that he had been known to scale steep mountain heights bearing a sheep on his shoulders. His cynical effrontery was such that he openly boasted of his crimes. On his death one cold grey November morning, I was [chosen] to make the post mortem, and on laying open the skull I found on the occipital part, exactly on the spot where a spine is found in the normal skull, a distinct depression which I named *median occipital fossa*, because of its situation precisely in the middle of the occiput as in inferior animals, correlated with the hypertrophy of the *vermis* known in birds as the middle cerebellum.

This was not merely an idea, but a revelation. At the sight of that skull, I seemed to see all of a sudden, lighted up as a vast plain under a flaming sky, the problem of the nature of the criminal—an atavistic being who reproduces in his person the ferocious instincts of primitive humanity and the inferior animals. Thus were explained anatomically the enormous jaws, high cheek-bones, prominent superciliary arches, solitary lines on the palms, extreme size of the orbits, handle shaped or sessile ears found in criminals, savages and apes, insensibility to pain, extremely acute sight, tattooing, excessive idleness, love of orgies, and the irresistible craving for evil for its own sake, the desire not only to extinguish life in the victim, but to mutilate the corpse, tear its flesh, and drink its blood." [Pp. xiv–xv.]

This description forms the core of Lombroso's theory of the "Criminal Man," which is briefly summarized in Chapter 9 (page 197). What concerns us here is that this point of view *at the time of its inception* was a very progressive one: it led to the advocacy of different types of treatment for offenders with varying psychological characteristics. Followers of Lombroso were thus among the first proponents of probation, parole, indeterminate sentences, the juvenile court, experiments with youthful offenders, and other measures of modern penology. Lombroso himself firmly supported these ventures, especially in the United States, where many of them originated.

CRIME AND ANATOMY

The progressive label which applies to Lombroso's demands for individualized treatment does not apply to his biological orientation. In an elaborate study of 3,000 convicts, the English physician Charles Goring (1913) demonstrated that Lombroso's biologically inferior criminal was — in the words of James Thurber — a "mythical beast." No differences in anatomical characteristics (with the possible exception of a difference in size and weight) could be found between carefully drawn samples of law-abiding citizens and institutionalized offenders.

Early texts in criminal psychology, like that of Healy (1915), include physique as one of several factors leading to crime. Some contemporary investigators, including Sheldon and Eleanor Glueck (1950, 1956), have related body type to delinquency but have stressed the complex relationship between physique and other causes of crime.[3]

---

[3] Lombroso's original "criminal man" has recently been represented only in the esoteric writings of Sheldon (1949) and Hooton (1939). Hooton has even outdone Lombroso in that he has described a large number of "criminal men." Thus, "Massachusetts criminals are notable for thick beards, red-brown hair, dark brown, green-brown and blue-gray eyes, whites of eyes discolored with yellow or brown pigment flecks," and so on, whereas Tennessee criminals have "thin beards and scanty body hair, light brown shade of hair, blue-brown eyes with speckled or diffused irides, foreheads with little or no shapes, . . ." (Hooton, 1939, pp. 57–58). Hooton also lists different body types for different types of crimes, for different ethnic origins, and for different states of sanity. In all instances, he makes the gratuitous assumption that his differences point in the direction of biological inferiority of criminals. Hooton draws the moral from

THE EVOLUTION OF CRIMINAL
PSYCHOLOGY

Generally speaking, nineteenth-century views of crime differ from modern ones in their mechanistic picture of cause and effect. In contrast to the free-will conceptions which prevailed through the eighteenth century, criminal behavior had come to be seen by the positive criminologists as a simple and direct result of such factors as biological make-up, intelligence, poverty, and climate. If a person was generously endowed with predisposing factors, his criminal behavior was as inevitable as taxes. Prediction of criminality became a simple matter of locating the presence of favorite causal factors. If a person possessed too many of these, no treatment was assumed to be possible. Neither love nor communality needed to be lost between these predestined offenders and the predestined nonoffenders who made up the decreasing bulk of humanity.

Both the simplicity and the fatalism of this view have gone the way of all reassurances. Today, each offender is seen as the result of a complex interaction of causes extending into every nook and cranny of his past and his current experience. Diagnosis and treatment have thus become a truly monumental task, which we are barely beginning to face. Before we discuss the current status of criminal psychology in subsequent chapters, it may be helpful to characterize briefly the two schools of thought which have entered into today's view of the problem.

THE PSYCHIATRIC AND
SOCIOLOGICAL VIEWS

Modern criminal psychology owes its origin to sociology on the one hand, and to psychiatry on the other. Each of these disciplines has been concerned with a special type of offender, and each has derived principles which have joined to make up the "modern" view of crime.

---

this fable that criminals should be permanently segregated and that many should be prevented from having children.

For other illustrations of primitive views of crime causation, mainly biological theories current in the United States between 1890 and 1915, see Fink (1938).

Two hypothetical cases follow. The first — Charles Jones — represents the crime problem as seen by the sociologist. The second — Richard Smith — depicts the "psychiatric" viewpoint:

Charles Jones

At the relatively tender age of twenty-five, Chuck has managed to spend better than ten years behind bars. He began his career as a member of an organization entitled "The Tough Braves," which engaged in extramural activities of various sorts, including automobile thefts and after-hour shopping in closed stores. As a result of this — and because of a tendency to avoid school — Chuck spent several years at local institutions for juvenile delinquents. He graduated into an adult institution during a jurisdictional dispute between the "Braves" and the "Fighting Marines," when he disabled several of the enemy with a home-made shotgun. Subsequent felony convictions included burglaries, unarmed robberies, and an attempted rape.

The probation report reveals that Chuck is of slightly lower than average intelligence but of relatively normal personality. He is the oldest of twelve children. His father was an unskilled laborer who migrated to a large northern city from the Deep South, and held a succession of low-paying jobs. When Chuck was five years old, his parents obtained a divorce, and Chuck's mother married an unemployed alcoholic. She later separated from her second husband and had to make a meager living taking in laundry.

Chuck has grown up in slums and correctional institutions. His only friends are his associates in the streets and in prison. His vocational qualifications are nil, although he is currently taking a course in welding.

Richard Smith

Dick is serving a life sentence for first-degree murder. He has a prior conviction for felonious assault, as well as a juvenile record. He was first brought to the attention of authorities at the age of eight, when his parents found that they could not control him. The culminating episode was Dick's setting fire to the family dog — a winsome, long-haired cocker spaniel — and watching the animal perish in agony. Only two weeks before, Dick had worried his school principal by narrowly missing a woman teacher with a large boulder he had thrown at her. Placed in a private institution by arrangement of the juvenile court (see Chapter 11), Dick proved difficult to handle. In one of his weekly escape attempts, he seriously injured a kindly old janitor named Pop.

Shortly before his first felony conviction, Dick spent six months under observation in a mental hospital, and was released because of overcrowded conditions at the hospital. It was several weeks later that Dick broke a beer bottle over the head of a stranger who had "called him names." Two years after his release from prison for this offense, Dick strangled his fourteen-year-old girl friend, whom he suspected of unfaithfulness.

The Rorschach Test and other instruments administered to Dick during his presentence investigation and in prison showed him to be emotionally unstable and explosive. He seemed to have specially pronounced feelings toward persons in authority. He regarded such people with fear, hatred, defiance, and suspicion. Interviews established that Dick felt strong resentment toward his father, whom he described as strict and unkind. The father had spent a great deal of time away from home, and Dick felt that he "just hasn't given a damn" for his family. Dick expressed feelings of affection for his mother, who had long since passed away on a vacation trip to Europe.

Chuck's antisocial behavior would be attributed to his under-privileged circumstances as a child. Thrown into the gutter by a lack of home life, with no guidance except that provided by his misguided peers, Chuck is seen drifting into a sequence which leads almost inevitably from delinquency to crime. Dick, on the other hand, has been impelled to crime by feelings which have their origins in early frustrations and disappointments. Whereas Chuck *learned* to be a criminal, Dick was *predisposed* to antisocial conduct by a deeply warped personality which combined bitter hatred with an inability to keep feelings under control. When carried to its extreme, Dick's problem could place him in the "sociopathic" category discussed in Chapter 12. In any event, Dick would seem to require some form of psychiatric treatment. Chuck, on the other hand, should clearly "unlearn" his antisocial habits, and should never be returned to his unfavorable environment.

Recent thinking has shown this scheme to be impractical. Psychiatrists are almost impossible to come by (even at exorbitant salaries), and conventional psychotherapy cannot occur in authoritative prison settings. Nor can slums be eliminated or families relocated for the benefit of individual offenders.

It also became apparent on closer examination that there is less difference between people like Dick and Chuck than might originally appear. Although Chuck may certainly be described as a product of his environment, his reactions to his environment must have played a part in determining the result. He may have felt frustrated and thwarted by conditions which might not have the same effect on other boys. (If this were not the case, every underprivileged youngster would land in prison.) It would also be overly optimistic to assume that Chuck's years of unfortunate experiences have not left a substantial mark on him that must be dealt with.

Dick, on the other hand, through a lifetime of reactions to pressure, could probably manage to create an unfavorable environment for himself. He has almost certainly antagonized his respectable friends, and he has become part of a circle or "subculture" of professional criminals and other antisocial people. Even if his emotional problems are eliminated, their past consequences might drive him back to crime.

THE LEGAL FRAMEWORK
FOR CORRECTION

In practice as in theory, correction today is in its infancy. "The punitive notion is still dominant, despite the shift in its justification from the purpose of retribution to the alleged purpose of prevention" (Waite, 1943, p. 33). This problem will be considered in Chapter 13, but a general overview may be helpful.

In many countries, such as those of the British Commonwealth, a person found guilty of a felony knows roughly what treatment to expect. The judge fixes a prison term corresponding to the gravity of the offense, in the tradition of Bentham and Beccaria. About the only other facts concerning the offender he may take into account are his age, which determines the type of institution to whose care he is committed; and his past record. The judge is certainly not concerned with the felon's intelligence (unless the offender is definitely feeble-minded) or his personality (unless he is a raving lunatic) or his social history. If the prison rehabilitates, it must do so during the time period fixed by the offense. Few personal characteristics of the offender are taken into account in setting the "time clock." Correctional reform has occurred in the shape of fewer and shorter prison sentences.[4]

In the tradition of positive criminology the average American

---

[4] For a description of English sentencing procedures, see Halsbury's *Laws of England* (Simonds edition) X, 434, 486-521. Also see H. E. Palmer, Principles of punishment, *Crim. Law Rev.*, 1957, pp. 155 ff. and E. J. Horsford, Sentencing power of quarter sessions, *Crim. Law Rev.*, 1958, pp. 172 ff.

judge will try to learn whatever facts about the offender seem relevant for gauging the nature and duration of the treatment he requires. Thus the judge, before passing sentence, may order a presentence investigation, consisting at least of a case history obtained through interviews, and sometimes including psychiatric reports and diagnostic test results. If this information promises hope, the judge may tend to put the offender on probation. If not, he has other ways of taking individual differences into account. If the offender is a juvenile delinquent and appears before a juvenile court, various types of treatment facilities may be available. (See Chapter 11.)

If the offender is an adult under the law, he is more formally disposed of. We may recall the cartoon of the two middle-aged offenders asking the judge, "Your honor, can't you look at us as middle-aged juvenile delinquents?" (Banay, 1949, p. 57.) Since this possibility does not exist, the alternative to probation for adult offenders usually is prison.

The Dilemma of Parole[5]

In most American jurisdictions, the length of a person's stay in prison is at least in part determined by a parole board. Parole has been defined as "a method of selectively releasing an offender from an institution prior to the completion of his maximum sentence, subject to conditions specified by the paroling authority, a method whereby society can be protected and the offender can be provided with continuing treatment and supervision in the community" (National Conference, 1957, pp. 65–66).

In theory, parole makes possible the release of a prisoner whenever he is rehabilitated. No person need remain in custody if he has been converted into a respectable, law-abiding citizen. On the other hand, dangerous offenders upon whom treatment may not have made sufficient impact can be retained until their correction is accomplished. When a person is released on parole, his treatment need not be abandoned. He remains under the supervision of a parole officer, who not only has the task of watching over him, but also can provide various types of assistance and support. Such assistance could range from personal counseling and therapy to help in locating a job.

There are many reasons why this theoretical picture does not

5 I am grateful to the Michigan Parole Board, and especially to my late friend, A. Ross Pascoe, for many opportunities to observe parole in practice and to contemplate its potential.

conform to practice. One major reason is that it presupposes that effective "treatment" does occur in prisons. As Chapter 13 shows, this assumption is unjustified. In fact, there is reason to suspect that prison routine is not only sterile and uncomfortable, but frequently stultifying.

Penal institutions today range from chain gangs and prison camps in which inmates are maintained in pitifully subhuman condition — to small, minimum security intensive treatment settings like the Michigan camps for youthful offenders described in Chapter 14. The *average* prison lies somewhere in between. It tends to be an institution which officially subscribes to the practice of rehabilitation and *claims* to provide treatment, but does nothing of the sort. One former inmate relates:

As I sat in my cell, year after year, reading the articles, books and speeches in which penologists were enunciating this [rehabilitation] doctrine, I waited eagerly for some sign of change in the actual administration of the prison. But nothing happend. I waited in vain.

For I am obliged to record the fact that, during the years I spent in the state prisons of New York and Massachusetts, not a single attempt was ever made to reform me, and that I did not see a single attempt officially to reform criminals as an aim of prison administrative policy. [Nelson, 1933, p. 43.]

If no treatment at all is provided, the best time to release a person becomes arbitrary, unless aging or discipline mellows him or he *spontaneously* changes for the better.

Another factor that may work against parole is the sentence. Lenient sentencing, or the habit of letting people plead guilty to relatively minor offenses, may result in periods of confinement too short for observation or for treatment. If the minimum sentence is long and close to the maximum, on the other hand, it may leave no time for the person to be paroled.

Parole authorities are also subjected to many pressures. The public urges caution. When a paroled offender commits a crime, the officials who released him stand accused. (For many years, the *Chicago Daily Tribune* sported the slogan "Abolish Parole!") While the public and press demand the retention of prisoners, the wardens of overcrowded institutions urge liberal release policies. Parole boards are sensitive to both these pressures. In some states, they respond to one and they release no one; in others, they grant releases freely. In neither case is the cause of rehabilitation served.

Clearly, the presence of treatment-oriented features in the correctional process is useless if other parts of the process lag behind.

TWO TRENDS IN CORRECTION

Several of the following chapters implicitly or explicitly raise questions about current practices in treating offenders and point to directions for future developments.

One of the most obvious trends in the correctional field is the tendency to give younger offenders the benefit of innovations and experimental programs. Parole was first established in the United States at the Elmira Reformatory in New York, an institution for juveniles. The Juvenile Court was a radical departure from formal criminal trial procedures. The first such court (Chicago, 1899) had jurisdiction over children up to 16 years of age. For a discussion of the present-day juvenile court, see Chapter 11.

More recently the youthful offender (the offender in his late teens and early twenties) has become the object of special attention. In England, for instance, the Borstal System was established around 1910. Institutions comprised in this system provided vocational training of various sorts, and generally tried to get away from the extreme regimentation of prison life. They attempted "to study the individual lad, to discover his trend and his possibility, and to infect him with some idea of life which will germinate and produce character, controlling desire and shaping conduct to some more glorious end other than mere satisfaction or acquisition" (cit. Fry, 1946, p. 157).

In the United States, interest in the youthful offender dates mainly to the Youth Authority Corrections Act drafted by the American Law Institute (1940). The purpose of this model legislation, as stated in its very first paragraph, was "to protect society more effectively by substituting for retributive punishment methods of training and treatment directed toward the correction and rehabilitation of young persons found guilty of violation of law." This objective has led to many interesting experiments, including the Michigan program described in Chapter 14.[6]

The logic of treating the youngest offenders first is inescapable. There is almost universal agreement by crime experts of every persuasion that the roots of criminal behavior are embedded very early in life. If past experience piles up around the offender in cumulative

---

[6] In addition to official efforts on behalf of young offenders, many private ventures could be mentioned. Probably the most famous early experiment is the one carried out at the Hollabrunn Institute by Aichhorn (1955).

fashion, early roots — fertilized by the slum, the prison, the dishonest society, or the unhappy home — can soon grow too large to unearth. The more promptly a remedial environment is brought to bear, the better the chance of preventing adult criminality, and the less strenuous the task. Early diagnosis and treatment must thus be one of the prime objects in correction.

Another current aim in correction is to define "treatment" very broadly. The sophisticated layman frequently steps in — in place of the psychiatrist, the psychologist, or the social worker — as a correctional therapist. (See Fenton, 1958.) One obvious reason for this liberal approach is the magnitude of the task and the scarcity of professional help. A more convincing reason is that just as it does not take professional personnel to engender antisocial tendencies, it does not require professional persons to undo the damage. The unhealthy environment which promotes delinquency is offset with a restituting environment. This environment should consist of people who can be perceived by the offender as a "natural" social group and therefore accepted as such. It must make up for the deficiencies of persons in the offender's past, with acceptance and support provided by sympathetic persons in the present. August Aichhorn anticipated this philosophy when he wrote that "the more the life of an institution conforms to an actual social community the more certain is the social rehabilitation of the child" (Aichhorn, 1955, p. 117).

It has also been argued that since the offender develops as a result of cumulative concentrated pressures, the rehabilitative effort, to be effective, must be equally concentrated and unmitigated. It does not suffice to expose the correctional candidate to short bursts of positive relationships between vast stretches of social vacuums (or worse). *A total, continuous therapeutic community* is needed. (See Chapter 14. See also the discussion of half-way homes for alcoholism in Chapter 16.)

A WORD OF CAUTION

It must not be assumed that the two trends described above constitute avalanches which threaten to engulf the traditional penal system, or are likely to result in wholesale reductions of the criminality rate. Such efforts currently take place on an extremely small scale, and in the context of institutions that act at cross-purposes with them. Moreover, criminal psychology has not yet advanced to the point where offenders can be sorted into meaningful groupings for treatment in separate institutions. We are only beginning to isolate complex types of causal patterns like those described in Chapter 11, and are still groping in our efforts to obtain measures of criminal tendencies, such as are needed to select the best candidates for treatment (see Chapter 10).

Finally, many types of offenders are not easily reached by any presently discovered methods. The offenders discussed in Chapter 12, for instance, are frequently diagnosed as "sociopathic" because they seem unresponsive to all treatment.[7] The drug addict (see Chapter 15) and some alcohol offenders (see Chapter 16) are physically and emotionally dependent on their habits to the point where even intensive efforts to rehabilitate them are notoriously ineffective.

But none of this is the main ground for pessimism about the future of correction. It would still be possible to make tremendous strides with more amenable correctional subjects. Large-scale attempts to rehabilitate offenders, however, encounter strong public and official resistance.

TREATMENT AND THE PUBLIC

Social psychologists concerned with social change have written a great deal on the subject of resistance to change. It is an interesting fact that no matter how urgent or ripe or necessary a reform may be, one can expect some public and official opposition to it. The reasons for this opposition have to be carefully investigated; one cannot convince people to permit change unless one understands why they oppose it.

In the case of opposition to correctional reform, one must remember that, as we have already noted in Chapter 1, many people tend to feel very impatient and intolerant with offenders against the social order. During the last few weeks before Caryl Chessman's execution, Governor Brown of California received telegrams such as "My Daughter Will not Be Safe Until He Is Dead" and "Don't Be Swayed By All Those Bleeding Hearts."[8] In response to outbreaks of juvenile delinquency, public-opinion polls show a heavy majority of the public favoring all kinds of restrictions on teenagers, including the right of teachers to paddle them in schools.[9]

---

[7] Here too, however, as pointed out in page 291, the "therapeutic community" has been tried with success.

[8] *Time*, February 29, 1960.

[9] *Public Opinion News Service*, January 16, 18, 1960.

Rare indeed is the person who can read the details of a cold-blooded crime of violence without catching himself musing about how the culprit would look strung up by his feet over a slow fire. This is an intimate, personal feeling. We are not prone to question it. When we have this feeling we rarely ask ourselves whether anything constructive is gained by compounding violence through retribution.

It is such feelings as these which constitute the backbone of public resistance to correctional reform. People are very likely to argue that crime must be expiated and discouraged through "deserved" punishment. They also tend to maintain that formal treatment programs constitute an open invitation to crime. This argument is based on the implicit premise that luxurious hospitals or playgrounds are the only alternative to prisons. It fails to envisage the lengthy, arduous, intensive process which would in reality be involved. It makes no allowance for the necessary restriction of freedom, and for the required institutional control and supervision.

The argument is also based on the outdated conception of human nature discussed earlier in this chapter. If crime were the result of free conscious resolutions based on calculations of personal profit, the point might be well taken. But such explanations, and the penal systems based on them, have failed us. This failure has not received enough publicity.

The fact that sound rehabilitation does involve fairness, sympathy, consideration, and understanding should not of itself arouse opposition. It might offend punitive desires, but it could meet with the support of the fellow feeling, the capacity for empathy (especially with the underdog) that we all possess. The same surge of indignation that resulted in the abolition of torture and the whipping post could be summoned to eradicate the less dramatic inhumanity of the large walled prison. This again, however, requires publicity.

It is obvious that the press and other mass media of communication can affect people's attitudes by the types of coverage they give to crime and correction. It has been argued that newspapers have tended to excessively emphasize sensational descriptive detail instead of placing the burden, as they could, on an understanding of the background and personality of offenders (Kobre, 1957).

Instead of waiting for prison riots to expose destructive features of the penal system, mass media could communicate a feeling for life within institutions on a day-to-day basis. The frustrating existence of the predelinquent slum dweller, the lack of opportunities which await the "ex-con," the impersonal fare of courtroom justice could all be brought into the public domain. Such information could easily set the stage for acceptance of reform, especially if intimate portraits of experimental programs in action were also provided.

Depiction of delinquency from the delinquent's point of view might also help provide a basis for national crime prevention on the part of community agencies. The following excerpt from an interview with a former delinquent, published in *The New Yorker*, illustrates this possibility:

"To tell the truth, I can't say *any* teachers ever helped me in *nothing*," he replied. "I used to get the feeling they don't *want* nobody to learn. You know how it is—after you've read yourself blue, they give you a test to show how you never understood. Then you flunk, and they start the rigmarole over. The way things is, a guy can go to school for the rest of his lifetime and never learn enough to keep him awake. It's like a guy I used to have for a friend—ten years out of school, and he couldn't sign his name. That's school for you." (Harris, 1957.)

This glimpse of one delinquent's unsatisfactory school experiences provides an indication of the fact that schools could play an important role in helping to prevent delinquency, which they now sometimes stimulate. Public awareness of the problem could generate pressures to this end.

One could cite many instances of journalists, radio commentators, film producers, and other practitioners of mass communication who have constructively reported on problems in the area of crime and correction. An arbitrarily chosen illustration is a series of articles written by Harrison Salisbury for *The New York Times* about juvenile gangs in New York City (Salisbury, 1958). Salisbury exposed many facets of the gang problem, including the subtle relationship between the adult community and the juvenile gang. John B. Martin also illustrates the point. His articles about the Jackson prison riot, later collected in book form, provide an insightful picture of the prison problem (Martin, 1954).

TREATMENT AND VESTED INTEREST

Another source of opposition to reform are public officials. Legislators and others who control the allocation of expenditures tend to favor activities which are more visible to their constituents — and of more concern to them — than are prisons. Officials in the system at times defend their own actions as almost God-given in their unimprovable perfection. Any proposed innovation is liable to be seen by some as naïve and unrealistic; by others, as directed against them personally.

Officials also sometimes confuse what they ought to be doing with what they actually do. Wardens who rule over purely custodial establishments may talk at correctional meetings about the most advanced rehabilitation techniques, thus conveying the impression that their charges reside in a hospital atmoshere. In a recent trip to a woman's prison the writer was regaled with a lecture about the unlimited educational opportunities at the insitution. The "educational opportunities" of the average inmate turned out to be a forty-hour week of pushing carts or stacking sheets in a giant laundry.

These types of apologetics and self-deceptions can again be neutralized by publicity. Reporters need to investigate actual practices rather than to publish handouts, tables of organization, or other canned publicity. On the other hand, they cannot afford to make unsubstantiated charges which might have been corrected by checking both sides of a story. The line between yellow journalism and reform journalism is a narrow one and must be kept in mind, since reform journalism is an effective tool of change, whereas yellow journalism can retard progress. What is needed from the media of communication is a sympathetic portrayal of the human problems in correctional settings.

EPILOGUE

Not all change is constructive change. In considering new programs for the treatment of offenders we must take care to avoid magic solutions or straw grasping. We must beware of the temptation to do *anything* for the sake of doing *something*. Theories should be sound. Implementation should be preceded by pilot projects, evaluations, and research. *However, if the choice is between lethargy and haste, the latter may prove to be the lesser evil.* Wherever fellow human beings are maintained in degradation, humiliation, and suspended animation, the overready acceptance of hope is preferable to the cynical defense of tradition.

References

Aichhorn, A. *Wayward youth*. New York: Meridian Books, 1955.

American Law Institute. *Youth Correction Authority Act official draft.* Philadelphia: The Institute, 1940.

Banay, R. S. The psychopathic adolescent offender. In *Current approaches to delinquency, Yearbook*. New York: National Probation and Parole Ass., 1949.

Barnes, M. E. *The story of punishment*. Boston: Stratford Co., 1930.

Beccaria, Cesare Bonesana, màrchese di. *An essay on crimes and punishment*. Philadelphia: Philip H. Nicklin, 1819.

Bentham, J. *An introduction to the principles of morals and legislation*. Oxford: The Clarendon Press, 1907.

Fenton, H. *An introduction to group counseling*. New York: American Correctional Ass., 1958.

Ferri, E. *The positive school of criminology*. Chicago: Charles H. Kerr & Co., 1910.

Fink, A. E. *Causes of crime*. Philadelphia: Univer. of Pennsylvania Press, 1938.

Fry, Margery. The Borstal System. In *Penal Reform in England*. (English Studies in Criminal Science, Vol. I.) London: Macmillan, 1946.

Glueck, Sheldon, & Glueck, Eleanor T. *Unraveling juvenile delinquency*. New York: Commonwealth Fund, 1937, 1950.

Glueck, Sheldon, & Glueck, Eleanor T. *Physique and delinquency*. New York: Harper, 1956.

Goring, C. The English Convict: A statistical study. London: His Majesty's Stationery Office, 1913.

Harris, E. They can be different than they ever knew. *The New Yorker*, September 7, 1957.

Healy, W. *The individual delinquent*. Boston: Little, Brown, 1915.

Hooton, Earnest A. *Crime and the man*. Cambridge, Mass.: Harvard Univer. Press, 1939.

Kobre, S. *Behind shocking crime headlines*. Tallahassee: Florida State Univer. Press, 1957.

Lawrence, J. *A history of capital punishment*. London: Low, Marston, 1928.

Lombroso, C. *Criminal man*. New York: Knickerbocker Press, 1911. (a)

Lombroso, C. *Crime: Its causes and remedies*. Boston: Little, Brown, 1911. (b)

Lynd, R. S. *Knowledge for what?* Princeton, N. J.: Princeton Univer. Press, 1946.

Martin, J. B. *Break down the walls*. New York: Ballantine Books, 1954.

National Conference on Parole. *Parole in principle and practice*. New York: National Probation and Parole Ass., 1957.

Nelson, V. F. *Prison days and nights*. Boston: Little, Brown, 1933.

Salisbury, H. E. The shook-up generation. *The New York Times*, March 24–30, 1958.

Sheldon, W. H. *Varieties of delinquent youth*. New York: Harper, 1949.

Waite, J. B. *The prevention of Crime*. Ann Arbor: Univer. of Michigan Press, 1943.

Wigmore, J. H. *A kaleidoscope of justice*. Washington, D. C.: Washington Law Book Co., 1941.

HANS TOCH
JACOB GOLDSTEIN

9 The Development of Criminal Predispositions

Every crime expert is occasionally asked questions such as — "How do people become criminals?" or "What *really* causes crime?" This is the type of inquiry to which no ready replies are available. As Vold (1958) states the case, "There is no entirely adequate or generally accepted theory of criminal behavior" (p. 305). Another authority (Cantor, 1932) puts it this way: "It may be critically maintained that not one single generalization has been formulated on the basis of fact in terms of which the tendency to commit certain crimes can be predicted or the conditions generating them controlled" (pp. 68–69). Dressler (1959) characterizes the situation rather amusingly as follows:

But surely there *are* experts who know what causes crime and delinquency? If so, they do not agree in their findings. Here, according to testimony given before legislative committees between 1954 and 1958 by presumed experts, are causes of delinquency: Too much corporal punishment; not enough corporal punishment; underprivilege; overprivilege; too little familial affection; too much familial affection; absence of recreational facilities; too much leisure time; lack of education; over-education; tough police; lenient police; feeble-mindedness; intellectual brilliance; neglectful parents; oversolicitous parents. Some authorities testified that comic books incited to delinquency; others, that they had no demonstrable effect upon children. A California Assembly subcommittee heard a Stanford University professor of law say that it is not known whether sex deviates become such through reading pornographic literature or whether they read the literature because they have psychological problems. At the same hearing, a minister argued that sex-mad magazines are creating criminals faster than jails can be built.

Broken homes were adduced before investigative bodies as causal factors, while testimony to the contrary was also introduced. Use of narcotics or alcoholic beverages was advanced as a potent influence at the same time that other witnesses asserted they accounted for but little delinquency.

Other causes which had "yea" and "nay" advocates were: Biological inferiority; modern advertising; pay-as-you-go plans that divert a disproportionate share of the family income to keeping up with the neighbors; the doctrine of easy money; our materialistic culture; the credo of success; and the American cultural value of resistance to authority of any kind." [Pp. 85–86.]

For some crime experts, these conflicting explanations can still add up to a description of the causes of crime. Thus Abrahamsen (1952) suggests as two basic "laws" of crime causation: (1) "A multiplicity of causative factors which vary qualitatively and quantitatively go into the making of criminal behavior"; and (2) "Since these causative factors differ from case to case of criminal activity, there can be no one rule given as to its causes. The causation of criminal behavior is a matter of relativity" (p. 53). Although to some extent this is obviously true, the questions arise, How relative is relativity? Is there anything we *can* say about how criminal behavior arises? In this chapter, we shall briefly review some of the things people have in fact said. We shall also worry a bit about their right to say anything at all.

THE NATURE OF "CRIME"

When we ask how people become criminals, we must first assume that we know what we mean by "criminals." If we take a "legalistic" viewpoint, this question presents no problem: A criminal is a person who violates the criminal code in the jurisdiction under which he lives. Thus a "criminal" in Massachusetts is a person who breaks a law of Massachusetts, or who violates a federal law. He may in fact do both, as when he robs a bank. One problem which immediately arises with this definition is that the same person, committing the same act, might be a "criminal" in Massachusetts, but not in New Hampshire. Another problem is that the bulk of the population of Massachusetts would be "criminals." Any person playing cards for money, for instance (and this form of social sport is not unknown in Boston) violates a Massachusetts statute. Massachusetts, like other states, also forbids sexual behavior which is freely indulged in by local residents (Kinsey, Pomeroy, and Martin, 1948). An interesting fact cited by Sellin (1938) is that in one part of Mexico 73 percent of the marriages are clearly "criminal" under the law (p. 22). Similarly, in the American South and among southern migrants in the North, it is also not uncommon to see family arrangements which the law would clearly regard as bigamous. Such contrasts between laws and practices are cited by sociologists and psychologists who would prefer to define "crime" as behavior which is antisocial, that is to say, directed against the interests of society at large; or as a violation of the moral standards of the group. Anthropologists also like to define crime in terms of violation of moral standards, because this definition is applicable to primitive communities which have no written code.

Whichever the definition of crime, a practical problem comes up when we try to locate the people we have defined as criminals, so that we can study them. Even if we accept the legal definition, we have limited access to lawbreakers who are not apprehended. And there are many reasons for suspecting that the offenders we capture cannot adequately speak for their colleagues at large. Psychoanalysts, for instance, have pointed to an unconscious "wish for punishment" as one of the motivating factors in crime (Reik, 1945). They cite example after example of illegal acts which seem designed to invite attention to the "guilty" party. Police officers are frequently puzzled by "bad check artists" who carefully endorse checks with their correct name and address. If there is an unconscious wish for punishment, it would be excessively represented (by its very nature) among culprits who "get caught." This would increase the relative proportion of people with emotional difficulties among our prison population, compared to criminals at large.

Intelligence may also be a factor which is related to whether an offender is likely to avoid discovery. An examination of available culprits could therefore give the mistaken impression that the "average criminal" is not very bright (a view which was widely held until fairly recently).

We might also get a false picture of the prevalence of certain *offenses*. Some acts (like exhibitionism, for instance) lead to apprehension in almost every case. Others involve relatively little risk of capture. Similarly a person who violates repeatedly is more likely to be captured than the "one shot" criminal, and thus it might falsely appear as if every offender was a chronic recidivist.

Finally, the strong biases of the law (already discussed in Chapter 1) must be taken into account. As Shakespeare remarked in *King Lear*

> "Robes and furred gowns hide all. Plate sin with gold,
> And the strong lance of justice hurtless breaks;
> Arm it in rags, a pigmy's straw does pierce it." [IV, 6.]

A study of captured offenders enhances the apparent prevalence of crime among lower socioeconomic groups. It also defines as "criminals" any people toward whom the arm of the law exercises special attention at any given time.

If we are to study "criminals" we also have the problem of locating a group of "noncriminals" with whom to compare them. This turns out to be more difficult than it looks. Several studies have shown that the average "respectable" citizen is far from law-abiding. One survey of 1,700 people, for instance, indicated that the typical middle-class male has managed some 18 adult offenses (Wallerstein and Wyle, 1947). An informal survey of a class of police officer candidates credited them with a public debt of 2½ years apiece.[1] Whom are we to use as a "control group" to study imprisoned law breakers? Great caution must obviously be exercised in contrasting those of us who are in prison with those of us who are not.

SPECIFIC OR GENERAL CAUSATION?

The next problem we must face is whether it is possible to find principles which shed light on *all* crime, or if not, what groupings of criminals are to be explained.

It has already been noted that the nature of the crime does not give us very much information about the offender. It makes little sense to speak of the psychology of *the* burglar or *the* murderer or *the* juvenile delinquent. Groupings within crime categories, however, have been very successfully discussed. Psychiatrists, for instance, have written many case studies of certain types of psychotic murderers; Chapter 11 in this volume discusses various meaningful groupings of juvenile delinquents, such as gang boys and aggressive nonsocialized delinquents; in Chapter 17 we shall see that some sex offenders are also emotionally ill, whereas others are not.

The same categories of offenders may sometimes be sensibly grouped in different ways. Thus, we can discuss alcohol offenders (Chapter 16) in terms of whether or not they are addicted to alcohol, or in terms of the drinking groups to which they belong. The point is that different sortings can lead us to different types of explanations. If we discuss alcohol offenders in terms of their addiction or nonaddiction, for instance, we may be led to place emphasis on physiological factors; if we look at the group memberships of alco-

---

[1] We are indebted to Robert Scott for this information.

holics, we may emerge from our efforts with a discussion of the role of socioeconomic class.

One problem with sorting people within categories of offenses is that we are likely to end up with groupings which may make it more difficult to discover psychological characteristics which cut across offense categories. "Psychopathic personalities," for instance, as discussed in Chapter 12, could not be diagnosed. Instead, we should talk about "psychopathic confidence men" or "psychopathic thieves." Similarly, if traits like "aggressivity" or "impulsivity" were fairly universal among people who commit crimes, this could not be discovered as long as one worked within types of crime. Neither would one ever be able to arrive at measures on the basis of which we could predict delinquency, such as are discussed in Chapter 10.

It thus becomes desirable to tackle the problem of crime both in terms of specific "types" of offenders (with whom we can work closely and whom we can try to understand intensively) and in terms of fairly broad characteristics of offenders in general. If the latter seems difficult to justify, it may help to recall our definition of crime: we can remember that however much crimes vary in detail, they do involve a violation of law or of the informal rules of society (depending on which definition one prefers). One can therefore assume that people who violate such rules — and who do so at the risk of being punished if they are discovered — might tend to be somewhat different in their personality or make-up from people who take more trouble to conform to the rules. At least, such has for many centuries been the fond hope of the legions of social scientists of every persuasion who have been concerned with the problem of crime causation.

THEORIES OF CRIMINAL PREDESTINATION

In the preceding chapter we traced the origins of criminal psychology to the Positive School of Criminology headed by Cesare Lombroso. It was this group of scholars who firmly maintained that treatment of criminal behavior must be based on data about the psychology of the offender. Personal characteristics of the criminal, rather than the nature of his crime, were seen to be the relevant facts.

Another reason why Lombroso could be regarded as a progenitor of modern psychological views of crime is his emphasis on crime *causation*. In the days when the free-will conception was prevalent, the question, How do people become criminals? seemed silly. It seemed obvious that those who transgressed against the moral code *chose* to do so, and that nothing lay behind their choice except spontaneous perversity. Criminals were seen to have a criminal *disposition*, and the question of *pre*dispositions never came up. The only exception to this rule was the conception of mitigating circumstances, such as when a person was possessed by devils (in medieval times), or if he was clearly insane or incompetent (in the days of classical criminology).

In his philosophy of crime causation, Lombroso was a strict determinist. He described criminal behavior as a "natural phenomenon" which he felt was "as necessary as birth, death, or conception" (1911b, p. 377). For Lombroso the most prevalent criminal was the born criminal. Such a person, said Lombroso, could be identified by physical characteristics or "stigmata": an asymmetrical face, unusually large or small ears, a low, receding forehead, and prominent eyebrows, jawbones, and cheekbones. The fact that the long list of Lombroso's physical stigmata calls to mind the image of lower animals is not an accident. Influenced by evolution, Lombroso regarded these features as "atavistic," which means "inherited from early ancestors." Lombroso conceived of his born criminal as an individual who had retained characteristics of his prehuman relatives, with uttter disregard for evolutionary developments in the interim.

Physiological and psychological stigmata were also listed by Lombroso as "atavistic" characteristics. Among these were insensibility to pain; sharp vision; the ability to recover quickly from wounds; a great resemblance between the sexes; laziness; a complete lack of shame, honor, remorse, and pity; recklessness; excitability; a passion for gambling and alcoholic drinks; vanity, and a special conception of God. There were also habits, such as tattooing; an excessive use of gestures; and an addiction to picturesque language (Lombroso, 1911a, 1911b). Lombroso saw a substantial area of overlap between the born criminal and the epileptic, and regarded epilepsy as an important cause of crime.

Although Lombroso described criminal types other than his born criminal, and although he discussed (especially in his later writings) many causes of crime, his emphasis always remained on biological causation: "The study of crime does not lessen the fatal influence to be assigned to the organic factor, which certainly amounts to 35% and possibly even 40%; the so-called causes of crime being often only the last determinants while the great strength of congenital impulses remains the ultimate cause" (1911b, p. 376).

Whichever the combination (it varies markedly among Lombroso's followers), criminal behavior was seen as completely predetermined. This is a general characteristic of the theories of criminal behavior which was current in the late nineteenth century and early twentieth century. It is even shared by investigators who were otherwise completely opposed to each other. Thus Goring (1913), whose sophisticated statistical study of English convicts was intended to demonstrate that Lombroso's "stigmata" were not widely evident in prisons, simultaneously maintained that crime was almost entirely a product of heredity.

The most famous exponent of the view that crime is a result of heredity is probably Robert Dugdale, who in 1877 published his study of the Juke family. In the course of an inspection tour of county jails in New York State, Dugdale had come upon six members of this family:

These six persons belong to a long lineage, reaching back to the early colonists, and had intermarried so slightly with the emigrant population of the old world that they may be called a strictly American family. They had lived in the same locality for generations, and were so despised by the reputable community that their family name *had come to be used generically as a term of reproach.*

That this was deserved became manifest on slight inquiry. It was found that out of twenty-nine males, in ages ranging from fifteen to seventy-five, the immediate blood relations of these six persons, seventeen of them were criminals, or fifty-eight per cent; while fifteen were convicted of some degree of offense, and received seventy-one years of sentence. ... The crimes and misdemeanors they committed were assault and battery, assault with intent to kill, murder, attempt at rape, petit larceny, grand larceny, burglary, forgery, cruelty to animals. With these facts in hand, it was thought wise to extend the investigation to other branches of the family, and explore it more thoroughly. [Dugdale, 1910, p. 8.]

Dugdale embarked on a careful study of seven generations of Jukes. He found, among the less conventional members of this family, 200 thieves and related criminals, 280 beggars, and 90 prostitutes. In 75 years, the family had cost the state an estimated $1,300,-000. Dugdale assumed that the generous prevalence of criminality in the ranks of the Jukes could only be interpreted as a function of heredity. He recognized "environment" as a secondary, contributing factor, which works in the same direction as heredity. For instance, he describes the living conditions of the Jukes as a contributing cause of their high illegitimacy rate:

They lived in log or stone houses similar to slave-hovels, all ages, sexes, relations and strangers "bunking" indiscriminately. One form of this bunking has been described to me. During the winter the inmates lie on the floor strewn with straw or rushes like so many radii to the hearth, the embers of the fire forming a center towards which their feet focus for warmth. This proximity, where not producing illicit relations, must often have evolved an atmosphere of suggestiveness fatal to habits of chastity.... Sometimes I found an overcrowding so close it suggested that these dwellings were the country equivalents of city tenement houses. Domesticity is impossible. The older girls, finding no privacy within a home overrun with younger brothers and sisters, purchase privacy at the risk of prudence, and the night rambles through woods and tangles end, too often, in illegitimate offspring. [Pp. 13-14.]

Another line of evidence which was followed by the advocates of hereditary predetermination was the study of twins. These studies were intended to show that if one member of a pair of identical twins embarked on a criminal career, the other member of the pair was *predestined* to do likewise. The best known of these studies — that of the German physiologist Johannes Lange — is revealingly entitled *Crime and Destiny* (1930).

Heredity was also seen by many as exercising its predestination indirectly. Thus several early studies (for example, Goddard, 1914) purported to demonstrate that criminality was a result of feeblemindedness. The same claim was made for "imbalance" of the endoctrine glands (Schlapp and Smith, 1928). "Moral insanity," the grandparent of the modern concept of psychopathic personality (see Chapter 12), was regarded as an inherited deficiency. Alcoholism was similarly cited.

The proponents of constitutional, hereditary, or biological causes of crime did not have a monopoly on the view that crime was an inescapable consequence of powerful forces. The early advocates of environmental or social causation talked of crime in a similar fashion. Quetelet, who is considered to be the first "social criminologist," formulated a "thermic law of delinquency," according to which crimes of blood would result from southern climes whereas crimes against property would be produced in the North. "Society prepares crime," he stated; "the criminal becomes its executive" (cit. Quiros, 1912, p. 19). Kropotkin, the author of a book on prisons published in 1890, went even further: "Take the average temperature of the month, and multiply it by 7; then, add the average humidity, multiply again by 2, and you will obtain the number of homicides that are to be committed during the month" (cit. Quiros, 1912, p. 34). Economic statistics were repeatedly used to support the argument that crime is a function of deprivation or prosperity. One famous study, that of Georg von Mayr, found an increase of one theft per 100,000 persons for every half-penny increase in the price of rye in Bavaria (cit. Sellin, 1937). Hundreds of other authorities, including Charles Dickens, made a strong case for the proposition that proverty is the direct, exclusive, and sufficient cause of crime.

THE MULTIPLE-FACTOR APPROACH

The multiplication of crime experts who steadfastly maintained favorite causes of crime led to the development of theories in which many such factors were added together. A picture emerged of crime resulting from a long list of causes (which varied with the expert), with the provision that the proportions of ingredients for particular criminal concoctions could vary. Thus climate might play a dominant role in stimulating crimes of violence in the South, whereas crimes such as those of Shakespeare's *Richard III*, might be predominantly the result of a degenerate physique:

> Deform'd, unfinish'd, sent before my time
> Into this breathing world, scarce half made up,
> And that so lamely and unfashionable
> That dogs bark at me, as I halt by them;
> Why, I, in this weak piping time of peace,
> Have no delight to pass away the time,
> Unless to see my shadow in the sun
> And descant on mine own deformity;
> And therefore, since I cannot prove a lover,
> To entertain these fair well-spoken days,
> I am determined to prove a villain.... [I, 1.]

The two best-known advocates of the multiple-factor approach were Healy (1915) and Burt (1925). Healy enumerated 138 factors, and found that most delinquents could be adequately described by invoking one major and two minor factors. His most important factor was "mental abnormalities and peculiarities." Burt enumerated 170 factors, which he classified into nine categories.

The multiple-factor approach survives today in the shape of the delinquency prediction tables constructed by Sheldon and Eleanor

Glueck (1930, 1934, 1937, 1950, 1959). These tables list background and personality factors which are presumably related to actions one wishes to predict. The tables vary, because factors which make it likely that a delinquent succeeds on parole may be different from those which ensure that he will behave himself in prison. The usual Glueck table lists five factors, and gives a numerical "score" for each, showing the extent to which it "predicts." (For further detail, and for a discussion of this method, see pages 236 ff. in Chapter 10.)

THE DEVELOPMENT OF CRIMINAL PREDISPOSITIONS

As suggested in Chapter 8, the mainstream of modern criminal psychology can be viewed as a product of two tributaries. The first of these is the psychiatric or psychoanalytic viewpoint; the second consists of various theories which may be described as sociological or social-psychological. Despite differences between these two schools of thought (which have been generously emphasized by them) they have an important common concern. This concern is with the development of criminal predispositions.

According to the dictionary, the word "predisposition" stands for "the condition of being inclined beforehand to do something"; it denotes "a pre-existing favorable state of mind." When referring to diseases, the word suggests that a person is liable to succumb to the first microbe which happens along.

If we adopt these meanings, we would talk about the "development of criminal predispositions" when we deal with the formation of needs or attitudes which render a person susceptible to crime, which "incline him beforehand" to criminal behavior. We would not think about "what causes crime" *directly*, but about how a person acquires psychological characteristics that increase the probability of his behaving in an antisocial fashion.

The Sociological View

Unfairly and simply stated, the sociological view of the development of criminal predispositions is that these predispositions are learned by the developing person from the people who surround him. While some sociologists have been mainly concerned about the people who intimately surround the very young child (its family), other sociologists have taken a broader view; some have shown that every human being with whom the growing person comes into contact, however indirectly, may help to teach him antisocial attitudes, habits, and ways of thinking.

A first step in studying crime in this fashion is to explore various types of human surroundings, with a view to locating the ones which seem to exercise the most pernicious influence. A group of Chicago sociologists followed this procedure in their own city (Park, Burgess, and McKenzie, 1925). An area which seemed to them to be an especially undesirable neighborhood for a growing child was the West Side district immediately south of the Loop. This type of location was characterized by them as a "zone of transition" from residence to business use:

> Here are to be found the slum or semi-slum districts of American cities where play is crime. Boys' gangs, juvenile delinquency, poverty, desertion, bad housing abound. The areas of first immigrant settlement are located here, as Little Sicily, the Ghetto, the Black Belt, from which their most enterprising numbers are seeking to escape. Close along the Central Business District, and following out along the main thoroughfare, are the rooming house districts with their mobile and mixed population of youth and old age, aspiring and defeated individuals, pleasure seeking Bohemians and hard working students, rural Fundamentalists and radical freethinkers, and of law abiding citizens and professional criminals. [Burgess, cit. Shaw, 1929, pp. 19–20.]

In 1921, a delinquency expert named Clifford Shaw set about the task of carefully pinpointing the residence of 100,000 Chicago school truants, juvenile delinquents, and adult offenders. He published the results of his labors in a volume entitled *Delinquency Areas* (1929), which is today considered a classic, although some of the findings are controversial. Shaw found that his offenders were "largely concentrated in certain areas adjacent to the business districts and the large industrial centers." He concluded that "since delinquents are largely concentrated in these characteristic areas, it may be assumed that delinquent behavior is very closely related to certain community situations which arise in the process of city growth" (p. 204). Specifically, Shaw suggested that the *disintegration* of community life in the zone of transition creates "criminal patterns" which come to "shape the attitudes and behavior of persons living in the area. Thus the section becomes an area of delinquency" (p. 206).

How is this delinquency taught? Shaw illustrates the process in a group of case studies published under the heading *Brothers in Crime* (1938). The studies center about five brothers who grow into delinquents on the shores of the Chicago River. According to Shaw, delinquency for these youngsters started as a game played with other children in similar circumstances. Rather than go to school, the brothers and their friends would browse through department stores in the Loop, stealing inconsequentials. Such early influences were reinforced by the teachings of all manner of people with whom the boys came in contact later in life. The family influence, which might have counteracted these teachings, was too weak to be effective. The family was far from close, and no affection or loyalty was lost in its bosom. The parents had neither the time nor the desire to exercise control. Thus, these five "careers in delinquency, from the first simple acts of stealing to the more serious crimes which occurred in later years, represent a gradual process of informal training, education, habituation and sophistication in the process of stealing" (p. 350).

Many students of crime, besides Shaw, have emphasized the crucial role of the gang as an "antisocializing" agent. Survey studies, such as Thrasher's *The Gang* (1936) and Whyte's *Street Corner Society* (1943), have described these highly complex organizations in great detail. Several theories have been developed to explain why these play groups exist, why they take the form they do, and how they go about the business of training delinquents.

One of these theories, formulated by Albert Cohen in *The Delinquent Boys* (1955), stresses that an obvious characteristic of the gang "subculture" is its opposition to some of the dominant values of "respectable" adult society. This "negativistic" attitude which permeates the gang finds expression in malicious delinquent behavior, such as deliberate destruction of property. Stealing, for instance, is frequently combined with vandalism, as in the following incident:

"We would get some milk bottles in front of the grocery store and break them in somebody's hallway. Then we would break windows or get some garbage cans and throw them down someone's front stairs. After doing all this dirty work and running through alleys and yards, we'd go over to a grocery store. There, some of the boys would hide in a hallway while I would get a basket of grapes. When the man came after me, the boys would jump out of their places and each grab a basket of grapes." [Cit. Cohen, 1955, p. 29.]

Cohen assumes that this type of conduct represents an expression of protest. The protest is directed against a society which keeps working-class children and their parents in underprivileged circumstances. Other characteristics of gangs seem to Cohen to be designed to compensate the slum boy for opportunities he does not find elsewhere.

Cohen thus assumes that society at large plays a negative role in the process of "teaching" delinquency. Others (like Shaw) have regarded this assumption as unnecessary. They have argued that criminal attitudes and criminal behavior are simply learned from intimate associates, as are other types of attitude or conduct. Just because we view criminality as antisocial does not mean that it is learned to *spite* us, or even that our presence is considered. Vold (1958), who seems to hold this view, puts it this way: "The acquiring of attitudes favorable to crime — and the learning of criminal behavior patterns — is just as 'normal' a psychological process (is, in fact, the very same psychological process) as that of learning the way of life approved of by law-abiding society" (pp. 186-87).

Occupying a middle ground between the social protest theory and the simple learning theory is the type of conception typified by Sutherland's well-known principle of "differential association." According to this view, the developing criminal is exposed to a variety of groups, some of which are procriminal, while others are anticriminal or neutral. The criminal learns his criminality from *all* his associations, not merely from broken homes and delinquent gangs. Some of his teachers may never even have visited a "delinquency area," or seen a member of a juvenile gang. Sutherland's professional thief (1937) for instance, "is part of the underworld and in certain respects is segregated from the rest of society" (p. 206). He remains aloof from his neighbors because he does not care to publicize his vocation; he is on good personal terms with other thieves so as to exchange services, technical data, and gossip with them — he also derives his professional status and identity from this membership; he "cultivates" the clients from whom he eventually steals; he has noncriminal friends who accept him as a person, although they may know him as a thief; he has a cooperative arrangement with dishonest politicians; finally, he is a full-fledged member of society at large. In fact, "his interest in money and in the things money will buy and his efforts to secure 'easy money' fit nicely into the pattern of modern life" (p. 209). Learning of crime occurs in every one of these relationships, including those with noncriminals. "White collar" criminality provides examples of how crime can develop among the most favored segments of society, where it is perpetuated in the midst of wealth and respectability (Sutherland, 1956).

More than any other group, the family has been talked about as the place where criminal predispositions develop. Much has been made of the large incidence of broken homes in the backgrounds of juvenile delinquents. From the sociological viewpoint, an important effect of the broken home is to limit supervision of the child, enabling it to fall freely into the arms of the gang. The family has also been suspected of directly transmitting antisocial attitudes. Among others, the Gluecks (1930) have presented data suggesting that well over 80 percent of all offenders are exposed to delinquents at home.

It is fair to say that in the literature today, the broken home is no longer viewed as the key to crime. The assumption that the family teaches crime has also lost much of its popularity. The average statistical breakdown (e.g., Michigan, 1959) suggests that nine of ten offenders do not have the benefit of delinquent relatives; when such a relative does turn up, he usually is a person of the same generation as the offender's.

It would be foolhardy to infer from this that the family is not involved in the development of criminal predisposition. To explore the family's most important effects we have to enter the domain of the psychological or psychiatric clinic.

The Psychoanalytic View

According to Wertham (1941), Freud once remarked after reading an analysis of a murder case, "Now we know everything — except why the murder was actually committed" (p. 193). Those who approach criminal predispositions from a psychoanalytic viewpoint frequently accuse their sociological colleagues of the very same type of omission.

Why don't all slum dwellers, or all children from broken homes, or all gang members eventually land in prison? How can respectable citizens as well as seasoned convicts emerge from the same families? How can social influences be invoked to explain the misdeeds of people from law-abiding backgrounds? Such are the questions psychoanalysts and psychiatrists ask in order to make the point that sociological theory requires supplementation.

Psychoanalysts assume that the essential predispositions to crime are *not* learned attitudes and skills, but deep-seated feelings and conflicts which persist from early childhood. The people who are responsible for the development of such predispositions are the parents. In the words of Abrahamsen (1952), "we may say that the causes of a child's delinquent behavior may be traced to his parents, particularly to his mother's emotional attitude toward his early instinctual manifestations" (p. 27).

Probably the most dramatic indictment on record of parents who cripple their children emotionally is Aichhorn's classic *Wayward Youth* (1955), first published in 1925. This book describes the warm, human attempt by a small group of dedicated people to rehabilitate delinquent children of the unsocialized aggressive variety (see pages 245 ff. in Chapter 11). The children involved in this experiment were a most unpleasant sort, as illustrated by the following excerpt:

> We can differentiate two kinds of hate reaction. One type hates the environment quite openly, without any attempt at concealment. This hate varies in quantity from a mere intimation to open repudiation and deadly hate. When we group all these reactions together we see their similarity.
>
> The second hate type appears less often. It is concealed and is harder to recognize. This group is obliging to the point of insistence, friendly to a degree of unpleasant intimacy, self-conscious to the point of arrogance. They are liars and intriguers; they tyrannize over their comrades in secret. All that they do and say becomes understandable when we recognize their hatred.

Aichhorn's explanation leads us to the parents:

> I have always found that this hate is a reaction to an unsatisfied need for love. In many cases it is objectively justified; in others it arises only from the child's subjective feeling. *In the first type, the hate is the result of too little love, a repudiation by the parents. In the second, the hate comes from another source; the parents, disappointed in each other, expend too much libido on the child.* The child feels that this love is not given to him for his own sake and reacts to it by becoming dissocial. Each group expresses its hate in a characteristic way: Open insubordination to the point of brutality in one group; underhanded intrigue to cowardly murder in the other. [Pp. 127–28; italics added.]

The main criminal predisposition which psychoanalysts describe is the inability to control impulses: "The criminal carries out in his actions his natural unbridled instinctual drives; he acts as the child would act if it only could" (Alexander and Staub, 1956, p. 30); "he is not able to give up immediate pleasure in favor of later pleasure" (Aichhorn, 1955, p. 1952).

Thus, according to psychoanalytic theory, the criminal does not differ from the noncriminal in his basic make-up. We are all born with antisocial needs which, if freely followed, would embark us on horrendous criminal careers. In early childhood, however, as a result of parental training, most of us develop effective checks for these impulses, whereas the potential criminal does not. In somewhat more technical language, he has a weak *ego*, or one whose effectiveness is reduced by emotional conflict.

In psychiatric literature one also frequently encounters interpretations of specific features of crimes in terms of their presumed unconscious symbolic significance for the criminal. In mental exercises shared by the analyst and his patient, every detail of the offense can be related to events in the offender's early childhood. If a woman has been murdered, it may be routinely revealed that she acted as a stand-in for the murderer's mother (Lindner, 1955), but a sex reversal is not out of the question. The following excerpt represents the ultimate in permutation:

> In that moment he understood with his feelings why he had stolen all those cars. At the same time, however—and this is more important— *a car in itself had a meaning to him. In a symbolic way it represented his mother.* Since he could not get her, he had to have a substitute, and a car was that substitute. Hence his thrill every time he drove a car; hence his continuous stealing. [Abrahamsen, 1952, p. 23; italics added.]

It would be a serious error to assume that this type of explanation represents the essence of psychiatric thinking about crime.

The Subculture versus the Ego

Illustrations were provided in Chapter 8 to suggest that psychiatry and sociology have tended to concentrate on different types of offenders. At first glance, it might seem as if this possibility could provide the ideal resolution for the controversy between the two schools of thought: psychiatry could explain the Leopolds and Loebs, the psychopathic personalities, the angry young men, the psychotic murderers of noble birth; sociology could regard as her exclusive province the slum-bred juvenile delinquents who follow invariant sequences leading from joyrides to burglaries. One could even speculate about the relative prevalence of the two types of offenders. This possibility is illustrated by the following article from a large prison newspaper, in which a "sociological" offender seems to be contemplating with distaste the prospect of being swamped by his "psychiatric" counterparts. The item, entitled "Young punks gall an 'old pro' yegg," was written by Sidney J. Harris:

> He is an old-fashioned criminal I used to see occasionally when I was a reporter nearly 20 years ago. A quiet round-faced man, he was a first-class burglar and safe-cracker, but otherwise a quiet decent sort of chap.

"I don't know what's got into young fellows these days," he shook his head mournfully as we had a cup of coffee together. "They're monsters, not human beings. I wouldn't spit on the best of them.

"In my day, a thief was a thief. He did his job and went home and tried to enjoy himself the same way other men would. He didn't like violence, he didn't hate anybody, and he wasn't trying to prove anything.

"Now I see these punks all over the streets, and they're enough to make an honest thief's stomach turn. They don't have any brains, and they don't have any heart either. All they can do is hit and shoot and curse.

"With a couple of drinks they'll knock off a cab driver for 10 bucks in change. What do you writing fellows call them—psychopaths?"

"How do you account for the difference?" I asked him.

"Who knows?" he shrugged. "Something has gone out of them. They don't love anything, and they even seem to hate themselves. They don't have families or hobbies, as we used to. They don't even seem to want to be successful—just noticed—and that's the surest way to get caught."

"Then you think they want to get caught?" I suggested.

"Sure," he said. "They want to prove how tough they can be, even walking to the chair. What's the point of 'punishing' punks like that? You've got to straighten out their mental kinks when they're small, or you can't do anything with them at all.

"The old bunch I used to know are mostly dead," he sighed. "Ah, they were fine fellows, some of them, a pleasure to talk with.

"It's a funny age we're living in, when a professional thief can't bring himself to associate with the scum running around these days." [*The Spectator*, January 16, 1959.]

A typology of offenders may prove to be the answer to the controversy between the sociological approach to crime and the psychoanalytic view of it. Cohen (1955) states this point, and enumerates two alternative solutions:

It may be that we are confronted with a false dichotomy, that we are not really forced to choose between two conflicting theories. There is the possibility of two or more "types" of juvenile delinquents, each the result of a different kind of etiology or causal process: one, let us say, predominantly subcultural and another predominantly psychogenic. There is the possibility of subcultural and psychogenic "factors" simultaneously but independently at work in the same personality, each providing a separate and distinct "push" in the direction of delinquency, like two shoulders to the same wheel. However, we are especially interested in a third possibility, namely, that in the majority of cases psychogenic and subcultural factors blend in a single causal process, as pollen and a particular bodily constitution work together to produce hay fever. If this is so, then the task of theory is to determine the ways in which the two kinds of factors mesh or interact. [P. 17.]

What might be required, in other words, is a description that provides a meeting ground between *motivation* and *socialization*.

THE STUDY OF PREDISPOSING
ATTITUDES AND FEELINGS

One way of looking at the etiology of criminal predispositions which bridges the gap between the couch and the slum is to view the offender's developing problems as he himself perceives them. We can study the pressures which the sociologists describe without neglecting personal differences by recognizing that "influence," if it is to be effective, has to be *felt* and translated into personal meanings and needs. The psychiatrist B. Glueck is quoted as having remarked, "a factor cannot become a cause before it is a motive" (cit. Bovet, p. 20). What this means is that neither deprivation, nor lack of supervision, nor the bad advice of playmates nor the harshness of a severe father can produce delinquency directly. These pressures must first be experienced as pressures; they must stimulate resentment, frustration, anger, despair, cynicism or any of the other feelings, attitudes, purposes, and values which predispose toward delinquency.

The study of antisocial feelings and attitudes is compatible with the "sociological" approach because it deals with psychological reactions to the unhappy situations and unsalutary influences which sociologists describe. The "psychiatric" view is also implied: identical pressures may occasion different reactions in people whose emotional "susceptibility" varies because of different experiences in early life.

Crime may be said to occur at the crossroads of adversity and debility. In the words of Banay (1948) it "is a reaction to unenurable internal pressures suffered by the individual" (p. 219). Probably the best evidence for this view is the monumental study of delinquency conducted by William Healy and Augusta Bronner in psychiatric clinics of three large cities. In this study, in which delinquents and nondelinquents within the same families were compared, it was found that delinquency resulted whenever a child felt that it could not carry out its purposes and gain its satisfactions in socially acceptable ways. Delinquency, in other words, was a substitute for positive ways of satisfying needs.

According to Healy and Bronner (1936), a delinquent child tends to be desperate. As one views such a child, one is struck by "the immense amount of discoverable emotional discomfort that clearly has been part of the story of the origins of delinquency" (p. 7). Most of the delinquent youngsters studied by Healy and Bronner differed from their nondelinquent brothers and sisters in that they felt rejected, unloved, thwarted, disturbed, and generally unhappy. Whether in any particular case the parents had actually done anything to provoke this, or whether the feeling was mostly the child's doing, is a question we need not ask. The answer is irrelevant to the practical problem of locating the psychological roots which give birth to the criminal act.

These psychological roots are unique to each offender. Healy and Bronner illustrate this with reference to truancy:

One boy may be avoiding a situation in which he feels inadequate and discouraged; another has developed out of family life antagonism toward all forms of authority—school representing one form; another has such need of recognition that, even though he does not dislike school he truants in order to be a "regular fellow" with his companions; still another is the victim of peculiar anxieties which make the classroom hateful to him. [1936, p. 6.]

Thus we can ask about each offender in turn, What is he trying to accomplish? What do his offenses mean to him? How does he, personally, view his antisocial acts in the context of his own purposes, attitudes, and values? Such questions require individual attention and study of every antisocial person. They mean that "we must individualize each offender, attempt to uncover, from a study of his background, what made this man act this way this time" (Dressler, 1959, p. 101).

The results of this type of inquiry make treatment possible. Of course, we may only rarely be able to solve the offender's problem as he sees it. However, we can frequently change his attitudes or feelings. If we cannot revolutionize the world or undo past damage, we can often convince people to adopt relatively congenial and harmless solutions to even the most heartbreaking dilemmas.

References

Abrahamsen, D. *Who are the guilty?* New York: Grove Press, 1942.

Aichhorn, A. *Wayward youth.* New York: Meridian Books, 1955.

Alexander, F., & Staub, H. *The criminal, the judge and the public.* Glencoe, Ill.: The Free Press, 1956.

Banay, R. S. *Youth in despair.* New York: Coward-McCann, 1948.

Bovet, L. *Psychiatric aspects of juvenile delinquency.* Geneva: World Health Organization, 1951.

Burt, C. *The young delinquent.* New York: Ronald, 1925.

Cantor, N. F. *Crime, criminals and criminal justice.* New York: Holt, Rinehart and Winston, 1932.

Cohen, A. K. *Delinquent boys.* Glencoe, Ill.: The Free Press, 1955.

Dressler, D. *Practice and theory of probation and parole.* New York: Columbia Univer. Press, 1959.

Dugdale, R. *The Jukes.* New York: Putnam, 1910.

Glueck, Sheldon, & Glueck, Eleanor T. *500 criminal careers.* New York: Knopf, 1930.

Glueck, Sheldon, & Glueck, Eleanor T. *One thousand juvenile delinquents.* Cambridge, Mass.: Harvard Univ. Press, 1934.

Glueck, Sheldon, & Glueck, Eleanor T. *Later criminal careers.* New York: Commonwealth Fund, 1937.

Glueck, Sheldon, & Glueck, Eleanor T. *Unraveling juvenile delinquency.* New York: Commonwealth Fund, 1950.

Glueck, Sheldon, & Glueck, Eleanor T. *Predicting delinquency and crime.* Cambridge, Mass.: Harvard Univer. Press, 1959.

Goddard, H. H. *Feeblemandedness: Its causes and consequences.* New York: Macmillan, 1914.

Goring, C. *The English convict: A statistical study.* London: His Majesty's Stationery Office, 1913.

Group for the Advancement of Psychiatry, Committee on Forensic Psychiatry. *Psychiatrically deviated sex offenders.* Report No. 9. Topeka, Kan.: 1949-1950.

Healy, W. *The individual delinquent.* Boston: Little, Brown, 1915.

Healy, W., & Bronner, Augusta. *New lights on delinquency and its treatment.* New Haven: Yale Univer. Press, 1936.

Kinsey, A. C., Pomeroy, W. B., & Martin, C. E. *Sexual behavior of the human male.* Philadelphia: Saunders, 1948.

Lange, J. *Crime and destiny.* New York: C. Boni, 1930.

Lindner, R. Songs my mother taught me. In *The fifty-minute hour.* New York: Holt, Rinehart and Winston, 1955.

Lombroso, C. *Criminal man.* New York: Knickerbocker Press, 1911. (a)

Lombroso, C. *Crime: Its causes and remedies.* Boston: Little, Brown, 1911. (b)

Michigan Department of Corrections. *Who are they?* Pamphlet No. 3. Lansing: 1959.

Park, R. E., Burgess, E. W., & McKenzie, R. D. *The city, the ecological approach to the study of the human community.* Chicago: Univer. of Chicago Press, 1925.

Quiros, C. B. *Modern theories of criminality.* Boston: Little, Brown, 1912.

Reik, T. *The unknown murderer.* New York: Prentice-Hall, 1945.

Schlapp, M. G., & Smith, E. H. *The new criminology.* New York: Liveright, 1928.

Sellin, T. *Research memorandum on crime in the depression*. Bull. No. 27. New York: Social Science Research Council, 1937.

Sellin, T. *Culture conflict and crime*. Bull. No. 41. New York: Social Science Research Council, 1938.

Shaw, C. *Delinquency areas*. Chicago: Univer. of Chicago Press, 1929.

Shaw, C. *Brothers in crime*. Chicago: Univ. of Chicago Press, 1938.

Sutherland, E. H. *The professional thief*. Chicago: Univer. of Chicago Press, 1937.

Sutherland, E. H. *The Sutherland papers*. Bloomington: Indiana University Press, 1956.

Thrasher, F. M. *The gang*. Chicago: Univer. of Chicago Press, 1936.

Vold, G. B. *Theoretical criminology*. New York: Oxford Univer. Press, 1958.

Wallerstein, J. S., & Wyle, C. J. Our law-abiding lawbreakers. *Probation*, 1947, **25**, 107–112.

Wertham, F. *Dark legend*. New York: Duell, Sloan & Pearce, 1941.

Whyte, W. F. *Street corner society*. Chicago: Univer. of Chicago Press, 1943.

10 The Gauging of Criminal Predispositions

If some personalities are more likely to become delinquent than others, we should be able to devise "personality" measures that predict future criminal actions. When we secure measures of traits that contribute to delinquency, we are in an enviable position to combine humanitarianism and economy: we can guide persons away from the criminal life and its attendant misery; and we can reduce our loss to crime and our expenditure in coping with criminals.

One possible application of a prediction instrument is to identify potential offenders before they have become delinquent. Predictive measures, for instance, could be employed in the school system to detect the presence of criminal predispositions in children. Children with such predispositions could then be given special training or treatment.

Measures of delinquent characteristics can also be useful in screening possible offenders from sensitive positions. The military, for instance, may wish to reject recruits who have a high probability of getting into trouble. Banks, law-enforcement agencies, and other establishments which offer special temptations could reduce their difficulties by screening out the criminally predisposed of their candidates for employment. The aim of this screening, of course, should be to guide such persons into positions where temptations are fewer, not to dump potential troublemakers into someone else's lap.

A second use of prediction measures is less obviously practical. The discovery of diagnostic patterns of personality among delinquents should lead to increased insight into the causes of crime. With this increased understanding, prevention programs may shift their emphasis from the prevention of delinquency as such to the elimination of factors that lead to crime. This would involve a shift of interest from coping with criminal personalities to preventing their occurrence. While holding to this possibility, however, we must remember that large-scale cultural changes may be required; these can be produced slowly, if at all.

Measures that predict early misconduct may also be useful for evaluating our treatment of offenders. For example, if we administered a delinquency potential measure before and after a group counseling program in a prison, and found a shift from the criminal to the normal end of the scale, we would have an indication of our program's success.

Such applications rest on the discovery of effective measures; this in turn depends on the validity of the hypothesis that a person's personality can predispose him to criminal activity. From the viewpoint of psychology, the most reasonable position probably is one that hypothesizes a contribution by personality to the aggregate of influences responsible for criminal behavior. The extent of this contribution will limit the degree to which predisposition to crime can be measured by psychological instruments. Had psychologists a well-stocked store of precise measuring instruments, the contribution of personality to criminal behavior could be determined by a few extensive but simple studies. As matters stand, the tools are themselves fallible; they rarely yield precise measurements. For this reason, when we fail to predict delinquency, we cannot say whether the failure occurred because personality is unrelated to delinquency, or whether the instruments used to measure personality were so poor that their use concealed a genuine relationship.

The prediction of delinquent behavior by psychological measures has not been spectacular to date; yet the belief that personality factors contribute to criminal misconduct is repeatedly asserted by experts in the field. Given this state of affairs, we must not overlook the possibility that our psychological instruments are defective. Taken merely as measures of differences among individuals, personality scales must meet certain basic requirements if they are to be trusted. The same requirements apply with equal force to the things we wish to predict. Before turning to predictive devices, therefore, we should consider first how delinquency stands as a variable to be measured.

DELINQUENCY AS A CRITERION

Psychologists use the term "criterion" to describe whatever they attempt to predict. In the present instance, the criterion to be predicted is one based on information regarding delinquent acts of varying seriousness. A criterion of this kind is itself a measure; it may be accurate and precise or inaccurate and vague. When a criterion is precise and accurate — in technical terms, *reliable* and *valid* — it is, in principle, predictable. Should it lack reliability and validity, it is inherently unpredictable. A number of factors related to the criterion of delinquency act to reduce its validity and reliability.

The commonest criterion of delinquency is the dichotomy of "confined versus nonconfined." Individuals in prisons, jails, and reformatories are assumed to be more delinquent than those more fortunate in their place of residence. While this criterion is sensible, it suffers from certain drawbacks so far as prediction is concerned. To begin with, the law-enforcement process is not infallible. Among the confined population are some who have been wrongly convicted, while the unconfined group contains a fair number of individuals who belong in jail. To the extent that justice miscarries, the reliability of the criterion is lowered and its predictability reduced in proportion.

A second limitation occurs because individuals are imprisoned for a wide variety of offenses, many of which have little in common so far as personality is concerned. Wife-murderers, confidence men, statutory rapists, thugs, homosexuals, income tax violators, bookmakers, bribe-takers, narcotics addicts, abortionists, counterfeiters, swindlers, extortionists, fences, second-story men, bank robbers, and contemptuous witnesses all are classed together with a host of other offenders into the category "confined." Yet differences in most personality traits are probably no greater between confined and nonconfined persons than they are within each group.

To improve accuracy and precision in the criterion, we might attempt to enlarge the dichotomy of "confined versus nonconfined" so as to include an estimate of the seriousness of offenses. Apart from the formidable scaling problems involved — is larceny worse than rape? — the more refined criterion is handicapped by judicial proceedings that may mask the relative seriousness of criminal behavior. As Newman (1956) points out, some convictions represent a compromise between defense and prosecution; the felon pleads guilty to a lesser charge in order to escape prosecution for a more serious but harder to prove offense. The notorious Al Capone, for example, was associated both personally and administratively with a wide range of the more aggressive and lucrative crimes; yet his most serious conviction was for income tax violation, an offense of little concern in delinquency prevention campaigns.

The methods used to establish the criterion of delinquency, it appears, are unsatisfactory on several counts, and its prediction from psychological data, as from other types of information, is bound to be less than perfect. To be sure, the influence of errors in the criterion may be small or moderate rather than large; this must be the case if prediction of misconduct is to be feasible.

RELIABILITY OF A PREDICTOR

Reliability sometimes is described as the degree to which an instrument provides precise measures of individual differences. A scale may be reliable, therefore, even though we are unable to identify just what it is that is being measured. A reliable measure is said to provide a stable score. If we measure a sample of subjects next week, a highly reliable scale will assign them approximately the same scores as were obtained today. Whenever a psychological variable is thought to be stable over time, measures of it should have high *test-retest* reliability; that is, a high correlation should hold between results of the two temporally separated applications of the instrument. If, on the other hand, either or both sets of scores are subject to much random error, their correlation[1] will be low, indicating lack of reliability. We cannot make much use of scores that fluctuate widely over relatively short intervals of time; hence high reliability is a necessary condition for useful prediction.

A low correlation between test and retest, however, may not always indicate random error in the measuring instrument. Real changes in the underlying psychological variable may take place to reduce the test-retest correlation. If the dimension being measured is one that can be expected to change in individuals over time, alternatives to the test-retest method are useful. One technique is to use *parallel forms* when the measure lends itself to such treatment. Certain widely used intelligence tests, for example, have two forms constructed to include similar, but not identical, content. When subjects are given both forms of the test, the two sets of scores will correlate

---

[1] The "correlation" between two measures is "perfect," when, by knowing a person's score on one of the two measures, we can predict his exact score on the second measure. The correlation is zero when knowledge of one score does not help to predict the other score. Correlations may be less than perfect but better than zero, indicating that some relationship exists between the scores. The extent of the relationship is given by a "correlation coefficient" computed by simple techniques. In general, the higher the correlation the better the prediction.

highly if the measures are relatively free from random error. The parallel-form approach, however, is rarely used with personality measures. The alternative in such cases is to employ an *internal consistency* coefficient.

To estimate internal consistency, we must have a scale with separately scorable parts. Some measures of delinquency potential, for example, consist of questions to be answered as either "true" or "false." A subject's score is the number of responses he makes of the kind classified as delinquent by the authors of the scale. If answers to such items were determined by a toss of the coin, individual differences in scores would be produced entirely by chance. To discover whether something of this kind occurs with actual scores, or whether they represent underlying psychological dispositions, an *odd-even* or equivalent estimate of reliability is used. Separate scores are calculated for the odd items and the even items. When little random error is present, these scores will correlate highly. Should scores on the even-numbered items prove unrelated to scores on the odd-numbered items, however, the measure is unreliable.

VALIDITY OF THE PREDICTOR

Validity is sometimes described as the degree to which a scale measures what it was designed to measure. It is proper, nevertheless, to think of an instrument as having and lacking many validities. A yardstick, for example, is a valid measure of height, not weight. An intelligence test is a valid predictor of years of future schooling and school grades; it is much less valid as a measure of future social adjustment. Furthermore, a measure that predicts delinquent behavior is a valid measure of delinquency potential regardless of its original aim.

The psychologist wishing to demonstrate that his scale is a valid measure of delinquency potential usually selects one of two methods. Most convincing is *predictive validity*. The procedure is simple. The scale is given to a sample of nondelinquents who are followed for a number of years until an appreciable number have become delinquent. If scores on the scale discriminate those who became offenders from those who did not, the scale has predictive validity.

Because prediction studies take time and effort, most measures first are validated by a method that compares scores of groups known to be different on the variable to be predicted. A measure that makes this kind of discrimination has *concurrent validity*. Most demonstrations of validity for measures of delinquent personality traits have taken the concurrent form: scores of confined and nonconfined persons are compared to discover the degree to which the scale distinguishes between them.

High concurrent validity is a hopeful sign that the author of a scale is on the right track, but it does not guarantee his measure will have predictive validity. Because it involves the comparison of normals with offenders after they have been convicted, concurrent validity may reflect the influence of factors that *result from* rather than *precede* delinquent behavior. Take, for example, the question: "Are you often bored?" When known delinquents are found more likely than normals to answer "true" to this query, is the result consistent with our impression of the delinquent personality as relatively aimless and thrill-seeking, or should we attribute the difference to the fact that prison life is boring? The flaw in concurrent validity is even more clearly illustrated by questions that ask in one way or the other: "Have you ever been in prison?" A measure with several items of this type ought to be effective in discriminating between prisoners and normals, but useless in predicting the career of subjects who have not yet committed crimes.

We need evidence of predictive validity before we can apply psychological instruments in real-life situations. And predictive validity must be imperfect because of the flaws in the criterion of delinquency. It will also be lowered to the extent that the measuring instrument is unreliable. For this reason, a report of the validity and reliability of a scale should be incorporated in the manual of any predictive measure. Individuals responsible for the selection of psychological instruments can find no more authoritative source of information on the strengths and weakness of current devices than is provided by the *Fifth Mental Measurements Yearbook* edited by O. K. Buros (1959). This encyclopedic volume contains multiple evaluations of commonly offered psychological measures as well as extensive bibliographies for very nearly all devices given wide distribution. The evaluations of measures of delinquency potential, it may be added, almost always criticize the manner in which concurrent validity is treated by the authors of these measures as equivalent to predictive validity.

THE BASE-RATE PROBLEM

Delinquency — as expressed by such criteria as confinement or police record — is not a common state of affairs. While this fact is fortunate for society, it is less desirable as far as prediction studies are concerned. We can use a valid scale more effectively when half the population is delinquent than we can when only a few percent become criminals. The proportion of individuals in the population who fall into the category to be predicted establishes the "base rate." Meehl and Rosen (1956) have presented a formal treatment, later corrected in certain details by Cureton (1957), of the effect of base rates on accuracy of prediction. The main elements of their analysis can be illustrated by a fictitious example.

Suppose that Nation Q has a serious delinquency problem in its 100,000 man Interplanetary Force. From psychologists expert in galaxian personality traits, the authorities in charge obtain a pencil-and-paper delinquency potential scale. Preliminary research indicates that it has high internal consistency and test-retest reliability as well as considerable concurrent validity. Encouraged by these findings, the personnel office begins a large-scale prediction study. All new recruits take the scale and are followed to the end of their enlistments. The results show that a score of 50 or more on the scale was obtained by 60 percent of recruits who later became disciplinary offenders, whereas only 5 percent of normal recruits scored that high. The scale, it is clear, has predictive validity. How will it do in application?

Imagine first that the delinquency rate is so high that half of the men in the Interplanetary Force become offenders during their enlistment. If all who score 50 or more on the scale are rejected as recruits, the delinquency rate should drop 60 percent with a loss of only 5 percent of useful men. Where the Interplanetary Force numbered 50,000 good men and 50,000 delinquents before the scale was introduced, its application with a cut-off score of 50 will produce a force of 20,000 delinquents and 47,500 normals. With only a slight reduction in the number of solid astronauts, a tremendous decrease in the frequency of space offenders is effected; 2,500 normals are dropped in order to get rid of 30,000 delinquents.

The effectiveness of the scale in the preceding example is based on a delinquency rate optimal for prediction. Suppose the contrary is true, that the base rate is something more typical of modern armed forces, say 5 percent delinquency. Under this condition, only 5,000 of the men will become offenders. Using the same scale and cutting score as before, the authorities now must reject 4,750 good men in order to eliminate 3,000 potential delinquents. Whether or not the scale should be employed for screening in this last condition depends on several nonpsychological factors: how easy recruits are to come by, how expensive it is to lose a good recruit, how costly it is to deal with a delinquent after he gets into trouble, and how much an offense damages the Force.

The base rate is as important in real-life situations as in this imaginary application. It is not enough to know that a psychological scale can predict criminal activity. To evaluate the measure completely, we must have information regarding the degree to which it discriminates between future delinquents and normals, how common delinquency is in the population, and how important it is to forestall delinquency at the cost of misclassifying an individual who will not become an offender. Methods of predicting future delinquency that ignore the problem of the base rate usually seriously overestimate their practical effectiveness.

TYPES OF PSYCHOLOGICAL MEASURES

Not all measures that have been employed as possible predictors of misconduct properly come under the heading "psychological." Among these are such devices as the social worker's rating of situational factors, the sociologist's estimate of socioeconomic status, and the physical anthropologist's indices of skull shape and physique. Truly psychological instruments can be grouped into three categories: (1) *inventories* or self-report questionnaires, (2) *psychological tests*, and (3) *projective tests*.

An *inventory* is a collection of statements or questions dealing with one's present and past attitudes, beliefs, and behaviors toward oneself and others. Inventories are easy to administer; the subjects merely read the statements, called *items* in the argot of psychologists, and mark a standard answer sheet so arranged as to limit drastically the range of possible responses. Commonly, only a choice of "true" or "false" is offered, a restriction that many feel obliterates shadings of meaning that may be important. Other inventories allow the subject more leeway and use a numerical scale of agreement and disagreement by which he can indicate the extent to which an item expresses his view of matters. Answers to inventory items, it should be added, are never "right" or "wrong." What, for example, could be a universally correct answer to items like these: "I am easily awakened" or "I would like to hunt polar bears"?

When an objective standard can be employed with every answer to mark it correct or incorrect, we have a psychological test. For instance, "Is Paris closer to Antwerp than to Vienna?" is a test item. For *everybody*, the correct answer to the test item is "yes." It would be silly, on the other hand, to say that a "yes" or a "no" is universally correct for an inventory question such as "Do you like loud, noisy parties?" or "Do you ever suffer from upset stomach?" Tests, especially if individually administered, permit a wider range of response than is possible with an inventory. Answers to individual intelligence tests, for instance, have been scored for such diverse characteristics as accuracy of information, correct solution of problems, speed, quality of performance, and fluency.

Projective tests, our third category of psychological instruments, combine relatively ambiguous material with instructions that encourage the widest range of responding to it. The latitude permitted the subject, of course, makes scoring his responses a task that requires the services of a professional psychologist. Most projective tests, moreover, are designed to be given to one subject at a time by a highly trained administrator. In order to reduce difficulty in scoring and to make group administration possible, some experimental versions of well-known projective tests have altered the method of administration so as to allow a standard answer sheet to be used in group testing. These measures are comparable to more widely used group psychological tests that utilize the multiple-choice format for securing answers in an easily scored form.

If a psychological instrument is to screen potential delinquents, the inventory has several advantages over its rivals. First of all, there is the fact that inventories usually are easiest to administer. Second, the scoring of an inventory is so simple that a clerk can handle hundreds of records in a relatively short time. Both of these characteristics make the inventory ideal for large-scale applications.

The inventory has the additional advantage of being easily prepared for specific tasks. Inventories used to predict delinquency, for example, can readily be made to cover material that experience, intuition, or psychological theory indicate is related to criminal behavior. Constructing a specific psychological test for delinquent tendencies, on the other hand, would require considerably more pains, and the same is true when a special projective test is wanted. For this reason, the literature on delinquency abounds with reports of specially devised inventory measures, whereas investigations employing psychological tests or projective tests are not only fewer in number, but have had to utilize measures originally developed for quite different purposes.[2]

CONSTRUCTING AN INVENTORY MEASURE

Inventories frequently are devised by a highly *empirical* procedure. Five steps may be followed: (1) development of a "pool" of items, (2) collection of answers by subjects, (3) analysis of these responses to secure a provisional scale, (4) "validation" of the provisional scale, (5) refinement of the measure. To be sure, not all inventory scales are manufactured in just this way. When an investigator has reasons for believing that items of a particular type will predict his criterion, he may dispense with the first three of these steps. If the abbreviated approach is to succeed, however, the aspiring inventory maker must possess insight into the nature of the behavior he wishes to predict and be both discerning and lucky in his choice of items. Because this armchair short cut rarely is more than partially successful, the purely empirical method is resorted to most frequently.

THE MMPI: AN EMPIRICALLY DERIVED INVENTORY

The empirical method of inventory construction is responsible for the Minnesota Multiphasic Personality Inventory, or MMPI, the most widely investigated of our true-false paper-and-pencil personality questionnaires. The MMPI is a product of the psychiatric clinic; hence its many diagnostic scales deal with standard neurotic and psychotic patterns of behavior. One scale, however, is of special interest in the present context because it measures personality traits of patients diagnosed as Psychopathic Deviates (see Chapter 12). Such individuals are thought to constitute an appreciable portion

---

[2] The predominance of inventory measures in this field is apparent in Kvaraceus' review covering psychological measures of delinquent tendencies reported through 1953, in Chapter 5 of *The community and the delinquent* (1954).

of prison populations. The MMPI Psychopathic Deviate Scale, usually abbreviated as *Pd*, is, for this reason, a promising measure to apply in prediction of misconduct. The procedure followed in devising this scale, like the others in the MMPI, is an excellent example of the empirical approach to scale building.

Construction of the *Pd* Scale

The authors of the MMPI, Starke R. Hathaway and J. Charnley McKinley, began with a large pool of items — over five hundred in all. Written on the basis of clinical experience, study of psychiatric examination forms and case-taking directions, coverage of psychiatric textbooks, and a survey of earlier personality measures, these items express such a large number of important human characteristics that the person taking the inventory gives himself, in effect, a broad psychiatric and psychological interview.

The second step involved the collection of responses of normal and deviant individuals. The latter group for the construction of the *Pd* scale consisted of patients diagnosed as psychopathic deviates in a mental hospital. "All had long histories of minor delinquencies" (McKinley and Hathaway, 1944), but there were no neurotics, psychotics, or major criminal types among them. Stealing, lying, truancy, sexual promiscuity, drunkenness, and forgery were common behaviors in this group. There were more women than men, perhaps because of our cultural preference for treating psychopathic men in prisons rather than in clinics. Normal subjects used for comparison purposes were married Minnesotans in addition to high school graduates applying for admission to the University of Minnesota.

The third step began after deviant and normal subjects had taken the MMPI. From inspection of the proportions of deviants and normals endorsing each item in the inventory, provisional scales were established that discriminated between the two groups.

Step four consisted in scoring these provisional scales for each subject and contrasting the results for deviants and normals. The *Pd* scale is the fifty-item measure that best separated these two types of individuals. It discriminated between persons previously known to differ with respect to psychopathic tendencies; hence its original validity is of the *concurrent* variety.

A technical point arises here. When we use the groups from whose responses a scale is developed to validate the measure, differences between the groups tend to be inflated because items that differentiate subjects by chance alone are allowed to contribute to the scores. For this reason, further validation, called *cross-validation,* is desirable. Step five, therefore, consisted in giving the MMPI to a new group of patients diagnosed as psychopathic deviates, and to a sample of 100 males who had received a similar diagnosis in prison. Scores of these deviant individuals then were compared with those of the original normal sample (it would have been even better to obtain a new group of normals for this comparison).

The analyses of these last results securely establish the concurrent validity of the *Pd* scale. Although directed at the diagnosis of psychopathic deviation as it is seen in clinics, the *Pd* measure was even more successful at distinguishing between prisoners and normals. This concurrent validity of the *Pd* measure has been repeatedly confirmed by later investigations.

The way MMPI responses are scored was governed by differences between responses of deviates and normals. The more common response among deviates is "keyed" on the *Pd* scale; an individual's raw score is the sum of such deviate answers. This means that the higher the *Pd* score, the more a subject resembles a psychopathic deviate.

The practice of basing the scoring system on empirical results maximizes the degree to which a given scale will separate deviants from normals. The psychologist who employs this method is willing, in principle, to score "false" as diagnostic even though he had expected "true" to be the deviant response. This procedure, call *criterion-keying,* and the discarding of nondiscriminating items can weaken the relation between the final scale and any theoretical rationale that may have governed its original development; hence interpreting or understanding what it is that accounts for the success of the scale, assuming it proves useful, may be difficult and subject to controversy. The purely empirical approach, in other words, may achieve practical ends at some sacrifice of insight into just what is being measured in the area of personality.

Prediction with the MMPI

The *Pd* scale, unlike the majority of similar paper-and-pencil measures of delinquent tendencies, has been shown to possess a certain degree of *predictive validity.* The relevant data were collected by Hathaway and Monachesi (1953) in their well-known study of juvenile delinquency. Two years after administering the MMPI to a sample of 4,048 ninth-grade boys and girls in the public schools of Minneapolis, Hathaway and Monachesi checked county and city records and found that 591 — some 22 percent of the boys and eight percent of the girls — had appeared before the courts or police. That these percentages are high is a reflection of the rather broad definition of delinquency employed in the investigation. The delinquents were classified into three levels according to the seriousness of their offenses:

I. This level of misconduct is used to denote those who committed repeated offenses such as auto theft, burglary, grand larceny, holdup with a gun, and gross immoral conduct (girls), accompanied by less serious offenses. . . .

II. This classification involves the commission of only one serious offense such as auto theft, grand larceny, or gross immorality, or more than one less serious offense such as petty larceny, immoral conduct, assault, disorderly conduct. . . .

III. The youngsters placed in this class had committed minor offenses such as destruction of property (especially when this was connected with play activities), drinking, one or more traffic offenses (escapades involving speeding, driving without a license, and/or going at high speed through a stop light or sign), curfew violation, and immoral conduct. . . . [Hathaway and Monachesi, 1953; p. 110.]

Nearly half of the 591 members of the delinquent group had become offenders before the MMPI was administered. The predictive validity of the *Pd* scale, therefore, must be determined by analysis of the scores of those subjects whose first record of misconduct postdated testing; such individuals are true "predelinquents." Mean *Pd* scores for the predelinquent boys are shown in Table 2 together with the mean score obtained by a subsample of 200 boys in the nondelinquent group.

TABLE 2

Average *Pd* Scores of Predelinquent and Normal Boys

		Delinquents		Normals
	Category I	Category II	Category III	
Mean Score	63.4	62.5	60.8	58.4
Number of Cases	12	96	79	200

Because there were relatively few predelinquent girls in their sample, Hathaway and Monachesi combined the data for Categories I and II. The average *Pd* score for the girls in these two classes was 64.7, and 64.6 for the girls in Category III. The control group of 200 nondelinquent girls had a mean *Pd* score of 58.4. Differences between delinquents and normals, except for those in the mildly delinquent Category III, are too large to be attributable to chance alone. There is also a tendency among the boys for the more seriously delinquent to receive higher *Pd* scores.[3]

It is clear from these results that the MMPI *Pd* scale can predict misconduct in young people with no record of delinquency up to the time of testing. *Pd*, moreover, is not the only MMPI measure that forecasts later misbehavior. The Hypomania scale *(Ma)*, which deals with overactivity, also discriminates predelinquents, in Categories I and II, from normal youngsters.

The MMPI contains scales designed to reveal careless or deceptive answering. When scores on these scales are too high, the record is invalidated and not used in comparisons of the sort described above. Approximately 12 percent of the boys and 8 percent of the girls who later became delinquent had invalidated records, as compared to 6 percent of the boys and 5 percent of the girls in the normal group. Invalidated records, it appears, predict later misconduct to a limited degree, because they are more frequent among children who become delinquent in the future.

The Hathaway and Monachesi results indicate that delinquency is to some extent predictable with a paper-and-pencil personality inventory. Yet if we ask how accurate these predictions are — how much better than blind guessing — the answer is not overly encouraging. The differences between scores of predelinquents and normals, while real, are rather small to be useful in immediate application. Furthermore, the problem of the base rate emerges at this point.

The difficulties besetting prediction of delinquency can be illustrated by a hypothetical example using these real-life MMPI results. Suppose that we had attempted to conduct an experimental delinquency-prevention program in Minneapolis at the time Hathaway and Monachesi gathered their MMPI records, and that a good fairy had whispered to us that invalidated MMPI records would be found to predict later misbehavior. "Select those youngsters who give invalid records," she advises, "and you will increase the number of predelinquents in the group you pick for training." What would happen if we had followed her suggestion?

---

[3] It is customary to present MMPI scale scores in transformed values. The inventory contains tables for converting raw scores into scores with means of 50 and standard deviations of 10 in the normative samples. The data in Table 2 have been transformed.

To begin with, although invalidated records are twice as common among predelinquent boys — 12 percent as compared with 6 percent of normals — the difference is not large. Then, too, the base rate for delinquency subsequent to administration of the inventory is low: only 187 boys became delinquent out of a total group of 1,683 who had no records of misconduct up to the time Hathaway and Monachesi tested them. Of these 187 predelinquents, only 27 gave invalidated records, while there were 101 such records among the returns of the 1,649 normal boys. Our training program using as subjects all boys with invalidated records would therefore deal with 128 boys, 101 of whom would not need our attention. Normal boys would be about three and a half times as common as predelinquents in this special group.

Of course, we would be even worse off if we did not use any selection device and merely took boys as they came until our experimental group was filled. In such a case, we would train nearly eight normal boys for every predelinquent. Selecting candidates by use of this one MMPI measure, it seems, does reduce the number of normals who are mistakenly classified as predelinquents; however, the reduction is not as great as we might desire. Further, even if the program is completely successful, we reduce the delinquency rate by only 12 percent. Eighty-eight percent of delinquents, having valid records, escape our attention until their misconduct later brings them into conflict with society.

We might have bettered the last figure in our hypothetical program by selecting on the basis of *Pd* and *Ma* scores as well as on invalidated records. If we had used all three of these devices, the percentage of the predelinquent group that would have been chosen for training would rise appreciably, but whether or not the ratio of predelinquents to normals in the group selected would differ very much from that obtained with invalidated records alone is doubtful.[4]

To increase the precision of diagnosis with the MMPI — to ensure that predelinquents rather than normals are chosen for training — two alternatives to the procedure just described are of potential merit. The first is to use the *profile* of scores on the standard MMPI scales, that is, to describe each record according to which of the scales are high and which are low for the individual. The second is to devise

---

[4] It is not possible to estimate the needed figures from the data that Hathaway and Monachesi provide. It seems unlikely, however, that a drastic reduction from the 3½ to 1 ratio would be achieved by use of *Pd* and *Ma* in addition to invalidated records.

a new scale aimed specifically at the prediction of misconduct as it appeared in the Minneapolis sample.

Considerable attention is given by Hathaway and Monachesi (1953) to the contribution of profiles in helping us *understand* the dynamics of delinquent behavior. Detailed information is also presented on the frequency of various profile types among delinquents and normals. In an inventory with as many scales as the MMPI, however, even the simplest classification of profiles must necessarily be extensive. To segregate MMPI profiles according to a relatively simple scheme that takes account of which scales are highest and next highest for each subject, Hathaway and Monachesi (1953) use one hundred different categories.

How good prediction from this classification of profiles would have been in the Minneapolis sample unfortunately cannot be estimated from the published frequencies of the profile types, because the Hathaway and Monachesi (1953) data are based on all delinquents, that is, the records of individuals who became delinquent after testing are pooled with those of boys already delinquent. The same confounding of concurrent and predictive data occurs in a study by Rempel (1958) of the validity of a more mathematically precise method of employing profile information obtained for the subjects in the Minneapolis study. His delinquent group consisted of all boys whose misconduct ranged from moderate to serious up to four years after the original administration of the MMPI. Using a sophisticated analysis, Rempel found that 69.5 percent of the delinquent and 62.3 percent of the normal boys could be correctly identified by a mathematical formula describing their MMPI profiles.

While Rempel's formula may represent the most effectiveness for the method of profile diagnosis because it is based on responses of boys already delinquent as well as on predelinquent records, the number of normal boys diagnosed as having delinquent personalities is still large. If our hypothetical training program had used Rempel's formula for selecting its candidates, we would have chosen a group of approximately 170 delinquents and predelinquents and 410 normals out of the Minneapolis sample of boys. Roughly 2½ normals would have been given training for every boy who needed it. Not the most efficient selection, perhaps, but better than the ratio of nearly 4½ to 1 that would hold if the inventory was not used.

The standard scales of the MMPI, including *Pd,* deal with personality characteristics that may predispose to or inhibit delinquent behavior, but these scales were not designed to predict misconduct of the sort encountered in the Minneapolis study. It is possible, therefore, that an effective empirical MMPI scale could be developed for the specific task of predicting later delinquency. In a discussion of the results of a second two-year follow-up of their subjects, Hathaway and Monachesi (1957) list 33 MMPI items that discriminate predelinquent from normal boys. These items could be combined into a provisional delinquency scale to be refined in the usual manner. Since only 11 appear on *Pd* and *Ma*, the 33 items might have predictive properties appreciably better than the two standard scales. Since no information on scores, when these items are used as a single measure, is given by Hathaway and Monachesi, the validation of the items as a scale remains a task for the future.

At this point, evidence on the predictive power of MMPI measures comes to an end.[5] Whether or not accuracy of prediction of delinquency by the MMPI can be improved is a question that must be settled by data not yet reported. There is, of course, no reason why useful predictive instruments may not be devised outside the regular MMPI format. There are several pencil-and-paper measures for which concurrent validity has been demonstrated; some of these may have better predictive validity than Hathaway and Monachesi have shown for MMPI scales. But the MMPI is important in the present context simply because it is one inventory for which evidence of predictive validity exists. By using its discriminating items and adding others to cover particular areas of personality more thoroughly, better predictors may yet be developed. For this reason, we need to consider what kinds of content the discriminating items of the MMPI deal with.

Predictive MMPI Content

One way to describe the content of discriminating items and scales is to make a rational classification, that is, to read the items and group them according to the sense they seem to make. Inspection of the 33 most predictive items reported by Hathaway and Monachesi (1957), for instance, reveals that 6 deal with various aspects of disturbed relations in the home, 6 with difficulties in school, 6 with a need for thrill and adventure, 3 with sex, and 3 with tactics to follow when in trouble. The content concerned with family and school is, to be sure, what a study of the literature on delinquency would lead us to expect. That responses of delinquents to such items reflect poor real-life home and school adjust-

---

[5] Delinquency among prisoners, that is, misbehavior during confinement, seems predictable by use of the MMPI. Paton has cross-validated an empirical MMPI measure for this purpose (1958). Data on the base rate unfortunately are missing.

ment is suggested, for example, by an investigation by Wirt and Briggs (1959), who surveyed records of social agencies and interviewed parents of a subsample of the subjects in the Minneapolis study.

The psychologist seeking to construct a better scale must consider the possibility of writing items to deal with content that is sketchily covered by Hathaway and Monachesi's items. The fact that six of their predictive items describe disturbed home conditions ensures that a subject from such an environment is likely to reveal the fact, whereas if only one item covering home conditions is offered, the information may not be too reliable. Responses to six items concerned with the same area of behavior ought, other things being equal, to give more precise information than is obtained when only one is used.

There is little point, on the other hand, to add items that repeat content already adequately covered by a scale. Clearly, some type of systematic classification of items is needed. One approach is to consider the relations among responses before attempting a classification by content. Items can be grouped according to the way answers to one are related to responses to others. When replies to a particular set of items are correlated, that is, when knowing how subjects answer item A helps us predict how they answer B, C, and D, we can hypothesize that the four items reflect the operation of a single source, dimension, or *factor* of personality. Psychologists who seek this sort of information about items usually employ one of several versions of a computational method known as *factor analysis*. Once the empirical groupings of items are disclosed by factor analysis, items associated with each factor are studied to provide clues as to the nature of the underlying source of variation.

Two recent investigations have employed factor analysis to uncover the dimensions underlying scores on the *Pd* scale. One is a study by Comrey (1958) of responses of normals and a variety of psychiatric patients. The other, by Astin (1959), employed records of hospitalized drug addicts. Despite differences in the composition of their samples and methods of factor analysis, their results are in fair agreement. Both find that certain *Pd* items reflect a systematic tendency toward feeling of persecution. Another factor observed in both studies concerns the occurrence of episodes of unaccountable cheerfulness and liveliness. Astin's factor of Social Maladjustment, however, is split in Comrey's analysis into separate factors of Delinquency and Anti-Social Behavior. Similarly, Astin's Neuroticism factor appears as factors of Shyness and Neuroticism in Comrey's study.

Limitations of Inventories

Although they share with all measures that might be applied to the problem of predicting delinquency the difficulties that arise from the nature of the criterion and its complex causation, inventory scales posses some specific inherent weaknesses. The most obvious of these concern the extent to which responses reflect the state of affairs as an unbiased observer might report it. Are the answers of subjects true? Certainly there is nothing about the questionnaire that compels a person to be accurate in his self-portrayal. A considerable body of research and theory suggests that some subjects can and do consciously or unconsciously distort their answers so as to appear either better or worse than they really are. For this reason, the MMPI, unlike many other paper-and-pencil inventories, includes scales that attempt to measure the extent to which subjects bias their scores by presenting themselves in unrealistically favorable or unfavorable lights.

Another well-known but usually unheeded source of trouble arises because individuals vary in the extent to which they endorse or reject items regardless of content. Some subjects, for example, are more likely than others to answer "true" to questions dealing with "liking" things, apparently above and beyond what it is that is liked (Hanley, 1959). When a personality scale contains many items worded in the same fashion, to include terms that call for individual interpretation of meaning (for example, "often," "certainly"), influences of this kind, called *response sets*, may systematically alter scores. If, on the other hand, a measure is composed of items with many different wordings, responses will be affected by a host of influences having little to do with the general content of the scale. For these reasons, it seems idealistic to hope that great precision in diagnosis is possible with any inventory scale. It is possible that measuring devices which do not suffer from the inherent weaknesses of inventories will prove more accurate in predicting delinquency. Among these are psychological tests and projective tests. Unfortunately, relatively little has been reported thus far regarding their effectiveness in the area of delinquency.

PSYCHOLOGICAL TESTS

Intelligence measures are the classic examples of psychological tests. The relation between intelligence and criminality has been the subject of controversy for decades. In a survey of studies of intelligence and delinquency conducted in the United States and Great Britain over the past forty years, Woodward (1955) concludes: "The average I.Q. of delinquents in the U.S.A. and Great Britain has been estimated at 92, and it appears probable that the difference between this figure and the general population norm (of 100) is accounted for by the association with delinquency of that constellation of cultural factors which adversely affects the test score" (p. 299). The average difference of eight points that may hold between delinquents and normals may be due in part, in other words, to such facts as that delinquents tend to come from intellectually deprived backgrounds where low IQs are common. Should this be the case, a group of offenders from lower socioeconomic levels may be no more different in IQ from a normal sample than is the case where nondelinquent lower-status subjects are compared with normals.

Regardless of the origin of the relation between intelligence and delinquency, confirmation of its existence means that IQ scores might be useful in predicting misconduct. Unfortunately, comparisons of the intelligence test performance of normals and delinquents typically involve concurrent rather than predictive validity, and ignore the problem of the base rate. An example of test differences between known delinquents and controls illustrates these points. Zakolski (1949) gave a battery of tests to 50 industrial school and 50 public schools boys. Mean scores on three well-known measures of ability are shown in Table 3.

TABLE 3

Scores of Delinquent and Control Boys on Ability Tests

Trait	Test	Delinquents	Normals
IQ (verbal)	Otis	82.6	92.7
IQ (nonverbal)	Revised Army Beta	85.5	95.9
Mechanical Ability	MacQuarrie	36.3	54.7

From Zakolski, 1949.

We can generalize these results — the Otis scores, for example — to real life only if two assumptions hold: concurrent validity must approximate predictive validity; and subjects must be representative of delinquent and normal boys in general. If these conditions are met, we can expect approximately one half of predelinquent boys to score 82 or less on the Otis. From additional information that Zakolski gives about spread of scores in his groups, we estimate that roughly 16 percent of normal boys will score this low.

How accurate will the test be in a prediction study where the expected rate of delinquency is 10 percent? In such a situation, if we test 1,000 boys not yet offenders, 10 percent will later become delinquents. A score of 82 or less should, therefore, pick up 50 of the 100 predelinquents and 144 of the 900 normal boys. Nearly three nondelinquents would be misclassified for each predelinquent correctly identified. Our level of accuracy is of the same order as that achieved with the MMPI in the Minneapolis study.

This degree of effectiveness, of course, is heavily dependent upon the correctness of our dubious assumptions. It is unlikely that any test will have as high predictive as concurrent validity. Zakolski's subjects may not be representative of the general populations of delinquents and normals. The figure of 10 percent for the base rate probably is too high. Our estimate of accuracy, therefore, surely errs in the direction favoring the use of the test.

These qualifications apply to a study by Jones, Livson, and Sarbin (1955), who show that institutionalized delinquent boys obtain lower scores than controls on a "perceptual-completion" measure, the Street Gestalt Completion Test. In this device, familiar objects are shown by partly completed drawings; the task is to identify the subject of the drawing. Perceptual completion is one of many ability factors; it is possible that comparisons of delinquents and normals on standard measures of other abilities may uncover particular types in which delinquents are especially deficient. The work in this area is interesting but essentially exploratory.

A recent development in the field of personality is an increased interest in psychological tests that measure traits other than ability. Under the leadership of Raymond B. Cattell (1957), a host of psychological tests have been developed to cover what appear to be rather distinct personality traits. When basic research on these new measures is completed, their use in preliminary comparisons of delinquents and normals can be expected. A test of this general type, devised by Cassel (1952), has been used in a concurrent validity study.

Cassel and Van Vorst (1954) gave the Cassel Group Level of Aspiration Test to samples of delinquent boys, delinquent women, and high school seniors. Our "level of aspiration" is the performance we seek to achieve; our past successes and failures affect this level, and people differ in the extent to which their aspirations are affected by their past experience. The Cassel test consisted of eight identical parts in which the subject draws circles at the top and bottom of each of a series of X's arranged four rows to the page. Before commencing any part, he makes a "bid," that is, estimates how many X's he will complete within a 30-second time limit. Overbidding is penalized, but one can earn a score no greater than the bid. The size of the bid, past performance, and past bids may be compared in a number of ways. Cassel and Van Vorst report differences that seem related to dissimilar levels of aspirations in delinquents and controls. The problem of the base rate is not treated, but the authors are careful to describe their study as dealing with "in-prison" and "out-of-prison" samples.

Another investigation in the same vein is reported by Doctor and Winder (1954), who studied the performance of normal boys and institutionalized delinquents — matched for race, age, mental ability, and socioeconomic status — on the Porteus Maze Test, basically a measure of intelligence. Their results agree with earlier studies of the Porteus Test that show personality differences — as measured by a score based on such things as regard for instructions, impulsivity, and carefulness — between delinquents and normals. This "qualitative score" is not highly related to intellectual ability. In the Doctor and Winder study, some 70 percent of delinquents obtained high qualitative scores as compared with a value of 30 percent in the control boys. These findings, of course, are suggestive rather than definitive, for the reasons outlined with the preceding measures.

It appears that psychological tests might be employed in place of inventories in predicting delinquent behavior. Much basic research is called for, however, before putting such measures into practical application.

PROJECTIVE TESTS

The picture with respect to projective tests resembles that holding for psychological tests — findings are "suggestive," "preliminary," or "promising," without much hope of immediate applicability. One study, nevertheless, stands out as indicating possible usefulness. As part of an extensive investigation directed by the Gluecks (see page 237), using samples of 500 delinquent and 500 normal adolescent boys, responses to the Rorschach Inkblot Test were analyzed by Ernest Schactel and his late wife. Schactel (1950) reports impressive concurrent validity for the Rorschach Test when it is used by skilled clinicians.

The Rorschach Test (Rorschach, 1942) consists of ten cards, each showing an elaborate inkblot. Subjects are asked to tell what they see in the cards. The method of administration is standardized, and the test has been the subject of thousands of studies. The Rorschach is widely used in clinical work.

There are several scoring systems for the Rorschach Test. Purely formal aspects of performance may be scored by a number of similar schemes. One important score, for example, is the number of responses in which human or humanlike movement is described. Table 4 gives the frequency of such "M" responses in the normal and delinquent samples studied by Schactel.

TABLE 4

Number of "M" Responses to the Rorschach Test

Number of "M" Responses	Number of Subjects Delinquent	Normal
0	241	204
1	131	150
2	82	71
3	31	39
4	9	16
5	5	5
6	1	5
7 or more	0	10
Total	500	500

From Schactel, 1950.

While normal boys show the greater tendency to give "M" responses, the measure in itself is not very discriminating, especially if we generalize from the data to situations with a lower base rate. Better discrimination was obtained when the Schactels made ratings of several personality traits hypothesized as relating to delinquency in the kind of subjects being observed. Ratings of this type require the services of expert clinicians. The best discrimination, however, occurred when the Schactels, without knowledge of the status of the subjects, sorted the Rorschach protocols into "delinquent," "neutral," and "nondelinquent" categories, using as a guide their theoretical analysis of the kinds of personality characteristics that would produce delinquency in the milieu from which the subjects were drawn. Some 329 of 496 delinquents were correctly identified, while another 135 were classed as "neutral." Among 495 nondelinquents, 333 were classified accurately, while 121 were called "neutral." A diagnosis of delinquency was accurate in 66 percent of delinquent cases and fell on nondelinquents only 8 percent of the time. In a situation with a base rate of 10 percent, about one nondelinquent would be misclassified as delinquent for every delinquent properly identified.

It is clear that these highly trained clinicians were able to discriminate between delinquent and normal Rorschach record with surprising accuracy. Whether such efficiency would hold up in a truly predictive study with a realistic base rate is, of course, a matter that only empirical evidence can settle. Although such evidence can be obtained, the difficulty remains that clinicians who can make the discrimination as accurately as Schactel appears to have done may not be available for practical employment of the Rorschach. The impressive results of the Schactel study, for this reason, may be difficult to transform into real-life applications. The same difficulty holds for any projective test that requires evaluation by skilled personnel who are few in number.

THE GLUECK PREDICTION TABLES

The reader by this time will have formed an opinion of the merit of psychological measures for predicting antisocial behavior. Before closing the chapter, however, we ought to consider how the job can be handled with nonpsychological tools. The most widely publicized of these at present are the prediction tables devised by Sheldon and Eleanor Glueck (1950). Should these tables live up to claims that have been made for them, the question of whether or not to utilize psychological measures might become a dead issue.

The various prediction tables were developed by the Gluecks after decades spent in the study of criminal careers. The Social Prediction Table has been the most widely discussed; it employs ratings by social investigators of the following items dealing with conditions in the preschool years:

Discipline of boy by father
Supervision of boy by mother
Affection of father for boy
Affection of mother for boy
Cohesiveness of family

The Social Prediction Table is seen by the Gluecks as the most useful of their tables for the practical prediction of delinquency (Glueck and Glueck, 1956). Among their other tables, which do not markedly improve predictions from the Social Prediction Table alone, are some that incorporate psychological measures. These include the ratings of Rorschach Test responses discussed in the previous section, and scores on psychological tests. In addition to psychiatric ratings, other tables include such variables as birthplaces, nativity, and religion of parents; economic status; school behavior; and factors related to early antisocial behavior.

The chief evidence for the validity of the Glueck tables appears in *Unraveling Juvenile Delinquency* (Glueck and Glueck, 1950), a book reporting comparisons of 500 offender and 500 control boys. The two groups were matched with varying degrees of success for intelligence, age, place of residence, and ethnic origin. Striking differences were observed; results with the Social Prediction Table, for instance, led the Gluecks to assert that delinquent tendencies can be diagnosed with accuracy as early as the age of six.

While hailed by many (a symposium of reviews in the *Journal of Criminal Law and Criminology*, 1951, is mainly highly favorable), the procedures and conclusions in this Glueck study have also been severely criticized. Rubin (1951) raises serious objections to most aspects of the investigation, two being especially relevant to topics in this chapter. The first is that the delinquent boys the Gluecks observed are not representative of delinquents in general. Second, the Gluecks did not study delinquents when they were young, but rather extrapolated from data obtained after the boys had been institutionalized during adolescence. Criticisms by Shaplin and Tiedeman (1952) also relate to these points. In our terminology, these critics argue that the Glueck study has concurrent rather than predictive validity. Similar strong objections by Reiss (1951) include discussion of the base rate. The accuracy of the Glueck tables, he emphasizes, is based on a situation with equal numbers of delinquents and controls. When the base rate is set at a more realistic figure — 10 percent — the tables turn out to be far less discriminating than claimed. This criticism has been repeated by Walters (1956), who shows how a base rate of 2–4 percent makes prediction from the tables quite inaccurate. It is clear that even when the use of concurrent for predictive validity is ignored, the practical effectiveness of the Glueck tables has been greatly overestimated.

Studies of the true predictive validity of the Glueck tables are said to be in progress. Until these are fully reported, we can only turn to recently published evidence (Glueck and Glueck, 1959) concerning the usefulness of these tables in predicting the behavior of the 500 delinquent boys subsequent to the time they first were seen by the Gluecks. The data relate to behavior in various types of peno-correctional treatments instituted after the original study began. Table 5 lists the kinds of treatments, together with information regarding the predictive accuracy of tables specially devised for each type of treatment.

Table 5 conveys two impressions. For one, the content is incomplete, making the data difficult to evaluate in their present form. For another, the tables *seem* to be highly accurate in predicting "failure." The material can be clarified by making separate and complete tables for each kind of treatment. When this is done, however, the results lose much of their impressiveness. An example is provided in Table 6, which gives the complete results for straight probation. When the evidence is put into this form, we can readily evaluate the accuracy of the predictions. Among the 286 boys for whom failure was predicted as having a better than even chance of occurring, 270 actually failed. Of 10 boys predicted to have a less than even chance of failure, 4 did not fail. The predictions were correct, therefore, in 274 cases out of 296, slightly less than 93 percent of the time.

Impressive predictions, indeed! But what about the base rate? Most of the 296 boys on straight probation failed. If we had no Glueck table handy, our best prediction would be that every boy would fail. This prediction would be correct 276 times out of 296, a bit better than 93 percent accurate. It seems that we do slightly better without the table than with it!

Using the same procedure of predicting the most common behavior for all subjects concerned, we find in all categories that the prediction tables make a negligible contribution to accuracy of prediction. The best showing for the Glueck tables comes in the case of failure in prison: 80 percent accuracy with the prediction table as compared with 74 percent from the base rate of nonfailure. Despite the superficial appearance of great accuracy, it is clear that these data do not show that the methods employed by the Gluecks possess greater validity than has been characteristic of far humbler paper-and-pencil inventory measures.

TABLE 5

Comparison of Predicted versus Actual Behavior by Type of Treatment

| | | Actual Behavior | |
| Predicted Behavior | Total Number of Offenders | Serious or Persistent Minor Offender | |
		Number	Percent
More than even chance of "failure"			
Straight probation	286	270	94.4
Probation with suspended sentence	344	337	98.0
Correctional school	465	366	78.7
Parole	458	417	91.0
Reformatory	39	21	53.8
Prison	4	3	75.0

		Occasional Minor Offender or Non-Offender	
Less than even chance of "failure"			
Straight probation	10	4	40.0
Probation with suspended sentence	11	0	0.0
Correctional school	22	12	54.5
Parole	3	2	66.7
Reformatory	118	80	67.8
Prison	31	25	80.6

The small number of cases in certain categories is due to the nature of the sample which is made up of true juvenile offenders (serious or persistent minor).

From Sheldon and Eleanor Glueck, *Predicting delinquency and crime.* Cambridge, Mass.: Harvard University Press, 1959, p. 258. Used by permission of the publishers.

TABLE 6

Prediction of Behavior on Straight Probation

		Frequency of Actual Behavior		
		Occasional or Nonoffender	Serious or Persistent Offender	Total
Frequency of Prediction	More than 50% chance of "failure"	16	270	286
	Less than 50% chance of "failure"	4	6	10
	Total	20	276	296

CONCLUSION

The preceding pages indicate the difficulties that must be overcome if psychological measures are to become useful in combating antisocial behavior. The accuracy of the best of these instruments is not high, although appreciably better than chance. More important, the studies we have cited suggest these measures might be improved markedly, given sufficient attention. This has not occurred to date. While the number of psychological investigations of delinquency may appear large, deviation that leads to punitive detention has received only a fraction of the attention psychologists have given to deviation that leads to other types of treatment.

The contributions of psychologists to the field of delinquency, moreover, often have taken the form of "explanations" of misconduct rather than suggestions as to how society can cope with it realistically. Should the day arrive when practical means for dealing with delinquency are the main object of research, the improvement of psychological instruments for diagnosing the presence of criminal tendencies ought to play an important part in the effort. Past investigations, although inadequate in various ways, point to a useful role for psychological measures in the future.

References

Astin, A. W. A factor study of the MMPI psychopathic deviate scale. *J. consult. Psychol.*, 1959, **23**, 550–554.

Buros, O. K. (Ed.) *The fifth mental measurements yearbook.* Highland Park, N. J.: The Gryphon Press, 1959.

Cassel, R. N. *Cassel Group Level of Aspiration Test.* Los Angeles: Western Psychological Services, 1952.

Cassel, R. N., & Van Vorst, R. Level of aspiration as a means for discerning between "in-prison" and "out-of-prison" groups of individuals. *J. soc. Psychol.*, 1954, **40**, 121–135.

Cattell, R. B. *Personality and motivation structure and measurement.* Yonkers-on-Hudson: World Book Company, 1957.

Comrey, A. L. A factor analysis of items on the MMPI psychopathic deviate scale. *Ed. psychol. Measmt*, 1958, **18**, 91–98.

Cureton, E. E. Recipe for a cookbook. *Psychol. Bull.*, 1957, **54**, 494–497.

Doctor, R. F., & Winder, C. L. Delinquent vs. nondelinquent performance on the Porteus Qualitative Maze Test. *J. consult. Psychol.*, 1954, **18**, 71–73.

Glueck, Sheldon, & Glueck, Eleanor T. *Unraveling juvenile delinquency.* New York: Commonwealth Fund, 1950.

Glueck, Sheldon, & Glueck, Eleanor T. Early detection of future delinquents. *J. crim. Law Criminol.*, 1956, **47**, 174–182.

Glueck, Sheldon, & Glueck, Eleanor T. *Predicting delinquency and crime.* Cambridge, Mass.: Harvard Univer. Press, 1959.

Hanley, C. Responses to the wording of personality test items. *J. consult. Psychol.*, 1959, **23**, 261–265.

Hathaway, S. R., & Monachesi, E. *Analyzing and predicting juvenile delinquency with the MMPI.* Minneapolis: Univer. of Minnesota Press, 1953.

Hathaway, S. R. & Monachesi, E. The personalities of predelinquent boys. *J. crim. Law Criminol.*, 1957, **48**, 149–163.

Jones, D. S., Livson, N. H. & Sarbin, T. Perceptual completion behavior in juvenile delinquents. *Percept. mot. Skills*, 1955, **5**, 141-146.

Kvaraceus, W. C. *The community and the delinquent.* Yonkers-on-Hudson: World Book Co., 1954.

McKinley, J. C., & Hathaway, S. R. The Minnesota Multiphasic Personality Inventory: V. Hysteria, hypomania and psychopathic deviate. *J. appl. Psychol.*, 1944, **28**, 153–174.

Meehl, P. E., & Rosen, A. Antecedent probability and the efficiency of Psychometric signs, patterns, or cutting scores. *Psychol. Bull.*, 1955, **52**, 194–215.

Newman, D. J. Pleading guilty for considerations: A study of bargain justice. *J. crim. Law Criminol.*, 1956, **46**, 780–790.

Paton, J. H. Predicting prison adjustment with the Minnesota Multiphasic Personality Inventory. *J. clin. Psychol.*, 1958, **14**, 308–312.

Reiss, A. J. Unraveling juvenile delinquency: II. An appraisal of the research methods. *Amer. J. Sociol.*, 1951, **57**, 115–121.

Rempel, P. P. The use of multivariate statistical analysis of Minnesota Multiphasic Personality Inventory scores in the classification of delinquent and non-delinquent high school boys. *J. consult. Psychol.*, 1958, **22**, 17–23.

Rorschach, H. *Psychodiagnostics.* (2d ed.) Berne: Verlag Hans Huber, 1942.

Rubin, S. Unraveling juvenile delinquency: I. Illusions in a research project using matched pairs. *Amer. J. Sociol.*, 1951, **57**, 107–114.

Schactel, E. G. Some notes on the use of the Rorschach Test. In Sheldon & Eleanor T. Glueck, *Unraveling juvenile delinquency.* New York: Commonwealth Fund, 1950.

Shaplin, J. T., & Tiedman, D. V. Comment on the juvenile delinquency prediction tables in the Gluecks' Unraveling Juvenile Delinquency. *Amer. sociol. Rev.*, 1951, **16**, 544–548.

Walters, A. A. A note on statistical methods of predicting delinquency. *Brit. J. Delinquency*, 1956, **6**, 297–302.

Wirt, R. D., & Briggs, P. F. Personality and environmental factors in the development of delinquency. *Psychol. Monogr.*, 1959, **73**, No. 15.

Woodward, Mary. The role of low intelligence in delinquency. *Brit. J. Delinquency*, 1955, **5**, 281–303.

Zakolski, F. C. Studies in delinquency: I. Personality structure of delinquent boys. *J. genet. Pschol.*, 1949, **74**, 109–117.

WILLIAM W. WATTENBERG

11 Psychologists and Juvenile Delinquency

The psychologist can state three basic facts about juvenile delinquency: (1) As is true of any form of social behavior or misbehavior, delinquency is the result of the complex interaction of many forces — physical, intellectual, social, and cultural. (2) Boys and girls involved in misdeeds have personalities which can still be substantially modified. (3) Although much research has been done about juvenile delinquency, a great deal remains to be learned.

The most important fact of all is that delinquency is a complex phenomenon. It is an example of what the scientist would call multiple causation. For example, in the cases treated by the Judge Baker Foundation Clinic in Boston, the experienced team of Healy and Bronner (1936) found that on the average three or four causal factors would be operating, and that in each case the combinations might be different.

One convenient way of ordering the material is to examine some of the more frequent combinations of cause and effect. We may think of these as being verified clusters of characteristics, something like what physicians would call a syndrome. Before such clusters are described, however, a caution must be given: There is danger that the reader will think we are inviting the classification of young people into types, that it is possible to label each delinquent and put him into the proper pigeonhole for treatment. Rather, what we shall be doing is to portray a few of the many combinations which in varying degrees make up the total group we call delinquents. Although we shall rely to a large extent on the pioneering cluster analysis made by Hewitt and Jenkins (1946) from a statistical study of 500 cases brought to a child guidance clinic in Ann Arbor, Michigan, we shall supplement this with the findings of other investigators who have exploited the same general idea.

GANG CHILDREN

Numerically speaking, the most common "type" of delinquent is a young man or woman who gets into difficulties as one member of a group with whom he or she has pleasant, easy-going social relationships. These youngsters take a casual attitude toward laws. Their credo boils down to "Be loyal to thy friends." They will do "anything" for a friend, and they have many friends.

Superficial investigation shows that these young people come from easy-going, neglectful homes in areas where the delinquency rates are high. It is frequently pointed out that in such homes the young people are "unsupervised." Various investigators use different terms to describe these young people. Hewitt and Jenkins called them "socialized delinquents." In the well-known classification by Riesman they would be termed "other-directed." They fit the pattern Havighurst and Taba (1949) called "adaptive."

If we dig beneath the surface, we are likely to find that at a very early age these children were allowed to roam the streets and were trusted to their own resources. Early they learned to rely upon other children for safety and satisfaction. They came to be dependent upon contemporaries, not upon adults. There are two results: (1) their consciences are weak, extremely flexible; and (2) they have a deep anxiety, a dread of loneliness. They respond to their anxiety by becoming very skillful at securing and holding friends. So adept are they at casual socializing that they can and do keep their anxiety down by having social fun. They are hungry for friends and for excitement.

In the socially least favored areas of a city these young people become delinquent in large numbers. For one thing, the very circumstances of life for adults almost guarantee that most youth will go unsupervised. The pressures of earning a living and fighting poverty preoccupy the parents. Many are products of life on foreign soil or rural areas and do not understand city life. Furthermore, the dwelling units are small and overcrowded; to avoid having the children underfoot the adults encourage them to fend for themselves. As Clifford Shaw (1942), his colleagues at the Illinois Institute for Juvenile Research, and subsequent sociologists have shown, these neighborhoods are typified by social disorganization and by a tradition of delinquency. Daring and excitement are found most easily in conflict with rival gangs or with the police. This accounts for the fact that in general the lower the average family income in an urban neighborhood, the higher the delinquency rate. An unpublished study by the present author discovered a rank-order correlation rate above .90 for this relationship in Detroit.

Delinquency of this variety does not yield to strictly psychological measures. The gang boy or girl is a poor candidate for counseling or psychotherapy. Although there is a deep stratum of anxiety, the person's social skill prevents this from emerging in a form suitable for treatment purposes.

The most obvious tactic to follow with these young people is to remove them from a delinquent group and place them in one which is not delinquent. Unfortunately, in the neighborhoods in which most live this turns out to be almost impossible. The next best move is to attempt to bring an entire group under skilled supervision as is being done by the "detached worker" program inaugurated by the New York City Youth Board and copied in other places. On occasion this works well.

Failing some such salvage operation, what usually happens is that these gang youngsters continue to get into trouble until they are old enough to form enduring liaisons with the opposite sex. Then, in loyalty to sweetheart or spouse they stay out of trouble. As delinquents their careers seem unending; fortunately, adult criminality is not their line.

Experienced police and juvenile court officials are familiar with this pattern. They consider the individuals to be psychologically normal, and therefore rarely request psychological evaluation. In this they are wise; in most cases an elaborate psychological appraisal (anything beyond routine intelligence testing) would be a waste of scarce resources.

At the present state of our knowledge — which may, of course, change at any time — psychologists as such have little to offer. The reduction of this type of delinquency is more likely to grow out of the efforts of sociologists and group workers.

UNSOCIALIZED AGGRESSIVE BOYS

In contrast to the above group are the boys termed "unsocialized aggressive" by Hewitt and Jenkins (1946). Other workers have called them "ego-damaged." Probably the best full-length description is in Redl and Wineman's *Children Who Hate* (1951).

Composed almost exclusively of boys, this group is typified by explosive attitudes and a wide range of offenses. Their police records begin early, expand rapidly, and include everything in the book. They have little tolerance for any type of frustration, and their self-control is repeatedly burst apart by eruptions of rage.

The homes these boys come from are usually classed as "rejecting." Their mothers actively dislike them; if the fathers have not deserted, they are given to physical violence. In terms of the items which make up the Gluecks' Social Prediction Scale (1959), discussed in the previous chapter, (love of father for child, discipline by father, love of mother for child, supervision by mother, and family cohesion), these boys register scores that indicate delinquency and repeating are certainties. They live up to the predictions.

When seen close up, the parents of these boys prove to be violently ambivalent: They are capable of fierce protection of their offspring, and alternate this with brutal and impatient treatment. Lacking any security and confronting aggression, these children carry so heavy a load of hate that they cannot master it or their other impulses except for temporary delinquent purposes. In school, they are readily recognized even in the primary grades. They cannot settle down to work; they are enraged by minor setbacks; they see the world as united against them; they are cruel to other children; they are foolhardy little daredevils bereft of a sense of consequences.

Unless something is done, these violent and dangerous boys will develop into equally dangerous men. Throughout their lives they will menace other people and themselves. The evidence indicates that fifteen years after their first delinquency they will be in prison. Extensive experimentation conducted by Fritz Redl (1952) both at the Pioneer House in Detroit and under auspices of the National Institute of Mental Health in Bethesda, Maryland, has demonstrated that a well-designed treatment home can repair the damage to such boys and enable them to cope adequately with life problems.

Skillful work is required to identify those boys who could be helped by an appropriate program. The fact is that the explosions of anger which appear to be the key symptom can be caused by a number of conditions, each offering a different probability of successful treatment and each calling for a different disposition by the juvenile court. In some instances, for example, some types of incomplete brain development or brain damage may be responsible for the lack of control.

If brain damage is a crucial factor, a treatment-home program would hardly work. In such cases, sedatives administered under medical supervision may control the outburst. More likely, permanent institutionalization will be required. In other cases, mental illness (a psychosis) may be in the picture. Here commitment to a mental hospital or a treatment home for emotionally disturbed children is in order.

Most states almost totally lack adequate treatment homes. Here and there, heroic workers attempt to make do with improvised facilities — and too often fail. Few psychiatrists, psychologists, and social workers have been trained to man the necessary programs. As far as this group of boys is concerned we might as well be living in the Dark Ages, except for one fact: we know what can be done and what needs to be done.

Related to the lack of appropriate facilities goes delay in giving these children what treatment is available. We do not know for sure what could be accomplished if there were prompt action the minute such a child was spotted. When this could be done, at the age of five or six, his small size beclouds perception of danger. Even when he commits his first actionable offenses at seven or eight, people let themselves be beguiled by the vain hope that "he will grow out of it." Accordingly, at first he may be placed in a boarding home, or returned to his parents, or receive perfunctory probation. Precious years drag by. Meanwhile, the parents become more violently hostile, neighbors turn persistently punitive, classmates do battle at the least provocation. In school, scholastic difficulties and failures are piled on top of futile, impatient discipline. Years of war with a hostile world — and such a boy's conduct would turn all but the saintliest saints against him — etch aggression ever more ineradicably into the personality structure. A psychologist who could give the alarm early and be insistent in opposing temporizing and inconclusive measures suggested because the offender is "so young" may literally save a life.

"ACCIDENTAL" DELINQUENCY

Another contrast is provided by those young people who are caught in offenses which are definitely illegal and which resulted from lapses in judgment or from problems arising in the course of the child's normal development. Put differently, the young people are really normal in a basic psychological sense. Possibly they did not recognize the seriousness of what they did; possibly their deeds seemed innocuous because "everyone" they knew did the same thing (like adults driving four miles an hour over the speed limit) or they were copying what they felt to be sophisticated behavior of grownups. Having detected the offense, the police performed their duty of law enforcement. For some reason, the case reaches the court. What should be done?

In some instances, the offense is serious in its consequences rather than its intent. Some boys, for example, were dropping snowballs from an overpass onto automobiles speeding on an expressway. One startled driver lost control of his car. As a result, four cars were wrecked and three people went to hospitals. The boys were aghast at what they had unwittingly done. Their dismay at the event was doubled by being taken into custody and redoubled by their parents' reactions.

Probably this string of unpleasant consequences by itself would strengthen the consciences of these boys if they were normal children. This alone would guarantee that they would neither repeat this offense nor engage in any which was remotely similar. Generally, normal young people learn from being punished. More harm than good, however, is done if the punishment takes a form bringing them in contact with tough delinquents prepared to teach the tricks of true crime.

A second type of "accidental" delinquency results from discovery and apprehension of a young person for activities which, although illegal, are prevalent and usually undetected. The principal illustrations have to do with sex behavior, both homosexual and heterosexual. The Kinsey reports have confirmed many researches which were less ambitious. Sex activities of various kinds which would be clear violations of the law are very prevalent. Among boys, for instance, Kinsey has established that homosexual stimulation does not forecast adult maladjustment but does involve over 20 percent of adolescent males. Police statistics show that only a small proportion of the total incidents is detected. However, if accidental discovery does take place some adults will call the police, and the offenders quite likely will be brought to court.

A number of problems immediately emerge. First, the activity is clearly illegal; no law-enforcement officer or judge can condone it. Second, sexual activities of this nature are considered perverted, and there is always the possibility that a young person caught in such an act may develop abnormally. For these reasons, a case of this type is almost certain to be referred to a psychologist or a psychiatrist. What is his responsibility?

An experienced professional will realize at once that any recommendation he may make will be accepted only if all concerned are sure he has been thorough in his work. Therefore, he will act with care. Usually, he will test all youngsters involved and will do some detective work to discover who instigated the episodes, and how. It is possible that the principal instigator or the principal victim present sufficient evidence of emotional disturbance to warrant a referral for counseling or therapy. It is always possible that an adult exploiter has been active and that his apprehension should be recommended as a police measure.

In the majority of youths, however, it will turn out that personality structures are clearly within the normal range. In this event, some court official (possibly the psychologist) will make it clear to the young people that their conduct was unacceptable and that it is banned. Also, a conference with the parents must be held to help them recognize the incident for what it was and to resolve any doubts they may have. Care must be taken to settle any anxieties which might lead to real perversion. Usually this type of case is cleared up unofficially. (See pages 259–262.)

A different situation, one involving what the child development people now call "developmental tasks," is linked to the fact that many preadolescents are impelled to establish their psychological independence and freedom from childishness. They may choose to show resourcefulness or daring or both by acts of theft or vandalism. Usually, if the item taken is inexpensive or the damage is slight, the police settle the episodes satisfactorily by seeing that the loss is made good. Occasionally, however, the aggrieved party makes a complaint which must be taken quite seriously. If a school system, for example, has spent tens of thousands of dollars replacing stoned windows, it may decide to insist upon recourse to the courts. If the item taken is an automobile, court action may be mandatory.

The settlement of damages is not the task of a psychologist; his duty is the assessment of personality. In cases of this type, his investigation may show that the child is developing "on schedule," and that the behavior under review is an unfortunate outcropping of normal motivations. Clearly, repetitions must be prevented. Therefore, he will probably urge the judge to limit his disposition to an impressive verbal warning, possibly reinforced by probation.

He will declare against the use of facilities needed to deal with more disturbed or more seriously delinquent boys or girls.

A psychologist in a juvenile court, and any other to whom troubled parents may turn, must master the facts of child development. He has to know what normal youngsters are like in order to ascertain what is abnormal. More important, he may have to help his colleagues in the court, and parents as well, keep the incident in proper perspective.

Even the most normal adolescents do outrageous things. They will adopt ungainly or offensive clothing fads. Their language is often salted with slang and profanity. From time to time dance movements are almost obscenely suggestive. Young people will attempt bravado by smoking, drinking, and imitating adult vices. When seen in a youngster who we know has been delinquent, these acts may be viewed as delinquent or even as the cause of delinquency. Probation officers, attendants in detention homes, and police officers are apt to wage war on such conduct. Even an occasional judge will order an obnoxious haircut shaved off under the illusion that this will wipe out delinquency.

Campaigns of this nature will occasionally sweep through a community, and become epidemic among court workers. It is one function of psychological science to indicate at which aspects of a total situation we can most effectively use our limited resources. Psychologists have a duty to reduce to a minimum the misdirection of energy. They will recognize the perils of trying to eradicate normal behavior; they can also recognize even trained people's hope for magic solutions. So, when an occasional false hue and cry is raised, they will circumspectly do their part to restore perspective.

Another variety of "normal" delinquency arises over behavior which is symbolic of grown-up status — permitted to adults but forbidden to youth. Drinking and driving cars are two examples. Peripherally, there is behavior where adults are not usually apprehended, but young people may be, as in petty gambling or premarital sexual intercourse.

These activities are considered "sophisticated" by many adults; to an adolescent, they may be symbols of adulthood. The "You Must Be Over 21" sign in a bar is a challenge. Accordingly, in the same spirit with which many self-considered law-abiding citizens swigged during Prohibition days and laughingly called themselves "scofflaws," so many a teen-ager defies similar enactments applying to him. Moreover, he may receive tacit, if not active, encouragement from parents.

In those cases which reach the courts, and especially a court clinic, there may be complicating factors. In some cases the behavior is an aspect of a neurotic parent-child interaction which is moving toward more serious misbehavior; for some girls it is a prelude to sex delinquency. In other instances, the case has come to court because police are applying "selective enforcement." They have reason to believe the group taken into custody has engaged in other offenses.

The vast majority of the "sophisticated" offenders, however, will be recognized to be engaged in a "normal and natural" reaching for adult status; they are doing exactly what a psychologist would expect many adolescents to attempt. Indeed, the very fact that the activities are prohibited is, psychologically speaking, self-instigating of infraction upon the part of the original enactment. All this a trained psychologist knows. However, if he is an officer of a court, and the statute in question has been adopted by legislators who undoubtedly are cognizant of these very arguments, the psychologist can hardly take what is essentially a subversive course. Should offenders be brought to his attention, he must consider the offense to be just that. If examination reveals no verifiable personality or emotional defect in the young people, that fact he relays to the proper authority.

MOTHER-DAUGHTER FEUDS

Among some girl delinquents there is a subtle and potent interaction between mother and daughter. Indeed, in many such cases the mother is the person who made the complaint to police or court. A portion of the motivation, not always unconscious, for the daughter's offenses is spitefulness: she enjoys being a source of disgrace for the family and especially for her mother.

A close-up of the feuding within the home may suggest that the mother is gaining some satisfaction from her daughter's misdeeds. In one case familiar to the author, the investigating policewoman said the mother greeted the girl the morning after each date with the taunting question, "Are you still a virgin?" Who was suggesting what to whom?

Responding to so provocative a combination of nagging and

suspicion, the girl clutches the suggestive signs of sophistication, and uses them to goad her mother. There may be no laws against make-up and clothing fads, but smoking and drinking are obvious next moves. Almost inevitably, she gives substance to what once were groundless suspicions. She may stay out all night, or even run away. In either case there are almost certain to be sex episodes, and often promiscuity. In one way or another the mother learns of what is happening. The notation on the official papers may be "ungovernable behavior," "incorrigibility," "truancy from home," or "immoral behavior."

The hopeful thing about this pattern is the ease with which it can be corrected by good counseling or good social casework. As distinguished from the patterns earlier described, in this one the family conditions are still active. In many instances, either the mother, the daughter, or both may be helped to achieve insight. Such cases lie within the domain of the social worker rather than that of the psychologist. If the latter enters the picture at all it is to do some testing.

NEUROTIC DELINQUENCY

There are some cases where an inner conflict finds expression in delinquent acts. The existence of such situations is most readily recognized in suburbs and in middle-class neighborhoods. Where homes and family life are likely to be good, where there is little poverty, and few children are delinquent, the reasons for the bulk of delinquency no longer operate. Then it is easy to face the possibility that a young person's behavior satisfies unconscious motivations. The number of specific combinations is so great as to defy cataloguing. Not only that, but even people familiar with the field are forever being figuratively floored by unexpected patterns. For this reason we shall give only a sample of illustrations.

Now and again one encounters a very "good" boy who has been apprehended in a burglary. He readily confesses to a whole series; checking his story the police find the loot from a dozen or more "jobs" hidden in a closet or an attic. When they come to the police station or detention home the parents are flabbergasted by his attitude; rather than being remorseful or shamefaced, he seems relieved. If psychological treatment is given it is soon ascertained that the boy had a feeling he was wicked. His reputation

for being good — until the thefts began this was objectively justified — he regarded as deception. Trying to shed his reputation and
to obtain the punishment his inexplicable guilt demanded, he began
to steal and to pave the way for discovery and retribution.

More familiar, and less devious in their operation, are the ways
in which a young man who doubts his masculinity may resolve
his feelings of inadequacy. He can go in for sexual conquest; he
can provoke fights to prove his toughness; he can drive recklessly.

Another not infrequent chain is built around the fact that to
many young people of both sexes, one sign of being loved is to
have possessions. (Grownups often bring gifts to a child they like;
therefore, a child who has plenty of things must be a loved child.)
Fearing they are not loved — and indeed many truly are neglected
— they give themselves a counterfeit affection. They steal.

It would be possible to fill this book with case illustrations of
delinquents whose acts had neurotic origin. However, the three
rather commonplace examples cited above will suffice. Having
read them, a tough-minded doubting Thomas will have decided
that the author is another wacky psychologist; a trained psychologist or psychiatrist will start muttering about oversimplification.

The essence of the situation lies in exactly that contradiction.
The link between act and purposes is so involved and intricate as
to seem incredible, and yet it defies simple summary. Even while
doubting, the layman will talk of kleptomania, pyromania, and
nymphomania; the psychologists and psychiatrists wince when
they hear the words because they feel they can do little by label-
ing conduct.

Psychologists, along with psychiatrists, are called upon to deal
with the "neurotic" delinquents most frequently when the offense
seems senseless. As one veteran police officer put it, "I always try
to place myself in the position of the kid, and figure out what made
him do what he did. If I can't come up with a good answer then
I guess maybe he's cracked and bring him to the clinic." Essentially, this represents good judgment; the only problem is that
some youngsters whose offenses may seem understandable really
need clinic service.

Generally, in this type of case, psychologists enter the picture
by establishing the fact of emotional upset and by finding clues
as to its nature. Projective tests, such as the Rorschach inkblots,
the various theme-evoking pictures, and incomplete sentences are
used. Interviews with the parents and the young person are held

by either a psychologist, a psychiatrist, or a social worker. Case conferences pull together the evidence. If a psychiatrist is available he is the one usually called upon to establish the diagnosis, but he usually relies heavily on the material gathered by his colleagues.

If, indeed, there are significant neurotic overtones to the delinquency, psychotherapy of some type is required. Who conducts treatment is a matter differently decided in specific cases. Technically, this is the province of the psychiatrist. In public clinics, psychologists and social workers do the actual work under the supervision of the psychiatrist, who gives any medical treatment required. If a juvenile court is large enough to have a full clinic staff, the role of the clinic in giving treatment depends upon the volume of work. Priority is generally given to preparing recommendations on cases coming before the judge and the referees. In few cases is a backlog tolerated at this point. Accordingly, only if the clinic staff is caught up with this aspect of its function will it undertake treatment.

The type of psychotherapy required in undoing any neurosis is usually lengthy. What evidence we have shows that in cases where a child or a parent is seen only two or three times little is accomplished. One usually has to think of a program involving one or more sessions a week and extending over months or years. The exigencies of a court clinic render this prohibitive; accordingly, the tendency is to refer cases to a child guidance clinic or to a private psychiatrist.

MIXED PATTERNS

As stated earlier, the patterns of interaction described are far from a complete listing, and create a deceptively simple impression. Human beings do not fall into any simple classification scheme; whenever anyone divides children or adults into types, he quickly discovers that very few conform purely to any single type. Most combine characteristics of several descriptions. So it is with young people picked up by the police.

Among boys who are in gangs, for example, some carry a load of aggression, some are pathetic "fall guys" who feel comfortable being "dopey," a few may be genuinely inclined toward homosexuality, and so it goes. Among girls picked up for promiscuity, some may be feeble-minded victims of exploiters, some may be seeking to satisfy dependency needs, some may be daughters cold-bloodedly imitating prostitute mothers, and some may be finding pure physical pleasure. And it is not uncommon to find instances where a given individual's conduct serves several functions in his life.

Enough has been said now to make it clear why people who study delinquency regard it as a complicated phenomenon. In a particular child's life a significant role may be played by his intelligence, his physique, his body chemistry, his parents, his school, his church, his friends, his neighborhood, and all the social services and communication networks we call a community. To understand him fully we may need to tap the knowledge of a physician, a psychologist, a sociologist, a psychiatrist, or more probably a team composed of all. Once we understand him, if we are to help him we need to bring to bear the talents of policemen, teachers, judges, probation officers, social workers, psychologists, group leaders, clergymen, psychiatrists, parents — a task force tailored to his problems. If these people are ever to become more effective they need the knowledge discovered by research workers from many disciplines, explained and inculcated through all the media by which knowledge is spread among intelligent people.

In this massive, if complex, endeavor no one profession, no one science, no one category of specialist can go it alone. All must work together well and bring to bear the tools of thinking and operating in which each is best trained. The jobs of the psychologist are significant ones: to gather knowledge through research on personality dynamics, to provide verifiable information as to the intelligence and personality structure of individuals, to make recommendations as to program, and to conduct certain forms of treatment.

PSYCHOLOGISTS IN THE JUVENILE COURT

Figuratively, the juvenile court is a species of parent. The "delinquent" boy or girl who appears in the court is there to be protected and re-educated rather than to be judged and punished. Although the precise situation varies from state to state, juvenile courts are in the tradition of that aspect of British legal institutions administering to the helpless.

The juvenile court may embrace other functions as well as handling juvenile offenders. It may act as guardian for neglected children. It may oversee processes of adoption. The formality around which many courts function in respect to delinquents may be in this spirit: The court hears a petition that the young person be declared a delinquent and, therefore, a responsibility of the court. In essence, the parents having been unable to provide suitable character formation, the court steps in either to strengthen the hand of the parents or to entrust the child's future to other persons.

The relationship between theory and actuality varies widely. Some juvenile court judges comport themselves as would a magistrate hearing criminal cases. They think of themselves as dispensing punishment; the youngsters are expected to, and usually do, regard the court's dispositions as sentences. In other instances, the court functions much as would a mammoth and very complex social service agency. The judge may act as administrator for an establishment which operates a detention home, a supervision service for boarding homes, a child placement agency, a clinic, a family counseling center, and cottages for dependent children. In such instances most of the courtroom duties may be delegated to referees. A boy or girl coming before the latter type of court may be the object of a complex processing designed not so much to determine guilt or innocence as to work out a program calculated to find the causes of his difficulties and place in operation corrective or rehabilitative measures. Should some penalty be levied, it is imposed because this procedure is felt most suitable.

It is in a juvenile court which assumes almost a medical attitude that psychological services are most fruitfully utilized. Therefore, this section will be mainly concerned with what happens in such a context.

Intake

A juvenile, as defined in terms of chronological age by state statute, is generally brought to the attention of a juvenile court by the police. However, parents, schools or any interested citizen may file the requisite petition. If delinquency is at issue, the behavior so considered has been a matter for legislative enactment. Usually a juvenile code embraces all offenses covered by statute or ordinance and, in addition, specifies certain conduct felt to be a bad omen on the part of a young person. In the latter category may be placed disobedience, smoking, drinking, incorrigibility, associating with immoral persons, frequenting forbidden establishments, and truancy from home or school.

Usually the first step taken by the court is to assign a case for preliminary investigation to one of its personnel. In some cases there may be an intake official empowered to accept or reject cases. The decision on this matter is based upon court policies; the person designated is usually a social worker, a probation officer, or a legally trained referee.

Waiving Jurisdiction

Where the offense committed by a juvenile is very serious the first question the court may be asked to decide is whether or not to waive jurisdiction. Many juvenile codes set a minimum age above which the prosecuting attorney may ask to have a boy or girl placed on trial as an adult. The juvenile court judge must decide what to do. There are several highly justifiable grounds for waiving jurisdiction:

1. The nature of the offense and the possibility of repetition are such that the protection of society demands the offender be kept out of circulation beyond the age where the jurisdiction of the juvenile court ends. Waivers are frequently granted where the juvenile is accused of homicide, forcible rape, armed robbery, or aggravated assault.

2. Even though the offense is not quite so dramatic, the young person has a very long juvenile record and all the resources available to a juvenile court have been exhausted in vain. Not only has the youth failed to respond, but it is almost certain he will continue to do so. In addition, his or her presence in a training school might be corrupting to other young people.

3. The offender requires permanent institutionalization, probably lifelong, of a type not available to a juvenile court.

The extent to which psychologists are consulted in respect to the first two reasons varies with court policy. In most cases, the factual record and the opinion of the probation officers with firsthand knowledge are all the court requires for action. However, a number of judges insist upon a psychological evaluation. They regard a waiver as in effect a declaration that the youth's personality development is either substantially completed or else that the distortion is of a nature beyond reach of any facility the court can bring to bear. In medical gobbledygook, "The prognosis is bad."

Before making such a judgment, the court may require that its clinic make a thorough investigation. This usually means the psychologists will administer tests of personality structure; a psychiatric consultant will weigh the evidence.

In some cases it will be clear that the young man or woman is, in effect, an adult criminal. A young man may be a cool, calculating burglar; a young woman, a thoroughly professional prostitute. Their behavior is motivated by the attitudes we find in adult criminals. In other instances, the investigation reveals that the young person is psychopathic in the sense that he or she has a very weak conscience (super-ego) and therefore feels no guilt or anxiety. At the present time, the outlook for successful treatment for this type of defective personality is poor. (See Chapter 12.) Accordingly, from the viewpoint of broad social policy, the only hope is to set in motion the dual program of adult criminal courts: temporarily protect society by sequestering the offender and, by this demonstration of punishment, convince him that crime does not pay. In effect, psychological science says to the juvenile court judge, "Your honor, we give up. The personality of this young man or woman is such that this court can do nothing constructive. Maybe the criminal courts can do better; at least, they can protect society."

By contrast, there may be cases where, despite the nature of the offense, the young person may well respond to treatment within the time limits available to the juvenile court. For instance, a juvenile may have set a fire which resulted in a death. The clinic of the court may be reasonably certain that the emotional disturbance which led to the act is of a type in which currently known methods of psychotherapy will be successful. Both the psychologist and the psychiatric consultants look at the individual rather than at the offense. They utilize skill in evaluating personality and bring to bear the results of research which provide predictive indices. If these indicate that the young person can be straightened out, the psychiatrist or the psychologist advises the judge, "Your honor, we can save this boy or girl. He or she can be treated successfully. If you order the proper disposition we will not only protect society but add to it one more good citizen."

The third situation which may arise occurs where the offender is suffering from a serious psychiatric disorder but there is a problem in finding an appropriate institution in which to place him. A concrete illustration is provided by a boy who brutally murdered a little girl. It was soon established that, because of an early attack of encephalitis, he suffered from brain damage. Tests and psychiatric study indicated that, when subjected to heavy frustration, he could readily go into ungovernable rages and that his condition could be expected to grow worse. He needed to be institutionalized; unless some miraculous discovery is made, his stay will be permanent. None of the child-treatment facilities in his state were equipped to handle a patient so dangerous to others. None of the regular mental hospitals would accept him. The only place he could be sent was a hospital for the criminally insane, to which the juvenile court was not authorized to make commitments. Therefore, the juvenile court judge waived jurisdiction; he was tried in a criminal court, and sent to the appropriate hospital. In other instances, psychological testing and psychiatric evaluation will reveal psychotic conditions and point to probability of violence. When he has this finding, the action of the judge is guided by his knowledge of facilities, of their admission procedures, and of legal technicalities.

As indicated above, both psychological testing and psychiatric evaluation go hand in hand. Most court clinics have full-time psychologists. Psychiatrists are in short supply and command high salaries. Some court clinics have a full-time psychiatrist; usually, he is the clinic director. In other cases, psychiatric consultants are employed on a part-time basis, and a psychologist is the clinic director. The process by which the clinic arrives at the type of recommendation is one involving teamwork. Usually a social worker gathers family information through interviews, a psychologist gives and interprets tests, and a psychiatrist coordinates this information along with any medical data. Where commitment is at issue, there may be a legal requirement that one or more psychiatrists sign the recommendation. In other instances, a psychologist may make the presentation.

Unofficial Action

Year after year the statistics gathered by the United States Children's Bureau reveal that about half of all cases accepted by juvenile courts in the United States are handled on an unofficial basis. This means that an acceptable program for a given youngster was worked out and put into operation without a formal court hearing. Neither an official finding of delinquency nor a court order was required to put it into effect.

What has happened is this: The preliminary investigation revealed that the youngster's behavior resulted from either a situation or a psychological condition which could be corrected. Possibly the parents showed a clear willingness to take voluntary action. In other instances, a social agency of one sort or another either was ready to enter the situation or else was already active. The cooperation volunteered by the parents, the program being undertaken by the agency, or both, appeared sufficient to take care of matters. The fact that the case was in the court gave everyone a feeling of urgency. If this works, nothing more may be in order.

The basic procedure in unofficial cases is highly informal. Usually there is much telephone communication. Often, the closest approach to formality is a case conference at which court personnel and representatives of the various agencies which have dealt with or are likely to deal with the young offender and the family share information, ideas, and opinions. The goal is agreement upon a plan of action. It is understood that, if the agreement is approved by the court personnel, the court will back the plan.

Unless this backing requires a court hearing, the last step, as far as the court is concerned, is for someone connected with the court to interview the parents to make sure that they are willing to take whatever steps would constitute cooperation. In some instances a promise is exacted from them. This may be accompanied by either an implied or open ultimatum that "next time" more drastic action may be taken. With this, for the time being, the case is considered closed as far as the court is concerned.

To illustrate this process, here are two cases in which unofficial action was taken:

A girl was reported as having run away from home. She was found in a clubhouse maintained by a group of boys; immoral actions were charged. Routine intelligence tests showed she was feeble-minded. In a conference with a social worker from the clinic the mother revealed that, although application had been made to place the girl in a home for the mentally retarded, she had hesitated to put her daughter in an institution. With the discovery that the girl could be easily victimized the mother began to realize that she could not provide the protection that a good institution offered. Accordingly, arrangements were made to place the girl in such an institution; acceptance by the institution was verified. When notification that the girl had actually entered was received, the file was closed.

A boy was picked up for breaking school windows. His mother, a widow with two other children (both girls), seemed sincerely upset and offered to do whatever she could. A chaplain connected with the court reported that the boy's pastor had said the family was a good one and raised the possibility of help from a Big Brother organization of the boy's faith. Evaluation by the court clinic and consultation with the professional workers at the Big Brother office indicated that assignment of a Big Brother might work well. The mother had offered to pay for the damage. At a conference, the Big Brothers agreed to accept the boy; a representative of the school district declared he was satisfied with the arrangement; the court chaplain showed his approval; the court clinic's social worker agreed to talk to the mother. The mother said she would welcome the Big Brother, said she had sent a check to the school board, and expressed gratitude that she would not have to appear in court.

In essence, the misconduct of a young person brings to light a situation in which corrective action is both necessary and feasible. The fact that the young person is in the hands of a court symbolizes the seriousness of the situation. Parents and any professional personnel may be spurred to more intensive efforts. With court workers acting as catalysts, an agreement is reached as to who will do what. Frequently, there are reasonable grounds for believing either that a solution has been reached or, at the very least, that the proposal offers enough promise so that it should be given a chance before resorting to more drastic measures. For the time being, the formal powers of the court are held in reserve.

Psychologists enter the highly informal processes of unofficial action in many ways. As the person, usually a probation worker, making the preliminary investigation begins to size up the situation and holds the initial discussions, he starts to think in terms of action and finds he needs a psychological appraisal of the youngster involved. Once he has this, he may want the opinion of the psychologist on the proposed solution. In other instances, where a youngster was immediately referred for psychological testing, the court's psychological services may see a possible solution and take the initiative in developing the arrangements.

Almost invariably, when case conferences are held, psychologists are present; in some courts, these conferences are convened by the court clinic and held under its auspices. Official position, however, has little to do with the weight given to opinions and suggestions made in free give-and-take. If a psychologist is regarded as an impractical screwball or a pompous fool, his opinion will be largely ignored, or considered only in order to reduce the nuisance value of his opposition. Where a psychologist's relationships with other personnel are good and where there is confidence in the soundness of his judgments, his contribution may be decisive.

In sum, in unofficial court action, psychological knowledge and understanding can be at a premium. Whether advanced by a trained psychologist or by someone with a different title, facts and theories as to the causes of behavior and ways of altering behavior, as to personality structure, and as to corrective measures, are essential ingredients in the development of specific plans. The focus here is on the education or re-education of a young person; behavior is taken into account mainly to the extent that it tells about the person.

The term "unofficial" may give a false impression of the significance of this aspect of the work of juvenile courts and of work with juvenile delinquents. We cannot emphasize too strongly that unofficial handling accounts for half the volume of juvenile court activity. Observers familiar with the field tend to believe that this half is the more effective one.

Official Dispositions

In the vast majority of formal court hearings the young people acknowledge the actions of which they stand accused. In contrast to adult trials, the fundamental issue in juvenile court cases heard by judges or referees is what should be done with or for the person in court. Accordingly, it is rare to see an attorney, except where a request for waiver is being heard.

In some states, should a youngster declare he is not guilty of the charges, he has the right to request that a jury hear the evidence. For this reason, even where the juvenile court has its own courtroom one will see an occasional jury box. Court attendants wait for years in vain to see it occupied.

From the above it will be recognized that in the United States juvenile courts have earned a reputation for fairness and for living up to their purpose. These are courts which serve and protect youth; they are not courts from which young people must be protected.

The first order of business before an official juvenile court session, of course, is to ascertain the facts and circumstances of reported offenses. This done, the main concern is choice of disposition. There are a number of things the judge or his representative may do: dismiss the case, remand the child to custody of parent or guardian, administer a lecture, place the young person on probation, commit him to a mental hospital or home for the mentally retarded, place him in a boarding home, send him to a rehabilitative facility operated under religious or private (philanthropic) auspices, or commit him to a publicly operated training school. Many judges extend the official range of dispositions by attaching conditions either to probation or to "suspended sentences" to training schools. This extended range may include restitution, clinic treatment, psychiatric evaluation or treatment of a parent, placement of the child with a relative, enrollment in a private school or in a character-building agency, family cooperation with a social casework agency, change in the family's living arrangements, and medical treatment.

Because of the complex issues which may be involved, some states have established "youth authorities" which relieve local courts of some decisions, especially those requiring any form of commitment. If the court decides a young person warrants being removed from his home it orders him into custody of the youth authority. This has available as wide an assortment of camps, clinics, and institutions as can be managed. (See Chapter 14.)

In the more usual case, however, the judge or referee is the one who makes the disposition. Accordingly, at the time the formal hearing is held he must have at hand all the material he may need. This usually will include any report or recommendations made by the clinic, the court's psychological services, or individual psychologists. In the hearing, the judge or referee will seek to elicit any additional information he feels he needs. On occasion he may find that he needs more material. Should this be the case, he can always continue the hearing at a later time. Thus it is not unexpected for a decision to be withheld pending psychological testing or psychiatric evaluation, if either was not part of the records, or if either should appear more relevant after the hearing than it appeared before.

The judge or his representative is limited in his dispositions by the requirements of the establishment to which he might want to send young people. In a number of instances the judge can exercise persuasion but cannot issue orders. Religious institutions, privately operated rehabilitative facilities, and individuals operating boarding homes retain liberties upon which the court cannot infringe. Mental hospitals, homes for the mentally retarded, and even training schools may be operated by public agencies completely independent of the court.

The directors and superintendents of various facilities frequently limit intake so as to increase the success of their programs. (Some, of course, less defensibly, simply protect their own ease and that of their staffs.) A particular organization or institution may justifiably refuse to accept mental defectives, schizophrenics, psychopaths, homosexuals, or some other category of youth who would either disrupt their program or require precautions which would add prohibitive costs or nullify other efforts. For this reason, the juvenile court must be able to convince the institutions' intake officials that a given youth meets their requirements. Thus, when a judge or a referee hears a case he looks at psychological reports not only to decide what is the wisest disposition, but to decide whether he can make that disposition with some assurance that it can be put into effect.

The results of intelligence tests are almost always included in the psychologists' reports. If these show a boy or girl to be mentally retarded, placement in a special institution is called for. On the other hand, psychotherapy is usually contraindicated; many rehabilitative institutions feel they can be of little use to a boy or girl of low mentality.

Usually there is also personality testing; projective instruments, such as the well-known Rorschach inkblots, are utilized in many courts. If these indicate a psychotic condition, especially schizophrenia, evaluation by a psychiatric consultant is in order. Should the diagnosis be confirmed, the court will generally see that the youngster is sent to a mental institution or treatment home, unless the condition is so mild that the child can be treated while at his own home. Almost all rehabilitative agencies refuse even to attempt working with psychotic children.

The psychologist is also expected to pick up evidence that there may be brain damage. A suspicion of it will lead to a neurological examination. If severe brain damage is established, the court will place the young person either in a home for the retarded or in a mental institution, depending upon local practice. Schools and rehabilitative agencies are only rarely equipped to be of aid where brain damage has produced uncontrolled behavior.

If the psychological examination uncovers neurotic motivation, the scope of possibilities widens. Such youngsters may be treated in clinics, residential treatment homes, or rehabilitative agencies with psychological services. The disposition will usually be recommended in the psychological report.

Especially in the last-mentioned instance, considerable informal activity may accompany the preparation of the recommendations. The court's psychologists can be expected to have easy access to any psychologists employed at mental hospitals and rehabilitative institutions. They will know what are the policies and what data are likely to be decisive in completing placement. They will be able to interest their counterparts in special aspects of a particular boy or girl. Often the report placed in the hands of judge or referee will declare a preliminary agreement that a given facility will accept the child if the court orders his placement.

Summary

If it is remembered that the juvenile court is a publicly provided parent, that it acts as a father for young people whose natural parents have been unable to prevent delinquency, the role of psychologists is simplified. The court turns to psychology for help in making decisions as would a wise father or mother. There is no restriction on the use of this branch of science beyond that imposed by judgment. The court can and often does ask the psychologist to uncover whatever information will define difficulties and then to suggest courses of action.

PSYCHOLOGISTS IN TREATMENT INSTITUTIONS

More and more, psychologists are included in the personnel of treatment homes and rehabilitative institutions. Traditionally, they are on the staffs of child guidance clinics, homes for the mentally retarded, and mental hospitals. Primarily, these men and women perform service functions within the institutional setting: they give the tests upon the basis of which young people are admitted, they help to specify the program to which young people are assigned, and they serve as counselors and therapists. They often take part in the informal agreements with court personnel, and influence the development of other facilities.

Institutional workers tend to be also trained in research. They are likely to set up and carry through research. As will be recognized by the listings in *Psychological Abstracts,* there is a tendency for this research to concentrate upon experimentation with new types of treatment or variations upon accepted programs.

Here we are concerned with the effect of all this on the development of facilities for working with delinquents. First, as psychologists engage in studies of the predictive type, many agencies and institutions become more humble in their goals and more selective as to intake. Inevitably this means that other programs must be developed to care for those excluded.

A concrete illustration can be given in the case of a treatment home which must be nameless. Originally it was built around self-government by delinquent boys and was staffed largely by men rescued from Skid Row by a religious mission. It would take any boy referred by any court. A new director brought in psychologists, who quickly pointed out that the program was often wrecked by boys who proved to be either schizophrenic or of very low IQ. Also, as an experiment, the psychologists tried out group therapy. At this time, intake was altered to boys who were of normal intelligence and free from psychosis. Follow-up studies made by psychologists next revealed that boys who had been gang members usually were not influenced by the program. Meanwhile, a higher level of staff personnel was attracted. The director decided to experiment with special, remedial educational classes. The psychologists worked with the teachers in diagnosing scholastic difficulties and developing remedial procedures. Individual counseling is gradually replacing the group therapy sessions. The institution now performs a highly specialized function for a rather selected group. It is more successful, as indicated by recidivism rates. Other institutions, some of them new, are taking the boys it rejects and have had to develop special programs.

In larger organizations this same tendency to tailor programs to individual needs, or to restrict intake to individuals likely to adjust to a program, may be handled by running a number of programs side by side, and using a classification type of orientation at intake.

A special situation is developing in respect to preventive programs in school systems. In a number of school systems efforts are made to detect predelinquents. School psychologists are often involved in studying the high-risk children and working out programs for them.

OTHER ACTIVITIES OF
PSYCHOLOGISTS

Although the most direct use of psychological science in dealing with delinquency is personalized in the court psychologist, or in the trained personnel employed in treatment agencies, there are other ways in which psychology can enter the picture.

In a few locations, police departments utilize psychological consultant services in connection with their delinquency programs. As a rule, focus is likely to be on selection of officers for youth work. The psychologist gives tests and interprets their import for this type of assignment. A more extensive arrangement was established in Detroit in 1945, when Dr. Howard Lane was employed by the Police Department and asked to work as adviser to the then recently established Crime Prevention Bureau, which eventually developed into a Youth Bureau. This bureau over a period of fifteen years has engaged in cooperative research programs with psychologists on the staff of Wayne State University.

It is in the area of research that psychologists play their most influential role in the broad social attack on juvenile crime. As has previously been made clear, delinquency is the product of multiple causation. Research has tended to concentrate either upon the social conditions which produce geographic areas of high delinquency rates or upon the genesis of personality attributes of individual boys and girls. As far as thorough training in research techniques is concerned, highly developed skill is likely to be found mainly among sociologists and psychologists. Social workers and psychiatrists are attracted mostly by case-study types of activity.

The main contributions of psychologists at present seem to be concentrated in three main streams:

1. There is a good deal of interest in studying the cause-and-effect patterns which lead to delinquency; the type of cluster or syndrome description given earlier in this chapter is an example of objective reporting and pinning down of observations stemming from psychiatric theory but cast into more "scientific" mold by psychologists. In addition there has been much work on the potent aspects of parent-child interaction.

2. The second major line of psychological research has been in the development and use of instruments for the appraisal of the personality structure and psychological attributes of individual de-

linquents. In some cases, the tests are designed primarily for study of delinquency, as in the Kvaraceus Delinquency Proneness Scales. In other instances, devices such as the Rorschach inkblots, the Rosenzweig Picture-Frustration, the Bender Gestalt, or other standard instruments are tested for efficiency in selecting or predicting. (See Chapter 10.)

3. The third main line is the development and testing of treatment programs. Here, for instance, we may find a psychologist active in setting up a project to utilize group therapy. His contribution may be not only in the invention of a technique, but in the screening of individuals to go into the program as well as the experimental evaluation of the results.

SUMMARY

Juvenile delinquency is not a simple problem. Rather, it is a series of complex patterns of behavior, each of which has to be tackled somewhat differently. To be truly effective any program must be geared to differences among individuals and communities. In any over-all attack on the interrelated problems, the skills of many differently trained people will be required. We must utilize and respect the contributions which can be made by the clergyman and the social worker, the police officer and the psychiatrist, the judge and the teacher, the probation officer and the sociologist. To the diligent and inspired teamwork that is essential, the psychologist can bring concern about individuals, skills in appraising them, and training in establishing factual relationships.

References and Recommended Readings

Australian Council for Educational Research. *The adjustment of youth.* Melbourne: Melbourne Univer. Press, 1951, Chap. 7.

Bloch, Herbert A., & Flynn, Frank J. *Delinquency: The juvenile offender in America today.* New York: Random House, 1956.

Bright shadows in Bronzetown. Chicago: Southside Community Committee, 1949.

Cohen, Frank J. *Children in trouble.* New York: Norton, 1953, Chap. 6.

Davidoff, Eugene, & Elinor S. Joetzel. *The child guidance approach to juvenile delinquency.* New York: Child Care Publications, 1951.

Doshay, Lewis J. *The boy sex offender and his later career.* New York: Grune & Stratton, 1943.

Edelston, H. *The earliest stages of delinquency.* Edinburgh: E. & S. Livingstone, 1952, Chaps. 3–5.

Eissler, K. R. *Searchlights on delinquency*. New York: International Universities Press, 1949.

Fine, Benjamin. *1,000,000 delinquents*. Cleveland: World Publishing Co., 1955.

Glueck, Sheldon, & Glueck, Eleanor T. *Physique and delinquency*. New York: Harper, 1956. Chapters 1, 7, 11–16.

Glueck, Sheldon, & Glueck, Eleanor T. *Predicting crime and delinquency*. Cambridge, Mass.: Harvard Univer. Press, 1959.

Havighurst, Robert J., & Hilda Taba. *Adolescent character and personality*. New York: Wiley, 1949, Chap. 13.

Healy, William, and Bronner, Augusta. *New light on delinquency and its treatment*. New Haven: Yale Univer. Press, 1936.

Hewitt, L. E., & Jenkins, R. L. *Fundamental patterns of maladjustment*. Springfield: State of Illinois, 1946.

Juvenile delinquency. *Ann. Amer. Acad. pol. soc. Sci.*, January, 1949, pp. 32–54.

Kahn, Alfred J. *A court for children*. New York: Columbia Univer. Press, 1953.

Kvaraceus, William C. *The community and the delinquent*. Yonkers-on-Hudson: World Book Co., 1954, Chap. 4.

Louttit, C. M. *Clinical psychology of exceptional children*. New York: Harper, 1957, Chap. 10.

Mannheim, Hermann, & Wilkins, Leslie T. *Prediction methods in relation to Borstal training*. London: Her Majesty's Stationery Office, 1955.

Mays, John B. *Growing up in the city*. Liverpool: Univer. Press of Liverpool, 1954.

Neumeyer, Martin H. *Juvenile delinquency in modern society*. Princeton, N. J.: Van Nostrand, 1955, Chaps. 7–10.

Powers, Edwin, & Witmer, Helen. *An experiment in the prevention of delinquency*. New York: Columbia Univer. Press, 1951.

Redl, Fritz, & Wineman, David. *Children who hate*. Glencoe, Ill.: The Free Press, 1951.

Redl, Fritz, & Wineman, David. *Controls from within*. Glencoe, Ill.: The Free Press, 1952.

Safier, Benno, Corrigan, Hazle C., Fein, Eleanor J., & Bradway, Katherine P. *A psychiatric approach to the treatment of promiscuity*. New York: American Social Hygiene Ass., 1949, Chaps. 2–3.

Shaw, Clifford R., & McKay, Henry D. *Juvenile delinquency and urban areas*. Chicago: Univer. of Chicago Press, 1942.

Sheldon, William H. *Varieties of delinquent youth*. New York: Harper, 1949.

Slavson, S. R. *Re-educating the delinquent*. New York: Harper, 1955.

Stott, D. H. *Saving children from delinquency*. New York: Philosophical Library, 1953, Chap. 5.

Sullivan, Katherine. *Girls on probation.* Boston: Houghton Mifflin, 1956.

United Nations. *Comparative survey on juvenile delinquency. Part I: North America.* New York: United Nations, 1952, Chap. 3.

Willemse, W. A. *Constitution-types in delinquency.* London: Routledge & Kegan Paul, 1932. Chaps. 1, 3, 5–7.

ALBERT I. RABIN

12 Psychopathic (Sociopathic) Personalities

THE CASE OF ROGER HAYES [1]

Prior to the hearings by the Parole Board, the prison psychiatrist interviewed the inmate. His report reads in part as follows:

He is entirely without insight, feels that the law-enforcing agencies have persecuted him. . . . He has been a definite problem in the community and certainly has made little constructive effort, during his incarceration, toward self-improvement. This man presents a *sociopathic personality* disturbance, is a chronically antisocial person who does not profit from experience and who still shows marked emotional immaturity, lack of judgment, and a tendency to rationalize. In my book, he is a very unpredictable type of person. While he is not psychotic, he is the same unstable individual as at the time of admission; he is merely doing time, day by day, and has no goals for the future. He is very apt to return to his former pattern of behavior upon release.

The dismal diagnostic and prognostic picture drawn above is that of Roger Hayes, age twenty-seven, an inmate of the state prison who has been serving a four-year sentence for "larceny from a building and for breaking and entering in the nighttime." The reasons for the doctor's pessimism regarding Roger will become apparent when we examine his past history in some detail.

Roger was born on July 7, 1932, in a fair-size midwestern city. He is an only child. Father has been working at a semiskilled job in a local factory and mother has been operating a small laundry. Both parents have been working ever since he was born. He was brought up in part by a maternal grandmother with whom the parents resided until he was five years old.

---

[1] All the facts in this illustration are taken from an actual case, except the name "Roger Hayes," which is fictitious.

Birth and early development were quite normal. However, there was a good deal of inconsistency in his early relations. Grandmother was fairly strict with the child; mother, when she was around, cuddled him and overprotected him. Father ignored him entirely most of the time, except when Roger would do something that displeased him. Then his temper was uncontrollable and he would punish the boy severely; sometimes beat him "within an inch of his life."

The child began having difficulties in school as early as the second grade. He was extremely aggressive, disobeyed the teachers, threw objects at them, truanted frequently, and was expelled from three different schools by the time he was twelve years old. His schoolwork was very poor despite his average intelligence.

Some religious training was also attempted. Roger attended Sunday school for about two years, between 1944 and 1946. He was a disciplinary problem during the first year. The second year ended when he threatened to throw a paper cutter through the window of the principal's office. When the teacher tried to intervene and take the cutter away from him, he sustained such a severe injury to his hand that it required surgery.

After assaulting the eighth-grade teacher physically and after frequent truancies, Roger was finally expelled from the city school system in the spring of 1946. His parents placed him in a private school for problem boys. He lasted only two weeks at this institution. Upon admission he had been placed temporarily in the "very best cottage." On the first morning following his arrival he tried to run away, but the other boys prevented him from doing so. "His housemother laid her hand on his shoulder and started to explain to him that things like that are not done at this school; he whirled around and struck her with his fist. She turned him around and told him to please look at her and he started pummeling her so that the boys refused to have him in their cottage." He was placed in another cottage but ran away ten days later and hitchhiked home.

Several months later he was placed in the Boys Republic. Here he made a marginal adjustment, fought frequently with the other boys, truanted often, and finally did not return after 2½ months of intermittent residence. Then he began to get involved in a variety of criminal and antisocial activities in the community at large. On August 20, 1948, Roger came to the attention of the juvenile court authorities for "Breaking and Entering, and Theft." He was then committed to the Boys Vocational School, a state institution for delinquent boys. At this school he remained under fairly rigid discipline for about seven months. He was subsequently placed on parole and returned to his home community.

The subsequent seven years in this boy's life are marked by repeated delinquency and criminality and consequent encounters with the law-enforcement authorities. He never worked at any job for more than two months, not being able to hold onto the job because of his constantly getting in trouble with the police. A partial list of offenses and arrests, culminating in incarceration at the state prison, follows.

August 28, 1949 — Simple larceny (fine and costs)

October 30, 1949 — Drunk and disorderly; assault of an officer (fine and one-year probation)

November 8, 1949 — Robbery, unarmed (reduced to simple assault; fine)

December 3, 1949 — Assault and battery (fine)

December 28, 1949 — Violation of probation (60 days, county jail)

May 29, 1950 — Drunk; resisting arrest (60 days, county jail)

September 2, 1950 — Assault of officer; disorderly conduct and assault and battery (180 days)

February 5, 1951 — Violation of probation (90 days)

June 28, 1951 — Illegal possession of beer; drunk (90 days suspended sentence; to leave town for five years)

July 18, 1951 — Drunk and disorderly (same as above) (In another community)

September 1, 1951 — Investigation of unlawful operation of an Army vehicle (Returned to home community)

September 29, 1951 — Bench warrant (270 days, county jail)

May 24, 1952 — Drunk (fine and two years' probation)

August 3, 1952 — Frequents taverns (fine)

April 2, 1953 — Drunk and violation of probation (fine and 90 days)

August 12, 1953 — Violation of probation (60 days)

February 24, 1954 — Breaking and entering, two charges

April 5, 1954 — Breaking and entering, warrant

September 8, 1954 — Resisting arrest (on bail)

February 18, 1955 — Breaking and entering — nighttime; larceny from a building (5 to 15 years)

This is only a "partial" list, for other delinquents and criminals have indicated his participation in crimes which are not listed above and for which he was not arrested. The sentencing judge made the following statement regarding Roger:

There are very few individuals who, in my opinion, do not have any good qualities whatsoever, but if this man has anything good about him I have never discovered it. I do not believe, therefore, that there is any chance of rehabilitating him by any appeal to his better nature. I would strongly recommend that his confinement be made as rugged as possible.... In my opinion there is an excellent chance that this man will end up murdering someone or being killed by a policeman's bullet.

The doctor's report, quoted, in part, at the beginning of this narrative, appeared to be amply justified. However, Roger was paroled from prison in December, 1959. Following violation of parole due to a severe assault on a man in a tavern (breaking his jaw), he was returned to prison in March, 1960. Upon being asked by one of the prison officials why he came back as a parole violator, he said, "It was just one of those things. Just made a mistake like everyone else does."

The history of this psychopathic (sociopathic) personality indicates that this is an impulsive, uncontrollable individual, antisocial in his behavior, with no stability in his occupational life and with no plans for the future. He is incapable of conducting himself in a way that would permit him to remain in free society. He is a menace to his fellow men and demonstrates a life-long pattern of hostility, aggression, and antisocial behavior which appears unmodifiable. His numerous experiences and various punishments were apparently ineffective; he did not learn from those experiences or gain insight into his behavior. The pattern remains unaltered.

THE TERM "PSYCHOPATHIC" OR "SOCIOPATHIC PERSONALITY"

One of the most interesting, yet baffling, psychological disorders is what has been termed for a long time "psychopathic personality." More recently the term "sociopathic personality disturbance" has been introduced and is considered preferable, for it contains the emphasis on social maladjustment. The most recent *Diagnostic and Statistical Manual: Mental Disorders* (1952), published by the American Psychiatric Association, replaces "sociopathic" for the old "psychopathic" personality. According to this manual, "Individuals to be placed in this category are ill primarily in terms of society and of conformity with the prevailing cultural milieu, and not only in terms of personal discomfort and relations with other individuals." However, in much of the professional literature as well as in actual usage in diagnosis, the two terms — sociopathic and psychopathic personalty — are employed interchangeably.

The diagnosis of psychopathic personality has often been made negatively: by eliminating a variety of other mental disorders, the diagnostician was left with the category of psychopathic personality as a last resort. As a result of this frequent and traditional procedure, this diagnostic classification became a "catchall" or "wastebasket" diagnostic category.

PSYCHOSIS AND NEUROSIS

Severe mental disorders have long ago been recognized by laymen as well as by professionals. "Possession by evil spirits," "lunacy," and "insanity" are some of the older names for behavior that is irrational, deviant, and often dangerous to the person affected or to those in his environment. Insane persons were also those who, despite previous adequate capacity, were no longer able to conduct themselves or their affairs with "ordinary prudence." This defective adjustment, which did not exist at birth or in infancy but usually became manifest in adult life, was attributed to the malfunctioning of the psyche or the mind. Hence, the modern, medical-sounding term for insanity is psychosis — the disease or disorder of the mind.

Another major group of psychological disturbances has been especially recognized, described, and treated during the past fifty years. These disorders do not exhibit the grossly irrational behavior characteristic of the psychoses. They do exhibit, however, such symptoms as fears, anxiety, compulsive behavior, and a variety of somatic (bodily) aberrations which are "irrational" in the sense that there does not appear to be any good reason or obvious cause for their existence. Persons who suffer from neuroses are not usually incapacitated as are those who suffer from psychosis; neither do they ordinarily endanger themselves or others. The most outstanding aspects involve their own feelings of well-being; they are unhappy, uncomfortable, fear- and guilt-ridden people.

These two major categories of mental disorder — psychosis and neurosis — are very broad classifications. Because of the variety of symptoms, causes, and behavioral manifestations, there are many subclassifications under both. A detailed discussion of these would lead us too far afield. This general background will help us, however, to understand the negative diagnosis or diagnosis by exclusion which often underlies the name and description of psychopathic personality.

PSYCHOPATHIC PERSONALITY

Often, behavior was observed and symptoms were noted in people who were not readily classifiable in the two major divisions of disorder just discussed. Although their behavior may have been called deviant and even irrational, it could not be categorized as psychotic. The condition did not have the incapacitating characteristics and confusion of a psychosis. On the other hand, compulsive activity and other neurotic-like symptoms may have been present, yet unaccompanied by the underlying anxiety and guilt so characteristic of this category of disorders. The behavior of these people and their attitudes to their behavior made it impossible to fit them into the available categories. Thus a new dimension and a new category were introduced in the field — psychopathic personality. This procedure of exclusion from the major subdivisions of psychological disorder dictated the placement into the remaining "wastebasket" class of psychopathic personalities.

Yet we cannot merely say what psychopathic personality is *not*. We must attempt a description and definition of the term. Only then can we see more clearly how a person of a given set of behavior characteristics may be properly excluded from the other categories and placed into this one. The following pages will be devoted to this task as well as to a discussion of the several theories concerned with the genesis of this disorder which looms importantly in the field of criminal psychology.

HISTORICAL DEVELOPMENT OF THE CONCEPT OF PSYCHOPATHIC PERSONALITY

The great French physician and humanitarian, Philippe Pinel, who was a pioneer of the modern era of diagnosis and treatment of mental disorders (end of the eighteenth and beginning of the nineteenth century) early recognized the paradox from which the concept of psychopathic personality emerged. He referred to a form of disorder call *la folie raisonante*, madness or mental illness in which the reason or intellectual processes were relatively unaffected or not involved. Somewhat later, Jeàn Esquirol, another outstanding investigator in the field of mental disorder, spoke of *manic sans délire* — mental illness without confusion (Zilboorg, 1941). Thus, the phenomenon of extremely deviant behavior, combined with unimpaired intelligence and efficient mental functioning, was observed and described a long time ago.

It was not until 1835, when the English medical psychologist Pritchard published his *Treatise on Insanity and Other Disorders Affecting the Mind*, that we got a look at a category of disorders which was the immediate predecessor of our present concept of psychopathic personality. Pritchard introduced the terms "moral imbecility" or "moral insanity." Here we see the emphasis on abnormality in a particular sphere of human personality and behavior — the area of moral judgment and conscience. He described this disorder of "moral insanity" as "madness consisting in a morbid perversion of the natural feelings, affections, inclinations, temper, habits, moral dispositions and natural impulses without any remarkable disorder or defect in the intellect or knowing and reasoning faculties . . ." (Pritchard, 1835). The emphasis here is on the inadequate "power of self government" which prevents the individual from behaving with "decency and propriety" in society and in relation to his fellow men.

Consonant with the nineteenth-century vogue, the idea of some hereditary weakness as the basis for the development of this kind of condition was advanced. As a consequence of this hereditary theory, the term "constitutional psychopathic inferiority" emerged. Subsequently, the term "personality" was substituted for "inferiority." Also, since the evidence for the hereditary basis for the disorder was far from satisfactory, the word "constitutional" was omitted.

MODERN STATUS OF CONCEPT

What is meant by psychopathic personality? What are the traits and characteristics of this personality type? We shall try to list in detail the main features that may be attributed to the personality constellation involved, as well as some of the more detailed consequences that express these characteristics in everyday behavior and interpersonal relations.

The following represents an attempt at a picture based on a variety of sources (Cleckley, 1955; Henderson, 1939; Preu, 1944) including the author's clinical experience. Of the afore-mentioned sources, perhaps the most interesting and readable presentation, especially because of the case histories, is Cleckley's volume, *The Mask of Sanity*.

Conscience Absent or Inadequate

We noted above that Pritchard used the expression "moral sanity" and "moral imbecility." What he meant by this is a severe disturbance or virtual absence of moral judgment. This principle is still a major ingredient of any description of psychopathic personality today.

There are two major related aspects to this notion of defective conscience or, what is termed in psychoanalysis, superego. The first aspect is represented in the inability of the psychopath to apply the moral standards of society to his behavior; he cheats, lies, steals, does not keep promises, and so on. He has not absorbed the "thou shalts" and the "thou shalt nots" of his society and cultural milieu. The second aspect is that of absence of guilt. Guilt is an important part of any well-developed conscience. When a normal person violates the moral code he feels guilty; he feels unhappy and blames himself for the transgression. Aside from this emotional experience, guilt performs a warning function or a preventive function. People try not to transgress the moral code, for if they do they will feel guilty and unhappy — a painful experience to be avoided. Guilt is an unknown experience for the psychopathic personality with no superego. There is none of this automatic self-punishment that goes along with the commission of immoral and unethical acts. The psychopath continues to behave irresponsibly, untruthfully, insincerely, and antisocially without a shred of shame, remorse, or guilt. He may sometimes express regret and remorse for the actions and crimes which he may have perpetrated; however, these are usually mere words, spoken for the effect, but not really and sincerely felt.

The absence of guilt and remorse permits the psychopath to continue indefinitely his antisocial behavior unless people in his environment or the authorities decide to exercise some control. When confronted with his lies and dishonesties he will often try to rationalize them and give some plausible reasons for his behavior. However, these are for the most part *good* and, frequently, persuasive reasons, but *not the true* ones.

Roger Hayes, whose case we have described above, by constantly getting into difficulty with the law illustrates the notion that guilt was not a deterrent to his behavior. Moreover, he is ready with rationalization. "Everybody makes mistakes" was his explanation for parole violation.

Emotionally Immature—Egocentric

The young infant or small child is almost entirely concerned with himself, with his own wants and needs — come what may. He is egocentric — he is in the center of his own world; all that counts is the satisfaction and gratification of his desires. If frustrated he reacts impulsively to his environment. He may even lash out at the persons closest to him for their failure to grant his immediate wants. When the child grows up, he gradually becomes "socialized"; he learns how to adapt himself in a world full of people; learns to postpone his gratification and becomes aware of the needs of other people which, sometimes, may conflict with his own. He learns to make compromises and realizes that he cannot forever remain in the center of the world. The needs and feelings of others must also be considered; he learns to obey some rules which evolved in his society for the sake of its smooth functioning. He realizes what the consequences may be if everyone remains egocentric — pulling in his own direction. Thus, the egocentricity is relinquished and a more *sociocentric* orientation takes place as part of the process of growing up.

The psychopath never grows up in this respect. He grows up physically and is often well developed and attractive in appearance; he grows up intellectually inasmuch as he acquires many of the perceptual, motor, and conceptual skills which are necessary for the manipulation of the environment. However, he never grows up emotionally. He remains egocentric; that is — he is solely concerned with the fulfillment of his own needs and wishes *immediately*. Since, like the small child, he can suffer no delay or postponement, he becomes extremely frustrated when his desires are thwarted by the environment. Likewise, he proceeds impulsively to do and get what he wishes without consideration for others. And, when he does, as we noted above, there are no pangs of conscience to bother him.

Unlike the young child, however, the psychopath has developed and matured physically and has acquired many important skills which he can employ in the manipulation of his environment. Thus, he may bring many of these aspects of maturity to the service of his childish needs and impulse satisfaction; or, in the case of frustration, he may use them against other people who are in his way. Such situations often constitute the dangers to society and to ordered living that are embodied in the psychopath.

It should be added that, like the child, the psychopath has a defective self-control apparatus. The ordinary person, as a result of the socialization process, has developed the capacity of self-control. In instances in which he transgresses the social code he gets punished; this experience usually alerts him in other instances, so that transgression and consequent punishment are avoided. The psychopath, however, cannot learn from his experiences, for the capacity of self-control has never developed properly. Thus he may go on committing the very acts for which he was punished on one or more occasions previously. Past experience somehow does not affect his future behavior. The infantile needs are strong, the control apparatus is weak; the result is that behavior remains governed by the former, unguided by the latter.

Absence of Life Plan

In the previous section we pointed out that the psychopath essentially lives in the present — in the "here and now"; he wants what he wants when he wants it — immediately; he is unable to postpone gratification for the future or anticipate it. He is essentially also incapable of visualizing the future or planning for it. Since he lives in the present and is primarily preoccupied with it, he shows little evidence of any life plan, or of making any preparation for the future.

Life, for the psychopath, is a hit-or-miss affair. It consists of a series of episodes of impulsive acts which are not instrumental in long-range planning for a career, in the achievement of socially desirable goals, or in the attainment of stability of social, economic, and emotional status. Although he may at times resolve to follow a certain plan for his future, he fails in the actual realization of such a program. Too many immediate and temporary lures dissuade him from his chosen long-range goal; he never gets where he allegedly wishes to go, for the gratification of the immediate need and the impulsive reactions hinder such achievements. In this sense he remains self-defeating and can be described as a drifter — a boat without moorings on a turbulent sea.

The psychopath, therefore, moves about. He does not hold onto a job for any length of time, although he may be quite successful at it. Sudden outbursts against fellow workers, manager, boss, customers; flagrant manipulation of the truth and other kinds of dishonesty; unreliability and lack of a sense of responsibility are all part of the picture of an unstable and shifting employment history. This is a further illustration of the inability and lack of capacity to select, maintain, and follow some consistent life plan.

Lack of Capacity for Love and Emotional Involvement

The fourth and last major characteristic of the psychopath is his inability to establish and maintain genuine affectional ties and interpersonal relationships. As we mentioned earlier, emotionally he is an egocentric and impulsive child. He is concerned chiefly with his own needs and their satisfaction. He is in the center of his own world and cannot allow someone else to share the limelight. Being so concerned with and engrossed in himself, he has little genuine interest left for others. Other people are important to him insofar as they can be *used* by him, insofar as they are instrumental to his supreme end — self-gratification.

True friendship is not within the psychopath's experience. Although people may give him a great deal of love and affection, tolerate many of his vagaries, and exhibit nothing but good will toward him, he will not respond at all nor have in the least a similar consideration for them. He may betray them at the first opportunity and exploit their trust in him if it suits his purposes. He is incapable of making any sacrifices for or concessions to others, although others have made them in his behalf. The capacity for empathy and identification is lacking; he cannot place himself in the other fellow's shoes and imagine another person's feelings and emotional experience. Callousness and insensitivity to other people are characteristic.

The same holds true for love. He is incapable of genuine love and affectional involvement with another person. To be sure, he gets involved in sex and sexual relationships, but such alliances are devoid of depth and genuineness. There is little stability in such relationships, and promiscuity is the rule. He may profess true and undying love, just as he may exhibit the external appearances of friendship. However, it is all sham and not genuine, for he flits from one "true love" to another with few qualms and no remorse. The protestations of love and friendship may be accompanied by a great deal of outward display of emotion, ecstasy, and affection, but it is not the genuine article; it is superficial and employed as a device to gain certain selfish ends — trust, support, or sexual gratification.

Sex for the psychopath is primarily a matter of physical contact, uncomplicated by the emotion of love. Sexual activities are casual affairs without emotional involvement. Cleckley (1955) states: "One gets the impression that their amativeness is little more than a simple itch and that even the itch is seldom, if ever, particularly intense."

Let us now assay a brief summary of the major characteristics of the psychopathic personality. This statement will be positive in the sense that it will indicate what conditions must be met for a diagnosis of psychopatic personality to be made; it will deal with what it *is*, not with what it *is not*.

A psychopath is a person without a conscience, without the capacity to experience guilt, who is incapable of adhering to the rules and mores of society, who is impulsive and emotionally immature and egocentric, who is incapable of genuine interpersonal relationships, and whose pattern of life and life style is devoid of long-range planning and considered anticipation of the future.

PSYCHOPATHIC PERSONALITY AND CRIMINALITY

When we consider the set of characteristics which describe the individual with psychopathic personality we can readily expect him to get in trouble with the law. Anyone who is impulsive, does not learn from experience, is incapable of affection for others, and is lacking in an internalized value system or conscience is apt to run afoul of the laws set up for governing society. It is true then that many habitual criminals are psychopaths. Many a crime is being committed, often repeatedly, by persons who have a strong revenge motive, who "act out" repressed hostility, and so on. These may be largely neurotic reasons rather than stemming from the basic personality defect we call psychopathic personality. There are no precise figures on the relative proportion of psychopaths in the criminal population nor in the population at large. Precise diagnoses in the criminal prison population are hard to come by. The situation in the general population is, of course, even more difficult. One of the largest surveys of nearly 10,000 convicted cases at the New York Court of General Sessions, described by Bromberg and Thompson (1937), reports 6.9 percent of psychopaths. Similar percentages have been reported by others on adult criminal populations.

But the terms "psychopathic personality" and "criminality" are far from synonymous. As we noted above, the vast majority of the criminal population is nonpsychopathic. Also, there are many psychopaths in the general population who manage to stay out of the clutches of the law. Cleckley (1955) has presented a number of fascinating descriptions of the psychopath as a businessman, as a gentleman, as a scientist, as a physician, and as a psychiatrist, all of whom maintained themselves with varying degrees of precariousness in "normal" society.

Even more dramatic is the instance of the psychopath who is catapulted into a position of political leadership and prominence. Such a man was "Herman Goering: amiable psychopath," Hitler's right-hand man and one of the top leaders of the German Nazi movement. G. M. Gilbert (1948), who was prison psychologist at Nurenberg, gave a detailed description of this case.

THEORIES OF CAUSATION

The Constitutional Hypothesis

At the end of the past century the tremendous influence of biology and the idea of somatic causation has extended markedly to the realm of mental disorder. A number of disorders, and particularly that of psychopathic personality, were considered to have a hereditary or constitutional origin. The belief was that there was some defective genetic factor which was the cause of constitutional inferiority, which, in turn, produced the behavior defects represented by psychopathic personality. However, this theory did not progress much beyond the realm of belief, for scientific proof for its support was lacking. Although there are still some people who cherish this notion, in the absence of adequate evidence, most workers in the field have abandoned it.

The "Abnormal Brain" Hypothesis

Observation of children and adults following brain injury or disease affecting the brain showed certain changes in their behavior. The patients become more aggressive, overactive, emotional, irritable, and, often, antisocial. Since this pattern of behavior resembles the symptoms subsumed under the concept of psychopathic personality, the hypothesis was advanced that brain injury, disease, or abnormality may be the underlying cause of psychopathic personality. However, gross neurological findings, of the kind obtained in an examination of the various reflexes, were usually negative. The belief persisted that the abnormality may lie in the areas of the brain which have no effect on the usual reflexes but which have to do with emotional control and "the higher mental processes."

During the past several decades scientists have developed a new diagnostic technique for the detection of brain damage or abnormality. This method is known as the electroencephalogram, or in its abbreviated form — the EEG. Popularly, the tracings or the electroencephalographic recordings of this technique are also called "brain waves." Essentially this is a graphic recording of the electrical activity of the outer part of the brain known as the cortex.

The usual procedure in obtaining an electroencephalogram is to attach electrodes to the scalp and connect them with an amplifier. The electrical activity of the cortex is then transmitted to the electrodes, amplifier, and the recording apparatus, which registers the fluctuations in the electrical potential (the brain waves).

There are several types of waves which are considered important diagnostically. The *alpha* waves, which appear at the rate of 8–13 per second, are ordinarily found in normal adults. The faster *beta* and *gamma* waves have also been found in normal adults. However, the extremely slow *delta* waves, of less than 8 per second, are particularly found in the records of young children and pathological adults (Lindsley, 1944).

Abnormal EEG records are usually obtained in the convulsive disorders (epilepsies) and in a variety of other brain disorders, tumors, cell degeneration, and so on. It is not a perfect diagnostic tool: around 20 to 30 percent of normally functioning persons show abnormalities in their brain waves. Occasionally it is found that a brain disorder discovered during surgery or upon autopsy has eluded the electroencephalographer.

Be that as it may, some investigators have obtained a rather high percentage of abnormal EEG's with groups of subjects diagnosed as psychopaths. Earlier, children with behavior disorders were reported to show EEG abnormalities in 70–90 percent of the cases. However, there is some evidence that these abnormalities are of a temporary nature and tend to decrease with age (Secunda and Finley, 1942). As far as adults are concerned, Simons and Diethelm (1946) found that "psychopathic personalities with poor ethical standards and resulting social difficulties" all had abnormal records characterized by a slow wave (delta) rhythm. However, several other groups of psychopaths considered in the same study did not yield such consistent results. Most of those had normal records. Gottlieb *et al.* (1946) reported that 58 percent of their psychopaths showed "electrocortical abnormality"; such percentages are significantly greater than those found in normals. However, among their conclusions the authors also state that the "proportion of patients showing electroencephalographic abnormality appears to be greater when the mothers were judged maladjusted or alcoholic. . . ." Thus it is suggested that certain hereditary or early environmental influences ("maladjusted mothers") may be a factor in the production of abnormal electrocortical activity and psychopathic personality.

In a critical review of many investigations on the incidence of EEG abnormality among patients with mental disorders, Ellingson (1954) gives us a pithy summary which puts the whole issue of the relationship between psychopathy and abnormal electrocortical activity in a nutshell. His survey indicates that "EEG abnormality among psychopaths has been found with remarkable regularity" in 47 to 58 percent of the cases. He points out that this fact is not helpful in distinguishing psychopathy from other mental disorders, for a high incidence of abnormal EEG's is also found in a large variety of psychiatric diagnostic groups. Ellingson's conclusion is quite cogent. He states that "beyond differentiating the few organic cases which will be found, the EEG is of no value in the differential diagnosis of mental disorders or in personality assessment at the present time."

We must conclude that there is some electroencephalographic evidence of abnormal cortical activity in many psychopaths. This condition, however, also prevails in many other disorders. Many psychopaths show "normal" electrocortical activity and a sizable percentage of normals show abnormal brain-wave patterns. A statistical differentiation may be made, but no valid conclusion regarding cortical abnormality in psychopaths can be reached. The EEG is too imperfect an instrument for the purposes of finer discrimination and for determination of individual diagnosis. Moreover, the basis for such abnormalities as are found is not clear. Are they due to developmental retardation, to cortical damage, or to a combination of psychological and physiological effects? Or, is a combination of all these factors to be considered? No reliable answer can be given to these questions at the present state of our knowledge.

In closing this section a final comment is in order. Criteria for the diagnosis of psychopathic personality often differ markedly from one investigation to another. Consequently it is very questionable whether the reported results with the EGG relate to a unitary, homogeneous group of persons exhibiting the same syndrome and the same psychosocial difficulties. This issue, of course, is not solely of concern in EEG studies but in the entire area under our purview.

The Psychological Hypothesis

The psychological hypothesis concerning the causation of psychopathic personality is essentially a genetic-developmental one. Basically it proposes that certain experiences in childhood, especially in infancy, affect permanently the course of character formation which results in what is known as the psychopathic adult. The questions that one would raise immediately are as follows: What are the processes involved in the effects of early childhood experiences on later personality development? What, specifically, are those alleged experiences that make for the differences in the development of the normal and the psychopathic personality? In the sections that follow we shall attempt to answer these fundamental questions in the hope of elucidating the psychological hypothesis.

The human neonate, unlike the newborn of other species in the animal kingdom, remains relatively helpless for a long period following birth. In order to survive he needs constant care and attention, physical as well as psychological. No one will question the need of the infant for food, for protection against disease, and for physical comfort. However, in recent years the importance of "mothering" by the biological mother or her substitute has been emphasized. Mothering does not refer to the mere care for the child's physical needs which are usually the concern of a mother, but also to the psychological security which is provided by a mother; to the close and constant physical contact; to the readiness of the mother to minimize frustrations; to oral and sound responses which are reassuring, pacifying, and soothing to the infant; as well as to a constant and consistent relationship with a loving adult. This early relationship between mother and child is most significant for it serves as a prototype for interpersonal relationship in adulthood. This is the source from which the capacity to receive and feel affection, to experience genuine love, empathy, and consideration for others, evolves.

Another principle of paramount importance in early personality development is that of identification. Under the usual circumstances the growing child imitates the behavior of his parents and subsequently adheres to the demands they make upon him. The parents are all-powerful in the infant's and child's immediate experience. By acting like them he can therefore feel that he somehow becomes powerful himself. Besides, even in very young children the penchant for imitation is well known. As the child grows older, the parents ordinarily confront him with a number of "dos" and "don'ts," a number of obligations and prohibitions which further fashion his behavior. These dicta of behavior communicated by the parents are, of course, generally the transmitted standards and codes of behavior of their society or culture.

Implicit in parental demands, expectations, and prohibitions is also punishment in case they are not obeyed. The child feels the threat of withdrawal of love if he does not comply. Anticipation of parental disapproval is, according to some theories, a devastating experience for the child which he wishes to avoid at all cost. At any rate, he learns what he *must* do, or how he must behave — he becomes socialized, in order to avoid punishment and parental disapproval.

As the child grows older and continues to identify with his parents, he not only imitates their overt behavior but also begins to accept their verbal communications — the demands and prohibitions — as his own. It is said that the child "internalizes" parental standards via his experiences at home and via the process of identification. The parental demands no longer are experienced from outside himself, but become his own, a part of himself — his conscience. What had previously been "I must" has now become "I ought" (or I must not, or I ought not).

Not only do the parental demands become part of the child in the form of his conscience; the threat of punishment is part of the process as well. Now if an infraction of the internalized code occurs, "pangs of conscience" follow — an uneasy and anxious feeling which one would rather avoid (like loss of approval of the parents). These pains inflicted by the conscience for doing what one "ought not," or for not doing what one "ought" or should, are known under the name of *guilt*.

In the previous paragraphs we have sketched briefly the course of childhood development with respect to the earlier experiences via mothering, socialization, and identification. We have shown the origins of early interpersonal relationships and the sources of moral judgment, conscience, and feelings of guilt. We shall now address ourselves to the question, What goes wrong in this process in the childhood of the psychopath? This is the essential question of the theory of psychological causation, or of the "psychological hypothesis."

In a comprehensive review of a large number of studies that have been amassed during the past several decades, the British psychiatrist Bowlby (1951) presents quite consistent evidence concerning the effects of early maternal deprivation upon later personality development:

"(a) Lack of *any* opportunity for forming an attachment to a mother-figure during the first three years."

(b) deprivation of 3-6 months (sudden separation from mother) during the first few years of life.

(c) changes of mother-figures during the first few years of life.

Any one of the conditions listed above, according to Bowlby, "can produce the affectionless and psychopathic character."

Let us now return to our previous description of the mothering process and see how the absence of mothering, its interruption during the crucial years of infancy, or the lack of consistency in the mother-figure may bring about the abnormal development which results in the psychopathic personality.

If we consider the array of evidence summarized by Bowlby we can reconstruct the infantile experience under various conditions of maternal deprivation. Mothering, as described for the usual "normal" conditions, does not take place at all or, at least, not consistently. The infant is thus deprived of the opportunity to develop a close reciprocal affectional relationship with another human being. He grows up lacking the early model after which he can pattern his subsequent interpersonal relationships and contacts. Moreover, maternal deprivation is also of paramount importance in interfering with the normal identification process and with the formation of a superego or a conscience.

In the absence of a positive affectional relationship with an adult there is usually little motivation to imitate the adult or to "be like" him. Even of more crucial importance is the fact that the absence of an affectional relationship with one (mother) parent interferes with the capacity to develop a similar relationship with the other (father). Thus, the socialization process and the internalization of parental standards, which is the foundation of the conscience, are hampered and distorted. Parental disapproval has little emotional meaning to the child. He cannot lose parental love, for he never had obtained it. He has "nothing to lose." Consequently, he may often obey for reasons of physical punishment or for other external circumstances, but he does not make the required standards his own. He watches out for himself and tries to avoid punishment, but is not concerned with pleasing his parents nor with being like them, for he does not use them as a model. Thus he ends by obeying some "musts" but has no feeling of "ought" nor the pangs of conscience or feelings of guilt which accompany infractions — real or imaginary.

The psychological hypothesis, then, evolves a detailed developmental explanation as to how "psychopaths are made." It addresses itself to the genesis of the basic psychopathic traits we have detailed above — lack of capacity for love, lack of conscience and feelings of guilt, and so on.

McCord and McCord (1956), as a result of their extensive review of the literature, have suggested certain reservations with respect to the linkage between deprivation experience and psychopathic personality. They point out that although the evidence overwhelmingly attests to the fact that psychopaths have suffered from familial deprivation, not all children who are deprived turn into psychopaths. The nub of the matter is the amount and extent of deprivation. *Severe* deprivation or rejection by the parents seems to be the precondition for psychopathy. In milder situations the outcome of psychopathy is not inevitable.

The same authors also suggest a neurosocial theory of causation. They propose that a combination of some neurological anomalies, of the kind discussed in a previous section, and mild or not severe deprivation can produce the psychopathic condition. In the absence of the neurological abnormalities the outcome may be more favorable despite a not too severe deprivation or rejection. This hypothesis has some merit, for it helps to explain issues that have remained unclear. However, more research and empirical investigation would be necessary in order to test its validity. Also, the question of what constitutes *severe* or *mild* deprivation and rejection remains unanswered.

There is an increasing tendency among workers in the field to advance what might be called a "psychosomatic hypothesis." By that we mean a theory involving the interplay between psychological and constitutional factors. To state it concretely, the amount of frustration due to deprivation and rejection the child may be able to tolerate may depend upon his constitution and his central nervous system. Thus, *severe* and *mild* deprivation may be considered in relation to the capacity of the organism to cope with frustration.

TREATMENT OF THE PSYCHOPATH

After a survey of the nature and possible causes of psychopathy, as well as the problems with which it confronts society, the question arises, What can be done about it? Can this condition be cured, modified, or changed? By and large the answers to these questions have been quite pessimistic. Now and then a few rays of hope do appear.

Imprisonment of the psychopathic criminal has not aided in rehabilitation. The overwhelming evidence points to the fact that violation of parole and recidivism are the rule with these persons, rather than the exception. Other modes of temporary isolation from the community at large have been similarly unsuccessful. Hospitalization in state hospitals and other psychiatric institutions is usually of brief duration. Quite often the psychopaths shuttle back and forth from penal institutions to psychiatric institutions until paroled or discharged, to resume their misbehavior or criminality for which they were originally incarcerated. Frequently the prison authorities feel that these prisoners have psychological problems which should be treated in the state hospital setting. The psychiatric institutions return them to the prison, for past experience has shown that the ordinary hospital regime, including some psychotherapy or group therapy as well as the various ancillary methods of treatment, is of little value in attempting to change the psychopath.

Even more intensive psychotherapeutic programs of individual psychotherapy, including psychoanalysis, have been marked by considerable failure. McCord and McCord (1956) have reviewed some of the material in detail. Some success with hypnoanalysis, however, has been reported by Lindner (1944). In his book *Rebel without a Cause*, Lindner presented verbatim reports of a series of interviews with a psychopathic prisoner under hypnosis. During these sessions the patient brought up a great deal of material dating back to early childhood and even infancy, which unearthed the basis for his continuous rebellion against society. The basic theme of hatred for his father and incestuous wishes for the mother, however, is very similar to the underlying psychoanalytic dynamics in neurosis. The question may be raised whether Lindner actually was dealing with a psychopath of the kind described in the preceding pages.

A major obstacle to psychotherapy with the psychopath is that of lack of cooperation. Although the psychopath may go through the motions of "cooperating" with the therapist, they are for the most part mere sham and deception. Often he does not even pretend; he resists the therapist. Unless there is a genuine desire for personality change, some anxiety and guilt of which the psychopath is incapable, psychotherapy is of no avail. "You can bring a horse to water, but you can't make him drink it."

Cleckley (1955) concludes his book with some programmatic suggestions with respect to the treatment of psychopathic personalities. He feels that the treatment of psychopaths has not been given an adequate chance, for they were always regarded as belonging to some twilight zone between normality or sanity and abnormality. His proposal is that the psychopath be regarded as the psychotic is — an incompetent in the business of managing his life. Like the psychotic he should be hospitalized in special institutions or in special wards of existing institutions for intensive treatment and resocialization for as long as it is deemed necessary.

A therapeutic program somewhat consonant with the suggestions of Cleckley has been undertaken in England. Jones and his co-workers (1953) have reported on the Therapeutic Community, which consists of hospital units treating a variety of chronic conditions including psychopaths. In these "communities" made up of staff and patients, the inmates work in the shops, participate in discussion groups, are given vocational guidance and are absorbed into the Unit community which has developed "a culture of its own." These conditions, according to the report, are effective in resocializing the patients and in preparing them for rehabilitation in the "normal" society. Although there are no definite figures on the therapeutic success with psychopaths, there seems to be some basis for a measure of optimism.

In a sense this approach may be characterized as the group and milieu kind of therapy. The emphasis is away from individual psychotherapy and the individual patient-therapist relationship in the direction of structuring or creating an environment which is conducive to change of attitudes in the interpersonal sphere. "Milieu therapy" has become particularly popular in the treatment of delinquents and young psychopaths in the United States. Some of this work has received its impetus from the pioneering work of Aichhorn (1935) in Austria. Some outstanding examples of this type of approach are the Pioneer House in Detroit and the Wiltwyck School for Boys near New York. There is some evidence that working with younger psychopaths who may be able to form some new identifications (with staff members), with consequent attitude and character change, is more rewarding and is perhaps a deterrent to the formation of hardened adult psychopathy.

SUMMARY

The disorder of psychopathic (or sociopathic) personality has been recognized long ago as "moral imbecility" or "moral insanity." It is a nonpsychotic, nonneurotic condition in persons of about average intelligence or better. The main characteristics of the psychopath are described as follows: He is "an asocial, aggressive, highly impulsive person, who feels little or no guilt and is unable to form lasting bonds of affection with other human beings" (McCord and McCord, 1956).

There is some evidence of brain abnormality in many psychopaths. The hypothesis that early maternal deprivation and family conditions which interfere with adequate socialization and identification are responsible for the development of psychopathic personalities has received a great deal of support from many investigators.

Somewhat less than 10 percent of convicted criminals are true psychopaths. This is the extent of the linkage between psychopathy and criminality. Many psychopaths manage to remain in society with varying degrees of social and material achievement — their number cannot even be estimated.

Individual psychotherapy with psychopaths has produced very little favorable results. More recently developed group settings such as "milieu therapy" and the "therapeutic community" hold out greater hope in the treatment of psychopathic personalities, especially in the younger age brackets.

References

Aichhorn, A. *Wayward youth.* New York: Viking, 1935.

Bowlby, J. *Maternal care and mental health.* Geneva: World Health Organization, 1951.

Bromberg, W., & Thompson, C. B. The relation of psychosis, mental defect and personality types to crime. *J. crim. Law Criminol.,* 1937, **28,** 70–89.

Cleckley, H. *The mask of sanity.* St. Louis: C. V. Mosby Co., 1955.

Diagnostic and statistical manual: Mental disorders. Washington, D. C.: American Psychiatric Ass., 1952.

East, N. *Society and the criminal.* London: His Majesty's Stationery Office, 1949.

Ellingson, R. I. The incidence of EEG abnormality among patients with mental disorders of apparently nonorganic origin: A critical review. *Amer. J. Psychiat.,* 1954, **111,** 263–275.

Fenichel, O. *The psychoanalytic theory of neurosis.* New York: Norton, 1945.

Gilbert, G. M. Herman Goering: Amiable psychopath. *J. abnorm. soc. Psychol.,* 1948, **43,** 211.

Gottlieb, J. S., Ashby, M. C. & Knott, R. J. Primary behavior disorders and psychopathic personality. *Arch. Neurol. Psychiat.,* 1946, **56,** 380–399.

Henderson, D. K. *Psychopathic states.* New York: Norton, 1939.

Jones, M., *et al. The therapeutic community: A new treatment method in psychiatry.* New York: Basic Books, 1953.

Karpman, B. Conscience in the psychopath: Another version. *Amer. J. Orthopsychiat.,* 1948, **18,** 455–491.

Lindner, R. *Rebel without a cause.* New York: Grune & Stratton, 1944.

Lindsley, D. B. Electroencephalography. In J. McV. Hunt (Ed.), *Personality and the behavior disorders.* New York: Ronald, 1944.

McCord, W., & McCord, Joan. *Psychopathy and delinquency.* New York: Grune & Stratton, 1956.

Preu, P. W. The concept of psychopathic personality. In J. McV. Hunt (Ed.), *Personality and the behavior disorders.* New York: Ronald, 1944.

Pritchard, J. C. *A treatise on insanity and other disorders affecting the mind.* London: Gilbert and Piper, 1835.

Secunda, L., & Finley, K. H. Electroencephalographic studies in children presenting behavior disorders. *New Eng. J. Med.,* 1942, **226,** 850–854.

Simons, D. J., & Diethelm, O. Electroencephalographic studies of psychopathic personalities. *Arch. Neurol. & Psychiat.,* 1946, **55,** 619–626.

White, R. W. *The abnormal personality.* New York: Ronald, 1956.

Zilboorg, G. *A history of medical psychology.* New York: Norton, 1941.

ALFRED C. SCHNUR

13 Current Practices in Correction: A Critique

Correction is concerned with the management of the offender from the instant of his conviction to the instant of his release from all legal supervision. The generally professed goal of correction is to protect society by preparing men as rapidly and economically as possible to become useful, law-abiding, self-supporting, self-sufficient, independent citizens — men who obey the law because they want to and not because they are afraid not to.

This objective is not being very well attained. "At least 55 to 60 percent of the prisoners leaving prison today will return within five years." In some places, "the recidivist rate exceeds 70 percent" (Bennett, 1954, p. 10). Seventy percent of the fingerprints received by the Federal Bureau of Investigation's Identification Division are of persons who have records of previous arrests (Hoover, 1957, p. 45). Reliable figures regarding the recidivism of probationers and parolees are also disappointingly high.

Although correction is handicapped in achieving its goal by not knowing enough about how to achieve it, the record could be better if agencies were allowed to apply what is already known about correcting convicted law violators.[1] Unrealistic legal constraints imposed by legislatures and the failure of legislatures to implement knowledge already accumulated make it impossible for correctional agencies to achieve the maximum results that even contemporary knowledge and resources make possible.

Failure of legislatures to make effective correctional work possible and the failure of correctional agencies to achieve better results are, of course, partially explained by the interests, the values, the understanding, and the misunderstanding of the people in a

---

[1] The need for better knowledge is not developed in this chapter. For a detailed statement, see Alfred C. Schnur, Some reflections on the role of correctional research, *Law and contemp. Probs.*, 1958, 23, 772–783.

democracy. The people do not seem to know either what they really want done with criminals or what objectives they actually want served in dealing with them. Except for being apparently satisfied with measures short of extermination or life quarantine for almost all offenders, the people lack agreement on clear-cut objectives and means to achieve them. Almost all the objectives ever stated and almost all the measures ever applied in dealing with nonconformists since the beginning of recorded time are still employed in the management of law violators. Many different and often incompatible objectives are served at the same time, and many different and conflicting things are simultaneously done to, with, and for the lawbreaker. Procedures followed are frequently unrelated to the professed objectives; indeed, they are often related to other objectives. This is frequently true even when the actions are executed with the intent of serving the particular objective professed.

Although society does not know exactly what it wants accomplished or just how it wants its criminals handled, correctional agencies are obliged to make these decisions for society. Criminals are delivered to them for determinate periods of time. Correctional agencies are obliged to do something. They do do something. Both by their action and inaction — since failure to act is as much a decision as action — the correctional agencies define the objectives and the means of attaining those objectives with the resources provided them by society and within the constraints imposed upon them by society.

Consequently, confusion and inconsistency, lack of tested knowledge, and vacillation in implementing objectives are all factors which characterize the management of convicted law violators while they are subject to the correctional processes. An example is the conclusion of some officials that the administration of justice should be a system wherein, at minimum cost, (1) men are made to be sorry that they committed crimes, but (2) are glad, or at least contented, that they were processed (fined, placed on probation, imprisoned, or the like) and (3) as a consequence refrain from all all further crimes so that (4) through the example of their experience they serve as a perfect deterrent for all potential criminals. These ends bear the same relationship to each other as the expectation that a machine will operate without an energy source.

SUBSTITUTE GOALS

For some people, punishment, deterrence, vengeance, retribution, expiation, and the like, have become sufficient ends in themselves. A collection of vague themes included under an umbrella called "the protection of society" adds to the confusion because these vague themes are used both as rationalizations for pursuing substitute goals and as reasons for adopting scientific techniques to abolish crime.

The most popular, dangerous, and blinding substitute goal today is punishment. Punishment is advocated by many both as a goal in itself and as a way of protecting society.

Can One Get Even for Crime?

Although we are primarily concerned with whether or not punishment reduces crime, some of the other reasons used by the champions of punishment will be considered first. One reason given is that one gets even through punishment. Such use of punishment is often as futile as kicking with his already sore toe the chair one has stumbled over. One can never really get even. What is done is done and cannot be undone. Punishment does not restore life to the murdered, health to the assaulted victim, or property to the loser. Bootless attempts to get even through punishment, however, do often sacrifice the future welfare of others.

Do Criminals Deserve Punishment?

There are those who would punish because they feel that the criminal deserves pain for what he did. Everyone is aware of criminals whose crimes so outraged the community that no one seems capable of devising a punishment horrible enough and painful enough to satisfy an outraged society and the injured parties. Everyone is also aware of other criminals whose life experiences have been so filled with unpleasantness and misfortune that they arouse more sympathy than censure. When the correction specialist deals with such criminals, his only concern with the conditions producing the community's reactions is with the ways in which such conditions affect the possibility of future crime. In other words, the treatment accorded the criminal depends not on whether he makes people "mad" or "sad" but upon what will help to end a career in crime. As one consequence, although the one who makes us "sad" may suffer more than the one who makes us "mad," the objective in both cases would be the same — the ending of crime. Techniques effective in eliminating crime should be applied. Humanitarian considerations need not be referred to by the criminologist as the basis for his decision to discard punishment for its own sake, although it is patently clear that such considerations, particularly those relating to the dignity of man, would immediately rebel at the new lows reached in so many places today.

Does Punishment Deter?

Punishment is also frequently advocated as a basis for deterring others from the commission of similar crimes. History is replete with examples of the absurdity of this position. At one time pickpockets were publicly hanged in England. While the pickpockets were being disposed of, the police had to be constantly on the alert to prevent other pickpockets from taking advantage of these public gatherings.

Does Punishment Work?

Punishment does not even deter persons from committing further misdeeds while they are being punished. The use of the lash at one southern prison offers evidence. The necessity of beating the same man again and again at frequent intervals casts doubt upon its effectiveness. Crimes occur even in places for punishment. Prison riots throughout the country document this. Newspapers record crimes in our prisons that are committed by inmates and civilian employees alike. Punishment is ineffective as a means for ending all crime because some of man's behavior is not controlled by logic. Witness the great campaigns of the insurance companies and others against overweight. Full-page advertisements and other means of mass communication recount the dangers of obesity. How many people reach for another sweet as they read these advertisements? The horrible consequences of smoking tobacco and consuming alcohol are painted in lurid detail. The "drys" do their best to make everyone aware of the consequences of drink. But even in one so-called dry state, where counterpropaganda by the "wets" is at a minimum, there are hundreds of federal wholesale and retail liquor licenses, and the revenue received by the state black-market tax collector is considerable. This state also boasts one of the largest hospitals for alcoholics in the nation. If men were ruled exclusively by logic would the above statements be true? Would there be so many parking violations and so many red lights and stop signs being ignored? Would there be so much smoking in bed? One needs but to look at his own behavior to add countless illustrations of actions taken that were not ruled by the known consequences.

This does not mean that punishment never works. It does work under some circumstances. But to rush a convicted criminal to standard punishment immediately is as absurd as rushing for a bottle of aspirin for every ache and pain. Sometimes it works, and sometimes it does not.

Punishment for punishment's sake is a moral issue. Punishment for treatment's sake is a scientific matter. Such investigations of punishment's relationship to abolishing crime as have been made, although not conclusive, suggest that its crime-stopping value decreases as criminal behavior becomes more complex; that is, as it involves more and more of the personality. Use of punishment as a standard technique for abolishing all crime can in no way be defended.

WHAT DOES IT ALL MEAN?

Does this mean that the criminal should simply have his wrist slapped, be told he is a bad boy, and then be turned loose to continue his activity? Obviously, this would not profit society. The criminal is neither deterred nor cured. Should the criminal be made to suffer in an effort to balance the pleasure he is supposed to have had in committing the crime with the pain society can give? This does not profit society either. He is still a criminal, albeit a suffering one.

Criminology neither condones nor condemns the criminal but recognizes him for what he is — an unwanted product of society. (See Chapter 9.) "In this sense, if the criminal is a product — *we don't need to hate people any more*" (Taft, 1950, p. 304). When conviction is secured, search should be made for explanations for the criminal's behavior and for ways of changing these conditions.

The denial of individual responsibility for crime implies that many outside influences are responsible for crime, but it in no way implies either the excusing of crime or the coddling of the criminal. No matter how he became criminal, he is dangerous to the law-abiding people and must be treated in such a way that the law abiding need fear him no more. If treatment is now impossible the criminal should be quarantined for life or until such time as the kind of treatment is feasible that will make it possible to return him to free society. Correctional treatment for crime should in *one limited* sense resemble medical treatment. Medical treatment for pneumonia does not depend on whether the illness was a consequence of a drunken spree or of overwork. Cure is the important thing.

Recognition that many outside influences operating through individuals produce crime implies a recognition that other controlled outside influences operating through the same individuals can eliminate crime. Because crime is caused by experiences from birth onward, society should concern itself with these experiences and eliminate those inciting to crime through crime-prevention programs operated at least as vigorously as the programs for apprehending offenders. These crime-inciting experiences over which developing criminals have no control, and not the helpless developing child, should arouse society's wrath and indignation. Such experiences are the sources of crime.

The adult criminal should be viewed with at least the same charity that is now accorded juvenile delinquents (see Chapter 11); the adult criminal is but a juvenile grown older who has not been reached soon enough. Perhaps the adult should arouse more compassion than a child, since the adult has suffered longer at society's hands. Although it is more difficult, it is never too late to try to make the adult criminal into a substantial citizen. Society will find it is more economical to prevent criminality than to cure criminals.

TREATMENT BY TIME CLOCK

As we have already noted, correctional agencies are handicapped in achieving their objectives because they are not allowed to apply what we know about correcting offenders. Nonrealistic legal constraints upon correction begin with sentencing statutes that deny personnel involved in the process the opportunity to utilize contemporary criminological and correctional knowledge to best advantage. Nowhere in this country are the courts or correctional personnel allowed the discretion necessary for the proper application of treatment.

Upon conviction of the law violator, the court must first determine the kind of sentence. The court's discretion is often severely limited by statutes. Age, previous criminal record, and present offense are frequent curbs upon the choice of sentences. Depending upon jurisdiction and upon the limits set by statute, a judge may use one or combine several of the following possible kinds of sentences.[2] A sentence of death may be imposed. A price list established by the legislature may be used to fine the criminal. This monetary penalty may be combined with incarceration in an institution. Jail confinements are usually for less than a year, but jail time may last beyond a year if the fine is not paid. Penitentiary, prison, reformatory, or correctional institution sentences are usually for a year or more.

Under appropriate conditions, institutional sentences can be suspended. If a sentence is suspended and the judge concludes that the offender has behaved properly for a stipulated time, the judge may discharge the offender. The offender will then be considered as having "paid his debt to society" without serving a day in an institution and without paying one cent to the state. He cannot again be sentenced for this crime from which he has been discharged. Suspended sentences take various forms. Some suspended sentences include probation and some do not. (Probation will be discussed later in this chapter.) Should the court conclude, after a time, that the convicted offender is not behaving properly, the suspended sentence may be revoked. What happens at this point depends upon whether the court originally suspended the *execution* or the *imposition* of sentence. If the *execution* of sentence was suspended, the original sentence automatically becomes operative and the offender is delivered to the institution for the duration of his sentence. However, if the *imposition* was suspended, the court has the same discretion in imposing sentence that it had before placing the offender on probation. The court can, for example, take into account the offender's behavior on probation.

After the judge has first considered and decided upon the kind of sentence (from among the variations available), he considers the amount of sentence. Here we shall be concerned only with the length of sentence. The judge must set the time clock for treatment.

The treatment time clock is variously set by three types of sentences: *Absolute determinate* (definite, flat), *limited indeterminate*, and *absolute indeterminate*. Different degrees of discretion are afforded treatment personnel by these three general varieties of sentencing practice. The ideal relationship between time and treatment is provided by the *absolute indeterminate* sentence. No minimum or maximum amount of time is predetermined. All sentences, in effect, are from no time to life quarantine. The law violator can be

---

[2] All of the sentencing possibilities and variations are not discussed here. Only the most frequently used sentences are presented.

passed from one kind of treatment to another according to his and society's needs. He can be released from all treatment at the optimum time — when his probabilities for lawful behavior are at their peak and when it is reasonably certain that he will not again engage in crime. On the other hand, with this type of sentence the man need never be released if his probabilities for continuing his career in crime are excessive.

Nowhere in the United States does the absolute indeterminate sentence exist. The closest approximation occurs in those jurisdictions with the lowest minimums and the highest maximums wherein the judge, by setting the lowest minimums and the highest maximums possible under the statutes, in effect delegates all the discretion available to him to the correctional authorities. This represents the best possible use of the *limited indeterminate* sentence compatible with the treatment and discharge objectives of correction. The worst possible use is seen in the sentences of judges who set minimums close to maximums or maximums close to minimums. Even this, of course, is a little better than the *absolute determinate* (definite, flat) sentence. Jurisdictions using such sentences in effect set up a fair-trade price list without discounts for all crimes. The price is expressed in so many days, weeks, months, years, or in life or death. Upon the determination of guilt, the judge is obliged to consult the legislature's price list and impose the scheduled price. Such sentences take account only of the crime and previous criminal record, but at the same time prohibit the judge from taking account of the man, his needs, and his probabilities for lawful behavior under a variety of treatment conditions. One variation is found in some jurisdictions in which the judge has a limited range of time available to him but is obliged nevertheless to impose a sentence that is specific in amount of time.

Both the absolute determinate and the limited indeterminate sentences share the same fatal defect in varying degree. Both have the effect of setting for each man a date beyond which he cannot be detained and before which he cannot be released, no matter how imperfectly this date correlates with a man's potential for lawful behavior. The absolute determinate sentence is the deadliest to correctional treatment because it accords treatment personnel the narrowest range of discretion.

The treatment time clock set by the absolute and limited indeterminate sentence can be advanced only slightly by institutional authorities through the award of good time and extra-good time.

ADVERSE EFFECTS OF TREATMENT
BY TIME CLOCK

The time-clock concept of corrections is not good for probationers, prisoners, or parolees. Under the time-clock concept they know that they are going to be through with correction as of such a date, no matter what they do, short of committing a new crime. They know that their behavior can have only a limited effect upon the timing of their release. This encourages them to behave just well enough to accomplish this purpose — but no better. They see nothing to be gained if they behave any better. Correctional treatment consequently tends to be measured by inmates, not in terms of changes for the better produced in them, but by crossing out the days remaining before discharge on their calendars and time charts: 1,017 days to go, 1,016, 1,015, and so on until the final hour. A new day is heralded not for the opportunities that it presents but rather for the fact that it will soon be over — another day will be behind them, and can be X'd out. Time has little other real meaning for inmates. They tend to lose their perspective and live in a highly selected past or unrealistic future, but not in the present. Under the time-clock system, the most significant thing to an inmate about a day is that it has passed.

The time-clock concept has at least another bad effect upon the inmate and the society that is to be re-entered. It helps inmates to feel that their "debt to society" has been paid. This latter concept may encourage them to run up a new account. Some may even feel that not only has their debt been paid; society now owes them something — and then they proceed to collect it upon their release.

For some men the period of supervision is too short for any treatment to have an effect. Others have terms so long that not only is treatment impeded but whatever positive effect treatment has had is nullified. To secure maximum protection for society at minimum cost, the kind and length of supervised treatment should depend upon adjustment in a treatment situation in relation to a pattern of factors that indicate successful adjustment to a free life, rather than upon the kind and amount of punishment that will pay a supposed "debt" to society and retaliate for crime.

Treatment by the time-clock method wastes the resources of society and fails to protect society. First, the supervision of men who no longer need correction requires the wasteful expenditure of limited resources that could better be used on men who still need correction. Presently, when treatment resources are insufficient, this is a particularly poor use of them. Second, society is not protected by the required but premature release of uncorrected men.

Treatment time clocks prevent parole boards from doing the best they can with their present resources. Some parole boards have more discretion than others, but no releasing authority now has sufficient discretion in the timing of parole. All are prohibited from paroling men until the time clock says the men are eligible. The best time for parole may already have passed: the time remaining between release on parole and discharge from parole may be too short to help a man bridge the gap between imprisonment and unrestricted freedom. On the other hand, a man may be obliged to remain on parole either for the rest of his life or for periods beyond his successful correction. This, too, is a waste of correction's limited resources.

Preset time clocks impinge upon correction at other points. Some states provide no credit on the sentence for the time spent in jail between conviction and delivery to an institution. In some states no account of the time spent under probation supervision is taken in case of probation revocation and subsequent incarceration. No time is credited for parole supervision that ends in revocation and reconfinement. The words "concurrent" and "consecutive" make a significant difference in a sentence. If several sentences are imposed concurrently they all are served at the same time. If they are imposed consecutively, they are served in turn until the full time is completed. The words "consecutive" and "concurrent" also affect the quantity of good time. It is usually better to get one ten-year sentence than two five-year consecutive sentences. More good time off the sentence is granted in the second year than in the first, in the third than in the second, and so on. After completing one consecutive sentence a man usually begins all over again at the minimum first-year good-time rate.[3]

Criminals tend to have a very formal concept of justice — a feeling that all men who engaged in the same objectively observable behavior should receive exactly the same penalty. This would be as poor a policy, of course, as the present policy which produces the dis-

---

[3] One inmate I knew had the nickname "85" because seventeen consecutive five-year sentences had been imposed upon him. Had he been given one eighty-five-year sentence, he could be released several years earlier, as well as be eligible for parole. His multiple sentences, although the first he had ever received, classified him as a repeater and made him ineligible for parole consideration.

parity in sentencing that can be better explained by studying judges than by studying criminals. Contemporary correctional objectives are incompatible with both ways of disposing of cases. It is not suggested here that sentences should be equalized for what appear to be the same crimes, but it is suggested that treatment should be prescribed, irrespective of time, to meet the needs of society and of the total man. Such a dispositions program, of course, may yield even greater apparent discrepancies for what appear to be the same crime, since the length and type of treatment will depend on differences in the needs of the men being treated and not on differences in sentencing practices or judges. This should focus the criminal's attention upon his own readjustment and readiness for release instead of upon some relatively rigid release date set by a man who could not anticipate the offender's response to treatment. With the treatment time clock turned off, treatment by deadline ends, and treatment compatible with correctional objectives can begin.

PROBATION: THE FIRST PHASE OF CORRECTIONAL TREATMENT

For some men correctional treatment commences with probation. Probation is designed for men who are safe to have loose in the community and for men who do not need the treatment resources of a correctional institution. When the above criteria are met and the granting of probation does not contravene the public's attitude toward the offense and the offender and thus jeopardize the whole probation service, probation is indicated.

Best practice obligates the court to secure and study a presentence investigation report for every guilty man. Ideally, the presentence investigation is conducted by a probation officer (counselor) who knows the variables of crime well enough to know what to look for, who knows the significance of what he sees, and who knows what to do about all of it. A presentence investigation represents a thorough diagnostic case study of the subject and a prognosis in relation to correctional and other resources.

In consultation with the probation officer after considering the report, the judge may choose whatever disposition he wishes within the statutory limits. Some states prohibit the granting of probation to men who have committed particular crimes and have particular kinds of previous criminal records. There is tremendous variation in this throughout the country.

Should the judge elect probation, the sentence is suspended upon condition of observing the rules established by the state and by the court. To help the probationer solve his problems and make a law-abiding adjustment, a probation officer is assigned to him. The officer has the additional responsibility of reporting to the court progress in adjustment and any rule violations. The rules that a probationer must observe vary considerably from jurisdiction to jurisdiction. In some areas they are so restrictive that a law-abiding man would be hard put to observe all of them. More is expected of the probationer than of the free citizen. If the behavior is unsatisfactory, upon review of the record the court may choose to revoke probation and the suspended sentence and commit the man to a correctional institution, the second phase of correction, according to the sentencing practices of his jurisdiction.

CRITIQUE OF CURRENT PROBATION PRACTICES

Probation really remains to be applied in the United States. Much of what is called probation shares only the name with the real thing. An unfortunate consequence is that real probation suffers the discredit produced by imitation.

Although all states have probation laws, the probation laws are not always realistic. Moreover, probation is not properly used in some states with good laws. In some jurisdictions men are on probation who should be in prison and men are in prison who should be on probation. Either error is expensive and destroys the efficient and effective attainment of correction objectives.

Many of our probation officers are not prepared for the responsibility of their assignment. They do not know what to do nor how to do it. Those officers who are qualified are ineffective and frustrated because their case loads are so excessive that they do not have the opportunity to apply their knowledge and skills.

Proper probation has not advanced as rapidly as it should because it has been judged by inadequately implemented substitutes for the real thing. One rather widely accepted standard of service is that an officer's maximum load should consist of no more than ten presentence investigations a month or the supervision of fifty cases. Rare is the officer whose work load is that light. In the case of unqualified officers, it is perhaps just as well that the loads are so excessive that they can only shuffle paper.

Should the probationer behave appropriately for the proper length of time, the time clock stops and the court discharges the offender. When he is discharged from the sentence he cannot again be restrained with more time for that offense. Indirectly it may affect him if he commits another crime: the price for the second crime is higher in some states than that for the first, and up to a certain point each subsequent crime costs the offender more. In the event the probation is revoked, the offender enters a correctional institution, the second phase of correction.

INSTITUTIONS: THE SECOND PHASE OF CORRECTIONAL TREATMENT

For some men confinement is their first experience with correction. For others it is the second phase because they arrived indirectly as a consequence of violating probation. Still others are returning to institutions from correction's third phase for violating their paroles. Many men who are confined in institutions should be either on probation or on parole. Institutions should be reserved for men whose freedom must be thus restricted in order to protect society and for men who can benefit from institutional treatment. If the correctional objective is accepted, there is no other legitimate reason for confinement.

The institutional experience is not conducive to treatment. Treatment is accomplished within institutions in spite of the situation and not because of it. Confinement is necessary for some men to protect society from them; yet confinement cannot be justified as a desirable treatment medium. Its necessity for societal protection is its only reason for existence. Much of what is called treatment in prison and parole is actually concerned with undoing the fact of prison. More time and resources are expended in undoing the destructive effects of incarceration than are expended in making a constructive impact.

This presentation is concerned with some of the more common things that happen in prison which can have an effect upon postrelease behavior; it does not explore the total problem of institutional operation, or the means of preventing escape and maintaining good order.

Arrival at the institution is a formidable experience for the inmate-to-be. Rarely is he prepared to accept the prison experience, particularly if he is a first offender.

In the reception area, a thorough strip-search of the new prisoner is conducted to make certain that no contraband is entering the institution. After being dispossessed of his clothing he is obliged to bathe, and he is issued institutional clothing and supplies, and finger-printed, photographed, and assigned an institution identification number. Some prisons immediately merge the new arrival into the general inmate population with an "orientation lecture" of the following type as his only preparation for prison:

You are here. We are here to see you stay. Let's make it as easy on each other as possible. You don't cause us any trouble and we won't cause you any. You can have just as easy or just as hard a time as you want to make it. Don't be mad at us. We didn't have anything to do with your getting here, but we have everything to do with the kind of time you do here. Go easy on us. We'll go easy on you. The way to get on here is to do what you are told to do and keep your nose clean and your mouth shut. The less you have to do with others the better. Don't go getting too friendly. Don't get any bright ideas. We can make it harder on you than you can make it on us.

Best practice, however, requires that the new prisoner be housed in an admission-orientation unit, reception center, diagnostic depot, quarantine section, or isolation unit for diagnosis and instruction. Such programs usually require several weeks. During this time, the classification personnel learn as much as they can about the offender by studying him and accumulating data from outside sources. Whether the man is studied or not, he cannot be merged into the general institutional population until medical personnel can certify that he has no communicable disease and is ready at least for general duty. Clues as to his custodial classification are also collected and analyzed. Until sufficient data are secured and studied to determine how safe or unsafe he is and whether he needs special housing and supervision because he has sex problems or other difficulties, it must be assumed that he requires close custody.

While institutional personnel are learning about him, the prisoner is also learning about the institution. He is oriented to the place. He finds out what is expected of him and what he can expect of the institution. He finds out what facilities for improvement the institution has and how he can make use of them. During this period, he may receive a handbook and letters of advice and information from the institution's head. Institutional personnel lecture the inmate and answer his questions. They may take him on a guided tour of the institution. He may see slides or motion pictures to help him understand the institution and his place in it.

The institutional treatment person whose role most closely resembles that of the probation and parole counselor is the classification officer. He is also variously titled a counselor, guidance officer, institutional parole officer or agent, psychologist, sociologist, social worker, correctional classification officer, case-worker, and so on. Whatever his title may be, all institutions which make any pretense at individualization through classification have a man who, in effect, is a treatment manager.

The treatment manager has the responsibility for mobilizing the institution's resources in diagnosis and treatment. He is charged with seeing that a treatment plan is carried out according to staff decisions. He notes progress, and recommends alterations when they are needed. He is continuously involved in diagnosis and treatment, and its revision. Through him the inmate makes contact with the treatment forces of the institution. To him the inmate is presumed to look when he needs help, advice, and counsel.

Preparation for the man's release begins as soon as he arrives. Every activity should be focused on making him fit for release. This post-release function begins during the reception process when the treatment manager schedules the newly arrived inmate for diagnosis by the available experts in human behavior. Sometimes the treatment manager is alone in performing the diagnosis. He may have psychiatrists, psychologists, sociologists, chaplains, physicians, dentists, vocational educators, academic educators, vocational specialists, and the like, available to carry out the diagnoses peculiar to their professions and to make their recommendations for treatment. When the available experts have completed their diagnoses and prognoses and made their recommendations for treatment, he has the responsibility for pooling and organizing all the information secured from the local experts, from the outside sources, and from his own observations into an admission summary with recommendations regarding how the available resources can best be used to produce the greatest positive change in the subject. This admission summary is circulated to the diagnostic staff, administrative representative, industrial representative, and the heads of custody and of treatment (or their delegated agents) sufficiently in advance of staffing the case in a classification committee meeting that all members of the committee can familiarize themselves with the content before the meeting. At the meeting the case is presented and discussed; decisions are made as to the ingredients of the main treatment program which the treatment manager will be expected to implement. Unfortunately, such decisions all too frequently are made on the basis of blind hunch, faith, intuition, whim, dramatic circumstance, anecdote, and so-called common sense, when they should be made on the basis of the uncommon sense that emerges from scientific analysis.

The man is given a custodial classification of maximum, close, medium, or minimum which affects his housing, work assignment, movements, and supervision. His job placement is determined. Decisions are reached regarding the prisoner's educational program. Provisions are made for religious participation and counseling if available. Vocational training may be a part of the job assignment or an independent activity. Recreation and library programs are determined. Plans are made regarding individual therapy; medical and dental treatment; participation in Alcoholics Anonymous, Dale Carnegie clubs, social education, group psychotherapy, writers' clubs, and similar activities.

Following the decision of the first classification committee meeting or a reclassification committee, the inmate sometimes can appear before the committee to learn about his program and have an opportunity to make constructive criticism of it in the event that there may yet be some significant factors that the committee has not considered. This does not mean that inmates have a veto power over the treatment plan. They are brought before the committee simply to assure that as little as possible is overlooked in developing a program.

Whenever alternatives in a man's program are available, the classification committee makes the decision. It is through classification that the prison program is individualized and in a real sense the prison experience made different for every man. The committee's decisions on treatment are never fixed and final because a treatment program is only a tentative thing. When there seems to be sufficient reason to consider a revision in the program, the man is reclassified by the classification committee.

The implementation of the treatment program varies. Professional staff members are never available in sufficient numbers. In some institutions, treatment facilities are nonexistent or embryonic; in others they are fairly well developed. A few prisons may appear to have reached the zenith in correction, but, in fact, all our prisons have a long, long way to go before they do what should be done. For many men in many prisons the prison experience amounts to little more than being counted in at the beginning of the sentence and being counted out at the end. The time between is often either a blank or a totally unpleasant memory.

JOB PLACEMENT — CROSS-PURPOSES

Job placement is considered first because in many prisons it is the dominant factor, with all else secondary. Extreme confusion and cross-purpose are typical of the work assignments of prisoners. According to the treatment purposes of classification, a man should be assigned to a job when such an assignment constitutes the most constructive use of his time in relation to his post-release behavior. The particular job that he gets should serve his needs.

It is unfortunate that some institutions focus on maximum production at any cost — at any cost to the inmate. A consequence is that the production of goods rather than the production of men becomes the chief end of industrial and agricultural operations. Employment is often rationalized in one way or another, after the fact, in terms of treatment objectives. This may be no more than congenial self-deception. Neither treatment goals nor production goals are effectively and efficiently served. The program is not right for the man; the man is not right for the program.

A favorite rationalization for a job assignment that has little or no treatment implications is that "it teaches good work habits." This is not supported when the per capita production efficiency of an inmate is compared with that of a free employee. Inmates are often "taught" sloth, habits of evasion, how to "soldier" on the job, how to give the appearance of working, and similar habits.

Another favorite justification for doing what industry wants done anyway is to call work "on-the-job training." At one time, the expression had both humorous and tragic implications in a southern prison. No matter what work the inmate did before he came, no matter where he came from or where he was going upon release, no matter whether he liked it or not or whether he had seen cotton before or not, each man was given "on-the-job training" in cotton growing. Southern field hands who had worked in cotton fields for years "learned" all about cotton; northern transients who had never seen cotton before learned all about it. For what purpose? Many prison work assignments utilize men who know all there is to know about the assignment and have nothing to gain from the job except keeping their hands in and not losing whatever skills may be involved. Some men know nothing about the assignment and care even less because it will have no conceivable value for them upon release. Such production programs as have merit should be correlated with a realistic analysis of the labor market.

Even the fullest possible benefits from such industry as are available are frequently ignored. By occupying a man with the same assignment continuously, productive efficiency is maximized; but the man becomes too specialized. In the interests of the man, he should be rotated periodically in order to achieve the maximum training benefits that can accrue.

The equipment used for the limited production programs in some institutions is commonly obsolete so far as competitive industry is concerned. Working with such equipment does not particularly benefit a man in seeking employment upon release. The industrial world has passed by both him and the prison. The values of such work for post-release adjustment are minimal.

Abandonment of various production programs, such as the manufacture of binder twine, when they become too unprofitable offers proof to the lie that they were ever intended for rehabilitation of the offenders. If they were good programs to begin with, their failure to make an adequate profit is not particularly pertinent to the problem of continuing or abandoning them. Some production programs which may produce the greatest long-range profit to society may mean a loss in actual operation.

Many people concerned with correctional institutions are primarily concerned with operating them at minimum cost, irrespective of consequences. Making things to sell or to consume locally is one way of reducing cost. Institutional administrators cater to these interests and boast about how much the men have produced. This is, of course, shortsighted. The larger social interest in lawful behavior after release means that the only relevance of what goes on during institutional confinement is its impact on post-release behavior. Contemporary institutional production operations serve neither the public interest nor production goals well. Analysis of production, in terms of the prison labor supply and its cost of maintenance, indicates that such operations suffer in comparison with production outside prison. In spite of having a labor supply for which the state has to pay only room, board, security, token wages, and the cost of the amenities, prisons are not self-supporting. This failure to measure up well with competitive productive enterprise is often excused in terms of the character of the labor supply, or explained away by saying that, after all, the men are being treated.

In actual fact, treatment and other activities are usually subordinated to prison industry. Prison production is usually in the driver's seat. Other activities usually must be organized around it rather than its being organized around them. Once prison industry has swallowed up what it can, the other programs are free to compete for the man's time.

Idleness is one of the things most feared by prison administrators. Treatment has probably made more rapid headway because of this fear — helped by restrictive legislation and business and union pressures on production activities — than because of the belief of the administration in the importance of treatment itself for post-release behavior. This can be seen in the featherbedding of jobs in an institution. When industrial operations in prison were cut back because of elimination of markets through restrictive legislation, treatment began to make headway: it occupied inmates' time. "Keep them busy at something — just anything — and they are less liable to cause trouble" is the philosophy of some administrations.

One way of determining whether or not there is correlation between public relations correctional philosophy and operating correctional philosophy is to note the emphases and the priorities when the institution is explained to the visiting public. The measure of a prison should be the quality of the men released and not how many tomatoes and string beans were canned, how many manure spreaders were made, how many pounds of cotton were picked, or how many license plates were manufactured. Our prisons are failures both as industries and as treatment centers. The goals of neither are being served. If treatment is to be abandoned for industry, our prisons require much improvement to accomplish industrial objectives to any meaningful degree.

TREATMENT IS AN ISLAND

Treatment is typically what is done after the institution's self-interest in other activities has been attended to. Inmates can utilize the treatment resources when their activities do not conflict with other institutional assignments or with the prison routine.

The treatment manager and his fellow diagnosticians are usually too overloaded with sheer numbers of clients to prepare adequate diagnostic and prognostic statements. The number of cases to be disposed of at the classification and reclassification meetings is generally too large to permit proper consideration and disposition. The classification officer ordinarily is responsible for implementing the treatment programs for too many inmates to do it adequately. Treatment is a compromise all the way with what correction people know should be done.

One consequence is that often more time is spent manipulating paper routine involving inmates than is spent in face-to-face or mind-to-mind relationships with inmates. Paper inmates get treated while the real inmates get lost in the regimen of the institution.

Treatment personnel customarily must perform in a hostile atmosphere generated by inmates and noninmates alike. Treatment personnel, popularly known as "head shrinkers" or by other appellations intended to degrade or belittle them and their role, are regarded as intruders upon an otherwise well-disciplined order. Their wanting to do things differently at the expense of upsetting smoothly running routine is considered, at the least, bothersome.

Undesirable relationships are sometimes generated by the hostility directed toward treatment personnel by other staff and inmates. These two populations may define treatment personnel as people who help the inmate do what he wants to do in the institution or help him to secure a premature release. Inmates who seek out classification personnel may become suspect as stool pigeons (rats, squealers) who try to join the administration against the rest of the inmates, unless they have prepared the onlookers to believe that they are trying only "to work" the treatment man they see. They frequently protect their prestige by denouncing the treatment man as unfair or foolish. Generally, they cannot take the risk of publicly acknowledging that anything really worth while occurs during treatment, even though they may feel they were helped and would like to return for more treatment. Treatment must proceed against such a backdrop.

Frequently, custodial personnel resent the presence of the treatment men and find satisfaction in egging inmates on to negative definitions of treatment. Inmates play the angles with susceptible personnel by playing one staff member against another. This is only one of the serious consequences of the typical schism between custody and treatment.

Treatment is not supported in many institutions that profess to have treatment, since custody is entrusted with the veto power over treatment activities. Custody can usually succeed in exercising such vetoes without reasonable explanations. Custody is not required to expand on the usual reason that "it is not wise for the safety and security of the institution." Institutional treatment personnel are tremendously outnumbered by custodial personnel and others who are employed to prevent escapes, to keep good order, and to do the necessary institutional housekeeping and maintenance. The vision of nontreatment personnel is likely to be shortsighted.

Some prisons maintain a treatment staff of sorts for window dressing. It is then that treatment is really considered a joke by inmates and other staff alike. The administrator looks upon treatment as part of those things necessary to keep do-gooders off his back, to placate the relatives, and to make believe he has the interest of the men at heart. In these institutions, treatment staff are neutralized by having their time consumed by nontreatment activities, public-relations assignments, paper work, and other trivia.

Significant results cannot be expected from the employment of treatment personnel if they alone, of all the personnel, are concerned with treatment. Every employee should reinforce by his actions the objectives that the treatment personnel are trying to accomplish.

Treatment personnel in some institutions are looked upon as living lies by most of the inmates because they are more concerned over getting along with their fellow employees than they are with treating inmates. One result is that they often outdo custody in restricting inmates.

The classification officer's role should include helping the inmate to understand himself, helping the institution personnel to understand the inmate, and helping the inmate to make constructive use of his time and of the institution's facilities to the end that he becomes ready for release.

Religion

Religious representatives have long been affiliated with correctional institutions. They have not always had an opportunity to use religious experiences for rehabilitation. Historically, and currently to a lesser degree, prison chaplains are called upon to perform dual roles and to fill the gaps caused by unimplemented ideas. Their time often was — and is — so consumed in trying to fill nonreligious deficiencies that they often have little opportunity to do that for which they are prepared. Prisons would have been longer without educational programs, libraries, recreational programs, and other meaningful prison activities if chaplains had not taken charge of these programs.

Church services are provided in prison, and some religious counseling is available, but chaplains are usually expected to spread themselves too thinly. In a sense they have the choice of doing a little for many or much for the few.

Education

Meaningful educational programs provide a foundation upon which rehabilitation can be built. Although prisons are not considered complete without an educational program, too many institutions are satisfied with having just enough of an educational program to enable them to say that they are doing something in this area. Institutions which have the facilities usually require that a man remain in the educational program until he has achieved functional literacy.

Many prisons enlist the better-educated inmates to instruct the less educated. Inmate teachers need not be used unless it is impossible to have civilian instructors. The only excuse for such an educational program is that otherwise nothing would be done. Educational programs, although often better implemented than other treatment programs, are not operated with adequate facilities or sufficient personnel. Those prisons which have outstanding educational programs are the exception rather than the rule.

Customarily inmates must inconvenience themselves to take advantage of whatever educational opportunities exist. Securing an education is usually made difficult for the prisoner rather than attractive to him.

Libraries

Only the mind is relatively free in prison. Through well-planned libraries, treatment personnel can take advantage of this fact by helping inmates to make constructive use of some of their time. This resource is important, since men left to themselves often turn to vices.

Professional librarians are rarely employed and book collections are seldom planned. Too often the available books were received through donations and book drives. To be sure, these are ways to secure books, but they are not necessarily the ways of getting the right books. The resulting collection is usually almost useless, outdated, and unsuitable for rehabilitation purposes. Better planning, better book acquisition, and better utilization of this treatment resource are needed if it is to have a meaningful impact. Even well-equipped libraries provide treatment for a pittance when compared with the cost of other programs.

Recreation

Inmates are granted some time to use for recreational purposes. Often *time* is all that is given. Guards are frequently used to operate recreational programs. Few prisons employ men who are professionally trained in recreation leadership.

Planned recreation often amounts to little more than the competition of various prison sports teams with teams from the outside. This provides limited opportunities for sports participation for the few who are team members but only spectator sports for the rest.

Prisons vary tremendously in their recreation programs. A few are well equipped to provide recreation opportunities for the men that want them and to encourage others to make use of them. Typically, however, this is another area in which the full potential for growth is not even approximated.

Group Therapy

A relatively recent admission to the prison is a trend toward group programs variously known as group therapy, group psychotherapy, guided group interaction, "group," and the like. Although some prisons have professionally operated programs, most do not. In such instances, the only contribution of the group-program seems to be the presence of a civilian in the type of "bull session" prisoners have been having since the advent of prisons.

Self-Improvement Activities

Various interest groups that have both a recreational character and a self-improvement character are allowed to operate in some institutions. Alcoholics Anonymous is probably the most prevalent. Dale Carnegie Clubs, writers' clubs, drama groups, bands and orchestras, choruses, hobbyists, and the like are also found in many prisons. This permits men to occupy their time pleasantly and reduces the administration's fear of idle men.

Psychiatric services are rarely available to an institution. When psychiatrists are available, they are not usually involved in treatment. They are typically concerned only with emergencies.

PAROLE: THIRD AND FINAL PHASE OF CORRECTIONAL TREATMENT

The relationship between the parolee and the parole officer is very much the same as that between the probationer and the probation officer. The conditions of parole and probation are very similar and are intended to serve the same purpose. Failure to live up to the conditions results in confinement.

The decision to use parole or to return a parolee to an institution is made, of course, by a different authority — the parole board instead of a court. The decision is a group decision instead of the decision of one man. The parole decision is made by people much more familiar with institutions than are the judges.

Just as the court is restricted in the use of probation and in sentencing by statute, the parole board has similar restrictions. A certain minimum amount of institutional time must have been served before an inmate comes under the releasing jurisdiction of the board. If he has committed particular crimes or has a previous record the parole board may never be able to release him.

Just as best probation practice requires that a thorough case study known as a presentence investigation precede a decision to use probation, best parole practice requires that a preparole investigation be conducted to ascertain fitness for release and adequacy of plans for after-release. This, along with the accumulated institutional case records and the presentence investigation, is considered by the board prior to its decision.

Although approved employment is usually required both as a condition of release on parole and as a condition of continuation on parole, such opportunities tend to be very limited.

Best practice also requires that the inmate appear before the board. Parole is indicated when the board concludes that it is reasonably safe for him to be released, when he is at his peak in readiness for release (more likely to be a success if paroled now than later, or released at his maximum discharge date), and when he can no longer benefit from institutional incarceration.

Should the decision be for release, the man on parole is then handled much as a probationer is. Often parole supervision is no more than record keeping and surveillance. Seeing that a parolee stays out of trouble is not enough. He should be helped to stay out of trouble. Simply checking up on a parolee and making certain that his monthly report sheets are in on time develops into a cat-and-mouse game between the parolee and the officer.

The amount of time on parole is dependent upon the parolee's minimum and maximum sentences. Some states require that he serve the difference between his release date and his minimum sentence. Others make the man serve until the maximum. Still others keep the man on parole for the rest of his life. In a few states, a parolee who makes a satisfactory adjustment may be discharged from his parole previous to its expiration. Every parolee must be discharged when his maximum sentence expires.

Parole is not used to best advantage. Parole board members are inclined to play it very safe because they have so often been the scapegoats whenever an active parolee or a one-time discharged parolee commits a new crime. Then the agencies of mass communication feel it their public duty to point an accusing finger at the parole boards. "This would not have happened if it had not been for those naïve soft-hearted sentimentalists who are easy prey for every hard luck story." The pressure is real, and in the interests of the parole process, the parole board must be realistically aware of how the public will react to its decision to release. Self-inflamed presses have often been responsible for the increase in the restrictions imposed on parole. A significant point often easily ignored by such newspapers and other self-appointed guardians of the public order is that nearly every parolee who commits a crime would have been released without supervision at a later date. With parole there was at least some hope that he would be a better citizen because of parole supervision than he would have been without it, with a simple discharge at the expiration of his sentence when the time clock had run out.

This kind of destructive activity has helped to keep parole from reaching its objective, in part by causing parole boards to release men on parole who do not need it — who would be law abiding no matter how released — and to refrain from releasing men who really need the supervision, but with whom the parole board is unwilling to take the risk. Parole boards are obliged to play it safe, and some may play it entirely too safe.

The parole process is often handicapped in the same way that probation is handicapped with unqualified board members and officers. Case loads, too, are excessive.

Release on parole varies from insignificant percentages of the total number released, to parole releases being almost the only way anyone is released. Even in such states where parole is the typical release, however, parole is not always used well because so many of the men are actually on parole for only a very few weeks. If, at any time, during the parole period the man does not behave as he is expected to, he may be reconfined in an institution. In some states he receives credit off his sentence for parole time. Occasionally he even receives the same good time deductions that he would have received had he been in prison. In some states no credit is given for parole time when the man is reconfined.

In some jurisdictions parole violation is a bar to a man's being paroled again. In other jurisdictions, such a man may be released whenever the board feels he may be successful.

Society is usually made less rather than more safe, in the long run, by the parole board's understandable feeling that it must cater to public opinion. Although this has the effect of making the batting average of parole much higher than it would otherwise be, the batting average of the correctional process as a whole is lowered: men who would benefit from the use of parole have been denied it and, as a consequence, commit more crimes than they would have committed had correctional authorities felt free to use their resources to best advantage. The same situation, of course, exists for judges and their use of probation.

In all three phases of correction the lack of sufficient qualified personnel often means that the real man is lost, and only paper probationers, paper inmates, and paper parolees are shuffled about. The correctional process has been merely an interlude of timed unpleasantness that has temporarily postponed and occasionally intensified the criminal career of its clients.

AFTER CORRECTION, WHAT?

In the beginning of this chapter, the correctional objective was defined as the protection of society through the act of preparing offenders for release from legal supervision as rapidly and economically as possible, as useful, law-abiding, self-supporting, self-sufficient and independent citizens. It was also recognized that this goal was not being attained.

Just how much can society expect from the correctional processes? Many of the men have not been long exposed to the inadequately implemented processes.[4] Half of the men who are committed to prison today will be released within twenty-two months. Many of these men are released not because they have reached the correctional objectives but because their release is required by law.

---

[4] For detailed discussion, see Alfred C. Schnur, The new penology: Fact or fiction? *J. crim. Law, Criminol. Police Sci.*, 1958, 49, 331–334; and Federal Bureau of Prisons, *National prisoner statistics: Personnel in state and federal institutions*, 1958, 1960.

Are the correctional processes a success or a failure? Many of those released from the correctional processes will continue their criminal careers. Half of the men who leave prison today will be in prison again for a new offense within five years. Others will arrive later. Some will commit crimes and avoid apprehension or conviction. Some will refrain from crime.

Who deserves blame or credit for the successes and the failures? There are at least two ways of looking at this: (1) Whatever success there is was not to be expected. Were the offenders not failures when they entered the correctional process? It would be natural to expect them all to continue to be failures. The fact that some succeeded is a bonus. (2) On the other hand, should any fail after being exposed to the correctional processes? They are supposed to have been rehabilitated before release.

In some cases the correctional processes can indeed be held accountable to some extent. It is, however, an oversimplification of human behavior to give correctional personnel either all the credit for the successes or all the blame for the failures.

It would not be realistic to blame them for all the failures even if the correctional processes were perfectly implemented. After all, the releases from such a perfect program re-enter an imperfect society that made criminals out of them originally. These influences are still in vicious operation. Part of the price for the freedom of the strong to enjoy their vices is paid by the crimes committed by the weak. A man released who is highly resistant to crime can often be expected only to resist so much of the crime-inciting conditions. His success or failure is affected by the weakness and strengths of the social conditions into which he is released. A less resistant man released into conditions with more strengths than weaknesses may be more successful than the strongly resistant released into very weakening conditions. The fact is that success or failure of correctional clients is to be explained by both the correctional process and the experiences in the release situation.

Some sectors of our society expect the correctional processes to immunize a man from a criminal career for the rest of his life, no matter how contagious the social situation is. They feel the ineffectuality of the correctional processes is documented whenever a one-time client commits a new crime, no matter how many years separate him from the correctional process. This is expecting more of correctional treatment than is expected of medical treatment. Physicians are not called quacks for every recurrent attack of illness.

As long as society refuses to remove the legal impediments to effective treatment, hesitates to implement contemporary knowledge, neglects to provide for the discovery of additional knowledge, and fails to control adequately the social and economic conditions productive of criminal behavior, accountability for recurrent crime (recidivism) must be shared by society with the correctional processes.

References

Bennett, James V. Evaluating a prison. *Ann. Amer. Acad. pol. soc. Sci.*, 1954, **293**, 10.

Hoover, J. Edgar. The challenges of crime control. In National Probation and Parole Association, *Parole in principle and practice: A manual and report.* New York: The Association, 1957.

Taft, Donald R. *Criminology: A cultural interpretation.* New York: Macmillan, 1950.

Recommended Readings

General Correction

Grunhut, Max. *Penal reform.* New York: Oxford Univer. Press, 1948.

Tappan, Paul. *Contemporary correction.* New York: McGraw-Hill, 1951.

Probation

Chute, C. L., & Bell, Marjorie. *Crime, courts and probation.* New York: Macmillan, 1956.

National Probation and Parole Association. *Guides for sentencing.* New York: The Association, 1957.

Institutions

Alexander, M. E. *Jail administration.* Springfield, Ill.: Charles C Thomas, 1957.

American Correctional Association. *Manual of correctional standards.* New York: The Association, 1959.

American Prison Association; Committee on Classification and Casework. *Handbook on Classification in Correctional Institutions.* New York: The Association, 1947.

American Prison Association, Committee on Classification and Casework. *Handbook on pre-release preparation in correctional institutions.* New York: The Association, 1949.

Clemmer, D. *The prison community.* Boston: Christopher Press, 1940.

Parole

Giardini, G. I. *The Parole Process.* Springfield, Ill.: Charles C Thomas, 1959.

National Probation and Parole Association. *Parole in principle and practice: A manual and report.* New York: The Association, 1957.

ROBERT H. SCOTT

14 The Youthful Offender: An Illustration of New Developments in Correction[1]

The juvenile court is fully dealt with in Chapter 11 of this volume. It is a protective court, with procedures and services modified to meet the special needs of children. The stern practices of the criminal court have been relaxed, children are carefully separated from other offenders, and records are kept from the public. Juvenile training schools, often operated by Departments of Social Welfare rather than Corrections, care for the child when committed. This protection ceases when the upper limits of the court's jurisdiction are reached. When the child reaches sixteen or seventeen or eighteen — whatever the limits of that jurisdiction specify — he becomes an adult offender.

About forty years after the juvenile court movement began in the United States, a book was published (Harrison and Grant, 1938) that threw a flicker of light on the 16–21 age group in trouble with the law. It revealed to some and reminded others that these youths (most not yet old enough to vote) were subject to the same procedures as the most hardened or vicious adult offender. A seventeen-year-old boy who had wired a car for a joy ride could be in prison with murders, pimps, and gangsters. Moreover, the stamp of a felony record and the brand of an ex-convict could follow this young man for the rest of his life, making jobs difficult to get, military service virtually impossible, and casting a shadow over him,

[1] The opinions expressed in this chapter are those of the author. They do not necessarily represent the views of the Michigan Department of Corrections. Grateful acknowledgment is made to Professor John Barker Waite, distinguished pioneer in the field of youth correction, for many of the ideas discussed here. The author is also grateful to the Michigan Corrections Commission, and to Gus Harrison, Director of the Corrections Department of the State of Michigan, for having made it possible to put many ideas into practice.

his wife, and his children in the normal associations and satisfactions of life.

Change was difficult, however, in the face of the undeniable fact that some young "punks" (to borrow a term from another school of thought) were clearly vicious, hardened, or degenerate. Then and now stories of brutal, senseless beatings and thrill killings are frequently reported in our press, and youth gangs are known to roam the streets of our big cities. The public is horrified and threatened by the crimes of these youngsters, and is indignant over the callous indifference and calculating affront to decency and humanity they often show. Charges of "coddling" and cries of "let's get tough!" are frequent public reactions, in opposition to proposed reforms.

In this context, a committee of the American Law Institute[2] drafted a model Youth Authority Act designed to provide a means for correcting the youthful offender, the 16–21 age group. The story of the act and its subsequent applications in various jurisdictions is well told in *Five States: A study of the Youth Authority Program as Promulgated by the American Law Institute* (Beck, 1951.)

It was first applied in California in the early 1940's, and a few years later in Minnesota. The major provisions of the act may be summarized as follows:

1. It vested in a board, committee, or authority the entire disposition of a case after adjudication (the court could no longer determine whether or not to place the offender on probation, or decide the length of his sentence, or designate the institution to which he was to be committed).

2. It provided for reception center facilities to which the offender would go for diagnosis and a decision as to his disposition. (This was coupled with a wide range of available institutions and programs.)

3. It provided for the prevention of delinquency and youthful crime as a function of the Authority rather than as a general responsibility of child welfare.

The provisions of the act were not uniformly applied; moreover, they were considerably modified in various jurisdictions. Comparisons are difficult because no two states have identical provisions. Perhaps the greatest deflection from the original purpose of the act was the inclusion of the juvenile delinquent group. Indeed, in a

---

[2] William D. Lewis, Director of the Institute, chairman; John Barber Waite, Professor of Law, University of Michigan, recorder.

majority of the states which have adopted the act, its provisions are restricted to the juvenile delinquent and do not cover the youthful offender for whom the act had been intended.[3] A more traditional approach to the administration of criminal justice to youthful offenders than is embodied in the Youth Authority Act is presented by Paul Tappan in his book *Crime, Justice, and Correction* (1960). This traditional approach has been recently revived in the Model Penal Code of the American Law Institute.

CHANGES IN ADULT CORRECTIONS

While the Youth Authority was being developed and applied, changes were taking place in the treatment of the adult offender. Some of these have been described in Chapter 13 of this volume. For our purposes, they may be summarized as follows:

1. The development of classification for treatment (as well as custody)

2. The introduction of psychiatry and psychology as bearing upon concepts of causation and treatment

3. Emphasis upon education and special programs such as the chaplaincy, recreation, and activities, such as radio and television

4. The development of the indeterminate sentence

5. Improved standards of selection and training of personnel

6. Civil service and merit systems

7. Reorganized Departments of Corrections to include probation and parole services

8. Development of camp programs

9. Introduction of counseling services to institutions

10. Improved standards and greater use of probation

11. Increasing use of presentence investigation to determine proper disposition

CHANGES IN JUVENILE CORRECTIONS

Corresponding changes had been taking place in juvenile institutions. Traditional concepts of harsh, repressive treatment were being

---

[3] For an excellent analysis of the experience of the act and the various difficulties it has encountered, the reader is again urged to consult Beck (1951).

replaced by modern treatment methods. Public attention was being concentrated upon this age group, and social-work philosophy and practice were introduced and integrated. Juvenile court services were improved and expanded to include trained probation staff and treatment personnel. The county jail was largely replaced by the children's detention home to hold children awaiting trial. (For greater detail, see Chapter 11.)

CHANGES IN POLICE SERVICES

Police departments began to see a need for personnel specially trained and qualified for work with juveniles. The importance of the first contact with offenders and the proper use of special legal procedures for handling juveniles were stressed. Police women tended to replace police matrons. Closer cooperation between police and social agencies in particular, and community agencies in general, came into being. Larger departments established Youth Bureaus consisting of officers detailed to handle delinquents. Many smaller departments strove to have at least one police officer especially trained for this purpose.

In some cases, police departments entered the field of treatment to a considerable extent. They established or encouraged recreational programs and summer camps. They undertook the supervision of delinquents by placing them "on visits" — a kind of informal probation. In some instances, social agencies were developed under police auspices in communities where regularly constituted agencies were too heavily loaded to meet the emergency cases referred to them by police. Rifle clubs, junior police departments, and similar activities were seen by police as ways by which the civic responsibilities of youth could be developed and hostility to the police reduced. Traffic safety and traffic patrols were fostered by police not only in relation to their traffic responsibilities, but also because these activities might have a bearing upon relations with children.

These ventures into treatment drew some criticism from social agencies, which felt that proper police functions were exceeded. Police countered by saying that they could not evade the responsibility for helping the troubled child. Probably the whole point of this controversy should be to see treatment of the delinquent as a continuing and not a segmented process. The importance of the police role is undeniable; contact with the juvenile can be constructive or destructive, depending upon the knowledge and attitude of the police officer.

CORRECTIONS' PROGRAMS FOR THE YOUTHFUL OFFENDER

This brief background brings us to the treatment of the youthful offender. The three fields of Corrections — juvenile, youth, and adult — tend to cross-fertilize each other. This is particularly true of youth and adult correction, since these two are so closely related. They are, in fact, in many cases, united; a Youth Division often is part of a general Department of Corrections. The state of Michigan follows this plan and will furnish us with most of our illustrations. Developments of Youth Corrections describe many of the changes in adult correction, for each of these fields borrows from and contributes to the others.

THE RELATIONSHIP BETWEEN CRIMINAL LAW AND CORRECTIONS

The juvenile court and the juvenile correctional field are much closer together than are criminal courts and adult correction. The juvenile court, when it does commit an offender to an institution, does so until he reaches a maximum age (usually nineteen or twenty-one), not for a definite sentence. The delinquent has not been found guilty of a particular crime so that treatment can be based much more on need than on an offense. A treatment philosophy is made more feasible. The juvenile institution usually has some discretion in the cases it will accept; an adult correctional institution normally does not. The continuing philosophy and practice of social work in the social agencies that prevent or treat delinquency, the juvenile bureaus of police departments, the juvenile courts that adjudicate the case, and the juvenile correctional agencies are much more consistent and continuous than the agencies concerned with youthful or adult offenders.

Youthful and adult offenders are subject to traditional police procedures of investigation, arrest, and apprehension, bail or confinement in a county jail awaiting trial, formal public trials, fixed sentences (although some form of indeterminate sentence is coming into increasing use); and, finally, either probation or sentence to a correctional institution. The offender receives a record that will usually follow him for life. He is stamped as a criminal and probably as an "ex-convict." The language and ritual of condemnation, rejection, and punishment are very evident. Change is difficult where old words are used, conveying sterotypes and carrying on traditional attitudes. Change is also made more difficult by virtue of the fact that divisions are of very long standing, and have deepened and widened over the years.

Some jurisdictions, especially California, Minnesota, and the federal government, have recognized the youthful offender as a separate legal category, and have developed special court procedures as well as correctional procedures for his treatment. This is an original Youth Authority concept. Other states (for example, New York) have adopted a Youthful Offender statute without accepting the total Youth Authority concept.

In considering the youthful offender program, one must remember that there are two distinct, but closely related parts — court procedure and correctional practice. We will be concerned in this chapter primarily with the latter, but the two are inseparable.

A CONCEPT AND PROGRAM
OF CORRECTIONS

The basic theory of correction, which has already been outlined in the previous chapter, is that crime is a violation of the community and that the prevention and the correction of crime are to be found in restoration to the community. (This must not be interpreted as meaning that every offender should be placed at once in the free community of society. Rather, he must become aware of the fact that he is, indeed, a responsible member of society with hope and potential for constructive, socially acceptable conduct.) This theory is at once simple and complex: it seeks to employ the insights and skills of the social and behavior sciences; it utilizes the knowledge and experience of Corrections administration; it undertakes to recognize the realities of life and is aware that some offenders are serious threats to society, which must be protected from them. On the other hand, it sees that not all offenders fall into this category and that many can be restored as useful citizens by means other than maximum security. Treatment is an individual matter, and begins with the way people are treated. This theory will be applied to various situations which are illustrated mainly from experiences in Michigan.

INSTITUTIONS

Reception-Diagnostic Procedures

Basic to the Youth Authority concept was the limitation of the court to a judgment of guilt or innocence. After this point, a central authority had the guilty offender diagnosed to determine his problems and potentials. This authority determined, on the basis of its diagnosis, whether to return the offender to the community on probation or to commit him to an institution. If the latter, the authority selected the institution best suited to his needs and society's, and recommended an appropriate program. The authority set a hearing date which, if all went well, would be the date of release. Program, place, and release date could be modified as circumstances warranted. This implied the development of a wide range of institutions and a variety of programs.

The underlying purposes of a reception-diagnostic center may be summarized as follows:

1. To provide a thorough evaluation of the offender's personality, background, and experience, and of the nature of the problem behavior

2. To determine which cases require institutional treatment

3. To release other cases directly to the community on probation

4. If an institution is indicated, to select the one best adapted to the offender's possibilities and needs, including the degree of security required

5. To develop a range and variety of institutions and programs sufficiently flexible to provide, insofar as feasible, for the varying needs of offenders

6. To determine the probable date of readiness for return to the community without the limitation of a minimum sentence

7. To separate the younger, less-hardened offender from the older, more-hardened offender. (Obviously calendar age is not the only criterion.)

As has already been indicated, most jurisdictions that have adopted the Youth Authority program have not fully adopted this principle of complete disposition. Courts did not view the invasion of their powers with enthusiasm. Consequently, most courts in states that follow some form of the Youth Authority program decide whether or not to place the offender on probation. If the court has not done so, the authority may do so at the conclusion of the reception diagnosis process. In Minnesota, for example, the Youth Conservation Commission (now a part of a unified Corrections Department) customarily releases about 25 percent of its incoming youthful offenders directly to the community on probation as soon as the offender has gone through the reception-diagnostic center. The experience has been favorable.

In Michigan, one such center, physically located at the State Prison of Southern Michigan but administratively separate from it, serves the entire Department of Corrections. All persons sentenced to imprisonment are received there for approximately thirty days of diagnosis and classification.

The reception center idea has been widely adopted throughout the United States by adult as well as youthful and juvenile Corrections. It represents a major trend in the whole field of Corrections. Three hypothetical cases will provide an illustration of how the center might function in Michigan.

Joe, nineteen, Pete, twenty, and George, twenty-one, broke into a filling station at night and took cigarets and small change (this offense could carry a maximum penalty of fifteen years in Michigan). The defendants all pleaded guilty. The presentence investigation revealed that Joe had once taken a car without permission when he was fourteen, had been placed on probation by the juvenile court, and had not been in trouble since. He might well receive probation. Pete had a long series of relatively minor offenses, including several small larcenies, and had been committed to a juvenile training school, where he had made a good adjustment. George, who had a somewhat similar record except that he had been involved in a "mugging" (unarmed robbery), had also been placed in a juvenile training school. While there he had escaped, stealing a car in the process. The court might commit both to prison. Pete received a sentence of from one to fifteen years. George, because of his more serious record and because he was the ringleader in the present offense, received a sentence of from three to fifteen years. At the reception-diagnostic center it was found that Pete had an IQ of 110 and possessed good manual dexterity, but had completed only the eleventh grade. He was within normal limits, emotionally and mentally. George, on the other hand, had an IQ of 85 and showed a tendency toward emotional instability. Because of his relatively good record and his educational potential, and because he was neither deviated nor disturbed, Pete was transferred to Cassidy Lake Technical School, which is an open type of institution for first offenders. It has an academic and vocational program where he could complete his high school. With the record of his escape, his relatively low IQ, and his personality problems, George was transferred to a reformatory for counseling and assignment to an industrial program.

Institutions for Youthful Offenders

A major goal of correction, insofar as institutions are concerned, is the development of a wide range of types (with various degrees of security), with appropriate programs in each designed to meet the needs of particular offenders. The large industrial institution is outmoded, although many such fortresses remain as monuments to our mistakes. The need is for small institutions, organized so as to permit the inmate to be treated as an individual and to allow him to observe the institution's interacting parts. A man can become lost in a large prison where the whole program tends to be restricted by the lowest common denominator — the difficult and disturbed people who are a minority of the population of our maximum-security institutions. The 10 or 15 percent who are troublemakers are largely responsible for many of the restrictions placed on the other 85 or 90 percent. Other arrangements are clearly necessary. Some of the institutions for youthful offenders and the programs furnished for them follow.

Reformatories. Reformatories represent the attempt of the past century to separate young offenders from older men. They have generally become traditional institutions with little to distinguish them from prisons except the age of the inmates.

For the youthful offender in Michigan this presented a special problem. When the Youth Division was established by the Corrections Act of 1953, there were only two institutions primarily for the young offender. One was Ionia Reformatory, which then housed about 1,200 inmates between fifteen and twenty-five years of age. It was virtually a maximum-security institution in that it had a wall, towers, and cell blocks. Its program included industrial shops, and academic and vocational education programs. The other institution was Cassidy Lake Technical School which was operated as a satellite of the Reformatory (although seventy-five miles away). It is of the open campus type, with no fences or towers, and is designed for selected first offenders. Inmates are on a trusty basis and are housed in nine-man living units. The program emphasizes education. (Cassidy Lake Technical School has since been separated from the Reformatory, has been enlarged to 250, and its program has been expanded.)

The picture clearly was out of proportion with the need for housing young offenders. Of Michigan's then approximately 8,500 inmates of all ages, some 35 percent were maintained in camps, farms, and trusty barracks. Of the total, over 2,500 were young offenders between fifteen and twenty-five years. Of these 2,500 young men, only 180 were *not* in prison. This meant that only 6 percent of the young offenders as compared with 35 percent of the general group received a type of treatment generally considered to be more beneficial and less repressive.

It seemed desirable to expand outside facilities for young offenders and to use the opportunity to experiment with program concepts and methods.

Camps. Camps for youthful offenders are not a new idea. California and Minnesota are among the leaders in this movement. Older readers will recall the Civilian Conservation Corp Camps, the "CCC Camps" of Depression days. While not for the correction of offenders, the camps provided valuable lessons in program and administration. Incidentally, interest in these CCC camps is being currently revived as a place for school drop-outs and youth not yet in trouble with the law but in need of constructive outlets and development of skills.

Before discussing Michigan youth camps, we must deal briefly with the general camp program of the Corrections Department. A joint Corrections-Conservation camp was established in 1948. The Conservation Department supplied forestry projects, equipment, and foremen. The Corrections Department built the camps, housed, fed, and clothed the men and generally administered and supplied them. Inmates were carefully screened for suitability for trusty status. From the first, the partnership was successful and the program expanded rapidly as a humane, economical way of caring for inmates, providing an efficient source of labor for important conservation projects. From the first, the tradition was "no guns." A very low walk-away rate attested to the care of selection and of administration. Now a total of thirteen camps housing more than twelve hundred men are operated in Michigan by the Camp Program of the Corrections Department.

Younger men were, for the most part, excluded from these forestry camps, and Cassidy Lake Technical School remained the only outside placement. It had been thought that young men would not work out well in camp situations, that they were unstable in behavior and lacked work skills. Earlier attempts to mix them with older offenders had not been entirely successful. The younger group had tended to be, in the eyes of the older inmates, a disrupting and disturbing factor. In secure institutions younger offenders were often regarded as more difficult to handle than older men and as requiring stricter discipline. In spite of these obstacles, the Corrections Commission decided to push ahead.

It should be stated at this point that our directions were not yet clear to us. There were certain fundamental ideas that we wanted to try: treating individuals as individuals, accepting the offender as a person, and involving him in his own recovery or restoration. We were also conscious of the reality factors in the situation: the need for careful selection of inmates (the difficult and disturbed did not belong here); very limited resources and personnel; and the surrounding community, which was hostile.

Our thinking was much influenced by Dr. Maxwell Jones's book, *The Therapeutic Community* (1953). This English psychiatrist had developed a residential treatment center for mentally and emotionally disturbed "industrial casualties." The center's program was built around the concept of the conscious cooperation of all elements within it for the welfare and development of the patient.

It was decided that group counseling would be a keystone of our program. There would be small groups — from six to eight members — nondirective, with freedom to talk about whatever the members wished, and with anonymity outside the group. What the individual said would *not* be held against him. The group counseling was not to be an artificial appendage, like an ornament on a Christmas tree, but hopefully an organic part of the whole camp program. It was here that a community concept could be brought into focus. The role of the group leader would be merely to keep the discussion within bounds, to see that it moved in the direction that the group desired and that its purposes and accomplishments were interpreted to the group.

We had discussed the pros and cons of voluntary versus involuntary group counseling sessions. To require the campers to attend would be one more irritating rule and might hinder the individual's necessary inward involvement. On the other hand, to seek volunteers would expose them to the charge of being "front-office men." Besides, the men who most needed help might well resist the idea. So we hit on a compromise. We would require all campers to attend twelve weekly sessions of one hour each. After that, they would be free to attend or not as they chose.

Basic to the program of group counseling were the "after sessions." For each hour of meeting with the group, we required the leaders to attend a similar session for leaders to discuss developments in the groups. We were careful not to mention group members' names in connection with anything that was said. We worked hard to maintain anonymity and to assure the camper that his confidence would be respected. We made only one exception — matters vitally affecting the security of the camp.

We stressed the need for sincerity on the part of the group leader and the importance of not pretending to know everything. We mentioned the testing process by which our acceptance was examined by the group. The avoidance of preaching and moralism was underlined. These and the simpler dynamics of the group situation were explained.

We learned a great deal in our initial ventures. For instance, one night, early in my own experience, in a group with which I was working we were talking about getting jobs after release. A member of the group commented on negative public attitudes toward hiring criminals. Another camper asked me, "Would you hire a man with a criminal record?" Without a moment's hesitation I said, "Sure!" He thought a minute. "Well," he said, "suppose you had ten men working for you. One had a record, the others didn't. Let's say some money was missing from the cash register. Would you suspect the man with the record quicker than you would the rest?"

That stopped me. I know perfectly well I would suspect him first. Yet if I said so, the group members would see my inconsistency and I would lose them. At that moment, the whole group counseling program seemed to be challenged, if not lost. If I said that I would not suspect the ex-convict first, I would be dishonest with them and myself. Neat evasions or rationalizations seemed out of place. With sinking heart, I said, "Fellows, you've got me, I'm not proud of it, but I would suspect him first." A lot of better things might have been said, but I didn't have the wit to say them. I felt miserable. But the group wasn't lost — we went ahead several strides in our relationship. Later, it seemed to me that the group sensed and honored my attempt to be honest, even though the members may not have agreed with me.

Some members of some groups hardly spoke at all and the leaders often wondered about the value of the experience for the silent. Yet we carefully avoided putting the silent member "on the spot." If he did not want to say anything beyond "Hello" and "Good-by," we did not try to make him. After all, the privilege of speaking is also the privilege of silence. And every once in awhile we were pleasantly surprised. A boy who hadn't said a word all evening would walk back to the mess hall with his leader and, on the way, would pour his heart out.

What would establish a relationship puzzled us. One night, I asked a group if we might record the session on tape for training purposes. I explained to them that we would not do so if anyone objected and that, in any case, we would play back the tape at the end to make sure that no one could be identified. If identification was possible, we would erase either part or all of the tape, as they preferred. One boy objected. It was George — a "hard case." He had come from the Reformatory, to which he had been returned as a parole violator. His offense, as I recall, was unarmed robbery. He was tough, cynical, and bitter, and he didn't try to hide his feelings. In the group he had been silent and suspicious in previous sessions. "That's okay, forget it," I said. "Well," he explained, "I got caught on one of these things once and I don't want it to happen again." I didn't press the point, but said that it made no difference, really. "Wait a minute," he said. "Did you tell us we could listen to the tape and then erase it if we didn't like it?" I replied, "That's right." He thought awhile and said, "Let's try it."

We did. The group quickly forgot its initial self-consciousness and the session went well. We stopped a little early to listen to the tape. When George heard his own voice he was fascinated. "Is that me?" he asked. By this time some of the other groups were breaking up and he yelled to several of his friends, "Hey, you guys! Get a load of this!" I don't think George would have let me erase that tape if I had wanted to.

From that point, George's attitude seemed to change. He appeared less bitter and resistant. Not long afterward I went with my wife and our eleven-year-old son to the Christmas party at the camp. My son soon became restless and wanted to explore outdoors. He asked permission. I hesitated, feeling a little uneasy (I apologize for the feeling). George heard what was happening and came over to me. "Let him go with me," he said. "He'll be okay." So I did, without a moment's further concern. George and I had come to know and trust each other.

CASE MANAGEMENT

Implied in correction is the necessity for individual treatment. The inmate needs to be seen as a person in terms of his problems and possibilities. The purpose of the reception center was to enable assignments to be made to place and program. This process needs to be continuous and to persist throughout the institutional experience. The primary responsibility of the counselor is to coordinate it. But the results of observation and experience should be communicated cated to all persons responsible for the inmate's development.

This principle has particular application in institutions small enough to permit staff to know and observe inmates throughly. In our first camp a device was used to get pertinent information to all staff, including Conservation Department crew foremen. The Youth Division staff psychologist prepared a short report on each camper. This report contained two headings: "Treatment Goals," and "Behavior to Expect." Terse, nontechnical language was used. For example, a report might state that Ed was easily discouraged, lacked the experience of success, and needed to discover the proper role of a man. The sheet might suggest that Ed be given encouragement for any progress made on a job. The advice would tend to head off any accidental discouragements for Ed caused by sharp or unthinking criticism for mistakes. Any camper might pose such a problem.

Another goal should be the case conference at which members of the staff outline a man's progress and development. The outcome of the conference should be interpreted to the camper by his counselor. Staff shortages and personnel pressures (we have a staff of only five for round-the-clock coverage of a camp) make it difficult to achieve these goals.

A CONCEPT OF REMEDIAL THERAPY

To us, a therapeutic community (Jones, 1953) meant a situation in which all efforts were related to therapeutic goals, and in which individual inmates reacted to those experiences in interacting with staff and with other inmates. Treatment is often superimposed upon custody by the administration. The result can be a split. At our camp, custody and administration were to be a part of treatment, and vice versa. One symbol and implement of this concept was the officer-counselor. Staff shortages had compelled us to consolidate both roles in one man. To some the roles seemed antithetical. We were fortunate in our choice of men to fill this job, for they have combined the duties successfully.

Treatment personnel need to recognize their custodial responsibilities and to cooperate with custody and administration. These are a part of the "givenness" of a correctional situation. Custodial and administrative personnel need to recognize the treatment and corrective goals of the institution and to cooperate toward these ends. Corrections officers and Conservation crew foremen can be a powerful influence upon men. The work of a psychotherapist can be undone in a moment by the thoughtless comment of a guard. Together they can constitute a powerful treatment team. This does not require extensive technical knowledge of human behavior on the part of the officer. It does involve a positive attitude toward inmates and an understanding of how the performance of his job affects them. By encouraging Ed when he made a small success, the Conservation foreman was contributing to Ed's treatment. In helping Joe control his impulsiveness, the Corrections officer is being an important part of the treatment team. Neither instance requires technical knowledge. The experience of a lifetime is a powerful teacher. (For a fuller discussion of this principle, see Vinter and Janowitz, 1959.)

Attitudes of the larger community surrounding the camp are also important. Volunteer lay group leaders can be valuable symbols of the community's interest and acceptance.

Another powerful source of influence is the inmate body itself. There are two cultures existing side by side in an institution. (For a full discussion of this point, see Sykes, 1958.) One is the culture of the administration, shared by its employees and made up of the formal goals and methods of any Corrections Department. In a large institution this may be divided into two or more parts. The first of these is the formal administrative hierachy with its echelons of command. The other is the informal group which takes its flavor and direction from the preferences, feelings, and perceptions of its members. Its channels of communication are the car pool, the coffee break, and the locker room.

The second major influence is the "culture of the yard." It is made up of and by the inmate body with its attitudes, unwritten rules, and penalties. Often it tends to resist the goals of the formal administrative culture. One may speculate on the reasons for this. Perhaps it is a desire to retain as much independence as possible. Perhaps it is a way of saying, "They can't do this to me." The resistance is seldom open and active. It is usually concealed and passive. But it is a powerful defense against attitude change. Inmate leaders tend to derive their leadership from the ability to thwart administrative goals without getting into trouble ("playing it cool").

At our camp, Camp Brighton, our goal was to involve inmates in their own treatment, to enlist the inmate culture in the task of positive attitude change. Part of this lay in the group counseling, part in the integration of the total program, but another important part lay in convincing inmates that we all shared the same goal — to get a man out and to keep him out. Once convinced of this, inmates tend to accept the goal and participate in their own recovery.

I remember Willie, an undersized, timid-looking youngster who will certainly never be a college president. Willie was suddenly transferred "back to the walls" one day. The reason given was that he was a sex offender. His formal charge had been burglary, but somewhere in the file there was a notation that Willie had been involved in rape. The camp investigated and it appeared that the case involved a girl his own age, and that there had been no element of force. Indeed, it was questionable whether an act had taken place at all: there was only the girl's story, and she had gone to a mental hospital soon after. The prosecutor had recommended no prosecution. There was never even a formal charge, but Willie was "behind the walls" by this time. The camp staff made these facts known and followed through on the task of getting Willie back. He was not a spectacular success at the camp but he managed to get along. The campers learned from this and other incidents that some people were concerned about them and would try to get them a "fair shake." At any rate, a later study showed that those identified in sociograms as being regarded as leaders by other inmates tended to support the formal goals of the camp.

THE CAMP AND THE NEARBY COMMUNITY

Soon after the camp's youth program was started, a petition was circulated in neighboring communities for the camp's removal. The director of the Corrections Department and some of his staff appeared at a hearing of the County Board of Supervisors to explain the program and the safeguards used in the selection of campers. The Director suggested a community relations committee. On the first night that the committee came to the camp, the members talked in the mess hall before the meeting. One man suggested, "Why not put up signs on the road saying, 'Danger, Prison Area. Do not pick up hitchhikers' "? Another added, "If there's an escape, why not notify the neighbors so they can put on the yard light and lock the doors?"

The first item on the evening's program was a tour of the camp, two by two, one guest to one camper. The second item was the regular group meetings with committee members divided among the groups (the campers had previously requested this chance). When the committee held its formal meeting later, there was no more talk about security, only about the program and how the story could be told to the neighboring towns. This community committee has been a great help in spreading understanding of the camp. It is a visible symbol, too, to the camp, of acceptance by the community.

Furloughs and Passes

On Easter Sunday, 1959, an unusual experiment began. Five families came to the camp, bringing dress clothes. Each left with a camper, returning at eight in the evening, having gone anywhere within a radius of fifty miles. Since then, every Sunday and holiday has seen a repetition of this event and all the men have returned. None have been in trouble. When parole is approved, campers may be given a 72-hour furlough to get used to the idea before the formal papers come through.

PROBATION

Probation is a constructive program for the supervision and treatment of selected offenders. It is described in more detail in Chapter 13. Comments here will be restricted to points particularly applicable to the youthful offender.

The percentage of offenders placed on probation varies considerably. In Michigan, the figure approximates 52 percent. In most states, it is lower; in a few states, higher. Generally the scale is weighted in favor of younger offenders because of their age and lack of experience, particularly of criminal experience.

In another sense, a part of the youthful offender group is disadvantaged by age and inexperience. Few are married; many have never held down a steady job. Most live at home; many have never completed high school and lack vocational skills. Some are fortunate in their home background; some are not. Where home conditions were bad, associations highly undesirable, and work habits and skills lacking, the outlook for success on probation was dubious. Courts were faced with the alternative of probation under unfavorable circumstances (even the best probation officer would find it difficult to supply these lacks) or commitment to a correctional institution. In such cases, even though the youth was otherwise potential probation material, he was at a disadvantage.

Some new attempts to solve this problem have been made by California and Michigan. A discussion of the latter's plan follows.

The Probation-Recovery Camp in Michigan

Legislation had been enacted in the early 1930's, as the result of a recommendation by Circuit Court Judge Parm C. Gilbert. His successor, Judge Earl C. Pugsley, carried the project into reality twenty-five years later. The Probation-Recovery Camp is named in Judge Pugsley's honor.

Camp Pugsley provides a place to which youthful offenders (not over twenty-two years of age when sentenced) can be committed for up to one year. The offender remains a probationer, under the control of the committing court, during his stay and after his return to the community. The young man comes directly to the camp without going through the Reception-Diagnostic Center and he cannot be transferred to any other correctional institution (except by return to the court as a probation violator or for the commission of a new offense). The Corrections Department, however, has authority to screen offenders to ensure their suitability for an open institution which has no provision for the care of the difficult or the treatment of the seriously disturbed.

The program of the Probation-Recovery Camp is similar in many respects to that of Camp Brighton. In fact, many of the ideas tested at the latter camp were applied at the new one. One particularly valuable concept was put into effect by the Corrections Commission before the camp was opened. Leading citizens from neighboring communities were invited to a meeting at which the philosophy, plans, and program of the camp were presented and comments and questions were invited. Community acceptance was expressed and later made evident in substantial ways.

One of these ways was a cooperative program with the public schools of Traverse City, Michigan, which was made possible by a grant from the McGregor Fund of Detroit. A vocational-counselor-coordinator was employed. Incoming probationers were screened to determine aptitudes. A secondhand school bus was purchased to transport probationers from camp to school four nights a week. Several vocational courses were offered.

Another offer of help came from the community. The Purvis brothers, who operated a welding shop in Traverse City, offered to teach probationers. Coffee and doughnuts went with the instruction. Welding soon became a very popular course, leading to good jobs for many. A local service club gave the tools for the camp workshop. Men from neighboring churches became lay leaders for the group counseling program. One leading member of the community donated funds to build a beautiful nondenominational chapel.

The foundation grant made it possible to furnish scholarships to interns from Central Michigan University. These students taught remedial classes, helped with recreation programs, and gave elementary counseling to probationers. An evaluation of the vocational program made under the grant pointed out its usefulness, especially when combined with other features of the program. The furlough and pass plan, later established at Camp Brighton, began at Camp Pugsley, where the probationers' excellent record for responsible behavior on pass made this extension possible.

Special Community Probation Programs

Many youthful probationers lack the skills requisite for rewarding employment. In the Van Dyke public schools, the director of vocational training speculated on a constructive use for shops and teachers that were idle during the summer months. He discussed this matter with a state probation officer who had a case load of youthful offenders (another experiment). Out of this discussion came a new idea — a summer training program for youthful probationers. The sum of three thousand dollars appropriated by the Macomb County Board of Supervisors was augmented by state aid.

Some twenty young probationers came to the course. Instructors, skeptical at first, grew enthusiastic about attitudes and potential skills. One teacher opened his own home to a probationer who would otherwise have had to drop from the course. "Duck cuts" were gradually replaced by normal haircuts. "Hey, teach!" as a form of address came to be replaced by "Mister . . . ." All of this took place by persuasion and without pressure.

Graduation was celebrated one year by a "cook-out" at the home of an instructor. Another year a canoe trip down the Ausable River was a high point of the course.

Skill are not the only goal. Attitudes are even more important. To help change feelings of bitterness and defeat to positive approaches to self and society, lay group counseling was employed. Members from the local Kiwanis Club furnished the leadership (and it has since been recommended as a service program by the international headquarters of those clubs).

Today many of the graduates of that first class are successful men. One has just graduated from college with an engineering degree; another is a highly paid designer with a large automobile manufacturer; yet another, at this writing, is on an important and responsible assignment at White Sands. Some have returned to the wrong road, but the program has paid for itself many times over, not only in money but in terms of lives that might otherwise have been wasted.

GROUP COUNSELING FOR YOUTHFUL PROBATIONERS AND PAROLEES

From the vocational classroom it was a short step to group counseling for youthful probationers. This program promises to be a useful tool for probation officers in appropriate cases.

A further step remained to be taken — group counseling for young men paroled from institutions. Some experts believe that the continuing supportive effects of a group would be an asset to the young man released from an institution. The pressures and anxieties accompanying new freedom might be eased by the knowledge that others have met them successfully. Dangers might be avoided by the shared experience of others. Attitudes could be changed by the corrective of a peer group. Other responsible experts feel that association among parolees is dangerous and must be avoided.

The successful experience of Alcoholics Anonymous in dealing with parolees encouraged experimentation. A small, carefully safeguarded experiment in group counseling for parolees was recently begun. A community Services Council has involved its Volunteer Bureau as a source of lay leaders, the YWCA and the YMCA have made meeting rooms available. If the experiment is as successful as a similar venture, the Restoration Club in Iowa, it will prove worth while.

GROUP COUNSELING FOR YOUTH IN COUNTY JAILS

County jails have not offered much treatment to the men and women confined there. The recent emphasis has been upon humane, secure treatment with segregation of offenders, but something remains to be done by way of a program to make this short-term experience as constructive as possible.

An experimental beginning has been made in two counties in Michigan. Group counseling for youthful offenders has been instituted by lay leaders from the community with assistance and supervision from probation officers. The results have been encouraging. Many possibilities exist here for constructive, inexpensive programs.

FOSTER FAMILY CARE FOR PROBATIONERS AND PAROLEES

Foster family placement has not been developed on any systematic basis for the youthful probationer or parolee. These methods are applied to the juvenile delinquent and to mental patients, but not to the offender. Often young men have been committed to the probation camp or have even been sentenced to prison in large part because of their living circumstances. After they are returned to the community, it is usually to no better circumstances than before. An alternative has been a cheap hotel. But four bare walls and too much time to waste are not good therapy for energetic young men who have learned poor methods of occupying themselves.

In Michigan a recent grant from a foundation has made possible a small experimental project in foster family care. This experiment will tell us something of the value of such a program for offenders (especially the youthful ones) and the ways in which these resources can be handled effectively. Again the community will take a direct share in the treatment of offenders — an important element in the process of recovery.

THE COMMUNITY'S ROLE IN CRIME PREVENTION

It is cheaper to prevent crime and delinquency than to treat them. A major school of thought leans heavily in the direction of general child welfare as the best over-all answer to the problem of prevention. The close relationship of dependency and neglect to delinquency argues for this, as does the fact that many social agencies, in providing services, are confronted with actual or potential delinquents. Another school of thought points out that, as a large proportion of resources are expended upon the well child, the serious delinquent may be deprived of the necessary attention and services.

There seems to be a tendency for individual agencies to concentrate so heavily upon the area for which each is responsible as to lose sight of the coordination of efforts. The individual can get lost in this process and fall into the gap between agency services.

No satisfactory answer has been found to this dilemma. But the tensions imposed by it have kept each position aware of the other and forced a merger of interests. Programs like the Chicago Area Project and the community work of the Illinois Youth Commission, which grew out of it, have brought the two positions closer together. New movements, such as the detached worker and services to the hard core of multi-problem families, tend to bridge the gap. Protective services to children need more attention, and the means already developed in some areas must be extended.

Future efforts need to be directed at the coordination of services. In this process probation and parole staff can take an important part.

COMMUNITY SERVICES BY PROBATION AND PAROLE IN MICHIGAN

In Michigan, the Corrections Department has been given the responsibility to cooperate with federal, state, and local agencies in the prevention of crime. Crime prevention must have strong roots in the local community, and parole and probation officers are a part of those roots. Probation and parole staffs are therefore taking an increasing part in the coordination of community services. In a number of communities Corrections staff are catalysts in the solving of local problems.

Along with the involvement of professional personnel should come the active participation by members of the general community. Laymen are too often regarded as "hewers of wood and drawers of water" in human welfare activities. Lay participation is often restricted to board membership, fund raising, errand running, and influencing public opinion. There is little direct lay involvement in the actual treatment process. Some notable exceptions exist. The work of the Grey Ladies is one example, the Big Brother program is another. I urge that greater attention be paid to the genuine involvement in appropriate ways of lay people in the direct helping process. Dr. Menninger has written brilliantly of the "therapy of friendship." Something of the sort needs to be extended and applied in more general terms to the community. Separation and isolation typify our fragmented culture. The signs of desire for genuine community are evident on all sides. The rediscovery of community may hold the seeds of an answer to the violation of community, which is crime.

SOME CLOSING WORDS ON INSTITUTIONS

In this chapter considerable stress has been laid on minimum-security institutions, especially camps. This emphasis may lead to the erroneous conclusion that camps are believed to be the answer to institutional treatment. This is not the case. A wide range of institutions is needed to provide a wide variety of treatment facilities and programs. The trend today is toward smaller units, permitting greater variety and specialization, coupled with the opportunity for more personal knowledge and observation of inmates. Sometimes these institutions are arranged in satellite constellations to permit the economy of general services (professional staff as well as physical facilities such as laundry, power plant, and hospital). In planning such facilities, care is used to maintain flexibility — that is, to avoid highly specialized institutions so rigid as to prevent changes to meet future needs.

Another requisite is provision for the more difficult cases that constitute a problem for the general population of institutions. Too often such cases are placed in isolation, with excessive restrictions, and with little opportunity for program. California has established adjustment centers within its larger youth institutions. These centers are, in effect, complete institutions within larger institutions. A full range of treatment and activity programs is provided, but security measures are increased. New York State has converted one of its institutions for older men into a center for more difficult younger cases. Not only are the inmates sent to the center benefited by the program provided there, but the general population is not restricted or threatened by the presence of difficult cases.

In Michigan original emphasis was laid upon minimum-security camps to bring the institutional picture into proportion, since most of the existing institutions provided only maximum security. Two years ago, however, a medium-security institution was partially completed. When finished, the new unit will provide space and program for six hundred young men.

PSYCHIATRIC AND PSYCHOLOGICAL SERVICES

Little has been said in this chapter about the contribution of psychiatry and psychology to the correctional process. Clearly the insights and techniques of the behavorial sciences play an important and indispensable role. In screening and evaluating cases, for example, the psychiatric team is of incalculable value. Provisions are made for the psychotic and neurotic in clinics provided for that purpose.

In the treatment of all offenders the psychological component is well-nigh indispensable. Progress should be evaluated continuously. If psychological services seem to have been placed in the background, it is only to emphasize the need of an integrated approach to correction which seeks to utilize all elements of the process and involve all persons in contact with the inmate, including lay persons and the inmates themselves. Outside the institution, the hope is to bring the total community into awareness of the destructive elements in the socializing process so that these elements may be converted toward positive aims, thus to restore to community those who are separated from it, whether inside or outside the boundaries of an institution.

CONCLUSION

1. The treatment of all offenders — juvenile, youthful, and adult — should be a continuum in which the community, its social agencies, and its police, judicial, and correctional agencies play an appropriate and necessary role.

2. Developments in the treatment of youthful offenders borrow from and contribute to the treatment of juvenile and adult offenders.

3. The most effective means of treatment are to be found in the coordination of institutional services and forces into a community approach that involves offenders in the process of their own treatment.

4. A variety of institutions and services is required in order to make treatment adaptable to individual needs.

5. Lay persons have an effective role in the direct treatment of offenders and in the prevention of crime.

6. Imaginative approaches can be developed that enhance existing resources and inspire new ones.

7. Crime is a violation of community and its prevention and treatment lie in development of and restoration to community. This process is both simple and complex, naïve and sophisticated.

References

Beck, B. A. *Five states: A Study of the Youth Authority Program as promulgated by the American Law Institute.* Philadelphia: American Law Institute, 1951.

Ellington, J. R. *Protecting our children from criminal careers.* Englewood Cliffs, N. J.: Prentice-Hall, 1948.

Harrison, L. V., & Grant, P. M. *Youth in the toils.* New York: Macmillan, 1938.

Honts, M. *From arrest to release.* Springfield, Ill.: Charles C Thomas, 1958.

Jones, M. *The therapeutic community.* New York: Basic Books, 1953.

Sykes, G. M. *The society of captives.* Princeton, N. J.: Princeton Univer. Press, 1958.

Tappan, P. *Crime, justice, and correction.* New York: McGraw Hill, 1960.

United States Department of Health, Education, and Welfare, Social Security Administration, Children's Bureau. *Police services for juveniles.* Washington, D. C.: U. S. Government Printing Office, 1954.

United States Department of Health, Education, and Welfare, Social Security Admnstration, Children's Bureau. *Administration and staff training in institutions for juvenile delinquents.* Washington, D. C., U. S. Government Printing Office, 1959.

Vinter, R., Janowitz, M. Effective institutions for juvenile delinquents: A research statement. *Soc. Ser. Rev.* 1959, *33,* 118 ff.

Waite, J. B. The Youth Authority Act. *Law and contemp. Probs.* 1942, **60,** 600 ff.

Part III
Special Problems in Criminal Psychology

HANS TOCH

Introductory Note

Drug addicts, alcoholics, and persons whose sex habits differ from those of other people tend to create problems for themselves and their associates. That is why such persons are discussed in treatises on social adjustment. Why should "criminal psychology" concern itself with these same people? And why, further, should they be placed under a common heading?

The obvious answer is that, although addiction and deviation *as such* are not our concerns as students of crime, actions taken by addicts and deviates sometimes come to our attention. For instance, although we are not interested in people's drinking habits, we must become concerned with persons who provoke fights or steal cars under the influence of alcohol. We may admit that someone's love life is his private domain, but we become involved when he recruits young people into unorthodox sexual practices. Similarly, if a drug addict maintains his habit through shoplifting, his addiction becomes of consequence to us.

Unfortunately, the matter is not quite that simple. Traditionally, the line between an offense and an unconventional act, between public disapproval and public retribution, between the enforcement of order and the enforcement of conformity, is a very narrow line. In Puritan England, in 1606, a law was passed against alcoholic intoxication, which started by describing the condition in the following terms:

> Whereas the loathsome and odious sin of Drunkenness is of late grown into common Use within this Realm, being the Root and Foundation of many Sins, as Bloodshed, Murder, Swearing, Fornication, Adultery and such like, to the great Dishonour of God, and of our Nation, and the Overthrow of many good Arts and manual Trades, the Disabling of Divers Workmen, and the general Impoverishment of many good Subjects, abusively wasting the good Creatures of God, *we decree* ... [Yale, 1924, p. 302]

This language makes it clear that sixteenth-century legislators not only saw a close link between alcoholism and conventional

351

criminality, but also took a dim view of alcoholic intoxication as such. Three hundred years later, an organization comprising a quarter of a million women collected a room full of signatures to a petition which beseeched "Honored rulers, representatives and brothers" in governments around the world to

> raise the standard of the law to that of Christian morals, to strip away the safeguards and sanctions of the State from the drink traffic and the opium trade, and to protect our homes by the total prohibition of these curses of civilization throughout the territory over which your Government extends. [Gordon, 1945, p. 71.]

A pamphlet published in 1912 by another group, mainly composed of members of the clergy, described taverns as follows:

> The saloon is responsible for most of the 60,000 girls who go astray into immoral lives every year.
> The saloon and the brothel are twin evils, and every man who votes for the liquor traffic is indirectly voting to create conditions which feed the social evil.
> The saloon is responsible for more vice, degradation, sorrow, tears, heartaches, and deaths than any other cause tolerated by Government. [Odegard, 1928, pp. 43–44.]

Partly as a result of such feelings as these, national prohibition was voted by Congress on December 17, 1917. The amendment became operative January 16, 1920. Drinking became a crime the next day, and remained so for thirteen years, creating the most crime-ridden period in American history.

In 1914, Congress passed the Harrison Narcotic Act, which in its application outlawed the purchase and possession of narcotics. As a result, "all drug users not under medical supervision became criminals overnight, not only nominally by the Narcotic Act, but in many instances actually. Instead of going to his neighborhood pharmacy for his supply, the user now had to consort with the underworld to get it" (Wilson, 1951, p. 328). According to one estimate an increase of some 1,500 percent took place in the addiction to opiates between 1914 and 1918 alone. Most states have emulated the federal government, and passed laws patterned after the Uniform Narcotic Drug Act (Howe, 1953, p. 7).

Sex has traditionally been subjected to regulation in Western culture: "Only in marriage," Judge Ploscowe writes, "is sex expression socially and legally acceptable. The jailer and the social censor cast their shadow across non-marital and extra-marital sexual behavior." Legislation of sex is in the tradition of ascetic Christianity, since "sex was evil to the early Christian, while the absence of sexual activity, virginity and chastity were great goods. All forms of sexual relations between unmarried persons were mortal sin. Even sexual thoughts unaccompanied by external acts were sinful" (Ploscowe, 1951, p. 1).

Most persons are filled with revulsion and disgust by *some* habit that they would like to be able to eradicate. One way in which they can do so is by pressing the passage of laws forbidding the habit. The next step is a legislatively fixed severe sentence that judges are forced to impose. A case in point is a Michigan statute which prescribes a twenty-year minimum prison term for anyone convicted of selling narcotics. The following scene in Detroit Recorders Court illustrates the result:

The prisoner, Robert Doster, dropped to his knees before Judge John P. O'Hara and tearfully begged for mercy.

Doster, who had no criminal record, was convicted of selling a matchbox full of marijuana to a police informer. He is an unemployed automobile worker.

"In our state and federal constitutions there are provisions which prohibit cruel and unusual punishments," Judge O'Hara said. "While I have no sympathy for dope peddlers, I think that in this case the supreme court should review the mandatory 20-year sentence." He advised Doster's attorney to appeal to the high court "on the inequity of a law which gives a judge no discretion in sentencing." [*The Spectator*, 1958.]

The law can also discriminate against deviants by making exceptions in the care it usually exercises in protecting the civil rights of suspects. Narcotics bureaus and vice squads indulge in permissive practices of search and seizure; these organizations also make extensive use of informers (sometimes referred to as "special employees"), who resort to all manner of underhanded stratagems to trap persons. It is also not uncommon for drunks, homosexuals, and other social deviants to find themselves in jail without the customary legal amenities having been observed.

Almost everyone involved in the legal and correctional process may reflect public feelings against deviants. Juries, for instance, have been known to take the personal habits of defendants into account in determining guilt or assessing the severity of offenses. Parole boards are traditionally sensitive to public opinion. What, for instance, if a paroled homosexual were to be found soliciting a minor? What if a paroled drug addict were spied vending opiates near a school? Considerations such as these can enhance the tendency to defer or to rescind parole.

How does the public exercise pressure? We have already illustrated that a most convincing means is to exaggerate wildly the social harm done by deviants. The unfavorable image of the alcoholic painted by advocates of abstinence, for instance, helped lay the groundwork for prohibition. The opponents of drug addiction could similarly "demonstrate that the menace of the drug addict is largely criminal in character" (Korn & McCorkle, 1960, p. 162). The drug addict is "depicted as a 'dope fiend'—a slavering sex-crazed sadist—rather than as a sick, disturbed, and maladjusted individual" (Brown, 1953, p. 270).

The list of fallacies perpetuated about sex offenders covers page after page in many reports on the problem. Among the most flagrant misconceptions are that sex offenders are usually oversexed, that less serious sex deviations tend to degenerate into serious ones, that "sex fiends" are widely prevalent, that sex offenders are bad parole risks, that sexual disorders are usually biologically caused or inherited, and that (paradoxically) these deviations are easily curable by known means (Hartwell, 1950; New Jersey, 1950). Unfortunately, myths about sex deviates sometimes are reinforced by relatively authoritative persons. J. Edgar Hoover, for instance, in an article entitled "How Safe Is Your Daughter?" has written: "The most rapidly increasing type of crime is that perpetrated by degenerate sex offenders. It is taking its toll at the rate of a criminal assault every forty-three minutes, day and night, in the United States" (cit. Ploscowe, 1951, p. 216).[1] Such a statement can easily provoke groundless hysteria. The same type of reaction would be appropriate to a text designed for police candidates (De River, 1958), consisting of luridly illustrated and unrepresentative case studies. The author groups under the heading "sexual psychopaths" relatively harmless practices such as masturbation and voyeurism, on the one hand, and extremely serious but very infrequent sex crimes, such as sadistic pedophilia (the erotically motivated torture and murder of children), on the other. Karpman, in reviewing the literature on the sex offender, has appropriately indicated that "some articles seem almost deliberately designed to perpetuate misconceptions and hysteria" (Karpman, 1954, p. 671).

What is the ultimate consequence of public "misconception and

---

[1] Judge Ploscowe points out that Hoover's estimate is based on rapes reported to the FBI by local police. Most of these incidents are acts of intercourse with underage girls who have given their consent without being legally entitled to do so.

hysteria", however motivated and perpetuated? Essentially, individuals whose acute personal problems have caused them to retreat into relatively self-destructive forms of social deviation are further alienated from society. At best, segregation in prison simply forces such people into temporary abstinence which leaves their problems intact. Unless spontaneous recovery occurs *(in spite of* prison), the released drug addict relapses into addiction, while his alcoholic cell mate heads for the nearest bar.

At worst, punishment may create or reinforce the types of reaction on which deviations feed, such as feelings of hopelessness, self-depreciation, and despair. Weak persons may grow weaker, bitter persons may find their cynicism multiplied. The human wreck who peeps into windows because he feels inadequate to more aggressive ways of sexual satisfaction may face prolonged incarceration under a law designed to cope with serious sex crimes. As a result of such (to him) incomprehensible deprivation of liberty, the voyeur's feelings of unhappiness and inadequacy may be increased (Hartwell, 1950, p. 23).

This type of situation implies the acute need for an understanding of deviant behavior, and of society's reaction to it through the criminal process. What do we know about the causation of deviations? What social problems do various form of deviation create? How does society "cope" with these problems? The three chapters which follow are designed to deal with these questions in relation to drug addiction, alcoholism, and sex deviations. In each case, the discussion will take us beyond the current situation, which is invariably tragic and muddled. In each case, we shall review thinking and research which hold glimmers of hope for treatment and prevention and for an increase in public understanding. This in turn may remove deviants from the pale of criminology and correction, where they do not really belong.

References

Brown, W. *Monkey on my back.* New York: Greenberg, 1953.

De River, J. P. *Crime and the sexual psychopath.* Springfield, Ill.: Charles C Thomas, 1958.

Gordon, Elizabeth P. *Women torch bearers.* Evanston, Ill.: Women's Christian Temperance Union, 1924.

Hartwell, S. W. *A citizen's handbook of sexual abnormalities and the mental hygiene approach to their prevention.* Committee on Education of the Governor's Study Commission on the Deviated Sex Offender. Lansing, Mich.: 1950.

Howe, H. S. *Narcotics and youth.* West Orange, N. J.: Brooks Foundation, 1953.

Karpman, B. *The sexual offender and his offenses.* New York: Julian Press, 1954.

Korn, R. R., & McCorkle, L. W. *Criminology and penology.* New York: Holt, Rinehart and Winston, 1960.

New Jersey Commission on the Habitual Sex Offender. *The habitual sex offender: Report and recommendations as formulated by Paul W. Tappan.* Trenton: 1950.

Odegard, P. H. *Pressure politics: The story of the Anti-Saloon League.* New York: Columbia Univer. Press, 1928.

Ploscowe, M. *Sex and the law.* Englewood Cliffs, N. J.: Prentice-Hall, 1951.

The Spectator. (State Prison of Southern Michigan, Jackson), September 5, 1958.

Wilson, D. P. *My six convicts.* New York: Holt, Rinehart and Winston, 1951.

Yale University, Laboratory of Applied Physiology, School of Alcohol Studies. *Alcohol, science and society.* New Haven, Conn.: Quarterly Journal of Studies on Alcohol, 1945.

CHARLES WINICK

15 The Drug Addict and His Treatment

Drug addiction is one of the most complex social problems of our time. Drug addicts represent a substantial proportion of the case load of the courts in a number of large American cities, especially New York, Chicago, Philadelphia, Pittsburgh, and Detroit, as well as in states like Texas and California. Drug addiction is practically nonexistent in the Middle West, the South, and the Northwest. Wyoming is the only state reporting no addicts.

Addicts who come to the attention of the authorities are generally accused of possessing or selling marijuana or heroin. Although there are a few jurisdictions in which it is a misdemeanor to be a drug addict, there are no accepted legally binding methods of demonstrating that a person actually is an addict. Therefore the addict usually comes to the attention of the authorities because he illegally has a drug in his possession. The line between selling and using drugs may be a very thin one because of the considerable extent to which users will become sellers in order to earn some extra money. The nonuser seller who is arrested is likely not to be the rich and crafty smuggler of popular legend, but merely a messenger (a "gopher," who goes for the drugs and gives them to the customers).

How many addicts there are is a subject on which there are no completely reliable data. The Federal Bureau of Narcotics stated in February, 1960, that there were 45,391 known drug addicts in the United States. The bureau's figures are, however, based on drug users who come to the attention of the law-enforcement authorities; there may be others who avoid detection and thus enumeration because their life situation or income is such as to permit them to purchase drugs without going "on the street" to "make a buy."

Even if there were only 45,391 addicts, the absolute number itself is somewhat misleading in terms of the cost to the community of its addicts. The typical heroin addict in New York (which has 45.7

percent of the known addicts) takes two or three "shots" a day, costing an average of perhaps $10 to $30 daily, or approximately $70 to $210 weekly. Most male addicts obtain the money to finance their drug use by stealing. Since the average cash value of stolen merchandise from a "fence" in the New York area averages 12 percent of its original cost, the typical addict may steal from $580 to $1,750 worth of merchandise in a week, or $31,000 to $91,000 a year. In order to maintain his addiction he becomes a kind of continuing one-man crime wave. Since most authorities feel that the figure of 45,391 addicts represents a minimum, it is obvious that such a large number of persons who are daily concerned with theft (or prostitution, if they are women) in the community cannot be treated lightly in any consideration of antisocial behavior. The figure of $350 million as the amount spent annually on illegal drugs has been suggested by the Federal Bureau of Narcotics. Other estimates have gone as high as $3 billion.

It can be estimated that perhaps slightly over half of the illegal narcotics smuggled into the United States is brought in by organized large rings; the rest is brought in by individual entrepreneurs, such as merchant seamen. The smuggling of heroin (heroin hydrochloride, the soluble version of heroin base) is an attractive business and because of its enormous profit justifies the great risk to those who engage in it. A kilogram (35 ounces) of pure heroin can be bought in France or Italy for between $2,000 and $3,000. In the United States it is immediately worth $8,000 to $9,000. If it is sold by the ounce it brings approximately $400 an ounce, or $14,000. If it is sold to the individual addict, it will be diluted ("cut") from 30 to 100 times, and can thus bring from $420,000 to over $1 million.

The individual addict usually buys a glassine packet or a small gelatin capsule (no. 5 size), which holds about a grain of the heavily adulterated heroin, from a "pusher" or "connection" (peddler). The peddler will usually ask for the money first ("up front") and will then go to his cache ("stash") and get the drugs. In order to avoid the risk of handling the narcotics himself he may conceal the drugs en route and tell the purchaser where to pick them up. All the circumstances surrounding the sale of illegal drugs are designed to make the task of law-enforcement officers difficult, so difficult that it is remarkable that they are as successful as they are in making arrests, especially since they rapidly become known to the drug salesmen. The narcotics police officers' increasing skill at their jobs as they get more and more experience is canceled, to a great degree, by the extent to which they become known to "pushers."

DEFINITIONS OF ADDICTION

Definitions of addiction are complicated by the different chemical actions of drugs which may be used by people in order to make themselves feel better. The opiates are the drugs most commonly used by addicts. Opiates are depressants, and all derive from opium. The opium poppy is not grown in the United States, and its legal growth and distribution is controlled by international agreement. Some 450 tons are produced legally for medicinal purposes, with another 2,350 tons estimated as going into the illegal trade.

Opium itself is generally smoked with a pipe. Although it was popular in the 1920's and 1930's in this country, opium smoking is now relatively rare, both because the price of opium is extremely high and because it is relatively difficult to prepare for use without an expert "chef." Morphine, an opium derivative, has great medicinal value because of its pain-relieving qualities. Codeine and dilaudid are also opium derivatives which are often prescribed by physicians for their analgesic qualities. Other widely used synthetic opiates include demerol and methadone. Heroin is about twice as potent as morphine and is the drug of choice of most of today's opiate addicts. It is completely illegal in this country, so that anyone possessing heroin is violating at least one law.

During the 1930's, heroin was usually administered by the user with a hypodermic needle directly into the flesh of the arm or leg. An ounce of "pure" heroin (about 87 percent pure) used to cost $25 to $40, and the typical addict would mix one part heroin to two parts of sugar of milk. With World War II, "pure" heroin became scarcer and the average purity of heroin dwindled to 1 percent. (One ounce of this diluted drug costs about $15.) The addicts then began to inject the heavily diluted heroin directly into a vein ("main line") in order to maximize its effect. This procedure, which is comparatively complicated because of difficulties in "hitting" a vein, has remained in use up to the present day, as the heroin which is sold becomes continually more diluted.

Another group of sedative drugs, the barbiturates, are widely referred to as "sleeping pills" and are sold on a prescription basis only. Until fairly recently, it was thought that barbiturates were not addicting. Research over the last ten years, however, has demonstrated that it is possible to become addicted to barbiturates and that this may be a relatively serious matter.

True addiction can only occur with sedative drugs and is primarily associated with the continued use of barbiturates and opiates. Addiction has traditionally been defined as being characterized by three separate but related phenomena: tolerance, habituation, and physical dependence. Tolerance is the diminishing effect of the same dose of a drug, or the need to increase the dose in order to get an effect similar to the initial one. Habituation is the emotional or psychological need which is met by the drug. Dependence is the body's need to get the drug, without which it characteristically responds with the abstinence syndrome, which was first measured by Himmelsbach and Small (1937).

The abstinence syndrome is a characteristic series of involuntary responses found in regular drug users deprived of drugs. In a mild form it includes watering of the eyes, perspiration, running nose, sneezing, and yawning. A moderate response includes pupil dilation, tremors, gooseflesh, and loss of appetite. In its more marked form such symptoms as fever, deep breathing, insomnia, blood-pressure increase, and restlessness are found. Severe abstinence symptoms include vomiting, diarrhea, and weight loss. A typical heroin addict will find the effect of his last "shot" beginning to wear off in about six hours; typical morphine addicts, in perhaps twelve hours; and a typical opium addict, after twenty-four hours. The abstinence syndrome manifests itself when the effect of the "shot" wears off. The typical addict takes from one to four shots a day.

There are drugs that are neither physiologically addicting nor depressants and that are used by some persons who are considered addicts by some legal though not by most medical classifications. These drugs may induce habituation even though they do not induce the tolerance and dependence caused by opiates. The most widely used of these stimulant drugs are marijuana, cocaine, Benzedrine, and peyote. Marijuana, which is both a stimulant and a depressant, is obtained from the flowers of the cannabis or hemp plant, which can be and has been grown almost everywhere quite successfully, even in city back yards. Marijuana is almost never prescribed by physicians because its action is so erratic. It creates a kind of lightness and humorous feeling and a distortion of the sense of passage of time, along with various unusual bodily sensations. Marijuana usually releases inhibitions and has been said to improve sexual potency. If he takes a large enough dose, the marijuana user becomes sluggish and may go to sleep. In one form or another, marijuana is used by perhaps a quarter of a billion people throughout the world as an intoxicant.

Cocaine, which is derived from the coca leaf, and the anesthetic qualities of which were partially discovered by Freud, has wide medical use as a local anesthetic. Addiction-prone persons are likely to use it as a stimulant. It is not too popular among addicts because it is very expensive on the illegal market, its effects are short-lived, and it may lead to an extreme anxiety reaction when the effects wear off. Addicts sometimes mix heroin and cocaine into a "speedball," which supplies the immediate "kick" of cocaine with the extended afterglow of heroin. This mixture is often also called a "love affair," with one of the drugs called a "boy" and the other called a "girl."

Benzedrine, the trade-marked designation for a drug pharmacologically more likely to be called amphetamine, is a synthetic drug that is a stimulant. It also reduces appetite. Peyote derives from a spineless cactus widely grown in Mexico and the Southwest and which has buttonlike growths. Peyote in its pure form (mescaline) has been used as a psychotomimetic drug to induce a temporary psychosis for experimental purposes. In addition to hallucinations, peyote can also lead to extreme anxiety and great gastric distress. Some very well-known writers for popular magazines, such as Aldous Huxley and Henri Michaux, have reported relatively agreeable experiences with peyote, but medical opinion would surely regard their reports with great caution. Physicians would be especially concerned about unsupervised experimentation with a drug such as peyote, which can induce a psychotic episode.

The last ten years have seen the proliferation of a variety of "ataraxic" or "tranquilizer" drugs, ranging from relatively mild drugs such as meprobomates (Miltown is the best-known example), to stronger drugs such as thorazine and reserpine. The permanent medical value of these drugs for nonpsychotics still remains to be confirmed, although they seem to have been very effective in facilitating the release of psychotic patients from state mental hospitals. The tranquilizers are not generally favored by drug addicts, unless their drug of choice is not available. Tranquilizers do not have the "kick" of a drug like heroin.

A drug user can only be said to be an addict in terms of the three criteria of tolerance, physical dependence, and habituation, if he uses an opiate or barbiturate. Only opiates and barbiturates lead to this classical three-dimensional response of addiction. Since over four fifths of the drug users known to the authorities in this country use heroin, they can clearly be identified as addicts. The persons who use the drugs which are nonphysically addicting, such as marijuana, are often called addiction-prone. The World Health Organization in 1950 developed a definition of addiction which attempted to include drugs traditionally used by addicts as well as by addiction-prone persons. The definition presents drug addiction as a state of periodic or chronic intoxication which is detrimental to the individual and to society and which is produced by the repeated consumption of a natural or synthetic drug.

Some very prominent Americans have been "medical addicts," or persons whose illnesses were so painful that their physicians regularly gave them addicting drugs. President Ulysses S. Grant had cancer of the throat and became addicted during the final stages of his painful illness. He even wrote a paper praising the pain-killing properties of cocaine. But there are relatively few medical addicts compared with the large number of persons who have become addicted for other reasons.

The federal laws make it illegal for a physician to provide drugs to an addict merely to maintain his addiction. If a patient is physically ill and requires drugs, a physician will give him drugs in accordance with the state and federal laws and with the regulations of the Federal Bureau of Narcotics. Physicians' major problems with drugs arise with persons who are not physically ill but who take drugs in order to cope with their problems.

HOW ADDICTS DEVELOP

How do addicts develop, if not for medical reasons? There are a number of different explanations, which is perhaps to be expected of such a complex syndrome as addiction. One explanation is *sociological* and emphasizes the social conditions which give rise to addiction. War and economic depression seem to be related to the onset of upsurges in the cycle of addiction. This cycle is almost a generation long. Thus, addiction reached a peak in the early 1920's, declined until the late 1930's, and assumed new importance by the early 1950's. In addition to the general social climate, there is also reason to believe that addiction is heavily concentrated in specific areas of a few large cities. Drug use is taught by peers of the new drug user, but, contrary to popular belief, the experienced user is often reluctant to "turn on" a nonuser. The first "shot" is seldom pleasurable; most people who take one or two "shots" do not go on to become addicts.

Studies of teen-agers in Chicago suggest that there is a special addict subculture which has its own values and which is well developed (Finestone, 1957). The "cat," or juvenile drug user in Chicago, tries to develop a "hustle," or any nonviolent method of making money which does not require work. He cultivates his "kick" or any activity taboo by the larger society which intensifies living, such as drug use.

Similar studies in New York have reported that drug users tend to cluster in cliques on the periphery of gangs (Chein and Rosenfeld, 1957). Both groups of researchers emphasized that the addict subculture is likely to be in those areas of the city which are the most deprived economically and which seem to have considerable family disorganization and high mobility, with populations which have recently arrived in the area and which lack effective adult controls. Being born in a particular delinquent area in certain big cities would therefore seem to make a young minority group member such as a Negro or a Puerto Rican, especially likely to be exposed to drug addiction. Although they have not been studied as extensively as teen-age addicts in Chicago and New York, there are more narcotics violators in Los Angeles under twenty-one than in the next ten high narcotic violation cities combined, including Chicago and New York City.

The sociological theories of drug addiction stress the social rather than the individual personality components of the addict. They assume that people *learn* to be addicts, rather than being predisposed to addiction by early childhood experiences. Lindesmith has suggested that a drug user becomes an addict only after he has undergone withdrawal and realizes that the drug removes withdrawal distress (1947). Another sociologist who studied marijuana intoxication found that young people remain marijuana users because of their going through a specific series of procedures which they come to associate with the pleasure of smoking marijuana (Becker, 1953). These sociological explanations of addiction and habituation stress that psychiatrists, who assume that addicts have a special personality make-up, usually study addicts only *after* they have become addicted, and they cannot really know, but only speculate on, what the premorbid personality of the addict may have been like.

The more *psychologically oriented* explanations of addiction recognize that a person's milieu has a good deal to do with his exposure to narcotic drugs, but they note that there are some people in every epidemic of a contagious disease who do not become contaminated, while there are some who do get the disease. The psychologist would attribute the relative immunity of some young people to drug addiction, even though they may be exposed to drugs in their neighborhood, to the relative strength of their personalities, or what the epidemiologist would call host-resistance. The young people who do become addicts, in this view, have personalities which are so disturbed that drug addiction is a symptom of their general maladjustment, and is one way in which they are expressing what is likely to be a severe character disorder.

[In *psychoanalytic* terms, the typical drug addict would be described as "oral-dependent" and "masochistic." This means that the addict relates to the world primarily through his mouth, and is unable to assume adult responsibilities. An oral person wants others to take care of him. Psychoanalysts have noted that the typical addict in large cities seems to take narcotics for the first time at around age sixteen, the age at which adolescents are traditionally confronted by the challenge of sex, and begin to think about their choice of a vocation. For some adolescents, the use of a narcotic drug represents one way of evading the responsibility of relationships with the opposite sex as well as the responsibility of selecting a career.]

[Most addicts are so busy seeking drugs and stealing, or engaging in prostitution if they are women, in order to support their "habit" that they have neither time nor opportunity to learn a vocation. The drug replaces the vocational decision, just as it replaces other decisions. The psychoanalytic view suggests that the typical young addict comes from a family in which there is a very weak and ineffectual father and a relatively strong mother. The mother is likely to be seductive as well as destructive, and to be rejecting in an overprotective way. Such a mother may actually have an unconscious need to keep her son on drugs, while protesting that she is eager for him to get off drugs. With a weak and ineffectual father and a strong mother, the addict would have difficulties in identifying with an appropriate adult figure of masculinity]

This difficulty in identification is used to explain why addicts generally have such disturbed sexual functioning. The young male adolescent does not have any model of a successfully functioning adult male with whom he can identify, whereas his model of a female is that of a special kind of aggressive temptress. Perhaps as a partial reflection of the difficulties in sexual identification related to this kind of family constellation, the young addict usually uses an opiate instead of sex, and his descriptions of the effects of heroin often include statements about its being a kind of orgastic sensation, especially in the stomach. It seems to be easier for the addict to buy drugs and thus have a sex substitute than to develop any relationship with the opposite sex. Rorschach studies confirm the addict's emotional constriction and sex difficulties.

Some psychiatrists experienced in working with addicts are not psychoanalytically oriented and do not subscribe to the theory that most addicts are "oral-dependent" types (Wikler, 1953). They suggest that addiction is a psychiatric disability, but one which can be adopted by a number of different kinds of disturbed persons. These theorists observe that the ingestion of opiates leads to a state in which such needs as pain, hunger, and sexual urges are substantially diminished, and that different kinds of people are able to respond to this method of coping with their primary urges. These students note that once a person becomes addicted, he can no longer be described in terms of his pre-addiction personality, because the use of the drug creates a new and unique response pattern.

There is disagreement between the way Chicago and New York investigators describe the juvenile addicts they have studied. This disagreement has served to highlight the continuing controversy in the field. The New York investigators subscribe to the psychiatric approach, and believe that all the addicts they have seen are "severely disturbed," with a weak ego, an inadequate superego, and poor masculine identification. The Chicago investigators question whether the addicts they have studied are "sick," and instead suggest that their drug use is a response to the realization that they will be denied participation in important activities because they belong to minorities. They therefore seek distracting activity, like the "kick" of drugs, as a means of escape.

Thus, sociologists describe addiction in terms of environment and exposure to a special subcultural way of life; psychoanalysts see addiction as flowing from oral dependence and specific kinds of parents; and some investigators see the addict as a person who has found drug use to be one method of coping with his needs. All three of these theories enjoy a certain amount of acceptance.

ALCOHOLICS AND DRUG ADDICTS

Alcoholics are also often described by psychoanalysts as being "orally fixated." Psychoanalysts assume that different kinds of "oral" persons are likely to become users of alcohol and opiates. They assume that those persons who become alcoholics experienced problems at the "oral biting" stage of their development and those who become drug users experienced problems at the "oral sucking" stage. The difference between the two is seen in a comparison of the traditionally boisterous and aggressive behavior of the alcoholic with the withdrawn and sleepy tendencies of the opiate addict. As Dr. Lawrence Kolb has said, the alcoholic will beat his wife, but the addict will be beaten by her. The drug addict does not have the capacity for the kind of violent crime with which he is often credited in tabloid newspapers. He steals, but his crimes are more likely to be crimes against property than crimes against the person. Thus he is more likely to be involved in a crime such as pickpocketing or shoplifting than in armed robbery. The drug addict is so afraid of his own aggression that he is likely to take drugs to quell it. (There have, however, been cases of gangsters going out to engage in a robbery who would take a "shot" of heroin in order to bolster themselves beforehand.) Many opiate users actually have difficulty in knowing if they are awake or asleep when they have taken drugs, and can hardly engage in much violent activity.

Students of alcohol addiction have frequently observed that there are few Jewish alcoholics. This has been explained on the basis of various cultural and personality factors among Jews. It is difficult to get accurate data on the number of Jewish drug addicts because the Federal Bureau of Narcotics does not maintain records of the religion of addicts. Records of the United States Public Health Service Hospital in Lexington, Kentucky, from 1953 to 1958 show that approximately 3 percent of the patients were Jews, which is not a disproportionate number. There is reason to believe, however, that there is a disproportionately high percentage of Jewish addicts, but that they are underrepresented at institutions and official hospitals. One possible reason for this is that the weak father—strong, overprotective mother pattern often found in addicts' parents is not uncommon in second-generation Jewish immigrants in America.

Another reason may be the Jew's stereotypical cultural tradition of unaggressive behavior and verbal mastery over situations, which might make the soporific qualities of opiates, and their users' special language, appealing. Another reason might be that drug addition is such a visible symbol of deviant behavior that the Jewish drug user is expressing the most extreme symbol of revolt against his or her parents. In much the same way, studies of Jewish unmarried mothers in New York have shown that such mothers often have Negro fathers for their children. Both the unmarried mothers and the drug addicts generally come from middle-class homes which are not in high-delinquency areas, so that the children's pathological behavior is clearly an expression of personality rather than the result of sociological factors.

Although drug users often regard alcoholics with contempt, there are some drug users who shift from drugs to alcohol and back again, depending on the availability of drugs. Alcohol is disliked by addicts not only because of its association with aggression, but because an alcohol user is likely to pass out after drinking too much. A drug user almost never passes out after taking an opiate, and can always maintain some kind of contact with reality.

The same kind of mutual group reinforcement which has proved to be successful in the treatment programs of Alcoholics Anonymous has also had limited success in the several chapters of Narcotics Anonymous which have been established in a number of large American cities. There is some difficulty in organizing such chapters because some addicts, rightly or wrongly, believe, because of the illegality of drug use, that they will be arrested if they appear in a semipublic place to discuss their addiction. By contrast, it is not illegal for a person to admit that he is an alcoholic.

There is no doubt that the three to four million Americans who are alcoholics constitute a more serious public health problem than do the smaller number of addicts. Alcoholics do not, however, engage in crime in order to maintain their "habit," and there are many industrial and medical groups engaged in study and research on alcoholism. Drug addiction, by contrast, gets no research support from any voluntary or industrial groups, and practically no research on addiction is supported even by government agencies. (For further discussion of alcoholism and its treatment, see Chapter 16.)

CRIME AND THE LIFE CYCLE

There have been many inconclusive discussions, beginning at the League of Nations in 1930, on whether the typical addict had engaged in criminal activity before he came to the attention of the law-enforcement authorities for a narcotics violation. The older addicts studied twenty years ago at the United States Public Health Service Hospital at Lexington, Kentucky, usually had no criminal record prior to their going to Lexington. The typical juvenile addict who came during the 1950's to Riverside Hospital in New York (the only hospital in the world for juvenile addicts) usually had a criminal record before admission to the hospital, suggesting that the kind of person becoming an addict had changed materially between the 1930's and the 1950's. To refer to the criminal record of addicts, however, may be somewhat misleading, because some of the violations for which they were arrested may have been thefts directly related to their need for funds with which to buy drugs. If they were not detected by police as addicts, there would be no way in which their stealing to keep up with their expenses for drugs would be listed as anything other than ordinary thefts.

The juvenile addicts, both in Chicago and in Riverside Hospital in New York, seem to be members of a delinquent subculture which is geared to crime and antisocial behavior. The addict subculture in Chicago seems to be more established and stable than that in New York. The use of drugs is one of several ways in which these delinquents express pathological tendencies. Experience with these younger addicts suggests that their pathology is imbedded so deeply in their personalities that it is difficult to reach them in any kind of therapeutic situation. Older addicts often seem to be easier to reach in a therapeutic relationship. Contrary to popular impression, both younger and older addicts seem to have average intelligence, in the 1930's as well as at the present time.

The bulk of the addicts who began to use drugs in the most recent epidemic since 1950 are young Negroes and Puerto Ricans. Sixty-one percent of current addicts are Negroes, and Puerto Ricans account for 5 percent of known addicts. Some may have begun drug use in order to be like the members of a gang or a social group to which they aspired, while others may have begun to use drugs in order to accentuate their individuality and to differentiate themselves from a gang or a social group. There are differences between the function served by drug use for a sensitive and shy young man and the function served by the same drug used by a roistering gang member. Also, whatever the functions served by drugs at the onset of addiction, these functions may begin to fall off by the time the user reaches his late thirties or early forties. There is reason to believe that there is a kind of "maturing out" of addiction on the part of many addicts. By the time a drug user reaches early middle age, the problems of sexual expression, creation of a family, and vocational choice are likely to be much less pressing. It is possible that the decline in drug use after middle age reflects the decline in the user's tensions occasioned by the gradual decline, once middle age is reached, in the possibility of meeting such serious demands of reality as marriage and a career. As in so many matters related to addiction, the lack of adequate data makes it necessary to speculate.

WHY TREATMENT?

That many drug users stop using drugs after twenty or twenty-five years of doing so does not, of course, mean that we should assume that there is little to be done while they use drugs. Since the drug user in our culture is usually a nonfunctioning and predatory person who has withdrawn from reality, he can hardly be said to be an admirably functioning and successful human being. Extensive medical research suggests that the regular use of opiates, when administered under medical auspices and in a socially approved situation, seems to have no deleterious effects on the body. The one study which came to a different conclusion found that regular opium users, who got their drugs legitimately on Formosa, died at a much earlier age than a group of matched nonusers (Tsungming, 1951), with the opium users dying at the rate of 65.5 per 1,000, while the rate for non-opium users was 26.1.

Wikler's research suggests that opiates satisfy primary needs, like sex, hunger, and fear of pain, and that the drug itself ultimately becomes a primary need. Modern mental hygienists tend to believe that anything like a drug which diminishes participation in central human concerns is not desirable as the central focus of an individual's life. Some recent research suggests that the either-or point of view on the effect of drugs is oversimplified, and that some people who take drugs regularly are enabled to function with the drugs, while others become "dopey" and inactive from drug use. The latter group has few defenders, but some physicians have said that it is hypocritical to give tranquilizers to patients to enable them to feel better and to refuse to give opiates to those people who can function with drugs. These physicians note that both the tranquilizer user and the heroin user take a chemical in order to feel better, but the first group gets full medical cooperation while the second group goes to jail.

TREATMENT PROGRAMS

Treatment programs in hospitals for narcotic addicts have had relatively discouraging results. Some of this may be a reflection of the understaffing of the few hospitals devoted to narcotic addicts. There are 1,500 beds for addicts at the federal hospitals at Lexington,

Kentucky, and Fort Worth, Texas, and both are understaffed. Some of the failure may reflect the lack of interest in addict patients on the part of the physician in private practice, who may also fear that he is violating the law by treating an addict. Addicts are not very likely to be able to pay for treatment after paying for drugs. Another element in the comparative failure of treatment may be the lack of a national citizens' or parents' organization to press for research and professional training of specialists. In spite of the enormous cost to the community of addiction, there is practically no research program of any consequence, except for a laboratory for pharmacological research at the United States Public Health Service Hospital in Lexington. Physicians' inability to treat addicts in private practice means that the normal flow of data from office experience is not available as a source of new and fresh treatment experimentation.

Perhaps the single most compelling reason for the lack of any simple and permanently effective treatment for narcotic addiction is that it is a chronic disease, like tuberculosis or schizophrenia. Like any chronic disease, it is very resistant to treatment, and quick recovery is unlikely. Withdrawal treatment, through which the addict is gradually withdrawn from opiates, can be routinely administered in hospitals, but most hospitals will not admit addicts.

By the end of one or two weeks after withdrawal, the former drug user's body has adjusted to no longer taking opiates. A few months of further bodily readjustment are necessary before the body has completely re-established its pre-opiate equilibrium. Many addicts have been withdrawn over a period of a few days, without the methadone which is usually used in hospital treatment. Where it is necessary to withdraw addicts in a nonhospital setting, tranquilizers are generally used. Addicts are often unhappy if they do not get methadone withdrawal. It is symptomatic of the addict's greater ability to absorb drugs that he usually can take about three times the dosage of tranquilizers which a normal person would find tolerable. After coming off drugs, addicts usually begin eating more and seem to begin getting colds and other "normal" ailments once more, for opiates often mask colds and other more serious ailments. Addicts usually suffer from insomnia for as long as six months after withdrawal.

The withdrawal treatment from opiate addiction is thus a relatively simple medical procedure. The reason that the treatment of addiction is difficult is that the great majority of addicts generally return to drug use and cannot stay away from drugs — they are "hooked." Estimates of the proportion of opiate addicts who have been in hospital treatment programs and who return to the use of opiates after an extended stay in a hospital range from 80 to 90 percent. The reason for the addict's return to drugs would be interpreted differently by sociologists, psychologists, and psychoanalysts. The psychological viewpoint would be that his personality is such that it prefers to cope with problems by taking drugs rather than face them directly. Once having tested the extent to which opiates provide surcease from daily problems, the addict tends to go back to drugs as soon as a difficult situation presents itself. Sociologists would explain this in terms of role behavior, and psychoanalysts in terms of oral passivity.

The addict's return to drugs is reminiscent of Freud's analogy to an army advancing into enemy territory. As it advances, small detachments of men and ammunition are left at strategic points on the terrain along the army's path. When the army faces severe opposition from the enemy, it is likely to retreat to the points at which ammunition has been left. Similarly, the addict has learned that opiates provide a permanently available method of coping with life problems. When he is confronted by a difficult situation, he can always solve it by reverting to the use of drugs, just as the army faces an enemy advance by retreating to previously prepared position of strength.

Most addicts who do revert to the use of drugs seem to have longer and longer periods of abstinence between their return to drug use. There are addicts who do *not* revert to drug use, for reasons which are not known, because of the lack of adequate research. Only 40 percent of the patients at the hospital at Lexington come back more than once, although some have come back for as many as twenty times. Some 14 percent of the patients at Lexington account for 42 percent of the total admissions. Some patients go to Lexington to withdraw so that they can re-establish their addiction at a lower dosage.

Whatever their other disagreements, there is complete unanimity among all students of addiction that there is not one community in the United States which has an adequate program of follow-up services for former drug users who have been through any kind of treatment or hospital activity, or even who have been in jail. The former user returns to his old haunts and the old specter of addiction reappears, since he has no group or agency working with him to help him withstand the easy road to solving his problems — what addicts call God's Own Medicine (G.O.M.). The former drug user's attempts to learn a trade and to rehabilitate himself in other ways are not likely to be sympathetically met by the community.

The general disinterest in and unfavorable prognosis for treatment of addiction can be seen in the refusal of most health insurance plans to accept addict patients, although they generally provide medical care for chronic alcoholism. The reason usually given for refusal to treat addiction is that relapse to the use of drugs is part of the disease. It is difficult for some health administrators to understand that relapse may not be discouraging in terms of treatment. A patient who reports his relapse to a physician may already be beginning to cope with it. With health rehabilitation difficult if not impossible, and medical resources closed to them, it may be expected that many addicts will drift back into their old habit.

CHANGE IN THE KIND OF PERSON WHO BECOMES ADDICTED

Before the Harrison Act of 1914, opium and opium derivatives were used freely by approximately 3,000,000 people, without prescription. This act and its subsequent modifications brought opium derivatives under federal jurisdiction. Prior to 1914, there were approximately three female opium users to every one male user. Curiously enough, there are now approximately three male to every one female user. It is possible that there are actually more female users than the one third reported, because police generally are less active in arresting prostitutes than they are in arresting thieves, and data on the incidence of addiction in women largely derive from arrests of prostitutes. Data on men addicts derive to a great extent from arrests of thieves.

Even if the number of women is somewhat understated, there is no doubt that there are now many more men than women addicts. Prior to 1914, women took opium almost as casually as they take cough syrup today. Most of these women stopped taking opium preparations within a reasonably short period of time, demonstrating that it is possible for some people to stop taking drugs where there is no profound need of the individual being met by the drug.

After (but not necessarily because) the use of opium and its derivatives became illegal, it became a favorite of lower-class whites in the South and in a few big cities. The typical addict of the 1930's was an itinerant white worker, perhaps thirty-three years old, with a grade school education. The typical addict of today is fifteen years younger and is a Negro living in a big city. Opium was smoked by some persons in the entertainment world and by some relatively wealthy people in the 1920's and 1930's, but its use has given way to the more widely used heroin. Another change has been the increase in the number of current addicts who seem to be associated with various other antisocial activities, as compared with the addicts of a quarter century ago.

One occupational group has remained fairly consistent in its illegal use of opiates — physicians. Approximately 1 percent of the perhaps 200,000 practicing physicians are opiate users, and it can be speculated that the same proportion were taking opiates twenty and thirty years ago. Physicians who take drugs may be the busiest and most successful practitioners. They clearly do not take drugs because they are unsuccessful but in order to meet some personality needs of their own, although many may have some organic ailment responsible for their addiction. It is possible that one kind of person who becomes a physician — compulsive and very responsive to status and goal needs — is likely, under some circumstances, to be especially aware of possible discrepancies between his self-concept and his actual achievement, and to take drugs in order to face such discrepancies or other feelings of personal inadequacy. Physicians' use of drugs is not necessarily due to their easy access to drugs; pharmacists have greater access to drugs and there are practically no pharmacist addicts, probably because the kind of person who becomes a pharmacist is likely to be quite different from the kind of person who becomes a physician.

Another occupational group associated with the use of drugs from the turn of the century consists of jazz musicians. The irregular working hours, performances in night clubs before semi-intoxicated audiences, association with the occasionally criminal elements of the booking and entertainment worlds, the unfinished nature of every jazz performance, the frequent recurrence of themes of masochism and sex in jazz music, and the heavily publicized drug use of some famous jazz musicians — all combine to create an atmosphere in which drug use may be accepted as part of the environment. Jazz has traditionally been a protest music and a vehicle of expression for musicians who have a dissident statement to make. Since the most conspicuous symbol of deviant behavior in our culture is the use of drugs, the jazz musician is thus in a deviant field and is italicizing his dissidence in taking drugs. Jazz musicians are the occupational group most heavily overrepresented in the addict population (Winick, 1960).

Most recently, attention has been given to the use of drugs by some famous "beatnik" writers and artists, who have written quite openly about their use of drugs. The drugs used by these writers serve to help keep them on an adolescent level of development, and clearly symbolize their withdrawal from reality and desire to avoid adult responsibility. Their formless writing bespeaks the same kind of nonseriousness. It is no accident that the heroes of Jack Kerouac's best-known novel, "On the Road," eat hamburgers and drink malted milk so frequently: by this excessive interest in the kind of chopped meat and milk drink traditionally associated with infants, they are expressing their preoccupation with infantile passive functioning. They want to be taken care of by society and still be free to scoff at society, like petulant infants.

The beatniks, the jazz musicians, and the addicts share a special language. This argot minimizes the expression of feeling and emotion. It expresses the addict's ambivalence toward the drugs, which both attract and repel him. Thus, a four-letter synonym for excrement is his term for heroin. The preferred state is one in which he is "cool," or detached. When on drugs, he is "stoned" and feels "crazy." This language expresses the hostility which the addict represses via the use of drugs. It also expresses the addict's peculiar values in which words mean the opposite of what they usually mean. Whether addiction is viewed sociologically or anthropologically, the drug user is clearly a person who has withdrawn from reality and wants to continue forever on an adolescent level, and his language helps him to do this.

Wholly apart from the modern pseudo artists and poseurs who have used drugs because of their lack of any artistic skill, there are a number of distinguished artists who have taken drugs. Among the famous artists who took opiates were Coleridge, De Quincey, Elizabeth Barrett Browning, Poe, Baudelaire, and Hans Fallada. The physician-author of the Sherlock Holmes novels (Dr. A. Conan Doyle) reported that Holmes averaged three "shots" a day of morphine or cocaine, after each of which he "sank back into the velvet-lined armchair with a long sigh of satisfaction." These creative persons surely did not "tune out on life" as most addicts do with drugs, but functioned quite successfully in their chosen fields. No one can tell how they might have functioned without drugs, but it can be said that they did not become talented *because* they took drugs, as many addicts believe, doubtless as a partial rationalization for their own drug use.

THE DRUG ADDICT IN THE COURTS AND PRISONS

The increase in drug addiction since 1950 has, in general, led to increases in the penalties provided for the possession or sale of drugs, both on the state and the federal level. The federal Narcotics Control Act of 1956 provides for a possible death penalty for the sale of narcotics to minors, and a minimum sentence of five years for selling narcotics, with no probation or parole possible. About one fifth of the prisoners in federal institutions for narcotic violations are marijuana smokers; most of the others use heroin. The proportion of narcotics violators in the federal prisons has risen every year (except from 1954 to 1955) during the period from 1946 (7.8 percent) to 1957 (15.5 percent). The average heroin violator in the federal prisons as of 1957 was serving a sentence of 5.7 years and the average marijuana violator was serving a sentence of 4.9 years.

Narcotics penalties have steadily increased in New York State from 1952 to the present. Of the state's 16,982 prisoners in correctional institutions in 1957, 3,432 were classified as regular users, and the proportion of drug offenders has increased annually. In the same state, drug offenders were committed at a higher average rate and placed on probation at a lower average rate than were most other kinds of offenders. Both on the federal level and in New York State, which has over 45 percent of the nation's addicts, the increased penalties have been associated with the arrest of more drug users each year.

Once in a prison, the drug addict is no longer an addict, since he is not taking drugs. He is a person who used to take drugs and is addiction-prone, and who is likely to have some behavior characteristics associated with his pathology. In federal usage, a drug user is called an addict until he has stayed off drugs for a year or more. In current medical usage, a drug user is regarded as no longer an addict if he has abstained from drug use for a period of five years, which is the period associated with recovery from any chronic disease. The Federal Bureau of Narcotics also uses a criterion of five years: if a recorded drug user has not come to the attention of the authorities in a period of five years he is no longer listed as a drug user, on the assumption that he would have come to the attention of the authorities within this period if he were still using drugs.

A few state correctional institutions have initiated special programs for former drug users, but none of these has been particularly successful. Usually, the former drug user engages in no special program or activities while in prison. Few prisons give former drug users any psychotherapy or otherwise attempt to cope with the underlying pathology which was probably linked with their commencement of drug use.

DRUG ADDICTION IN THE FUTURE

The last few years have seen narcotics programs which are both more punitive and less punitive than has been customary, and both extremes have reported considerable success. A number of vocal exponents of permitting physicians to supply drugs to addicts at low cost have aroused considerable sentiment for their point of view (Lindesmith, 1957). It has been repeatedly urged by various legislative committees that this approach be tried on a limited basis, but to date it has not. The employment of such a procedure involves some ambiguous questions of medical ethics. Physicians have generally believed, along with the late distinguished narcotics authority, Dr. Kenneth W. Chapman, that "drugs are not good for anyone ...giving drugs to all addicts is a last resort...." Physicians would have the responsibility of deciding which addicts were incurable and what their dosage should be, and whether such a dosage should be increased if the user wanted more than the amount prescribed for him.

Another procedure for liberalizing treatment procedures, and one which has been tried experimentally with limited success, has been the psychotherapy of addicts on an ambulatory basis, while they are still on drugs. Such procedures leave the question of cessation of drug use up to the patient, with no coercion from the psychotherapist. Using such procedures, the Musicians' Clinic in New York reported that all its jazz musician addict patients were off drugs for an average of thirty months, three years after the commencement of voluntary out-patient therapy. These patients were given treatment on an ambulatory basis, while still on drugs, and it was up to them to handle the problem of their addiction. The clinic grew out of the experience of another experiment in voluntary treatment, the Narcotic Addiction Research Project, which resulted in a working classification of addicts into two categories: those who function effectively on drugs, and those who do not function well and want to get off drugs but are "hooked" (Nyswander, Winick, *et al.*, 1958).

At the other extreme, there have been a number of proposals for making more stringent the current practices for coping with drug addicts. One direction, followed by some states, including New Jersey, has been to make it a misdemeanor to be a drug addict. New Jersey requires a convicted narcotics offender to register with the police and to keep the police posted on changes of address. This procedure seems to have resulted in an increase in the number of narcotics arrests, with some addicts going to states with less stringent penalties. The District of Columbia has made hospitalization for addicts compulsory and has established a high-security ward for addict patients.

The city of Oakland in California has experimented with the Nalline test for determining whether a person has taken drugs prior to the administration of the test. In a person who has taken an opiate in the day or so previous to administration of the synthetic drug Nalline, there will be a measurable dilation of the pupils as well as a miniature withdrawal reaction after taking a small dosage of Nalline. In Oakland the test is used to establish whether a convicted former drug user is or is not using drugs. Some physicians have objected to its use on the ground that it is a kind of chemical conscience, and that this kind of external threat is likely to interfere with any ongoing therapeutic relationship which a former drug user may be attempting to establish. Oakland authorities, however, report not only a decline in addicts but also a sharp decline in crimes usually associated with addiction, which they feel is related to their use of the Nalline test. In the three-year period (1955–58) since they began using Nalline, for example, they report a 21 percent decline in robberies, a 13 percent drop in burglaries, a 47 percent falling off in stealing from automobiles, and 25 percent fewer prostitution offenses.

The experience of Oakland has renewed interest in a suggestion made by a number of law-enforcement officials, and especially by Commissioner Harry J. Anslinger of the Federal Bureau of Narcotics. He has suggested that there be compulsory commitment of the drug addict (Anslinger, 1957). Such a law, Commissioner Anslinger notes, "would have to be enacted by state legislatures; it could not be federal because of the Constitution. . . ." The commissioner has documented the extent to which very severe sentences on peddlers have led to a substantial decline in the number of addicts arrested in such states as Ohio. He has consistently opposed providing drugs to addicts on any clinic basis, pointing to his estimate of one addict in 400 in America before the passage of the Harrison Act, whereas there is now one in 3,000. This decline in the proportion of addicts, the commissioner feels, is a reflection of the efficacy of the Harrison Act and is the best retort to the critics of his bureau's procedures.

The argument for compulsory treatment has received some support from the experience of the New York State Department of Parole's experimental project for providing close supervision to a limited number of parolees who had been in prison for narcotic violations. After three years, 42 percent of this group which received the supervision had remained off drugs, suggesting that this kind of intensive case work in an authoritarian setting may be effective with some former drug users.

Another development in the enforcement of drug-addiction laws has been the introduction, in a number of jurisdictions, of legislation which removes the judge's discretion in issuing sentences to drug users by providing for mandatory minimum sentences with no probation. This has raised the question of how police can reward the informers on whom they must depend for the bulk of arrests of other narcotics violators, if they cannot promise them a suspended sentence for cooperating and identifying their source of supply. Most arrested narcotics users will not cooperate by naming other users or sellers, but there are some who will. In some cases they may be encouraged to buy narcotics for their own use, so that police can watch them making the purchase and so arrest the seller. There have been cases in which drug-using informers were paid by the police in drugs, and thus maintained in their addiction.

Although many officials believe that it is unethical for police to promise anything to an informer, a substantial proportion of narcotics violators are arrested through such procedures. The growing inability of the police to promise informers a light sentence, because of the growing tendency toward mandatory minimum sentences, will surely focus new attention on the ethical and civil liberties aspects of arrests for drug violations as the question of how informers are to be paid becomes increasingly urgent. Recent court decisions have questioned the propriety of evidence obtained through wiretapping and have also raised important questions related to narcotics enforcement, since many narcotics arrests are based on wiretaps.

It is a sign of healthy differences in a controversial field that so many differences of opinion exist on the subject of dealing with addiction. Available facilities have, however, not kept up with the interest in discussing the addiction problem. The extent to which the problem is ignored in practice can be seen in the almost total lack of beds for adult addicts in the large cities which have the major problems of addiction. In the municipal hospitals of all three of these cities (New York, Chicago and Detroit) combined, there are not even one hundred beds for many thousands of addicts. The poor results so far obtained with treatment of addicts should not be discouraging, any more than poor results in schizophrenia or cancer research are keeping us from an extensive program of research and treatment in these fields. Unless we can mount the kind of concerted research and treatment program which ultimately led to the Sabin and Salk polio vaccines, our treatment of narcotics addiction will continue to be a rebuke to twentieth-century America.

The growing number of films, novels, and plays on the subject suggests that the general public is becoming more interested in narcotics addiction. Yet in terms of scientific knowledge of the psychology of addiction, we have not advanced much beyond the classical investigations of Terry and Pellens (1928) and Dai (1937).

Addiction is so complex that a wide variety of enforcement and treatment programs should receive experimental attention. No one approach is likely to provide a quick solution to the problem. We know that different kinds of people become addicted and it follows that they should get differential treatment programs. What can be done with those addicts who yield to no treatment is a medical decision that must be squarely faced. Mainly, however, we must resolutely confront and conquer the general disinclination to give the addiction problem the research attention it must receive.

References

Anslinger, H. J. Interview in *Modern Medicine*, Oct. 15, 1957, pp. 170–191; Anslinger, H. J. & Tompkins, W. F. *The traffic in narcotics.* New York: Funk & Wagnalls, 1953.

Becker, H. S. Becoming a marijuana user. *Amer. J. Sociol.*, 1953, **59**, 235–242.

Chein, I., and Rosenfeld, Eva. Juvenile narcotics use. *Law and contemp. Probs*, 1957, **22**, 52–68.

Dai, B. *Opium addiction in Chicago.* Shanghai: Commercial Press, 1937.

Finestone, H. Cats, kicks and color. *Soc. Probs*, 1957, **5**, 3–13.

Himmelsbach, C. H., & Small, L. F. *Clinical studies of drug addiction: II. Rossium treatment of drug addiction.* (Supplement No. 125 to the Public Health Reports.) Washington, D. C.: U. S. Government Printing Office, 1937.

Lindesmith, A. R. *Opiate addiction.* Bloomington: Indiana Univer. Press, 1947.

Lindesmith, A. R. The British system of narcotics control. *Law and contemp. Probs.* 1957, **22**, 138–154.

Nyswander, Marie, Winick, C., *et al.*, The treatment of drug addicts as voluntary outpatients: A progress report. *Amer. J. Orthopsychiat.*, 1958, **28**, 714–727.

Terry, C. E., and Pellens, Mildred. *The opium problem.* New York: Commission on Drug Addictions, 1928.

Tsungming Tu, Statistical studies on the mortality rates and the causes of death among opium addicts in Formosa. *United Nations Bull. on Narcotics*, 1951, **3**, 9–11.

Wikler, A. *Opiate addiction.* Springfield, Ill.: Charles C Thomas, 1953.

Winick, Charles. Narcotic addiction and its treatment. *Law and Contemp. Probs*, 1957, **22**, 9–33.

Winick, Charles. The use of drugs by jazz musicians. *Soc. Probs*, 1960, **7**, 240–253.

EARL RUBINGTON

16 The Alcohol Offender and His Treatment

Aside from motor vehicle violations, more persons are charged with drunkenness than with any other offense. The FBI reports more than a million arrests for drunkenness each year. Since these reports do not cover all police agencies, there are no doubt many more. These statistics also do not include other petty offenses such as vagrancy, disorderly conduct, and offenses against the family in which excessive drinking may play a role. Adding them to arrests for drunkenness makes a grand total of a million and a half persons charged with alcohol offenses.

Of course, the number of persons involved in all these arrests is considerably less than the number of arrests reported. "Repeaters," persons arrested as little as two or three times a year together with those who are arrested as much as ten or twenty times a year, shrink the actual number of persons committing petty alcohol offenses. Here, as with so many other social problems, a few persons have an influence in inverse proportion to their numbers: more than a third of all persons charged with drunkenness are recidivists or chronic alcohol offenders.

These offenders are charged more often and serve more sentences than all other types of offenders. At any given time, between 40 and 60 percent of the prisoners in the more than 3,000 county jails are serving sentences for drunkenness and/or its sister offenses. And the bulk of these prisoners are chronic alcohol offenders. After release, most of them will commit the same offense, only to get arrested, tried, convicted, and sentenced again to the same jail for another short-term commitment. This policy of processing alcohol offenders continually in and out of police stations, courtrooms, and county jails is called the "revolving door." The phrase describes rather aptly the problems which both drunkenness and alcoholism pose for the legal apparatus.

381

Chronic alcohol offenders are a small part of the estimated 4½ million alcoholics in the United States. Persons who experience difficulties from repeated and prolonged drinking are alcoholics. Abuse of alcohol over a long span of years results in numerous somatic, psychological, social, and economic difficulties. Results of repetitive drinking cumulate whether the alcoholic is aware of the connection between his drinking and its effects or not. Under this rather broad definition, the chronic alcohol offender is an alcoholic.

Yet most alcoholics, despite their other difficulties, manage to avoid arrest and imprisonment for drunkenness. "Respectable" alcoholics are less exposed to police action than are typical alcohol offenders because they are more often "hidden" alcoholics. Alcohol offenders, on the other hand, live in or gravitate to areas of high arrest risk, particularly for drunkenness. In this habitat, in which there is a very high tolerance for inebriety, there is also less pressure to conceal the growing dependence upon alcohol and the effects of that dependence. And, as that dependence becomes confirmed, pressures for concealment disappear.

Chronic alcohol offenders act out a career in which excessive dependency and drinking are cause and effect of each other. Increased frequency of drinking among offenders brings them into contact with other people and social agencies at an advancing rate and in relationships which are supportive; before, during, and after drinking bouts, offenders require social support. Ultimately, offenders forfeit their rights to conventional support when their drinking causes intensified and increased demands for support which disrupt everyday life; conventional society finally gives up on the offender and ostracizes him.

At the point of ostracism, offenders develop a need for even more support. It is at this point that many offenders gravitate to the places where they can find joint tolerance of dependence on people and on alcohol. In the furnished-room districts of small cities, in the Skid Rows of large cities, they find or create such tolerance as they need.

Between bouts, offenders require one type of support; before, during, and after bouts they require another type. Both types of support increase dependence on people and on alcohol. Jails and other establishments which serve declassé individuals begin to see more and more of them: dependence now extends to these agencies.

Increasing arrest among offenders is only one index of the rising social and economic costs of their maintenance and support. Beyond maintenance and support, few agencies report any success in breaking the pattern of dependency. Jails punish, welfare agencies support, hospitals treat; yet offenders continue in their dependent style of life. Drinking becomes only more excessive while dependency spreads in several directions.

Growth of alcoholism treatment services, rising costs of municipal administration, and urban redevelopment have once again brought alcohol offenders to public attention. How to treat them, how to lower the costs of maintaining them, how to plan for their orderly relocation are three major problems today. Central to the solution of these problems is an understanding of how offenders are dependent upon alcohol, people, and agencies.

This chapter takes up the question of how alcohol offenders solve the problem of their triple dependency and the consequences of these solutions. It discusses their characteristics, how they drink, how they come to and live on Skid Row, how their dependence on alcohol and on people changes, and how their dependency solutions may affect therapeutic efforts.

CHARACTERISTICS OF OFFENDERS

The significant social characteristics of alcohol offenders are partly consequences of a homeless life and partly preconditions of careers which culminate in dependency, excessive drinking, and frequent arrests for public drunkenness. Preconditions include recruitment from the most disadvantaged social classes, acquisition of numerous social stigmata, learning of social and technical skills which predispose to failure, and choice of heavy drinking as one adaptation to failure. In turn, these conditions set the stage for dropping out of conventional society and entering into the Skid Row way of life. For some, frequent arrests for drunkenness are antecedent to Skid Row life; for others, arrests are consequences of Skid Row life.

Generalizations about alcohol offenders and Skid Row require some caution. The available literature, however, permits at least the conclusion that alcohol offenders are all homeless men and that Skid Row is a locale in which homeless men live and drink in excess of community drinking norms. The few systematic studies of alcohol offenders suggest the following portrait. It must be kept in mind that this portrait is only a tentative one based on statistical averages and draws on a small number of studies (Bacon, 1944; Pittman and Gordon, 1958; Ullman, *et al.*, 1957).

In addition to being homeless, alcohol offenders are considerably older than the general population. While their average age is around forty-five, a large number of them are over fifty. The bulk of them are white and native-born. And they can be equally divided into two groups, one which never married, and another of men formerly married but now separated from their wives because of death, divorce, or desertion. Their educational attainment is slightly less than that of the general population, with older men having had less education than younger men. The great majority of them are currently employed, if at all, at unskilled labor; their religious affiliation is Protestant mainly, though eastern seaboard states have slightly higher concentrations of Catholics in the offender population. Considering their career patterns, it seems reasonable to find them both geographically and residentially more mobile than the general population. With advancing age, of course, there is an increasing tendency to settle in one locale. Finally, they are drawn almost exclusively from the lower social classes; their fathers usually had little education and low occupational status. (There is a small subgroup whose members have descended the ladder of social mobility mainly through excessive drinking. This small group is generally considered to be the best risk for rehabilitation.)

Offenders are about evenly distributed into three types of criminal careers. One type has been arrested solely for public drunkenness; another, for public drunkenness and related offenses, such as vagrancy and disorderly conduct. The last type has been arrested for serious offenses in addition to public drunkenness. It is generally believed that serious offenses occur earlier in the career, with a shift to arrests exclusively for drunkenness in later life (Pittman and Gordon, 1958).

As noted above, many characteristics of alcohol offenders are stigmata which predispose persons who have them to select deviant solutions to their problems. However, since many other persons might have similar stigmata and yet not select excessive drinking and dependency as solutions to their problems, these stigmata are neither necessary nor sufficient conditions for recruitment into the ranks of alcohol offenders. At present, the best guess is that if a group is available in which drinking is used as a major outlet for release of tensions, persons with backgrounds similar to that of the alcohol offender will choose such a solution.

The same reasoning applies to the history of emotional deprivation which so many offenders display in their early family background. Quite obviously many are products of depriving environments which include broken homes as well as unstable, disorganized families. Nevertheless, unless there is access, particularly in adolescence, to a group which uses alcohol beyond the community norms, products of such homes are more apt to select from other deviant solutions. Early backgrounds of offenders predispose them to select deviant solutions for acute personal problems, but do not guarantee that excessive drinking will necessarily be the choice.

DRINKING PATTERNS

There are two major categories of alcoholics — addictive alcoholics and habitual symptomatic excessive drinkers (Jellinek, 1952). Alcohol offenders fit into either one or the other of these categories. The drinking patterns of both types have many features in common. It is quite easy to confuse one with the other. In fact, many people believe that all alcoholics are addicts.

The main distinction between the two types of alcoholics is that at a certain phase in his drinking career, the addictive alcoholic reaches a point known as the "loss of control." Whenever such an alcoholic starts to drink, he experiences an imperious demand for alcohol and cannot stop drinking until he is either intoxicated or too sick to drink any more. He fights to obtain control over his drinking by many stratagems, all to little avail. Even when he tries long periods of abstinence and numerous changes in drinking patterns, once he starts to drink again, the insatiable craving for alcohol reappears and all control on amounts taken is lost.

There are alcoholics, however, in whom this insatiable craving is absent, and only its presence is a sign of addiction. The habitual symptomatic excessive drinker, despite his astonishing resemblance to the addict in all other respects, never loses control. He may drink daily to relieve symptoms, and there may be a marked effect of prolonged drinking on his organism, yet the habitual symptomatic excessive drinker never becomes addicted. He may endure most of the difficulties which the addict suffers because of excessive drinking, but he is not an addict. For he can stop drinking whenever he wants to, and can regulate the amounts he will consume in any given sitting. This provides him with a slight advantage over the addict: he does not have to erect elaborate rationalizations about his drinking nor does he lose control of the amount he drinks.

Both addict and habitual symptomatic excessive drinker are potential candidates for the state known as chronic alcoholism. After many years of prolonged abuse of alcohol, the alcoholic shows certain changes, some of them irreversible. In general, the physiological organism and personality have undergone transformation. Adaptation to the inner stresses of high intake, together with chronic intoxications, transforms the alcoholic. Usually, at this stage of the drinker's life cycle, all is subordinate to the drinking pattern. At the same time, alcohol tolerance has lessened to the point where relatively small doses induce intoxication.

Given the age structure of the offender population, there is little doubt that a sizable portion are chronic alcoholics. The older the offender, the more likely he is a chronic alcoholic. And given the relationship between advancing age and decreased alcohol tolerance, it is clear why drunkenness is the "crime of middle age." For as offenders age, they become intoxicated sooner and arrested for drunkenness more frequently. Offenders in early and late middle age also begin to make use of a variety of treatment facilities such as emergency rooms and state mental hospitals. This use, however, is mainly for treatment of acute alcohol intoxication or for severe withdrawal symptoms. Between treatment and jail periods, alcohol offenders revert to their pattern of drinking.

Among both addictive alcoholics and habitual symptomatic excessive drinkers, personalities with underlying psychopathology are probably distributed at random. At present, at least, there is little evidence to support the idea of a unique pre-alcoholic personality (Sutherland et al., 1960; Syme, 1957). On the other hand, there are definite signs of a post-alcoholic personality which appears superimposed upon the variety of personality types who become either addictive alcoholics or habitual symptomatic excessive drinkers. This personality, which many have regarded as the cause of excessive drinking because of its pronounced neurotic features, is actually an aftermath of excessive drinking itself.

ROUTES TO DEPENDENCY

Alcohol offenders have relatively few workable defenses against punishment, and their excessive drinking exposes them to a host of punishments. While some are self-inflicted, others are the expressions of the moral indignation of society. Frequent arrests for drunkenness are only one of a long series of harassments which mark the offender as a deviant and give him the self-image of an unworthy person. One response to punishment is additional drinking which, of course, only results in more punishment; another is flight. In either case, excessive drinking continues and punishments mount. The final flight is into sections of the city where one can drink excessively and avoid punishments.

Offenders oscillate between periods of sobriety (called "straightening out") and periods of inebriety (called "going on a drunk"). As the intervals between these periods narrow, the offenders disrupt the everyday life of others, particularly by their increased demands for help and support. Different milieus expel or ostracize them at different points in their drinking careers; the tolerance of increasingly dependent behavior in these milieus is one of the major factors determining when the offender will finally seek out Skid Row. Changes in age, status, and drinking patterns also affect the rate of descent into dependency on Skid Row. In general, there are three routes to this dependency: the drop, the slide, and the drift (Sutherland and Locke, 1936).

The Drop

The precipitous and rapid descent into Skid Row living is accomplished by addicts with underlying personality disturbances. In general, they are persons of middle-class background whose aspirations are far out of line with both their accomplishments and their abilities. In addition, their own particular milieu exerts strong controls against excessive drinking. A small portion of Skid Row recruits descend from this type of milieu. These recruits are of two types generally, the irregulars and the regulars.

The irregulars are very often addicts who have merely come onto the Skid Row scene during the later phases of an extended drinking bout. In order to obtain anonymity and escape from social punishment, they gravitate to the Skid Row quarter because of its permissive drinking norms. Once the drinking bout is over, they leave Skid Row and return to their original milieu. They may make a practice of this kind of "moral tourism" over a number of years, since they regard Skid Row as the safest place to conduct what they call "serious drinking." In essence, however, they are infrequent visitors rather than residents of Skid Row, comparable in some ways to lower-class workingmen who prefer to drink on week ends in Skid Row taverns.

The regulars are of two subtypes, the short-term resident and the long-term resident. The short-term resident may remain on Skid

Row around six months. During that time he drinks quite heavily, is often a solitary drinker, and maintains himself through casual and infrequent labor (on Skid Row called "spot jobs"). Ultimately, he gathers his resources together and often is able to leave Skid Row by affiliating with Alcoholics Anonymous. The other type of regular becomes a more permanent resident of Skid Row and drinks with persons of similar social background and drinking pattern.

Both regulars and irregulars are small in number. Their influence on and off Skid Row, however, is disproportionate to their incidence in the total Skid Row population. Considerable pathos attaches to the reports which journalists write about them. They are less apt to fall into the hands of the police; when they do, some of them have the shock of recognition, called "reaching one's bottom" in AA circles. Seeing how low they have fallen, they "surrender," and renounce alcohol completely.

The Slide

The gradual descent into Skid Row is the path taken mainly though not exclusively by married men of low economic status. Through a combination of economic reverse, family instability, and increased frequency of drinking, the husband leaves the family. Over time, his position in the family declines until the point of dissolution. Divorce, separation, or desertion are the major forms of rupture which precede the slide. In a few instances, men slide into Skid Row upon the death of their wives, or of their mothers if they are unmarried. Once homeless, many men who follow the slide route attribute their homelessness to drinking, although other factors sometimes loom more important.

For some, the first arrests for public drunkenness occur just prior to the family dissolution. These arrests often act as keys opening the door of Skid Row. For the majority of the sliders, conventional living has proved increasingly punishing and gradually less rewarding; at this point, Skid Row has great attraction because of its permissive drinking norms, its anonymity, and its relatively simple demands. In general, the sliders are in their later thirties or early forties.

The Drift

Drifters, for the most part, are younger men, most of whom are unmarried. Usually in their later twenties or early thirties, they display many forms of emotional instability. They quit school early and flee a depriving home environment. They are marked for failure almost at the outset because they enter the adult working world several years earlier than most adolescents and with a minimum of social and technical skills. Rebellious, they turn to low-status adults, who introduce them to heavy drinking as a way of proving one's masculinity. To "drink like a man" requires large amounts, which usually result in intoxication. Thus, these offenders come to the attention of the police quite early and an arrest record for intoxication merely adds to their disadvantages in obtaining and holding jobs.

These offenders are introduced rather early to a round of menial jobs, transiency, and heavy drinking. In addition, a small percentage develop quite rapidly into addicts. Soon Skid Row begins to look attractive. With the romanticism of adolescence, they tend to look upon it as "experience." Because of their early arrival on Skid Row, it is doubtful if they ever pass completely through the stages of adolescence into adult maturity.

THE SKID ROW SUBCULTURE

Men with different social characteristics and drinking patterns enter Skid Row by way of the drop, slide, or drift. And though they may enter at different stages of their careers, they face common problems. Incipient alcohol offenders, for example, are involved in "role-reversal": if they are to continue their style of life, they require a subculture which stands conventional values on their head. A subculture which permits continued reversal of roles, excessive drinking, and some measure of self-esteem can offer them solutions to their common problems (Rubington, 1958). Skid Row seems ideally suited to their needs.

Skid Row permits excessive drinking, tolerance of dependency, and sharing of good fortune. It imparts skills, including ways and means of obtaining a supply of alcohol, of avoiding social punishment, and of gaining help during alcoholic crises. In addition, its language communicates the special values of Skid Row. And, perhaps more important, one can find here a self-image which denies the failure and the stigma which the conventional social world attaches to Skid Row outcasts.

In the outside world, excessive drinking only led to massive social punishments. On Skid Row, it is the source of rewards and acceptance among one's fellows. In the conventional world, men are expected to be independent, self-sustaining, and self-reliant; asking for help or favors are signs of powerlessness, dependency. On Skid Row, men are expected to ask for help, particularly on matters pertaining to alcohol; and, considering the poverty of most homeless men, others are expected to give help, to share good fortune. In the outside world, men are expected to give a good account of themselves, to discuss their attainments, to show symbols of achievement. On Skid Row, men are not expected to be anything except good drinking companions; a moratorium on discussion of personal troubles and failures is strictly enforced and "personal questions" are forbidden. Since all have a vested interest in concealment or denial of past failure, conversations center on the immediate present. Where the outside world is future-oriented, Skid Row lives in a timeless present.

In the conventional world, men are expected to do something about their personal troubles. On Skid Row, men are expected to drink whenever their troubles weigh heavily on their minds. The consequence is that many Skid Row men, soon after arrival, experience a lessening of tension, a feeling of relaxation, all pleasant accompaniments of the cessation of thought.

Quite obviously, Skid Row is an "easy" rather than a "tough" culture. And for outcasts who feel powerless, downtrodden, and ill-equipped to meet problems of adult life, the solutions Skid Row offers to their problems appear most sensible. But, as with any subculture, deviant solutions create additional problems. Consequently, later on in their Skid Row career, many men become dimly aware that they have been caught up in a way of life which creates more problems than it solves. Fully socialized to the Skid Row style of life by then, many continue to use its techniques for solving their problems because they now feel there is no escape.

Drinking Groups

Homeless men, whether in furnished-room districts in small cities or in the Skid Row section of larger cities, distinguish between men who use alcohol and those who do not. They further distinguish between moderate and heavy users of alcohol. Among heavy users, a loose social system of drinking groups exists (Jackson and Connor, 1953; Peterson and Maxwell, 1958; Rubington, 1958). Within this system men are ranked by the style of their dependence on alcohol, on people, and on social agencies.

What appears to conventional society as a disorganized community is actually one in which manners and morals exist. They center on how the act of excessive drinking is carried out, and rank is proportional to performance. Both newcomers and veteran Skid Row habitués always confront the problem of choice; this they solve by joining those drinking groups in which their drinking pattern is accepted. As in any social group, self-images are more pleasant the higher one's rank. Considering the need to deny failure and dependency, it is understandable how men on Skid Row might want to exercise some care in the selection of drinking companions.

Symbols of social differentiation include modes of procurement of alcohol, beverage of choice (whiskey, inexpensive fortified wine sometimes called "Sneaky Pete," nonbeverage alcohol), standards of living, adherence to drinking group codes, use of Skid Row institutions (furnished rooms, inexpensive workingmen's hotels, flophouses, rescue missions, shelters, jails), type and regularity of employment, and behavior when drinking.

This system of drinking groups requires certain mechanisms of social support. At the top of the drinking hierarchy one type of support prevails; at the bottom, another. The top utilizes a system of "intensive" dependency; the bottom, one of "extensive" dependency.

The supports of "intensive" dependency recapitulate some features of the immediate family. A small group of drinkers associate closely in obtaining and consuming large supplies of alcohol, then weathering the alcoholic crises brought on by drinking bouts. These groups contain dependency in the groups and by so doing foster the illusion of independence. They believe they are entitled to more respect because of their greater ability to protect each other against arrest for public drunkenness, and to absorb dependency and other forms of deviant behavior. They will do all the things other men on Skid Row do only when forced to, and pride themselves on the fact that they "do not make a habit of it." They panhandle, drink wine when "sick" (in hangover), use flophouses and missions only when they are without resources. They are contemptuous of persons who use all the lesser-ranked Skid Row institutions with greater frequency. They believe that many men actually "ask for" arrests for drunkenness because they like being in jail. Finally, when their self-esteem is threatened severely, they point out that they are not "as bad" or as "bad off" as the men who employ the supports of "extensive" dependency.

The supports of "extensive" dependency bear a strong resemblance to the extended family. Men who fit their drinking pattern to this style of social relationship are acquainted with many more excessive drinkers and know of more social agencies to exploit between drinking bouts. In the system of extensive dependency, men establish a wider range of mutual obligations, distributed narrowly over many persons. In this system a man helps another person out during an alcoholic crisis and puts him under an obligation to repay the favor when the roles are reversed. These reciprocities are so widely distributed that a person always has a number of people to whom he owes favors and, in turn, a number of people who owe favors to him. In many respects, of course, it is an informal system of social welfare which provides resources for initiating and recuperating from drinking bouts.

The system provides support on condition that men continue drinking. The conventional world is willing to provide support only on condition that men stop excessive drinking. Thus many men "coming off a drunk" approach other men and ask them for money for food. At this point the suppliant is anxious to become sober. His prospective helpers, however, deny him any money for food but are most eager, anxious, and willing to share their present supply of alcohol with him. This system has some points in common with the drug addict subculture (Chapter 15), where some addicts introduce their friends and acquaintances to the "habit" so as to ensure another source of supply for themselves.

Orientation to supports varies with position in drinking groups. Intensive dependency seems oriented to maintaining and supporting excessive drinkers but makes allowance for ultimate departure from the system. Extensive dependency is likewise oriented toward maintaining and supporting excessive drinkers but is always pointed toward keeping its members within the system. Thus, drinkers in the system of intensive dependency are more apt to see themselves as alcoholics, to seek treatment for alcoholism a little more often, and to think more often of leaving Skid Row. Drinkers in the system of extensive dependency, on the other hand, are less likely to see themselves as alcoholics, much less likely to seek treatment for alcoholism, and less likely to think of leaving their present way of life.

Pressure to drink, as a solution to acute personal problems, provides motives for joining drinking groups. Prolonged abuse of alcohol, however, results in movement, in changes in position and roles within these transitory drinking groups. As people move in and out of drinking groups, they adopt new attitudes, practices, and values. The results, in time, are changes in their style of life.

Perhaps major factors in the reshuffling of groups and the downward movement of drinkers are arrests for public drunkenness. Frequent arrests for drunkenness disrupt drinking groups; barriers to contact which all groups seek to maintain are broken during incarceration. Stripped of resources and partners, men accustomed to intensive dependency come into contact in jails and other institutions with men who use the supports of extensive dependency.

In emergencies, manners and morals break down; fraternization between the ranks takes place. Offenders accustomed to intensive dependency now find themselves associating with lesser-ranked heavy drinkers who seem quite willing to defer to them. Finding themselves in the company of others worse off than themselves is a mixed blessing. Offenders accustomed to intensive dependency take comfort from the presence of the admittedly lower-ranked group. The high status accorded them deflects attention from the shock of jail punishment. Conversely, the men of low rank draw comfort from the fact that they are now permitted access to the company of the higher-ranked. Because of this symbiotic form of interaction, both are able to find evidence for denying social stigma, for not seeing themselves in their immediate situation as the conventional world sees them.

Both groups have strong needs to deny their increasing dependency, their failure in the eyes of the conventional world. Fraternization between ranks, first established in jails, recurs back on Skid Row, particularly when both groups face alcoholic crises. During their "up" periods, both strive to remain apart; during their "down" periods they come together. Need, more than anything else, breaks down the barriers between drinking groups and forces many to associate with persons ordinarily considered to be inferiors.

So long as a person consciously seeks out those "worse off" than himself, he can buy the drinks and appear the independent, strong figure. In a career which is literally degrading, this is often the last defense against the recognition of utter dependency.

TREATMENT OF THE ALCOHOL OFFENDER

All alcoholics motivated to regain sobriety require the support of a group. Their needs for support strain the bonds of everyday life. Only an organization of recovered alcoholics, like Alcoholics Anonymous, appears equipped at the present time to tolerate these powerful dependency needs, to accept the alcoholic without moral judgment, and to help him slowly to regain sobriety through a supportive relationship.

Moreover, most alcoholics believe that only another alcoholic can understand them. Barriers to the alcohol offender's making use of Alcoholics Anonymous are differences in heavy drinking patterns and social class background. Offenders who attend AA meetings do not see any resemblance between themselves and the persons who "tell their stories" at AA meetings. These people, from the point of view of offenders, talk, dress, act, and used to drink differently from the way they themselves do. The support which AA might extend to offenders is vitiated because of these negative perceptions.

Many offenders make a virtue of their suffering, believe they had it tougher than most AA's had, and that they were "tougher" drinkers. Whether or not this is another variation on the illusion of independence, it prevents offenders from establishing enduring contact with Alcoholics Anonymous. Moreover, their greater experience with jail punishment, coupled with ideas which prevent them from seeking other kinds of treatment for alcoholism, makes such people poor treatment risks.

All the problems of treatment and rehabilitation of alcoholics are only intensified and exaggerated in the case of the homeless alcohol offender. Members of Alcoholics Anonymous and patients at alcoholism clinics still have conventional group supports. They are more often married and regularly employed (Straus and Bacon, 1951). By contrast, the homeless alcohol offender no longer has a family or regular employment; the only supports he can count on come from men like himself, but usually on condition that he drink as they do and when they do. Whenever he makes an attempt to regain sobriety he suffers loneliness and social isolation. His need for affiliation propels him to seek out a group; but since the only groups he knows in which he can be both accepted and comfortable are drinking groups, he renounces sobriety as the price of acceptance.

This vicious circle is the force behind the monotonous Skid Row–Jail–Skid Row pattern. Homeless, penniless, poorly dressed, on his release from jails or hospitals the offender has no place to go but Skid Row. Strangers merely evoke powerful anxieties; alcohol offenders, like most social deviants, are hypersensitive, and see rejection all about them. These inadequacy feelings can be dissolved only in the company of a drinking group even when the offender has no desire to drink at all. And with advancing age, the offender not only goes through the doors of the jail more often; he has to make use of other agencies more often. Yet each time upon his release he faces the same dilemma. Sobriety means isolation; drinking means company and group support. Here, more than anywhere else, is the major barrier to effective resocialization of homeless alcohol offenders.

A new institution for the treatment of offenders, designed to cope with their acute release problem, has come into being in recent years. Called a *half-way house*, it is intended to provide a way station between Skid Row and "respectable society." The therapeutic philosophy of the half-way house is quite simple: It seeks to turn the offender's group supports away from inebriety toward sobriety. And it offers to do so by providing a group within the half-way house which will answer the offender's need for affiliation without making his acceptance in the group dependent upon excessive drinking.

The problem which the half-way house sets for itself is to shift the alcohol offender's triple dependence on alcohol, Skid Row persons, and social agencies onto key persons within the half-way house. And, in so doing, it seeks to provide its members with the rewards that may come from "sober" association. Where conformity on Skid Row meant excessive drinking, in the half-way house it means sobriety. In effect, half-way houses attempt to reverse the manner in which many offenders became habituated to alcohol. To cope with depriving environments which they were unskilled to handle, these offenders turned to groups where they could obtain release through excessive drinking. The half-way house obviously is attempting to teach offenders to replace alcohol with people as a means of solving their acute personal problems.

At present there are around thirty half-way houses in existence. Despite considerable variations, these are their common features: a small group of offenders, usually around twenty-five men, come together and live in a building which is staffed for the most part by recovered alcoholics. In this place, members try to maintain sobriety and to become self-supporting once again. The two most common techniques for achieving sobriety are group therapy (broadly defined) and personal counseling by staff members. To rebuild their confidence and self-respect, members pay rent or fees (the average is around $15 a week) and obtain outside employment. Some form of vocational counseling goes on, official or otherwise. If there is any fixed period of membership, it is generally around ninety days.

Half-way houses are a new type of social therapy center which invite alcohol offenders to join if they are interested in regaining their sobriety and breaking their attachments to Skid Row. All require abstinence, and the major cause of irregular discharge, as might be expected, is relapse before the period of membership is over. All seek to afford a protective environment, protecting the offender against his urges to drink, and against association with men who are currently drinking. All seek to provide a warm social climate in which acceptance in the group does not depend upon drinking. Very much like other forms of treatment and rehabilitation, acceptance now depends upon sobriety.

In many half-way houses, protection and acceptance are extended even after a member has "graduated." Several half-way houses have "graduates' clubs" and encourage their "alumni" to maintain contact after graduation, for they recognize that there is a serious half-way house release problem. To remain sober, the erstwhile alcohol offender must continue to associate with sober persons. Aside from fellow alumni, the only people whom he knows who are currently sober are in the half-way house, either as staff or as members.

Half-way houses which maintain a system of follow-up recording report a 35 percent success rate. Considering the numerous obstacles to successful treatment and reformation of offenders, this record is quite impressive: it is not uncommon for members of half-way houses to get drunk just prior to their "graduation" because departure from the institution means sobriety and isolation. In addition, as is probably well known, to give up drinking is extremely difficult; and if there are no substitutes for this alternately rewarding and punishing pattern, relapse is almost inevitable.

Since all half-way houses deal only with a small segment of the entire alcohol offender population, all utilize some system of selection in the hope of drawing members who are more strongly motivated to regain sobriety and who have, in addition, more resources for coping with the difficult transition from excessive drinking to a relatively stable and sober state. Consequently, upper and lower age limits are set, and attempts to screen out psychotics, feeble-minded, and physically handicapped persons are made. In addition, some attempts have been made to develop prognostic indices that might prove useful in screening candidates for membership. To increase their usefulness, half-way houses need to know which candidates are most apt to profit from the experience.

One explanation for the fact that some men profit from the experience while others do not has to do with Skid Row drinking groups and social relationships. Perhaps more than any other factor, the kinds of social relationships offenders sustained during their drinking careers determine whether or not they will profit from a half-way house experience.

While drinking on Skid Row, alcohol offenders made use of the supports of intensive or extensive dependency. In general, they solved the problem of choice of drinking groups by electing one of the two possible systems of supports. This problem of choice remains for the newcomer to a half-way house. After the initial period of adjustment, the newcomer may seek out and enter into a dependent relationship with one of the staff figures, or he can choose to avoid this kind of relationship with staff and, instead, enter into more extensive, casual relationships with other half-way house members. In either case, the two predominant styles of Skid Row social relationships recur within the half-way house.

Members who become emotionally involved with staff members gain the support to which they have become accustomed. Formation of such a relationship gives the staff person a chance to influence the member, slowly to change his attitudes toward drinking, to view it as a problem over which he can exercise some control. Small group supports of this kind work in the direction of sobriety, changes in attitude, in behavior, and ultimately in personality.

By contrast, members who avoid these relationships and who turn to other half-way house members chafe at half-way house rules, feel that they are being "regimented," and express a need to be "on their own." Intensive dependent relationships are either foreign to their nature or abhorrent. They begin to complain that they are "paying their way," to see themselves as self-supporting, thus in no need of counsel or advice from the staff. These tensions mount; for some, because of a vague awareness of their own dependency; for others, because they want to regain their independence. Members resolve these mounting tensions by suddenly "breaking out" (returning to excessive drinking).

Consequently, half-way houses are probably achieving greater success with alcohol offenders who sustain intensive dependent relationships while drinking, and who find it possible to re-create these relationships within the half-way house. Offenders who sustain extensive dependent relationships while drinking likewise re-create these same relationships within the half-way house. Though they may regain a degree of sobriety, they ultimately relapse when they feel the need to be independent. The half-way house may serve to reawaken long-smoldering dependency conflicts which some have always resolved by heavy drinking. In any case, lacking either skill or desire for intensive dependent relations, they revert to uncontrolled drinking after a short stay in the half-way house.

Half-way houses encourage members to be dependent in order to reach them. Some members, of course, use the half-way house only as a "drying out" station between drinking bouts. Others appear to be quite willing to become dependent upon the institution. Only those who enter the dependent supportive relationship with the staff appear to profit in substantial ways from the experience.

CONCLUSION

The price the alcohol offender pays for his deviant career is wholesale punishment, of which jail sentences are only one outstanding example. The rewards he gains are Skid Row solutions to his dependency problem. He finds associates who drink as he does, who help him out in times of crises, and who steer him to social agencies when he needs even greater support. As the offender ages, however, his tolerance for alcohol lessens, his dependency increases. Rather than continue in the downward spiral of Skid Row, some offenders seek a way out. But until recently few channels for returning to a niche in conventional society were open.

Recently, such a channel has appeared in the form of the half-way house, an innovation in the treatment of alcohol offenders. By means of social therapy, the half-way house seeks to make its members abstemious and self-supporting. Considering the numerous obstacles, half-way houses have already established a remarkable rate of success in supplanting the fellowship of inebriety with sober associations. As more half-way houses appear and as their experience widens, their success will no doubt increase.

The present discussion, ignoring many of the complexities of the alcohol offender problem, has examined the career of the offender, both over time and in cross section. This has enabled us to see that forms of inebriate fellowship, established in Skid Row drinking relationships, tend to reappear within the half-way house. If the form is intensive dependency, half-way house staff appear to be able to turn it to good therapeutic account. If the form is extensive dependency, relapse is more likely. Future work with offenders must consider how to use extensive dependency as a means of regaining sobriety.

References

Bacon, S. D. Inebriety, social integration and marriage. *Quart. J. Stud. on Alcohol*, 1944, **5**, 86–125, 303–339.

Jackson, Joan K. Types of drinking patterns of male alcoholics. *Quart. J. Stud. on Alcohol*, 1958, **19**, 269–302.

Jackson, Joan K., and Connor, R. The Skid Road alcoholic. *Quart. J. Stud. on Alcohol*, 1953, **14**, 468–486.

Jellinek, E. M. Phases of alcohol addicton. *Quart. J. Stud. on Alcohol*, 1952, **13**, 673–684.

Keller, M. Alcoholism: Nature and extent of the problem. *Ann. Amer. Acad. pol. soc. Sci.*, 1958, **315**, 1–11.

Peterson, W. J., & Maxwell, M. A. The Skid Road "Wino." *Soc. Probs*, 1958, **5**, 308–316.

Pittman, D. J., & Gordon, C. W. *Revolving door: A study of the chronic police case inebriate*. Glencoe, Ill.: The Free Press and Yale Center of Alcohol Studies, 1958, pp. 154 ff.

Rubington, E. The chronic drunkenness offender. *Ann. Amer. Acad. pol. soc. Sci.*, 1958, **315**, 65–72.

Straus, R., & Bacon, S. D. Alcoholism and social stability. A study of occupational integration in 2,023 male clinic patients. *Quart. J. Stud. on Alcohol*, 1951, **12**, 231–260.

Sutherland, E. H. & Locke, T. J. *Twenty thousand homeless men. A study of unemployed men in the Chicago shelters*. Philadelphia: Lippincott, 1936, pp. 207 ff.

Sutherland, E. H., Schroeder, H. G., & Tordella, C. L. Personality traits and the alcoholic: A critique of existing studies. *Quart. J. Stud. on Alcohol*, 1960, **21**, 547–561.

Syme, L. Personality characteristics and the alcoholic. A critique of current studies. *Quart. J. Stud. on Alcohol*, 1957, **18**, 288–302.

Ullman, A. D., Demone, H. W., Jr., Stearns, A. W. & Washburne, N. F. Some social characteristics of misdemeanants. *J. crim. Law, Criminol., and Police Sci.*, 1957, **48**, 44–53.

17 The Sex Offender and His Treatment

A sex offender is commonly defined as an individual who has committed a sex act that is legally banned and penalized in a given jurisdiction and has been apprehended and convicted for the commission of this act. As Kinsey and his associates (1948) indicate, most technical sex offenders (like most nonsex offenders) are never arrested or convicted for their legally proscribed sexual activities; if they were, perhaps 95 percent of the American male populace would at some time in their lives be jailed. Consequently, the term "sex offender" is generally employed only in connection with convicted offenders, and it will be used solely in this sense in the remainder of this chapter.

CLASSIFICATION OF SEX OFFENSES

In spite of the fact that many sex statutes contain a mass of detail about the acts they ban and are harrowingly specific in many instances as to what activity constitutes these banned acts (Sherwin, 1961), many statutes listing sex offenses are also, at least in part, vaguely worded and include such almost undefinable terms as "carnal abuse," "open lewdness," and "unnatural practices." These terms may — and often do — mean almost anything and they vary widely in meaning from one legislative jurisdiction to another (Ellis and Brancale, 1956). If we stop to unravel some of the semantic confusion created by the use of such vague terms, we find that the actual sex acts which are commonly prohibited and penalized tend to be these:

1. Forcible sexual assault — that is, a male's forcing a female to submit to his sexual advances but stopping short of coitus. Mild sexual assault includes such acts as intent to kiss, to embrace, or to look under a woman's skirt. Serious sexual assault includes intent to rape, to force oral-genital contacts, and the like.

400

2. Forcible rape — coitus with a female as a result of actual force or duress. Rape is often held to have been committed even if complete penetration has not taken place (Traver, 1959).

3. Statutory rape — coitus with a female under the legal age of consent (which is usually sixteen to eighteen years) even though it is engaged in voluntarily, without the use of force or duress.

4. Incest — coitus with a close relative, such as between a father and daughter, mother and stepson, or brother and sister.

5. Noncoital sex relations with a minor — noncoital contacts with an individual under the legal age of consent; or verbal sex acts with an individual under the legal age of consent (for example, talking about sex to children, impairing the morals of a minor, and the like).

6. Exhibitory sex acts — exhibiting the genitals to another individual in an active, aggressive manner; masturbating in public; urinating or defecating in public; appearing in public without sufficient clothing.

7. Obscenity — making indecent or offensive proposals to a member of the other sex; using improper language in public; disseminating material that is judged to be obscene.

8. Homosexuality — having sex relations with a member of the same sex.

9. Transvestism — dressing in the clothing of a member of the other sex and appearing in public so dressed.

10. Voyeurism or peeping — that is, spying on the sex relations or nudity of others.

11. Sex murder — finding sex arousal or satisfaction in the course of killing another.

12. Sodomy — having any kind of "unnatural" sex act, according to many statutes, including homosexuality, bestiality, or oral-genital relations between consenting men and women.

13. Adultery — coitus between individuals at least one of whom is married to another person.

14. Fornication — coitus, or at least habitual coitus, between two unmarried individuals.

15. Prostitution — engaging in coitus or other sex relations for monetary gain.

16. Pimping or pandering — soliciting males to patronize a prostitute; soliciting girls to work as prostitutes.

17. Brothel-keeping — managing a house of prostitution.

PSYCHOLOGICAL CLASSIFICATION
OF SEX OFFENDERS

Sex offenders need not necessarily be sex deviates or perverts and they may or may not be psychologically disturbed. Statutory rape, for example, or intercourse between underage individuals, is an exceptionally common occurrence in most parts of the world and is often psychologically normal. If, however, an adult male *mainly* or *only* has coitus with underage females and if he continues to do so in spite of the real danger of his being detected and legally penalized he is to be strongly suspected of being an emotionally disturbed person.

It is useful to differentiate between *sexually* and *psychologically* (or *psychiatrically*) deviated offenders (Group for the Advancement of Psychiatry, 1950; Ellis and Brancale, 1956). A sexually deviated offender is one who commits an offense because he is fearfully or obsessively-compulsively driven to some kind of sex behavior (such as homosexuality) which happens to be legally banned in his community. The fear or hostility which drives him to his offense is specifically sexual or linked to sex behavior. Thus, he may be afraid of failing in heterosexual affairs, or he may be hostile toward women and may therefore become exclusively homosexual.

A *psychologically* deviated offender is an individual who commits *any* offense, sexual or nonsexual, because he fearfully or rebelliously is driven to defy some public ordinance. Thus, a psychologically deviated offender may be afraid that he is weak and "unmanly" or may be generally hostile to people and he may therefore resort to stealing or arson — or to some sex offense, such as rape.

A given offender, therefore, may be either sexually or psychologically deviated; or he may be deviated in both respects. Some confirmed delinquents or criminals either are mentally deficient or have serious emotional disturbances, and that is why they continue to commit offenses which keep placing them in serious jeopardy. Many sex criminals are disturbed in exactly the same manner, except that their crime happens to be a sex offense. Many of them, in fact, commit a considerable number of nonsexual in addition to sexual offenses (Abrahamsen, 1950; Glueck, 1956; Guttmacher, 1951; Pollens, 1938; Karpman, 1956).

Sex offenders may be divided, therefore, into four main categories: (1) Normal sex offenders who are not sex deviates or psychologically disturbed (for example, many fornicators or adulterers). (2) Sexually deviated but psychologically nondeviated offenders (for example, voyeurs who may be sexually overshy but who may not be generally disturbed). (3) Sexually and pschologically deviated offenders (for example, compulsive exhibitionists who have a specific sex problem and who also are generally hostile and reckless and keep getting themselves into trouble). (4) Sexually nondeviated but psychologically deviated offenders (for example, psychotic individuals who masturbate in public or walk naked in the streets not because they have a specific sexual deviation but because they are generally emotionally ill and consequently do all manner of disorganized acts).

SEXUAL OFFENDERS AND SEXUAL DEVIATES

There is considerable confusion in the public mind, and sometimes in the professional literature as well, between sexual offenders and sexual deviates or perverts. Often the terms "offender" and "deviate" are used as if they were synonymous. As pointed out previously in this chapter, this is erroneous usage: An individual may be a grave sex offender (for example, a brutal rapist) and yet be completely unperverted. Or he may be extremely deviated (for example, he may be a masochist who comes to orgasm only when his partner whips him) and may never commit a statutory sex offense.

Sexual deviation or perversion could once be clearly defined as any persistent form of sexual behavior different enough from the normal of a given society to be judged pathological. Shifting legal, psychological, and social standards, however, have led to a confused definitional situation. Today, an individual's sex acts may be called deviated because they are statistically unusual, legally proscribed, socially disapproved, biologically nonprocreative, physically harmful, or psychologically self-defeating (Allen, 1949; Bailey, 1956; Bowman, 1952, 1958; Ellis, 1962; English and English, 1958; Karpman, 1956; London and Caprio, 1950).

All but the last two of these criteria for deviation quickly run into internal inconsistencies and extrinsic illogicalities. Thus, voyeurism (peeping) and frotteurism (rubbing aganst clothed members of the other sex in public places) are generally considered to be deviations — but they are statistically common. At the same time, rape and having coitus in a squatting position are statistically uncommon in our society — yet they are rarely considered to be perversions.

Defining sex deviation in terms of legal proscriptions or social disapproval also leaves much to be desired in the way of consistency and logic, since although no legal jurisdiction and practically no social group in the United States would penalize or severely condemn an individual who was able to obtain full sex satisfaction only when he behaved masochistically, and asked his sex partner to beat or humiliate him, virtually every psychiatric textbook and every practicing psychotherapist would agree that this kind of masochist was a full-fledged sex deviate. Again, although practically every court and every social group in our society would seriously criticize a common prostitute, almost no psychologist or psychiatrist would call her, just because she practiced her trade, a pervert.

As for defining sex deviation in terms of nonprocreative acts (as several orthodox religious groups still tend to do, although some of them have recently significantly changed their stand in this respect), such a concept becomes untenable since, by its standards, every married individual who regularly copulates with his spouse while employing contraceptive devices would have to be labeled a sex deviate.

Because the statistical, legal, social, and procreative methods of assessing sexual deviation run into serious difficulties, professional workers have tried to establish more sensible and objective bases for diagnosing perversion. One such basis may be arrived at if we focus on the possibility of the individual's defeating his own best ends and say that a person is sexually deviated when he regularly and arbitrarily defeats his own sex interests — that is, irrationally harms himself, physically or psychologically, by fetishistically engaging in or antifetishistically refraining from certain sex acts. Although this concept of sex deviation has (like all definitions) some difficulties of its own, and is not accepted by many penologists, sexologists, or psychologists, it does seem to be becoming more widely accepted than the previously listed definitions of perversion. In accordance with this definition, an individual in our society may be considered sexually perverted if he can, under *all* circumstances, enjoy only one special form of sexual activity; or if he is obsessively-compulsively fixated on a given mode of sex behavior; or if he is fearfully and rigidly bound to one or two forms of sexual participation; or if he persists, in a disorganized and self-defeating manner, in engaging in sex acts which destroy his own well-being (Guze, 1959).

A sex pervert, then, either inappropriately overinhibits himself and fearfully confines his activities to unusually limited modes of expression; or else he self-destructively underinhibits himself and (often with considerable hostility) engages in behavior which literally carries with it serious legal or personal penalties. Most sexual perverts are unusually fetishistic or antifetishistic in their range of sex objects (as sadists are only attracted to those who will submit to them or as pedophiles are drawn only to young boys). Or they are repulsed by a certain type of sex participation (as fixed homosexuals are often revolted by the thought of having sex relations with females). A minority of perverts are not fetishists or antifetishists, however, but impulsively and/or compulsively engage in several kinds of sex acts (such as exhibitionism, peeping, and sex relations with minors) which are socially banned and self-destructive. This minority is more likely to wind up as sex offenders than the majority of sex deviates who for years pursue their overinhibited activities without ever coming to the attention of the authorities.

It is most important that we distinguish between sexual deviation and so-called "unnatural" sex practices — by which is often meant extravaginal heterosexual relations between consenting adults, which are included as sex offenses under some omnibus "sodomy" statutes. Although it is true that any person who *only* or *exclusively* enjoys oral-genital or anal-genital relations and virtually never desires penile-vaginal copulation even when it is freely available is fetishistically fixated on such an extravaginal act and is therefore perverted, it is by no means true that anyone who enjoys nonvaginal relations *as well as* regular intercourse is similarly perverted. In fact, from a psychological standpoint, it may justifiably be said that some individuals who *only* engage in the most common form of intercourse and who under *no* circumstances would ever try extravaginal heterosexual relations are extremely fetishistic and fearful and hence tend, in a minor sort of way, to be deviated.

It is also important that we distinguish accurately between subclinical *tendencies* toward deviated behavior, which actually fall well within the normal range, and clear-cut, overt manifestations of perversion. Thus, almost all normal human beings have some masochistic and sadistic tendencies; and many of these perfectly healthy men and women have some difficulty in coming to orgasm unless they are reasonably aggressive on certain occasions or unless they, in phantasy or in fact, experience some degree of painful stimulation on other occasions. Particularly in the case of many individuals who at times have difficulty achieving climax, sadistic or masochistic tendencies are well within the range of normal sex behavior.

At the same time, when an individual can reach his or her acme of sex satisfaction only by resorting to extremely sadistic or masochistic acts — for example, by beating, or being beaten by, his or her sex partner up to and including the point where blood flows or physical injury results — there is reason to believe that normal sex tendencies are then being taken to excessive extremes, and the result may justifiably be labeled "sex deviation." Similarly, although most human beings normally have some degree of attraction to members of their own sex, when such attraction continually, exclusively, and compulsively leads to overt homosexuality, sex perversion may accurately be deemed to exist.

Tendencies toward plurisexual participations are the normal biological inheritance of virtually all human beings. It is only when these tendencies become overchannelized into specialized outlets or when they give way to disorganized and self-defeating pansexuality that we can correctly speak of the existence of sexual deviation or perversion.

Although most convicted sex offenders are distinctly perverted, in the sense just defined, many of them, such as those convicted of statutory rape, are not deviates; and of these nondeviated offenders, as noted above, some are psychologically normal (though perhaps at times more than a little rash in their activities) and others are nonsexually psychologically deviated. In any event, although sex offenses and sexual deviation significantly overlap, they are by no means the same thing and should not be indiscriminately lumped together.

INCIDENCE OF SEX OFFENSES

No highly reliable reports of the incidence of sex offenses have ever been published because of the difficulties inherent in gathering the necessary statistics. Most technical offenders, as pointed out previously, are never arrested; many of those who are arrested are not convicted in spite of the fact that they clearly committed a statutory offense; many of those who are convicted are allowed to plead guilty to a lesser charge (such as loitering, assault and battery, or disorderly conduct). Consequently, individuals who are finally convicted of a specific sex offense (and on whom we do have some statistics) represent only a relatively small percentage of those who actually commit a sex act that is legally banned in the jurisdiction in which they reside (Drummond, 1953; Guttmacher and Weihofen, 1952; Sherwin, 1949; Wolfenden Report, 1957).

Perhaps the best and most detailed study of sex offenses done to date is that by Radzinowicz and his associates (1957), who made a thoroughgoing investigation of offenses known to the police in England and Wales and estimated that in 1954 about 16,000 such offenses occurred. Of the known sexual offenses, the distribution of indictable cases was found to be as follows: indecent assault on females, 50 percent; attempts to commit unnatural offenses and indecent assaults on males, 21 percent; indecency with males, 13 percent; defilement of girls between the ages of thirteen and sixteen, 9 percent; unnatural offenses, 7 percent; rape, and the like, 2 percent; incest, 2 percent; and defilement of girls under the age of twelve, 1 percent.

In the United States there are about 40,000 arrests a year for major sex offenses and doubtless many more for minor offenses. The new Jersey State Police adds to its file of known sex offenders about 800 to 1,000 individuals a year. These offenders and their offenses are classified as follows: exhibitionism, 18 percent; rape (including statutory rape), 45 percent; perversion, 14 percent; commercial sex, 7 percent; unclassified, 16 percent (Tappan, 1950).

CHARACTERISTICS OF
SEX OFFENDERS

As virtually all modern authorities on sex offenders have stressed, there are many existent myths about the overimpulsivity, aggressiveness, and recidivism of convicted offenders. Some of the truths in this connection would seem to be as follows:

1. The majority of convicted offenders are found to be rather harmless, "minor" deviates rather than dangerous "sex fiends."

2. Only a relatively small proportion (about 20 percent) of sex offenders uses force or duress upon the victims of the offense.

3. When they are not psychologically treated, convicted offenders are found to be frequent repeaters of both sexual and nonsexual offenses, even though their rates of recidivism may be lower than those of nonsex offenders.

4. Very few offenders may truly be designated "sexual psycho-

paths": most of them, when intensively examined with modern psychological and psychiatric techniques of investigation, are found to be severely neurotic, borderline psychotic, psychotic, or organically brain-impaired. Studies at Sing Sing Prison in New York and at the New Jersey State Diagnostic Center at Menlo Park show that the majority of convicted offenders suffer from some type of mental or emotional disorder, though not usually so pronounced as to meet the legal definition of mental illness.

5. Aside from those convicted of statutory rape and incestuous relations, most offenders tend to be sexually inhibited and constricted rather than overimpulsive and oversexed. The great majority of them indicate distinct emotional immaturity.

6. Convicted sex offenders tend to show subnormal intelligence in a higher percentage of the cases, and bright normal or superior intelligence in a smaller percentage of the cases, than do members of the general population. Subnormal intelligence is particularly likely to be found among offenders convicted of statutory rape, incestuous relations, and bestiality and least frequently found in those convicted of forcible rape, exhibitory acts, and the dissemination of "obscene" material.

7. The majority of offenders are quite young, being in their teens and early twenties. From 50 to 60 percent of sex offenders are unmarried, although others are married, divorced, separated, or widowed. Most of the offenders come from relatively poor educational and socioeconomic backgrounds.

THE TREATMENT OF SEX OFFENDERS

Convicted sex offenders, largely because of their propensity to be arrested and convicted, are usually severely disturbed persons who cannot or will not confine their activities to legally accepted practices or who (perhaps more important) refuse to be sufficiently discreet and privately behaved about their legally proscribed activities. The mere fact that they are caught, and often caught several times, in their acts puts them in a distinctly different category from other technical offenders, such as adulterers and fornicators, who are rarely apprehended and convicted of any offense. In addition, many offenders (such as confirmed homosexuals) are, quite apart from the illegal nature of their offenses, psychologically deviated because of their own groundless fears and hostilities, and would require psychological treatment even if their acts were not legally banned.

The psychological treatment of sex offenders such as these is quite difficult in most instances (Buckle, 1949; de River, 1949; Ellis, 1956; Foster, 1947; Gurvitz, 1957; Rickles, 1950; Wolfenden Report, 1957). It requires a tackling and an undermining of the offender's general and sexual disturbances; and it involves, in the final analysis if not in the beginning of psychotherapy, a pronounced willingness on the part of the offender to work at his own improvement. Sex deviates and sex offenders, however, are notoriously uncooperative in this respect, and often receive so many neurotic gains or satisfactions from their aberrations that they have little or no incentive to work for basic changes in themselves.

Nonetheless, a defeatist attitude toward the treatment of sex offenders is not scientifically warranted. Several investigators, including the present writer, have found that sex deviates and offenders can be successfully treated both in institutions and in private practice, and that unusually good results can often be obtained if the therapist employs a highly directive, rational psychotherapeutic approach that shows the offender what his basic fear- and hostility-creating philosophies of living are, how they originated, how he is continually sustaining them in the present, and how he can examine, question, and challenge them so that they significantly change (Ellis, 1956, 1958, 1959a, 1959b).

As an example of what can be done in the treatment of a sex offender, we may consider the case of a thirty-two-year-old salesman who had been discharged from the armed forces for homosexual activity and had twice been arrested and convicted for picking up males in public urinals and inviting them to his room. He was not only exclusively homosexual in his activities but almost always assumed a feminine role in his relations with other males.

As in the case of many other homosexuals, this patient had an exceptionally dominating mother and a weak, ineffective father for whom he had no respect. He had always been afraid to date girls, although he was exceptionally good looking and had maintained buddy-buddy friendships with several females. On the single occasion when one of his female friends, who was seriously interested in marrying him, had encouraged him to have sex relations with her, he had gone into a panic state at the last moment and had run out of her apartment.

It was soon determined, after this patient had come for psychotherapy at the insistence of his lawyer and the probation officer, that the main factors in his pattern of homosexual behavior were (1) his hostility against his dominating mother and his enormous fear of being similarly dominated by another woman; (2) his conviction that he was just as inept as his father and that he could never compete sucessfully in business or social relations; (3) his ardent desire to identify closely with a strong, butch-type male, who would take the responsibility for being the active partner in sex affairs and would care for him, help him, and protect him from the harsh realities of life; and (4) his general feelings of rebelliousness against an unkind world that was forcing him to be more commercially and socially active than he (because of his fear of failure) wanted to be.

The therapeutic approach that was taken with this patient was to get him to question his assumption that it was frightful if he failed at any project or was rejected by someone whose approval or love he sought. He was forced continually to ask himself the questions: "*Why* is it so terrible to fail at anything?" and "What would *really* happen to me that is so awful if this or that person does not approve of me?" As is invariably true in these cases, he could give no sensible answers to these questions, since the assumed terror and horror of failing at a task or of being rejected by someone are merely the result of *definitions* in the head of the assumer and have little or no objective reality.

Once this patient started to contradict his own self-defeating philosophies of life, and to see clearly that there never *is* anything objectively dreadful about failure or rejection, he was induced (as part of the "homework" assignments that are commonly given to patients in the course of rational psychotherapy) first to become more aggressive and active in the homosexual relations which he still continued (though in a more discreet and less dangerous manner). Whereas he previously had only permitted himself to satisfy his partners sexually, in order to win their approval and protection, he was now able to be as much or more concerned about his own satisfaction and to refuse to participate any longer on a one-sided basis. Instead of the butch type of male he had previously sought, he began thinking about and going with more effeminate, passive males who were (because of their own severe emotional disturbances) vitally interested in satisfying him.

The next step was to get the patient to date girls and to make definite sexual overtures toward them. As is usual in these cases, he at first had many excuses and rationalizations for not making the dates or for not making any attempts at physical contacts when he did make dates. But all of these excuses were ruthlessly revealed and analyzed by the therapist and invariably the same motive was disclosed: the patient was still terribly afraid of failure, still morbidly concerned about immediate, guaranteed acceptance. Again and again his basic philosophies in regard to his dire need of approval were attacked, until he began truly to see that it did not make that much difference if he were refused or disapproved. Not only in the sexual-social area but in the area of his business life as well were his attitudes toward success and acceptance uncovered and assailed. Although his strong *desire* or *preference* for getting ahead in life was not attacked, since it appeared to be quite legitimate and realistic in the light of his underlying abilities, his translation of this desire into a grim *necessity*, and his convincing himself that he would be an utterly worthless human being if he did not enormously succeed — these assumptions and philosophies were revealed and seriously challenged.

The first significant breakthrough came on the business front. Whereas the patient had previously turned down all offers to better his position because he was terribly afraid to assume greater responsibility (and hence risk greater failure), after he had been in therapy for four months he learned about a better job opening and actively went after it, even though there was a good possibility that his present employer would discover that he was in the market for a new job and would show distinct disapproval. "Let him find out!" the patient said to himself and the therapist. "With the way he's holding me down and paying me so little right now, what have I got to lose?" "And if he gets angry at you?" asked the therapist. "So he gets angry! As you have helped me see, that's *his* problem. What can he do — kill me?" "Right. But suppose you don't get this new job, what then?" "So I won't get it. Can they kill me, either? And if I don't get that one, I'll keep trying till I get another. I'm goddam sick of being pushed around, since I now realize that that's what's been happening. No one pushes you very far, I see, unless you let yourself be pushed. So if I don't get this job, I'll jump at every single opportunity that comes along till I get another."

As might have been expected, the patient did get the job he was going after — largely because he was so determined to try for it. Then, a few weeks later, he not only made a date, for the first time, with a girl he thought was absolutely terrific, and from whom he would not have dared risk rebuff before, but actually was sexually forward with her from the beginning. Although at first he got nowhere with her, he persisted until he was having regular and highly satisfactory sex relations with this girl. After several subsequent affairs, he finally married and has lost all interest in having homosexual affairs. He has continued to forge ahead in business and has a few remaining remnants of his pathological passivity but no inclinations to identify with or be subservient to stronger male figures. Largely as a result of the therapist's getting him to challenge and attack his general philosophies of life, he has overcome his basic neurosis as well as the homosexual symptoms which were derivatives of this fundamental neurotic pattern of behavior. In the course of this type of psychotherapy, it is found that there are virtually no sex problems per se but that so-called sexual disturbances arise from general fears of failure, feelings of inadequacy, dire needs for approval, and other irrational philosophies of life.

The successful treatment of sex offenders and sex deviants has also been reported by a number of clinicians using a variety of other psychotherapeutic techniques. Practitioners who have successfully employed orthodox psychoanalytic and psychoanalytically oriented methods include Allen (1949), Fink (1954), A. Freud (1951), Gurvitz (1957), Hadfield (1958), Karpman (1956), Lewinsky (1952), London and Caprio (1950), Poe (1952), Robertiello (1959), Rubinstein (1958), and Shentoub (1957). Practitioners using Adlerian, Stekelian, deconditioning, and other psychotherapeutic techniques with sex offenders and deviates have also had a fair amount of success, as shown by clinical reports of Buckle (1949), Creadick (1953), Deutsch (1954), Foster (1947), Nedoma (1951), Srnec and Freund (1953), and Stekel (1930). From the increasing number of reports, such as these just cited, which keep appearing in the professional literature, it should be obvious that while the treatment of sex offenders is still difficult, it is by no means doomed to failure.

SOCIAL PROPHYLAXIS

On a social level, the prevention and treatment of sex offenses would be greatly aided if the citizens of any community and their duly appointed and elected police, judicial, and legislative officials would take an objective and scientific rather than a traditional biased and punitive attitude toward offenders. Individuals commit offenses not because they are blackguards or degenerates but because they are ignorant, mentally subnormal, or emotionally disturbed; and because they are often following normal psychophysical urges or drives which are mistakenly and cruelly limited and banned in many jurisdictions. If society would see to it that as many as possible of its members were raised so that they were minimally ignorant and disturbed and maximally permitted to engage in harmless sex acts, there would doubtless be a sharp decrease in the existing high number of sex offenders.

More specifically, for the best kind of prevention of, and treatment for, sex offenses the following general program is suggested:

1. Only those sex acts should be legally proscribed which involve the use of force or duress, an adult's taking sexual advantage of a minor, or public acts distasteful to the majority of those in whose presence they are committed. Sex acts other than these, which are engaged in private between two competent adults, should not be subject to legal processes or penalties.

2. All sex laws should be rewritten so that offenses are specifically and scientifically designated and defined in meaningful, consistent, nonoverlapping terms.

3. When individuals commit any sex offense that would be an offense under the two preceding rules, they should, after conviction but before being sentenced, be given a complete psychological examination to determine whether they are sexually and/or psychologically deviated.

4. All sex offenders, and particularly those who are diagnosed as being sexually or psychologically deviated, should receive psychological treatment either in their own community while they are placed on probation, or in a mental hospital or other facility that affords specialized psychotherapeutic care for sex offenders. If institutionalization is required, the convicted offender should remain in protective custody as long as he is regarded as being sufficiently psychologically deviated to constitute a menace to the rights and safety of his fellow citizens.

5. Under no circumstances should sex offenders (or, for that matter, nonsex offenders) be viewed as horrible, villainous criminals to be harshly punished as an atonement for their sins. Rather, they should be viewed as relatively normal individuals who are rash enough to get into occasional difficulty, or as seriously disturbed persons who are sufficiently disordered to keep getting into legal

414 • SPECIAL PROBLEMS IN CRIMINAL PSYCHOLOGY

difficulties because of their sexual behavior. In either case, education and treatment, rather than excoriation and punishment, should be the lot of these already sufficiently unfortunate individuals.

6. It is most necessary, for the prevention and treatment of sex offenders, that every community favor increasing, and improving the quality of, general sex education, so that children at an early age are provided with scientific, objectively stated sex information, and so that a much more liberal, socially sanctioned heterosexual participation by young people than now exists is heartily encouraged.

References

Abrahamsen, D. *Report on study of 102 sex offenders at Sing Sing Prison.* Utica, N. Y.: State Hospitals Press, 1950.

Allen, Clifford. *The sexual perversions and abnormalities.* New York: Oxford Univer. Press, 1949.

Bailey, D. S. (Ed.) *Sexual offenders and social punishment.* Westminister: Church of England Moral Welfare Council and Church Information Board, 1956.

Bowman, K. M. *Sexual deviation research.* Sacramento: Assembly of the State of California, 1952.

Bowman, K. M. Too many sex laws. *Nation,* 1958, **188,** 286–289.

Buckle, D. The treatment of sex offenders. *Int. J. Sexol.,* 1949, **31,** 1–8.

California sexual deviation research, January 1953. Sacramento: Assembly of the State of California, 1953.

California sexual deviation research, March 1954. Sacramento: Assembly of the State of California, 1954.

Creadick, R. N. Management of homosexuals. *South. med. J.* 1953, **46,** 455–460.

de River, Paul. *The sexual criminal.* Springfield, Ill.: Charles C Thomas, 1949.

Deutsch, Danica. A case of transvestism. *Amer. J. Psychother.,* 1954, **8,** 239–242.

Drummond, Isabel. *The sex paradox.* New York: Putnam, 1953.

Ellis, A. *The American sexual tragedy.* New York: Twayne Publishers, 1954. (a)

Ellis, A. Interrogation of sex offenders. *J. crim. Law,* 1954, **45,** 41–47. (b)

Ellis, A. The effectiveness of psychotherapy with individuals who have severe homosexual problems. *J. consult. Psychol.,* 1956, **20,** 191–195.

Ellis, A. *How to live with a neurotic.* New York: Crown Publishers, 1957.

Ellis, A. Rational psychotherapy. *J. gen. Psychol.,* 1958, **59,** 35–49.

Ellis, A. Treatment of a homosexual with rational psychotherapy. *J. clin. Psychol.*, 1959, 15, 338–343. (a)

Ellis, A. The treatment of a psychopath with rational psychotherapy. (In Italian.) *Quaderni di criminologuia Clinica*, 1959, 2, 173–184. Also published in *J. Psychol*, 1961, 51, 141–150. (b)

Ellis, A. *The art and science of love.* New York: Lyle Stuart, 1960. (a)

Ellis, A. There is no place for the concept of sin in psychotherapy. *J. counsel. Psychol.*, 1960, 7, 188–192. (b)

Ellis, A. Coitus. In A. Ellis and A. Abarbanel (Eds.), *Encyclopedia of sexual behavior.* New York: Hawthorne Books, 1961.

Ellis, A. Sexual deviation and anomalies. In *Collier's Encyclopedia.* New York: Collier's, (on press).

Ellis, A. and Brancale, R. *The psychology of sex offenders.* Springfield, Ill.: Charles C Thomas, 1956.

Ellis, A., Doorbar, Ruth R., & Johnson, R., II. Characteristics of convicted sex offenders. *J. soc. Psychol.*, 1954, 40, 3–15.

English, H. B. & English, A. C. *A comprehensive dictionary of psychological and psychoanalytical terms.* New York: Longmans, Green, 1958.

Fink, H. K. *Long journey.* New York: Julian Press, 1954.

Foster, A. W. Treatment of sexual offenders. *Marriage Hyg.*, 1947, 1, 77–80.

Freud, Anna. Clinical observations on the treatment of manifest male homosexuality. *Psychoanal. Quart.*, 1951, 20, 237–238.

Glueck, B. C. Psychodynamic patterns in the homosexual sex offender. *Amer. J. Psychiat.*, 1956, 11, 584–590.

Group for the Advancement of Psychiatry. *Psychiatrically deviated sex offenders.* Report No. 9, rev. Topeka, Kans.: 1950.

Gurvitz, M. Sex offenders in private practice: Treatment and outcome. Paper delivered at the American Psychological Association Annual Meeting, September 3, 1957.

Guttmacher, Manfred S. *Sex offenses.* New York: Norton, 1951.

Guttmacher, M. S., & Weihofen, H. Sex offenses. *J. crim. Law,* 1952, 43, 153–175.

Guze, H. What is sexually normal? Paper delivered at the Second Annual Conference of the Society for the Scientific Study of Sex, November 7, 1959.

Hadfield, J. A. The cure of homosexuality. *Brit. med. J.*, 1958, 1, 1323–1326.

Karpman, B. *The sexual offender and his offenses.* New York: Julian Press, 1956.

Kinsey, A. C., Pomeroy, W. B., & Martin, C. E. *Sexual behavior in the human male.* Philadelphia: Saunders, 1948.

Lewinsky, H. Features from a case of homosexuality. *Psychoanal. Quart.*, 1952, 21, 344–254.

London, L. S., & Caprio, F. S. *Sexual deviation.* Washington, D. C.: Linacre Press, 1950.

Michigan, State of. *Report of the Governor's study commission on the deviated crimnal sex offender.* Lansing: 1951.

Nedoma, K. Homosexuality in sexological practice. *Int. J. Sexol.,* 1951, 4, 219–224.

Poe, J. S. Successful treatment of a forty-year-old passive homosexual. *Psychoanal. Rev.,* 1952, 29, 23–36.

Pollens, B. *The sex criminal.* New York: Macaulay, 1938.

Radzinowicz, L. (Ed.). *Sexual offences.* London: Macmillan, 1949.

Report of the Committee on Homosexual Offences and Prostituton. (Wolfenden Report.) London: Her Majesty's Stationery Office, 1957.

Rickles, N. K. *Exhibitionism.* Philadelphia: Lippincott, 1950.

Robertiello, C. *Voyage from Lesbos.* New York: Citadel Press, 1959.

Rubinstein, J. Psychotherapeutic aspects of male homosexuality. *Brit. J. med. Psychol.,* 1958, 31, 74–78.

Shentoub, S. A. De quelques problemes dans l'homosexualité masculine active. *Rev. franc. Psychanalyse,* 1959, 21, 485–534. *Excerpta Medica,* 1959, 8, 12, 958.

Sherwin, R. V. *Sex and the statutory law.* New York: Oceana Publications, 1949.

Sherwin, R. V. Laws on sex crimes. In A. Ellis and A. Abarbanel (Eds.), *Encyclopedia of sexual behavior.* New York: Hawthorn Books, 1961.

Srnec, Dr., and Freund, K. Treatment of male homosexuality through conditioning. *Int. J. Sexol.,* 1953, 7, 92–93.

Stekel, Wilhelm. *Sexual aberrations.* New York: Liveright, 1930.

Tappan, P. W. *The habitual sex offender.* Trenton: State of New Jersey, 1950.

Traver, R. *Anatomy of a murder.* New York: Dell Books, 1959.

Index

Index

419